Murder in McComb

Murder in McComb
The Tina Andrews Case

Trent Brown

Louisiana State University Press
Baton Rouge

Published with the assistance of the V. Ray Cardozier Fund

Published by Louisiana State University Press
Copyright © 2020 by Louisiana State University Press
All rights reserved
Manufactured in the United States of America
First printing

Designer: Michelle A. Neustrom
Typefaces: Whitman, text; Helvetica Now, display
Printer and binder: Sheridan Books, Inc.

Library of Congress Cataloging-in-Publication Data

Names: Brown, Trent, 1965– author.
Title: Murder in McComb : the Tina Andrews case / Trent Brown.
Description: Baton Rouge : Louisiana State University Press, [2020] | Includes index.
Identifiers: LCCN 2019041542 (print) | LCCN 2019041543 (ebook) | ISBN 978-0-8071-7280-3 (cloth) | ISBN 978-0-8071-7365-7 (pdf) | ISBN 978-0-8071-7364-0 (epub)
Subjects: LCSH: Andrews, Tina, 1957–1969. | Murder—Mississippi—McComb—Case studies. | Trials (Murder)—Mississippi—McComb—Case studies. | Poor girls—Social conditions—Mississippi—McComb—Case studies. | Police corruption—Mississippi—McComb—Case studies. | McComb (Miss.)—History—20th century.
Classification: LCC HV6534.M384 B76 2020 (print) | LCC HV6534.M384 (ebook) | DDC 364.152/3092—dc23
LC record available at https://lccn.loc.gov/2019041542
LC ebook record available at https://lccn.loc.gov/2019041543

For my wife, Jennifer

Contents

Acknowledgments ix

Introduction: The Road to the Oil Field
August 13, 1969, and the Killing of Tina Andrews 1

1 "The Camellia City of America"
Managing Life in McComb, Mississippi 14

2 "The Weirdest Angles I've Encountered"
Investigating the Murder of Tina Andrews 39

3 Joe Pigott Receives a Call
Two Indictments and Initial Preparations for a Trial 53

4 The Summer of 1971
Developments on the Eve of the Trial 74

5 The *State of Mississippi v. Richard McIntosh*
Opening Salvos 94

6 "A Girl of Ill Repute"
Billie Jo Lambert Testifies 116

7 The *State of Mississippi v. Richard McIntosh*
The Defense Makes Its Case 147

8 The *State of Mississippi v. Richard McIntosh*
The 1972 Trial 173

9 After the Trials
The Fates of People and the City 201

Contents

10 Searching for Tina Andrews
Conversations and Rumors, but No Smoking Guns 224

Conclusion: What Happened to Tina Andrews? 252

Notes 269

Index 297

Illustrations follow page 134

Acknowledgments

More than any other project that I have undertaken, this book was built upon the generosity and help of others. It is my pleasure to recognize some of them here. First, thanks to Louisiana State University Press for publishing another one of my books. From the moment I took this manuscript to LSU Press, Editor-in-Chief Rand Dotson offered enthusiasm, patience, and wise counsel. This time I surely tried Rand's serenity on more than one occasion, but he never let me know it. LSU Press Director Alisa Plant runs an outstanding organization. As I have come to expect, everyone at the press provided expert work and care as this project moved toward publication. Thanks also to Jo Ann Kiser for her careful copyediting of the manuscript and to Denise Carlson for her excellent job of indexing this book.

Without the willingness of so many people to talk with me about the Tina Andrews story, there would have been no book. Special thanks to Carroll Case, who opened his home to me and spent many hours in conversation about our mutual interests in McComb. When Carroll said that I could call on him at any time, I knew that he meant it. So I did; he always answered. Justice James W. Kitchens and Brad Pigott offered vital information at critical stages. I owe them much more than a brief acknowledgment. Many thanks as well to Jackie Sue Andrews, Sue Williams, Clifton McGowan, Bennie Hayman, Dee Bates, Wayne Dowdy, Julian Prince, and Rita Watts, all of whom spoke to me about the Tina Andrews case or McComb's history. I appreciate their trust in me. This seems an appropriate place to say that the interpretations here are my responsibility alone. In Pike County, Mississippi, and elsewhere, a number of other people shared recollections about the subject of this book, helped me search for records, or otherwise provided significant assistance. They either intimated or insisted that they not be named here. I have respected their wishes, but nevertheless want to express my gratitude for all they did.

At the Missouri University of Science and Technology, Linda Sands was an enthusiastic listener whenever I wanted to tell her about the latest twists and turns in this story. Kayleigh Rodgers and Mackenzie Shields helped with newspaper microfilm, the transcription of interviews, and the conversion of my typewritten drafts (on an Olympia SM9, for those who are interested) into modern, editable form. The dean's office of the College of Arts, Sciences, and Business provided funds for rental cars, meals, and other necessities of my research trips to Pike County; I appreciate the support of deans Stephen Roberts and Kate Drowne. Thanks to Kris Swenson for her comments on an early draft of the introduction.

A special thanks once again to Vance Poole, a great friend and companion for more than two decades now. In the profession, Steve Reich and Mitzi Walker Jones expressed interest and enthusiasm about this project. I wish to acknowledge as well the insightful, thorough reading of this manuscript by the anonymous reviewer for LSU Press. If I could thank that person by name, I surely would.

My family offered love and support, as they consistently do. For more than two years, my head and heart and sometimes the rest of me, too, were in Mississippi. My children, Jack and Ellie, have never known a time when their father was not thinking or writing about the South. I am proud of all that they are and all that they are becoming. Readers of this book will see my deep connections with Mississippi. My family there always offered a warm homecoming. Longer than I am able to remember, my mother has provided unconditional love and steadfast care. The older that I grow, the more I appreciate all that she has given me. Thanks and love to Aunt Jackie, too. When she says that she is always there for me, I know it is true. When I am in Mississippi, they always ask when I will return. In significant ways, I have never left.

To my wife, Jennifer, I owe the greatest debt. She listened for a long time to my obsession with this story, insisted that I go home to Mississippi to follow its trail, and most important, has tolerated all my many faults. One of these days, I hope that I can offer her more than a few words of thanks in a forum like this one for all the love that she has given me over the years. This book's dedication reflects only a very little bit of what I feel for her. If my will can make it so, the best is yet to come.

Murder in McComb

The Road to the Oil Field

August 13, 1969, and the Killing of Tina Andrews

Her name was Tina Marie Andrews. In the summer of 1969, she was twelve years old. On August 13, Tina awoke at her parents' home on Oak Street in McComb, Mississippi, a small town in the southwestern part of the state.[1] It was not a school day. Children then still enjoyed most of August for summer vacation. Later that fall, however, under most circumstances she would have seen to her morning routine, left her house, and walked a few blocks, crossing south over Delaware Avenue to Otken Elementary School, where she would have been a fifth grader. Tina attended the new Otken, which had opened in 1959, not the old one, which had been located a mile or so east across town.[2] She was too young to remember that school.

Even if it had been a school day, though, she might not have walked to Otken, let alone been awake at an early hour. Nothing required Tina to go to school if she did not feel like it, or if her parents could not make her. Mississippi had repealed its compulsory attendance law years earlier, in the 1950s, in an effort to ward off integration of black and white schoolchildren. Consequently, in Pike County, where Tina lived, about one-third of the children dropped out before finishing high school.[3] Tina did in fact miss a lot of school. While she enjoyed seeing her friends there and tried hard to make new ones, she was not a good student. Her classes did not hold her interest, or she struggled with them for other reasons, and she had made poor grades the last two years.

On this August day, however, fifth grade and books and homework were likely not matters that concerned Tina. She had made other plans, ones that involved going out that evening. Despite her age, Tina was becoming experienced with the streets and nightlife of McComb. Some local people remember her as precocious, that "she was twelve going on twenty," and she was doing so without a great deal of interference or supervision. A contemporary of Tina's recalls: "She was beginning to get into all kinds of trouble. That worried her family, but they didn't seem to be able to do a lot about it. Tina sort of came and went just as she pleased."[4]

Downtown McComb, with its retail stores, movie theaters, cafes, and other spots for socializing, was about a mile from Oak Street. Tina would walk down there later, she decided. Her friends and most other people her age walked to get around town, too, unless they could catch a ride, maybe with an older brother or sister. Along State or Front Street, the heart of what was then still a vibrant commercial area, there always seemed to be a crowd to see and much to do, even for a girl her age. However, movies at the State or the Palace, or treats from the soda fountain at Gillis Drug Store, not to mention the clothes in the windows of women's stores like the Hollywood Shop, cost money. A girl like Tina, from a modest economic background, usually did not have much money for entertainment or other things that she wanted, and certainly she wished that she could have more.[5]

While Tina was young, she was attractive. Over the last year, she had grown up a lot. A little tall for her age, physically well-developed, with long brown hair, Tina seems to have craved affection and the adventures that she might have dreamed it would bring. In downtown McComb with her friends, it is not hard to imagine that they "would lean together to whisper and laugh secretly if someone passed who amused or interested them," as a contemporary writer said of adolescent girls.[6] Boys her age, as well as some who were older, had begun paying attention to her. Tina, like many other girls, enjoyed the idea of having boyfriends. Tina went out often these days, and stayed out late, sometimes practically all night, a fact that occasionally caused trouble at home. Once in a while she did not show up at all for a day or more. Tina had sisters and brothers, some of them still living at the house on Oak Street. The older ones went to school or they did not, like Tina, and they came and went without much interference from their parents. Tina was beginning to do the same thing. But her family questioned her about her comings and goings, and Tina learned that sometimes it was simpler just to leave, to return later, and to deal with any consequences then. So on that night, like other ones over the past year, she would get out whenever she found the chance.

Looking over her clothes, she chose a pink and white blouse. It was a new one, low-cut in both front and back, the sort of thing that showed off one's figure. Her sister Donna had purchased it at Gibson's, "Where You Buy the Best for Less," the discount store on Highway 51. Donna was almost two years older than Tina. She was fond of her sister and had used some of her recent birthday money to buy Tina that blouse. Many of Tina's clothes came from other people. Her bra was a hand-me-down from a friend of her older sister Winifred. That bra was a size 32B, and padded. Like a lot of used clothing, the bra showed signs of wear. However, Donna had helped her repair it with a safety pin. Tina also put on a pair of green shorts. Those shorts were not new, either. They belonged to a cousin of Tina's, who had left them at the Andrews house. But Winifred had fixed those shorts as well, sewing a button back on the pocket. These details about the clothing, simple matters of fact for a family without a great deal of spare income, would become important later, when Tina's sisters and the rest of her family needed to identify Tina's body.

As usual, that evening there was supper to prepare and then dishes to wash, chores that few girls her age enjoyed. So while their mother, Doris, left the cleaning up for Donna and Tina, Tina told Donna that she needed to use the bathroom. She did not come back right away. Their mother noticed that Tina was not helping in the kitchen. Donna told her that Tina was in the bathroom and had been there for a while. Her mother checked on her, but Tina was gone. Apparently she had slipped out, Donna said. Tina had done things like that before, so her family, while annoyed, was not overly anxious. But Tina would not slip out of the house on Oak Street anymore. In the fall, there would be no school or chores or questions from her parents about where she had been and what she had done. Her family would never see Tina alive again.

Leaving Oak Street, Tina walked east on Delaware Avenue toward downtown, where she decided to see what was happening at the Tiger's Den, located at the corner of Main Street and Railroad Boulevard.[7] All the teenagers went there; it had been a popular place as long as Tina could remember. You walked down a set of street-level stairs and entered a small door. Inside the Tiger's Den, you could play pinball, have a Coke, and listen to the latest records on the jukebox. "Crystal Blue Persuasion" by Tommy James and the Shondells was a big hit that summer, as were Johnny Cash's "A Boy Named Sue" and Neil Diamond's "Sweet Caroline."[8] The Tiger's Den was by design a spot for young people, and for years it had had a generally wholesome reputation. "By the late '60s," however, remembered one local resident, "some rowdy kids hung out

3

there. Police did come around, sometimes to keep an eye on what was happening and sometimes for other reasons, too."[9] But it was definitely not a bar, so they did not serve beer. Several establishments near downtown McComb did offer alcohol, though, as well as a more colorful clientele. In case things seemed slow at the Tiger's Den, then, there were other options. Tina had already begun to explore some of those places where older people gathered.

At the Tiger's Den, Tina met her friend Billie Jo Lambert. Billie Jo was thirteen, a year older than Tina, and lived in east McComb, the working-class district across town from Tina's street. She was the kind of friend you enjoyed seeing when you went out, where you could talk about things that interested or troubled you. There was another girl that Tina encountered at the Tiger's Den that night, too, Marjorie Parsons. She had been paying attention to a boy that Tina liked, one that Tina probably thought of as her boyfriend. So Tina told Marjorie Parsons that she needed to leave the boy alone, and Tina told her that fact in a frank and spirited manner. While some people might have enjoyed a scene or even a fight between two girls over a boy, the Tiger's Den was not the place for that sort of thing, Billie Jo decided. So Billie Jo intervened, telling Tina to come outside with her to cool off before things became carried away.

They walked south on Railroad Boulevard to the corner of Railroad and Canal Street. The girls probably did not think of directions in terms of points of the compass or even necessarily by street name. But they knew their way around McComb, navigating through landmarks such as businesses or familiar houses or the streets they recognized. It was a short walk to the corner of Railroad and Canal, just under two minutes, if you were not in a hurry. It was dark, but not late yet, and temperatures were mild that evening, particularly for mid-August in Mississippi.[10] A third girl walked with them. She had been with Tina at the Tiger's Den when Billie Jo arrived. They sat down on the curb to talk. Perhaps Billie Jo did not know that third girl, at least by name. There were always a number of people at the Tiger's Den, a companionable place. Many of them you knew from school or maybe church, but others you did not. Billie Jo later told many people, including two juries in the Pike County Courthouse, that she never did learn the name of that third girl.

Then a car pulled up. From what direction the car came, or what else the men in it had been doing that evening, or why particularly they stopped at that corner, no one ever said. Two white men sat in the front seat. Everyone else at the Tiger's Den and the other places Tina and Billie Jo frequented was white, too, as were they. One of the men asked the girls if they needed a ride home. The girls accepted the offer. Riding in cars with older boys was not a new experience for either Tina or Billie Jo, and perhaps it seemed to promise more of a good time than sitting on a curb downtown. The three girls climbed into the back seat of the car, which had four doors, so the men did not have to get out to let them in. One of the men, the driver, looked familiar to Billie Jo. Tina seemed to know the other man, the one in the passenger's seat.

The five of them drove west on Canal Street, then turned right onto North Broadway, a total distance of less than two blocks. They made a left onto Delaware Avenue, a major city artery, which carried them west, heading through and then away from downtown. They did not take Billie Jo home. She lived on Cherry Street in east McComb, the opposite direction from their route, but Tina's house was just off Delaware, so the ride seemed to be going as the girls had expected. Delaware Avenue took them closer to places that Tina knew, places to eat like Plantation Chicken, where forty-nine cents would buy you a lunch of one piece of chicken, fries, and a roll, and the Mr. Swiss Drive-In, with thirty Alpine flavors from which to choose. The other girl, the one whose name Billie Jo said she did not know, told the men that they could let her out. They had not gone far, only about a mile, and were just approaching the corner of Delaware and South James Avenue. To that point, the men in the front seat had not said much, but neither had the girls. Just after the third girl got out, they were close to Tina's street, Oak, which was two blocks west of South James. Tina said that they could let her out now, too, but they did not. They needed some gasoline, the men replied. There were indeed service stations on Delaware, but gasoline was not what the men had in mind. One of them told Tina and Billie Jo that they were not going to go home just yet.

Then the evening took a turn that Tina and Billie Jo had not anticipated. The girls insisted that they could walk home; they asked once more to be let out of the car. But again one of the men said no. Instead, they were going to go parking. Later, if they wished, he said, they could tell all about it to anyone who wanted to know. The man seemed pleased, or tickled, as they said in Mississippi, that men their age might enjoy some time alone with girls like Tina and Billie Jo. They continued to drive west out Delaware Avenue, crossing over the new highway, Interstate 55.[11] Across that highway, there were no more residential neighborhoods, businesses, or street lights. The girls began to whisper to themselves in the back seat. When they stopped, Tina and Billie Jo agreed, they would jump out of the car and get away from these men, to whom they decided they were not particularly attracted. But they were getting far from home, especially for walking, over two miles and more each minute from Billie Jo's house.

The girls repeated their request to walk home, but still the men refused to stop. They turned south onto Schmidt Road, a twisting lane the name of which the girls might not have known, but they probably did soon realize their destination. Then they turned onto a smaller dirt road, which carried them through pine woods and pastures. There were cattle gaps in that road. Finally, they reached their spot. It was a place, like many others in the county, where oil work was done; there was drilling equipment in the ground. In the daylight, one would have noticed trash scattered about. People dumped things in the field, including old furniture. That evening it was quiet and isolated, probably seeming even more so under the darkness of a new moon. Many people in town, even girls their age, knew the location to be a good place for couples looking for privacy. But the girls had had enough. When the car stopped, they were getting out and going home, one way or another. That is when the ride to the oil field turned deadly.

The moment the men stopped, Billie Jo stepped out of one side of the car; Tina got out of the other. Billie Jo had a clear shot toward the road that would take her back toward McComb and eventually home. Tina did not. She had to cross around the front of the car to get away from the men. When she did that, one of the men, the one who had been driving, grabbed Tina by the arm. Billie Jo heard Tina tell the "son of a bitch" to let her go. Infuriated, the man said that no one called him that name and got away with it. Billie Jo was moving quickly now, and it was dark. But she did look back in time to see the man who had grabbed Tina hit her in the face, and he struck her hard.

So Billie Jo began to run. She continued to run and then to walk as she made her way back to her home on Cherry Street, a distance of well over three miles. She was thirteen years old and scared. She did not stop at any house or business to ask for help, nor did she seek any rides, given how this one had turned out. When she arrived home, it was late, but Billie Jo did not check a clock to see what time it was. Because she had not been wearing shoes, her feet were swollen and bruised, and they hurt. People at her house were still up watching television. They were irritated at Billie Jo for being out late again. But no one, including her mother, wanted to hear excuses or any story about where she had been or what she had done. So Billie Jo said nothing to them then or for some time to come about what had happened that night.

Billie Jo Lambert never saw her friend Tina Andrews again. The driver of the car, the man who hit Tina in the face, had in fact hit her hard, so hard that he broke her jaw. Sometime after that, one of the men took a .38-caliber revolver, which he happened to be carrying, and shot Tina in the back of the head. Why he shot Tina, or what else they did to Tina before or after they killed her, Billie Jo could not have known. No one other than the three people left there in the oil field ever knew that. When the two men were done with Tina, they left her body, concealed under an old couch they had rolled on top of her. Then they drove away, going back to whatever else they had to do on a Wednesday night in McComb, Mississippi.

Over the next week, Billie Jo was anxious, but she had no idea what she should do. She did not know what had happened to Tina after she ran away from the oil field. No one asked her if she knew where Tina was, not Tina's parents, her brothers or sisters, or anyone else. She certainly did not hear from Tina or see her when she went out. She wondered too if either of those men might come looking for her. On that night of August 13, she thought that she heard someone outside her bedroom window, but she was not sure. She asked one of the men in her house to take a look, but he did not see anyone. But if sometime later she did see either of those two men from the oil field, what then? She spent a good deal of time wondering what she could do or say and to whom she might say it.

After a time, she decided why one of the men had looked so familiar to her. She had seen him around town. Sometimes, however, he was in a different car and wore different clothes, because he was a McComb policeman. That fact made things very difficult. Even if she wanted to say something about Tina, she could not go to the police. If a policeman had done that to Tina, what, she imagined, would they do to her if she talked? In September, when Tina's fate became clear, Billie Jo and her mother had a conversation about Tina. Her mother warned Billie Jo that she could get in a great deal of trouble if she told anyone else about that evening of August 13, so she should keep her mouth shut. So that is what she did for a long time. But Billie Jo thought about what had happened, and sometimes she dreamed about it. Those dreams about her friend Tina and those men and what she had seen in that oil field weighed on her mind. If things seemed bad now, however, over the next year they became much more complicated and in many ways worse for Billie Jo Lambert.

Saturday, August 23, 1969, was a hot day in McComb, with temperatures in the low nineties, typical for that time of year. The weather was humid as well, also common in a Mississippi summer. The aftereffects of Hurricane Camille, a phenomenal Category 5 storm that had struck the Gulf Coast the previous week, exacerbated conditions.[12] Around 9:30 a.m., Pike County authorities, including the sheriff's office and the police department, received disturbing news. Workers for the Sun Oil Company, checking property south of Delaware Avenue Extension that the company leased from the Hess Oil Company, discovered a badly decomposed body. Soon, officers of both departments, along with Mississippi State Highway Patrol investigators, an FBI agent, a local radio station announcer, a funeral home employee, and Pike County District Attorney Joe N. Pigott, were on the scene. A reporter for the local newspaper, the *Enterprise-Journal*, took notes and shot photographs. What the men saw in the oil field was grim. The body, "little more than a skeleton," apparently that of a young woman or a girl, based upon the clothing on and near the remains, was found partially concealed beneath a discarded sofa. "The oil field workers saw the skull protruding from beneath the sofa," the paper reported. A man who was present at the investigation scene recalled years later: the area was "just past Schmidt Road, through the cattle gap and maybe 110 yards to an . . . oil well site. . . . Bobby Bellipani [a McComb police officer and brother-in-law of McComb police lieutenant Ted Fleming] was there and he had a box of cigars, which we all smoked" against the odor of the human remains.[13]

Who was the person discovered in the oil field? McComb authorities were initially puzzled. Incredibly, at least four area women were currently missing or otherwise unaccounted for, and the investigation centered first on identifying which of those woman, if any, the body might be. Several possible victims were quickly struck off investigators' lists, however, and efforts then concentrated on discovering whether the victim might be "a McComb girl reported missing for the past 10 or 12 days." "We've checked every lead we have so far," said Pike County sheriff Robert "Tot" Lawson. "As of now we have only one missing person in the McComb area that it could possibly be." But neither Lawson nor anyone else released the girl's name.[14]

From the beginning, the case was considered a homicide, not a possible suicide or an accident. The killing of people in Pike County was not rare. Most grand juries during each year's two county court sessions considered at least one such crime. In the October 1969 term of the Pike County Circuit Court, in fact, the grand jury would hear evidence of four homicides, three rapes, and many other felonies.[15] The local newspaper would refer to the matter as "one of the most publicized homicide cases here in months," a testimony to the frequency of killings in Pike County.[16] But the murder of a young white woman, as this victim seemed to be, was not common. From the discovery of the body, this case would occasion much interest and speculation in McComb, a town that a few years earlier *Time* magazine had called "the toughest anti-civil rights community in the toughest anti-civil rights area in the toughest anti-civil rights state in the Union." After a crescendo of violence in 1964, local people, including the editor of the city's newspaper, recognized that McComb had earned a reputation as "the bombing capital of the world."[17] That recent history of violence—both public attitudes toward it and the roles that area law enforcement had played in it—formed the world in which Tina Andrews lived and died, and in which the search for her murderer took place.

Murder in McComb describes not only what happened to Tina Andrews but also why the aftermath of her killing unfolded as it did. However, this is not a book offering a solution to a cold case, because strictly speaking, the Andrews murder is not a cold case. Two men were indicted in 1971 for killing Tina Andrews. Two Pike County juries, in 1971 and again in 1972, heard two different district attorneys attempt to persuade them of the guilt of one of those men. For reasons not rooted solely in the evidence presented in court, neither jury convicted that defendant. Charges against the other indicted man were dismissed in 1972 and never reopened. No other charges were ever filed in the case. This account does not uncover fresh evidence to prove who killed Tina Andrews. What, then, does it offer? The heart of this book is a narrative about the brief life and death of a white, working-class girl. Tina Andrews lived in a community in which deep patterns of racial segregation—built, maintained, and challenged over the course of a century—were made extraordinarily more complex by the social class divisions that existed among its white residents.

Those tensions manifested themselves not only during the 1950s and 1960s, but also for years to come, as would be evident in the investigation and trials following Tina Andrews's murder.

In the early and mid-1960s, white McComb became more overtly aware of those social class divisions than they had been in many years. Disputes over how best to handle the racial challenges of the period exacerbated tensions within that community, exposing disagreements about matters of order, respectability, and other forms of behavior. In the aftermath of Andrews's murder, one can see those attitudes about the necessity and limits of control more clearly than at other times in the area's history. *Murder in McComb* examines the context of the community in which Andrews was killed, seeking there the reasons that no one was ever convicted of that crime. Such an examination reveals the operation of race and social class and presumptions about gender and respectability in a small southern town in the years during and immediately after what is generally considered the civil rights movement. It explores these social forces in the period after McComb and the Deep South had largely ceased to attract national attention. The tensions unleashed and amplified in the 1960s shaped the community for years to come. My hope is that the book will suggest how much remains to be written about the history of the Deep South in recent decades.[18]

McComb was fundamentally shaped by notions of racial difference. During Tina Andrews's life, fewer places in Mississippi evidenced a more palpable consciousness of living within a racialized social order. Black people there were intensely aware of that fact. Fewer groups of white Mississippians were more convinced that their way of life, as they thought of it, was more in need of protection from disorder. Fewer groups of white Mississippians practiced more sustained defense of that social order. "One seemingly unbreakable thread binds together almost all the white citizens of McComb and Pike County," wrote a reporter in 1965. In the mid-1960s, "no other Mississippi county was more united or determined in its resistance to federal civil rights laws. The whites are very serious about this."[19] On the face of it, the murder of Tina Andrews may not seem to have much to do with the violent resistance to social change that marked McComb in the 1960s. She was white, as were all the principal actors in the story, including the two men arrested for her murder.

Nothing suggests that anyone considered that a black man might have been responsible for her death, a logical, satisfying solution in other times and places in the South. But a passion for racial order and control profoundly informed the community in which Tina Andrews lived and died. The arrests and trials associated with the case, as well as local understandings and memory of the murder for years to come, unfolded in an area in which all basic institutions and attitudes had been formed in the crucible of race.

McComb, Mississippi, was one of the most notoriously violent centers of resistance to the civil rights movement from the early 1960s through a campaign of bombing in 1964 that brought national attention to the city.[20] The counties in southwestern Mississippi—Amite, Pike, and Walthall—were Klan country, notes historian Charles Payne, with a well-earned reputation among civil rights activists for being both "vicious" and "remarkably hateful."[21] White violence sought to thwart grass roots black resistance to Jim Crow, a resistance that had been growing in determination since the 1950s in ways that white McComb residents did not fail to notice. A young black McComb resident expressed the thoughts of many other local people in 1964 when he wrote: "For the last time, take your foot off my neck and give me my rights as a citizen."[22] Most of white McComb rejected, in one fashion or another, that claim to full black citizenship. Robert Brumfield, at the time the president of the local chamber of commerce, later recalled: "The way of life we had lived through the years was crumbling around us, and I'm sure I didn't like it."[23]

The violence that met the civil rights movement in Pike County in the mid-1960s was a reaction by many local whites—mainly but not exclusively working class—not only against black aspirations for social change but also against white McComb authorities' failure, as they saw it, to control the black population. At the same time, McComb's most influential citizens did not like night riders, bombings, and the kinds of violence that frightened investment. They resented the Klan and the bad publicity their terrorism had brought to the area, as much as many of them shared their basic aim of keeping black people subservient. Some Pike County residents were Klansmen. Most others, including the great majority of downtown businessmen and the jurors that heard the Andrews murder cases, were not. To civil rights activists and the national media, one white McComb person might have seemed much like another. But not so

in the eyes of whites there. Some white people were as worried about and re-
sentful of other whites as they were of black people. Insistence upon order and
control, then, could operate across social class lines as well as racial ones.

Local people understood too that matters of social class had something important to do with Tina Andrews's life and death, and with the trials of 1971
and 1972. "Tina was white trash. That's why no one worked too hard to find
out who killed her," a longtime McComb resident told me recently. The stories about the Andrews murder that have continued to circulate in McComb
over the decades speak not only to the social origins of Andrews as a factor
in the case, but also to those of the men alleged to be responsible, directly or
indirectly, for her killing. "Some of the best men in town were in it," another
person told me. "People are still scared to talk about it because of who they
were."[24] It is a rare small town in the Deep South that does not draw suggestions of corruption among a cabal of the well-connected. But the exercise of
power in McComb did not necessarily involve conspiracy. Matters of import
could be handled above board and confidently by people who had power. The
families of Tina Andrews and Billie Jo Lambert were not among those people.
But other people were. Tina Andrews was not murdered by a conspiracy of the
respectable. But the prominent and the powerful in the area did have a stake in
the outcomes of the trials of her accused killer. The social origins of Andrews
and Lambert deeply mattered in McComb. The arrests and trials after her murder display clear evidence of the importance of social class in Pike County,
Mississippi. In the eyes of some people in the community, Tina Andrews did
not matter very much because of who she was, an undistinguished child of an
undistinguished family.

A case such as this one attains a more general relevance through a detailed
examination of particulars, ones that set a specific problem—the life and death
of a white, working-class girl—within its historical moment, thus raising not
only human but also historiographical concerns that carry the story beyond
the limits of Pike County, Mississippi, in the late 1960s and early 1970s. Tina
Andrews's murder occurred at an especially inopportune time. Had she been
killed in the 1950s, her death would not have happened in a community in
which white tensions had been so recently revealed and were so much in need
of tempering. Had she been killed later, say in the 1980s, she would have died
in a town in which white residents had learned what could and could not be

preserved of the Jim Crow years, a place in which memories of white social class tensions in the 1960s had been muted, forgotten, or ignored. As Stephen Berrey has rightly argued, white Mississippians by the mid-1960s had heard for years "narratives" of "black deviance" and criminality that increasingly dovetailed with broader national concerns about the need for law and order to protect "the family, the nation, and the community from a nonwhite menace."[25] But the heightened vigilante violence in McComb in the mid-1960s also worried a number of local whites that the threat to law and order might also come from elements of the white community itself. By the late 1960s, then, many influential McComb residents believed that the time had come for the white community to close ranks and to trust in local authorities and institutions—other than the Klan itself—to maintain order. The system would work, they believed, if it were allowed to do so, and so they worked to ensure that it did. Such priorities and such a system ultimately offered little protection for a girl such as Tina Andrews.

Appreciating the habits of violence—practiced by the police and other area law enforcement authorities, by Klan organizations, by individuals, and by the power of the state itself—that had prevailed in Pike County, Mississippi, in the 1960s is vital to understanding Tina Andrews's fate and the story that unfolded after her death.[26] Violence, aggression, and murder marked the region in which she lived and died. Her hometown's culture and customs had been shaped and maintained within a deeply racialized social order. Tina Andrews was not killed because of her race, as many black Mississippians had been. But her death in 1969 and the murder trials in 1971 and 1972 occurred within social and political structures that were as strongly shaped by race as any others in the South. That violence exposed tensions within white McComb about the meaning of law and order that many people in that community were eager to resolve. In the work of white retrenchment that was occurring in those years, Tina Andrews's modest social origins made her expendable and made her a victim. No one has ever considered the murder of Tina Andrews as a civil rights–era case, but given the significance of race in McComb, Mississippi, it might be well to do so.

1

"The Camellia City of America"

Managing Life in McComb, Mississippi

It is a privilege to live in McComb.
—*Enterprise-Journal* (McComb, MS)

In 1964, McComb was "hell on earth."
—Local NAACP activist C. C. Bryant

McComb, Mississippi, where Tina Andrews lived and died, was a city of twelve thousand people, the 1970 U.S. Census would report, approximately the same population that it had in 1960, and not much less than it does today.[1] Pike County, just above the Louisiana line in the deep southwestern part of the state, contained 31,756 residents, 17,903 of them white and 13,867 of them black, making the county 56.4 percent white; only twenty-six people living there were neither black nor white, according to the official count at least. McComb itself had just over eight thousand white residents and about four thousand black ones. Like the rest of Mississippi, McComb had a long history of racial segregation, maintained by law and custom. But even by southern standards, Mississippi seemed grim. "Segregated Mississippi," observed Howard Zinn in 1964, "became as closed a society as slave Mississippi had been." A white civil rights activist recalled: "Though I grew up in deepest darkest rural Alabama, I was afraid of Mississippi."[2] In the 1960s, black residents of Pike County mounted a series of sharp challenges to that segregated society, and local whites defended, some of them violently, what most white Mississippians thought of as the southern way of life. Through the early and mid-1960s, the national media helped sharpen the image of McComb as a forbidding place. "Tensions are as great," reported the *New York Times* of McComb in 1964, "as anywhere else in the state."[3]

McComb also had a history of social class distinctions and periodic tensions that sometimes complicated the maintenance of the segregation that almost all whites agreed was the natural order of things. In the town, it mattered whether one were born black or white. But it also mattered, if one were white, whether one came from a solid, respectable social background or not. That sense of solidness and respectability was not entirely a matter of income. Behavior, presentation, and reputation counted for much in McComb and the rest of Pike County. Tina Andrews and her family did not come from such a respectable background. Neither did Billie Jo Lambert, Tina's friend, on whose word the state ultimately depended when attempting to bring the men arrested for Andrews's murder to justice. The deep history of race and social class in McComb, more than either of those two girls could have realized, informed the search for Andrews's killer, two trials for that crime, and the legacy of the case long after the trials concluded.

Founded in 1872, when the New Orleans, Jackson, and Great Northern extended its line north from New Orleans, McComb had long been shaped by the railroad.[4] Between 1870 and 1880, the population of the county grew by nearly 50 percent, as many early residents worked in the line's maintenance shops. In the twentieth century, the Illinois Central became a major employer in the area, with large shops located near downtown McComb, where until 1987 they provided steady work for several generations of Pike County men. The railroad shops not only repaired cars for the Illinois Central; they manufactured them as well, enjoying a significant period of growth in the 1920s and again just after World War II, when the refrigerated cars built there carried the Deep South's produce to northern markets.[5]

McComb City, as it was long known, had a notable blue-collar tenor and a white working class that had occasionally demonstrated a consciousness of its potential power. McComb men, for instance, had joined one of the state's first railroad unions. In 1911, those workers, along with others up and down the line, struck against the railroad, with Governor Edmond Noel eventually calling in the National Guard to quell the violence that erupted against both workers and strikebreakers.[6] The small railroad museum in downtown McComb now commemorates that strike, which otherwise does not loom large in the city's official stories about its past.[7] By 1904, the city also had a large factory, McComb Cotton Mills, typical of the deep southern manufacturing of the era that depended upon the light processing of local agricultural products.

In the 1930s, Hugh White, the son of a local sawmill baron and community booster, became governor of Mississippi. Governor White's "Balance Agriculture with Industry" program, a hope as much as it was an accomplished fact, did inspire the McComb area to some greater economic diversification.[8] Light industry and agricultural processing provided many blue-collar jobs in the county. The city never attracted the thriving development that its boosters had hoped for, but a number of small manufacturing concerns provided solid employment through the middle decades of the twentieth century. McComb, more than most other Mississippi towns its size, had a fair amount of steady wage work that drew people there from rural areas of surrounding counties.

Pike County also developed a small oil industry after World War II, with two wells operating in the county by the 1950s and others in the following decade.[9] "In 1958," boasted one local account, "the largest United States oil discovery for that particular year was made in Little Creek, an area near McComb." "Even now at night," waxed one 1970s description, "the traveler near McComb can easily see these lighted derricks resembling giant fire-flys on a warm spring evening."[10] Shell Oil operated a natural gas processing plant near McComb as well. In the 1950s, many area people imagined that gas and oil would propel the area into great prosperity, but it never did, at least for the average person. Emmitt Thornhill, a man prominent in the 1960s as a vocal opponent of the civil rights movement, was not an average person. He grew rich from his oil business, claiming that at one point his wells brought him $500,000 in a month, enough to buy a new Cadillac for himself and his wife every year.[11] Thornhill is one of those area men who became rich by anyone's measure, but never entirely respectable, a reminder that one's standing in the area was not measured only by the size of one's bank account.

Compared with Natchez and Vicksburg, cities to the west and northwest, McComb was not an old town. There were no grand antebellum homes in the city, no significant Civil War landmarks, other than a Confederate memorial in front of City Hall, and no remnants of Faulknerian plantations or great families gone to seed. Comparing the town to other Mississippi cities, Greenville journalist Hodding Carter wrote: "McComb lacks the antiquity and the aristocratic antecedents of a Natchez, the Midwestern industrial enlightenment of a Tupelo, the cultural eminence and cosmopolitan tolerance of Greenville, the political sights and sounds and odors of Jackson, and the relaxed amorality of Biloxi. The stamp of the roundhouse and the small farm's corn patch bite too deep."[12] Without an antebellum and Civil War past, McComb was instead forged in the struggles of Reconstruction, and that history mattered very much for the pattern of race relations in the town. Those post–Civil War years figured centrally in the stories that white McComb remembered about community and identity. One of the great lessons of that era, believed by generations of white Mississippians, was that "bossed mass Negro voting" during Reconstruction had proved a political and economic danger and a failure, one that white men had eventually corrected.[13] The system of racial segregation that had been created in the late nineteenth and early twentieth centuries, they believed, was not only essential to the maintenance of the local way of life, but was also satisfactory to people of both races.[14]

McComb had never been part of any Old South cotton kingdom, although Pike County did have a significant African American population, largely concentrated in McComb itself. That black population rose and fell over the decades, and in common with many other Mississippi counties, Pike County saw a significant drop in its African American population during the 1910s, as people left to seek better opportunities and relief from the oppressions of Jim Crow.[15] The town had also welcomed several generations of immigrants in the late nineteenth and early twentieth centuries, many from Italy and the Middle East. McComb's Hollywood Cemetery holds graves of families with names such as Serio and Abdallah. As was common in southern towns with a significant African American population, those southern European and Middle Eastern immigrants were quickly assimilated into and embraced a white identity. People do recall, however, that once tensions over the defense of Jim Crow became acute in the 1960s, occasionally some of those families would be challenged by anxious merchants who believed they were black people testing public accommodations. Such anxieties demonstrate one of the ways that the black challenge to Jim Crow revealed tensions and potential fractures within the local white community.[16]

McComb lies about eighty miles south of Jackson, the state capital. Just over one hundred miles south is New Orleans. Approximately one hundred miles southwest is Baton Rouge, Louisiana. People from Walthall County to the east and Amite County to the west came to McComb for goods and services that the very small towns in those counties could not offer. "The city's wholesalers and merchants [supplied] a radius of more than 50 miles and 300,000 people" by the 1970s, one account bragged.[17] McComb's geographic and economic circumstances were thus similar to many other cities in the Deep South: major regional cities within driving distance, while itself playing an important role on a subregional stage. By national standards, McComb could seem a small place. In its Mississippi context, however, it was a town of significant size. In the southwestern part of the state, it was one of the most important towns, a place whose importance overbalanced its raw size.

In the 1950s and 1960s, McComb still seemed centered on its downtown area. Driving east along Delaware Avenue, within less than a square mile one could find a healthy percentage of the city's white residential properties, McComb High School—the white high school, as the city's schools were until the early 1970s still essentially racially segregated—churches of the major Christian denominations, the city hall and police department, and a host of businesses. Most banks, automobile dealerships, and lawyers' offices were still downtown, too, along Broadway or Main or Canal. By the late 1960s, the downtown area had entered the economic doldrums. Some businesses of long duration had closed. "Right now much of downtown McComb is headed in the direction of a slum condition," warned newspaper editor Oliver Emmerich at the beginning of 1969. On a recent walk through the area, Emmerich had counted some forty-six vacant buildings, a sign that downtown was "suffering" and "degenerating."[18] By that period, most new commercial and residential development occurred in the western part of town, and in the 1970s would continue to push west out Delaware Avenue. By the 1970s, most people in McComb realized that downtown was dying. But in the late 1960s, that economic decline was not as fully apparent as it would be a few years later, and its businessmen still wielded considerable influence in town, reflected in their presence on the city board, as well as on the boards of directors of various banks and the hospital.

The city, at least the parts of it that a white visitor might see, was attractive. In the late 1950s, the McComb Garden Club organized an Azalea Festival, featuring a lighted tour of the houses in the city that featured those flowering plants in their landscaping. That festival was inspired, so the story went, by the traditional Japanese lighting of the cherry blossoms. The newspaper wrote:

"During the days and nights—particularly the nights—of McComb's annual lighted azalea trail, this area becomes a veritable fairyland. Nothing in Florida or California can surpass it."[19] The city also boasted of the great number and beauty of its camellia bushes, a variety of japonica. The city liked to call itself "The Camellia City of America," and also featured an annual lighted tour, or "trail," of those attractive blooming shrubs. Despite the town's lack of an Old South grounding, some kinds of nostalgic foundation stories were impossible to resist, and would have been catnip for white tourists of the era: "History tells us the story," ran one account, "of an old black woman affectionately known as Aunt Caroline, who lived in McComb and planted japonicas in her yard. She began giving both the lovely blooms and her productive cuttings to her friends."[20] Tourists and many local people relished such anecdotes, speaking as they did to warm feelings between the races.

The *Enterprise-Journal*, a vigorous booster of the city, reminded people that "it is a privilege to live in McComb." Many McComb people who grew up in the 1950s remain nostalgic about the community of their youth, a habit they share with other Baby Boomers. For young white people whose parents had a moderate income, life in the small town could indeed seem pleasant. That generation enjoyed, as did millions of other children of the post–World War II economic expansion, a stability and prosperity that previous McComb generations had not known.[21] The men and women there who were adults in the 1950s and 1960s had come of age during the Great Depression and World War II. "Those were not the good old days," one could hear from older residents of Pike County. "Those were hard times." More men than not, it seemed, had been "in the service" during the war, as everyone put it. Compared with the 1930s and 1940s, the early post–World War II years did seem good times, and one can understand why McComb people in those years prized order, stability, and the seeking of a good standard of living.

Many white McComb residents thought of their hometown as one in which people knew their neighbors, worked hard, and enjoyed an unmatched quality of life. The climate allowed children to play outdoors for most of the year, and many homes, before the era of universal air conditioning, had front porches that encouraged conversation and after-supper visits with neighbors. Typical of a town its size, McComb had neighborhood elementary schools, to which most children could walk and even return home for lunch. There was one high school for white students, which did much to forge what sometimes seemed common interests across social class lines. The annual football game against rival Brookhaven, a similarly sized town twenty miles to the north, was played on Thanksgiving Day in the 1940s and 1950s.[22] People dressed well for the game, as they did for college football games in the state, especially those of Ole Miss. What of the sports teams from the black schools? A McComb man who grew up in the era recalls frankly: "Few whites knew how the teams in the African American section were doing; even fewer cared."[23] Much the same thing could be said of the white population's general attitude toward their black fellow citizens.

It was possible to grow up in McComb, if you were white, without thinking very much about racial matters. If you did think about them, they seemed one of those facts that one took for granted, like the Mississippi summer heat. White McComb residents could easily believe, if they wished to do so, that race relations were settled and that black McComb understood its place and was basically happy with its lot, or at least resigned to it. The early and mid-1960s would change all that, however. From the perspective of black citizens in the area, the Jim Crow years were not happy days or a period about which one could feel the same nostalgia in later years.[24]

To the large black community in town, the one overarching fact was the Jim Crow society in which they lived, worked, and raised families. Downtown McComb businesses were racially segregated by law and custom until the mid-1960s, but only an unobservant person would imagine that changes in federal law brought a quick end to segregation in the Camellia City. Politics and elections were considered by practically all whites and by some blacks as well to be white people's business. Schools were separate and unequal. Always there was the threat of violence to attempt to ensure that African Americans knew their place and remained there. There were, especially by the 1950s, black residents who worked to change that pattern of life, but their efforts did not bear much fruit until the 1960s and beyond. In the meantime, as one Mississippi journalist put it gingerly, there was "no tradition in the area of that patriarchal regard for one-time black chattels, which can still be found, though decreasingly, on the plantations along the Mississippi River."[25]

Housing in McComb was racially segregated, a fact that would have seemed unremarkable to Mississippians. Black residents lived mostly in south Mc-

Comb, in neighborhoods such as Baertown, Silver City, and Harlem Heights. McComb had an ambiguous official relationship with its black neighborhoods. Only in 1961 had Baertown been annexed. By 1963, the city had second thoughts, with the city board strongly debating whether or not to deannex the area. Mayor Gordon Burt regretted having taken in the area, and he worried that residents would demand city services for which the rest of McComb did not wish to pay. "They'll want street lights," he predicted. Ultimately, the board did vote to keep the area.[26] In a pattern of development typical in small Mississippi towns, the city had given its south McComb residents not street lights, but instead the local sewage treatment plant. Baertown continued to rankle city fathers, and early in 1964 they revisited the issue, this time in fact voting to deannex the area, a statement of white McComb's dissatisfaction with recent black restiveness.[27]

Growing up in McComb in the 1960s and into the 1970s, one could still hear these black neighborhoods referred to as "the nigger quarters," a usage that allowed whites of all social classes to employ the nomenclature of slaveholding. The low price of black women's labor allowed very many white families, including those of modest middle-class means, to hire black cooks and housekeepers. A local young black resident wrote matter-of-factly in 1964: "The Negro woman earns her wages as a maid."[28] In scenes familiar to readers of *The Help* and other fiction set in the era, in the morning one could witness uniformed African American women arriving in white neighborhoods to work and care for other people's children. Black men, who did much of the yardwork for white families, were careful about the ways in which they interacted with white women; risks of misunderstandings were high. Did any affection develop from this employment? Generations of white children thought so. But at the end of the day, having observed a good deal about the families for which they worked, black people returned to their homes and families, about which white McComb understood very little.[29] By the 1970s, that pattern of black women's employment in white homes was changing. A local newspaperman recalled: "There was a local lawsuit in which the workers filed a suit seeking back Social Security payments. That 'pretty much ended the practice of hiring these workers on a widescale basis.'"[30]

During the middle decades of the twentieth century, a vital African American business district in the city centered on Summit Street. There were restaurants and other amusements, including the Lyric Theater, with an ice cream parlor and a drug store. Along Summit Street, one could shoot pool, shop for goods and services, and in the evening, enjoy music at the Harlem Nightingale, later known as the Elk's Rest. A local black businessman remembered, "It was a wide-open city. They had clubs, gambling, corn liquor, everything. . . . Dancing, partying, drinking. Clubs, clubs, clubs."[31] McComb was part of the southern "chitlin' circuit" traveled by black entertainers, some of them the best of that era. The list of acts that visited the city is staggering: B. B. King, John Lee Hooker, Muddy Waters, Lightnin' Hopkins, Marvin Gaye, Little Milton, Ray Charles, Fats Domino, Cab Calloway, Louis Armstrong, and Redd Foxx. These artists stayed in the Summit Street district in the Desoto Hotel, as would any other black traveler who did not have a local connection for a bed.[32] But again, white McComb, except for a few adventurous teenagers, knew little of this world, except for what they might read in a police report in the local newspaper. Decades later, McComb elected its first black mayor, Zach Patterson, a man who had grown up on Summit Street.[33] In the heyday of the "chitlin' circuit," that development would have been inconceivable to both black and white residents of the city.

McComb became the center of some of the most intense civil rights clashes of the 1960s, in Mississippi or anywhere else. The obstacles faced by local African Americans and those who assisted them were formidable. "The hazardous southwest area of Mississippi," noted the Student Nonviolent Coordinating Committee, was a "stronghold of white terrorist activity," a reputation earned in the period from 1961 through 1964.[34] Although most local whites were unaware of it, McComb and Pike County had seen persistent efforts in the 1940s and 1950s to organize grassroots resistance to Jim Crow, including attempts at voter registration. As John Dittmer shows, the same railroad that white McComb prized for the good jobs that it brought to the area also employed local black men, affording them "a degree of economic security." That security, thanks to union-protected jobs, meant some insulation from "local whites, who had historically applied economic sanctions against blacks who engaged in political activity."[35] As was the case in other Mississippi communities, there had been a chapter of the NAACP, founded in 1944. But also in common with other areas of the state, recruiting members in McComb was difficult. By the mid-1950s, however, the local NAACP branch showed signs of renewal, sparked by interest in the *Brown* decision of 1954 and strong leadership from local men (and railroad employees) C. C. Bryant and Webb Owens. Soon the chapter had more than one hundred members.[36] Still, "it was almost impossible," said Bryant, "to get anyone registered."[37] By the early 1960s, some of those longtime activists, along with a young generation of McComb people, determined to undertake a fresh drive for civil rights in the area.

The year 1961 brought evidence of black McComb's dissatisfaction with the status quo. Black direct action, some of it coordinated and assisted by national civil rights organizations and some the product of spontaneous local efforts, seemed revolutionary to most local whites and took most of them by surprise. As Wesley Hogan has argued, "Voter registration was just as threatening to the racial caste system as a sit-in or a Freedom Ride, so there was no meaningful difference between these kinds of actions."[38] Few McComb whites recognized the long-standing grievances that black McComb felt. Events of that year emboldened local black people and alarmed white residents, sparking white resistance that continued to grow through the middle of the decade. One of these developments was a voter registration campaign led by local activists in tandem with Student Nonviolent Coordinating Committee (SNCC) workers. Another was a sit-in at a downtown business, undertaken by young McComb people. Yet another sign of young black activism was a student walkout from Burgland High School. And finally, near the end of the year, was the attempted integration of the local bus station by Freedom Riders. No one in McComb, black or white, could recall a time of such fundamental challenges to the racial order.

Most people in McComb in the early and mid-1960s were not direct participants either in civil rights activism or in overt resistance to the civil rights movement. White McComb largely wished for matters to remain as they had been, convinced as they were that the system of racial segregation was either acceptable or something about which they could do very little. Black McComb wished for changes, but recognizing the forces that were arrayed against them, many black area residents sought to avoid acts they understood would invite violent retaliation. Others in the area, however, deliberately looked for ways to participate in what they recognized as a moment of significance. Some of them welcomed civil rights workers, tried to register to vote, or in other ways worked to achieve the citizenship denied to them. Other people, white men, concluded that standing pat or waiting for law enforcement officials or city fathers to do something about agitators was not enough. Some of those men joined the klaverns of the Ku Klux Klan that were beginning to organize in Pike County in the early 1960s. Others took matters into their own hands. But they little understood the black determination that existed in the city.

"Part of what made the McComb movement possible," observes historian Charles Payne, "was the ability of SNCC to plug into work that an older generation of activists had begun."[39] In 1961, longtime local activist C. C. Bryant invited Robert Moses and SNCC to undertake a voter registration project in McComb.[40] Moses was determined to show people like Bryant that civil rights activists from outside the area were willing to move in, stay there, and share the considerable risks with local people. Before coming to McComb, Moses had written to the Justice Department, asking if the Kennedy administration would make good on its promise to assist potential voters who faced violence or intimidation. Moses received assurances that it would; it did not. Many local people worked closely with these activists. Webb Owens, NAACP treasurer and a retired railroad worker, introduced SNCC workers to black community members, including Alyene Quinn, a local cafe owner. Owens urged Quinn to feed and assist workers in any ways that she could. Moses was joined by two SNCC field secretaries, Reggie Robinson, from Baltimore, and John Hardy, a veteran of the Nashville student movement.[41]

The main challenge for Bryant, Moses, and other activists was to persuade local people that registering to vote was worth the risk and to assist them in navigating the deliberately complex, intimidating registration process. The application form was lengthy, and the requirement that any potential voter might be asked to display an "understanding" of any of the 285 sections of the Mississippi constitution provided a flexible way for a white registrar to disqualify any black voter. A Pike County man who tried to register just after World War II recalled being told to "go back and study, brush up on your civics."[42] Reactions to potential black voters in the 1960s would not always be so cordial. Grim humor among local people suggested that a black person who attempted to register to vote could save everyone's time by burning his own house. Moses eventually accompanied sixteen determined would-be voters to the county seat of Magnolia.[43] Six of them successfully registered. People in the neighboring counties of Amite and Walthall asked for similar assistance in registration efforts, and Moses cooperated. Amite County proved a hard nut to crack. "It was bad in McComb and in Pike County," said C. C. Bryant, "but it was still worse in Amite County."[44] After a registration trip to the county seat of Liberty, Moses was pulled over by a highway patrolman, arrested for interfering with an officer, tried quickly, and fined. His sentence was suspended, perhaps because local authorities heard him telephone the Justice Department to report what had happened, and also in part because they were not sure what to do with a man like Moses, with his quiet but firm knowledge of his rights and a willingness to confront white authorities.[45]

That same summer, a number of McComb African Americans, too young to register to vote, took action of their own. Some teenage activists were impatient both with second-class citizenship and with what many of them perceived as their elders' caution. One argued that some older black McComb residents "are just plain afraid to get aside and let the young people of the community do what they want."[46] One of the things that young activists wanted was to conduct direct-action protests. On Saturday, August 26, 1961, Hollis Watkins and Curtis Hayes were arrested for "McComb's first sit-in demonstration," occurring at the F. W. Woolworth store, where Watkins and Hayes took a seat at the lunch counter and asked for service. They were arrested on breach of peace charges. The men said that their aim was to "awaken the entire community of McComb . . . we are tired of segregation." The local paper reported that the men were carrying various literature, including writings by Martin Luther King and Lillian Smith. "One of the Negroes had a copy of a paperback book, 'Nausea,' by Jean Paul Sartre, inscribed on the flyleaf 'Property of Bob Moses,' in his possession."[47] The Woolworth's sit-in arrest demonstrates that young activists' McComb work should not be sharply separated from that of the SNCC-assisted voter registration campaign, as SNCC activist Marion Berry had approached Woolworth's management the previous week about integration of the lunch counter. Some SNCC workers quickly organized a meeting to coordinate protests of the arrests. Equally clear was that white McComb authorities were well aware of the possibility of a growing sit-in movement. Upon hearing rumors that the now members-only McComb Library was a potential target, city board members requested that the library shut its doors. Police Chief George Guy had that same day sent officers to area cafes and other businesses with lunch counters, not sure where the challenge would strike.

The next challenge was not long in coming. On Wednesday, August 30,

Bobbie Talbert, Ike Lewis, and Brenda Travis were arrested for attempting to use the white waiting room after purchasing Greyhound bus tickets, a charge of "conduct designed to provoke a breach of the peace," which was becoming one of the favored anti-direct action tools of the period.[48] The three were arraigned and tried within two hours. One of the police officers testified that he "arrested the Negroes to prevent a disturbance." All received fines and four-month sentences, which in Talbert's case and likely because of a guilty plea, was suspended "pending good behavior." Lewis and Travis would remain in jail until October. Bob Moses displayed ambivalence about these direct-action protests. While he understood the desire of Hayes and Watkins to "do something themselves" that "they were enthusiastic about," he worried that local activists who had signed on for a voter registration campaign would be less interested in sit-ins and similar protests, especially ones that put young black people in harm's way. He also worried that the Justice Department would be less willing to offer support of sit-ins than of the violations of rights of would-be voters.[49]

In the late summer of 1961, the voter registration project piloted by Moses began to encounter violent resistance. On Tuesday, August 29, the same day that Hollis Watkins and Curtis Hayes were tried for the Woolworth's sit-in, Moses was attacked by the Amite County sheriff's cousin, Billy Jack Caston. Surprising most people, black and white, Moses filed charges against Caston. At the courthouse, the sheriff informed Moses and other witnesses that he could not guarantee their safety in the county. Caston claimed that Moses had started a fight with him. The Amite County jury acquitted Caston.[50] The murder of Herbert Lee, a black farmer, in Amite County in 1961, and other violent reactions against the work there and in Pike County, brought the voter registration project organized by Bryant and Moses to a halt. By the fall, few people were willing to attempt to register.[51] Ultimately, few voters were registered that summer, and the city developed a reputation among civil rights workers as a forbidding place. But many young workers who came to the city, including Chuck McDew, Charles Sherrod, and Marion Berry, later mayor of Washington, D.C., gained experience that proved useful. For everyone involved, the year 1961 seemed fresh territory. As Charles Payne puts it, "Going into Mc-Comb, there was no way that SNCC could have much sense of what it took to sustain an organizing drive in the hard-core South." The major lesson for

SNCC seemed to be that it was possible to get "a critical mass of local people to respond," that in itself a major accomplishment.[52]

McComb young people also developed a taste for direct action that year of 1961, and at least some older black members of the community and other activists, including SNCC organizers, determined to follow where the younger people led. When Ike Lewis and Brenda Travis were released from jail after their bus station arrests, they learned that they had been expelled from Burgland High School. In response, over one hundred students walked out of Burgland High, surprising white authorities, SNCC activists, and older community organizers such as C. C. Bryant. Some black parents were uncomfortable with their children's participation in this campaign. But other local activists did support the students, following them to McComb City Hall, where they kneeled and prayed. White SNCC field secretary Bob Zellner was beaten savagely there.[53] Moses and Charles McDew were arrested for contributing to the delinquency of minors. Brenda Travis was sentenced to an undetermined term in a youth correctional facility. Burgland's principal attempted to have his students sign pledges not to engage in any more activism, promising to expel anyone who did not return to classes. The students refused and turned in their books. The SNCC workers in the area set up a "Nonviolent High" for the students to attend. After a short time, Jackson's Campbell College took over the students' education.[54] Many black parents, displeased by this disruption of their children's schooling, blamed activists for the young people's involvement.

"Direct action ran head-on into the stone wall of absolute police power in Mississippi," one contemporary observer argued.[55] But in Pike County in the early and mid-1960s, who or what constituted police power? The police and sheriff's departments were the forces to which local whites looked to keep order, often defined as ensuring black compliance with law and custom. By the 1960s, a powerful, well-financed Klan also operated in southwest Mississippi. Black residents were aware that the line between Klan and other forms of policing was not sharp, as members of one organization could in fact be a member of the other. But McComb authorities in 1961 were determined that any unrest should be handled by legally constituted force. They were uncomfortable with white violence undertaken by free agents such as Klansmen.

But certainly there was in the area a tradition of violent white intransigence to any dissent on matters of racial order. Oliver Emmerich, the editor of the *Enterprise-Journal*, recalled incidents in which he had been physically assaulted for writing about matters of race. In 1950, Emmerich described the jailhouse beating of a young black man falsely accused of breaking into a business. A man later came to the newspaper office to confront him: "Why did you print that story about that nigger being whipped in the jail?" Emmerich replied: "If we do not stop these abuses ourselves the time will come when others will force us to correct them." In response, Emmerich "felt a hard fist strike the back of my neck, just behind my right ear. I plummeted to the ground—out cold." In 1961, when Freedom Riders tested public accommodations in McComb and were met with white violence, Emmerich "pled for law and order, and urged that an effort be made not to project an ugly image of the state." "The following Sunday morning a stranger walked up to me. He seemed agreeable enough. . . . He stopped me and asked me pleasantly, 'Are you the fellow who runs this newspaper here?' I answered affirmatively. Without warning, his fist crashed into my eyeglasses. I had just been released from the city hospital a couple of weeks before following a serious heart attack. My assailant later came to trial and was acquitted."[56]

The Freedom Riders, the occasion for Emmerich's plea for law and order in McComb and the subsequent attack upon him, arrived in the city at the end of November 1961, as part of their campaign to test southern compliance with Supreme Court decisions outlawing racial segregation on public interstate bus transportation. At the city's downtown bus station on November 30, a host of people prepared to meet the riders: national media, F.B.I. agents, local activists, McComb police, and a crowd of local whites. The bus arrived earlier than expected, and that white crowd beat the police to the station. When the riders entered the formerly white waiting room and took seats at the lunch counter, "the place seemed to blow up all of a sudden," said a bus station employee. The riders were "pushed and scuffled" to the "sidewalk and the street," where "they were central figures in a wild chase for several minutes."[57] The riders left that evening for New Orleans, but not before taking poundings from various members of the white crowd. In response, McComb's mayor, C. H. Douglas, issued a statement. First, he said, bus desegregation was a federal mandate, and while "we did not make it at a local level . . . it is our purpose to enforce it." Second, he characterized the activists as "outside professional agitators who come with the announced intention of remaining in our city until an incident is provoked and photographed." Third, he said that whites who had participated in the day's attacks had been arrested, as McComb authorities were determined to maintain order against any disruptive forces.[58] Finally, said the mayor, his town, "the Camellia City of America," was a "beautiful and enlightened community" that enjoyed "mutual respect and friendship" among blacks and whites. If McComb police were allowed to do their job without interference from federal injunctions or white violence, all would be well.

The violent reaction to the Freedom Riders in McComb reveals two fundamental matters about the community, ones that would shape the area's history through the 1960s. First, a number of area white men took action into their own hands, not waiting for the police or other legally constituted forces to meet racial challenges. Claude Sitton, reporter for the *New York Times*, argued that "some of these people really thought they were defending their way of life. They believed it. I don't question their sincerity." But others were simply men who relished the opportunity for aggression toward those they considered outsiders, whether black or white. Such men, said Sitton, were simply "thugs." "Sam Fentress of *Time* and a *Life* photographer were walking down the street and this thug comes up and knocks Fentress through a plate glass window . . . because the thugs were thugs and thugs will be thugs, it don't matter what." Sitton's comments also make plain another matter. Local people of influence and power understood that extralegal violence was bad for business. "Merchants at that time were calling salesmen coming to town and telling them not to come to town. It was too dangerous."[59] Over time, that division among white McComb residents over what constituted acceptable forms of resistance would become more pronounced, exposing tensions within the white community.

Events of 1961—the black school protest, the Freedom Riders, the local sit-ins, and the early efforts at voter registration—taught lessons to area whites. Some believed that area law enforcement agencies and the courts were sufficient tools, perhaps with some refinements in the way of enhanced criminal charges for anything that looked like civil rights activism, to handle challenges that they surely knew would come. Other whites, some of whom wore the uniform of one of those law enforcement agencies, believed that the time had come for stronger measures. Some of those men embraced one of the Klan organizations that had begun to revive in the state in the early 1960s. Again in 1964, as part of the Freedom Summer project, activists and local people attempted to crack the white hold on political power in the area. And again, organized violence met them.[60]

In the early and mid-1960s, matters of crime and criminality weighed upon the minds of many white McComb residents. They were concerned to counter national perceptions of the community as a lawless place. As historian Joseph Crespino argued, "An important part of the civil rights fight involved public relations, explaining to other Americans why southern segregation was reasonable, good, and proper."[61] As they had done for decades, many local whites asserted that racial segregation itself was the best bulwark against the breakdown of the social order. Responding to national media criticism of McComb, Mayor Gordon Burt said in 1963: "We vigorously and proudly practice segregation. We are the only people in the history of the world who have successfully evolved a formula under which two completely different groups have lived together in harmony, without mongrelization and assimilation." Black McComb was free and protected, argued Burt. Neither "our Negroes," he said, "nor the whites need police escorts to protect them from the hoodlum and criminal element spawned by the moral breakdown inevitably resulting from integration." If one wanted to see real criminality, asserted Burt, one should look to "the sociological experiment in integration" in "Washington, D.C."[62]

Black residents of Pike County, however, saw much evidence of local criminality and little of the harmony that Burt lauded. By the mid-1960s, just in time for the Freedom Summer of 1964, Pike County was thick with active, well-organized, and violent Ku Klux Klan organizations, operating under the auspices of the United Klans of America (UKA), which had formed in Alabama in 1961 and rapidly grew in strength through the Deep South. This Klan growth was a relatively new development. David Cunningham points out that "for a number of years the KKK in Mississippi was distinctive mostly for its absence." Determined to change that fact, however, the UKA's leader, Robert Shelton, conducted organizing drives and public rallies in McComb in 1964. Initially, the UKA tried to distance itself from the reputation for overt violence of the other major Klan organization operating in the state, the White Knights, who were responsible for the Neshoba County murders of James Cheney, Andrew Goodman, and Michael Schwerner. Shelton, noted a contemporary U.S. House of Representatives report on Klan activity, "publicly proclaim[ed] nonviolent intent."[63] However, a definite taste for violent direct action marked the Mc-Comb UKA klaverns, and in "a five month period beginning in June" of that year, "eight beatings, seven burnings, four shootings and fifteen bombings were reported in the area." The acts were carried out by some of the most determined of the area's Klansmen, operating as a "secret sect dubbed the Wolf Pack." Victims' names, one of those accused Klansmen later said, were sometimes drawn from a hat.[64]

The violence of 1961 had not prepared activists or journalists for what they would see in Pike County during the summer of 1964. Activist Cleveland Sellers, like others who came to work in the area, found southwest Mississippi hard to fathom. McComb was located, he recalled, in "an area some observers have compared to the 'ninth circle of hell.'" Area whites, he learned, "were willing to kill in order to keep the organizers from accomplishing their goals."[65] Claude Sitton, who as a civil rights correspondent for the *New York Times* had covered many of the hottest spots in the South from Virginia to Texas, agreed with this assessment of "dangerous" McComb: "It was small, condensed, you know, well, hell." People there "would kill."[66]

In 1964, the state of Mississippi experienced what white residents had been told would be an "invasion." Around one thousand college students and other volunteers came to the state to attempt to register black voters and to organize "freedom schools" to teach black Mississippians a variety of subjects, including basic civics. Largely because of McComb's reputation as a hard place, Freedom Summer organizers chose to work there in tandem with the town's long-standing cadre of local activists. Through May of 1964, Oliver Emmerich in the pages of the *Enterprise-Journal* urged his readers to avoid violence and to remain calm, a stance more responsible than that taken by many other state newspaper editors, especially the ones in the capital city of Jackson. On May 29, Emmerich wrote: "Our choice is simple. We can be smart or we can be outsmarted. Our people could become emotional and panic. We could even resort to mob action and with extreme hysteria find federal troops in our community. . . . We should all try to relax. Let the law enforcement officers handle the situation for us. They are willing. They stand committed. They insist that they are prepared. What more could we ask?"[67]

McComb police officers, like those in other Mississippi towns, prepared themselves for the invasion. The department purchased a new tear gas pistol, suitable for "close range work," which could be used to "control riots, flush fugitives from hiding, and break up demonstrations."[68] Through the summer of 1964, which writers then and later always refer to as a long, hot one, McComb erupted with a series of bombings so intense that the city became national news. Black homes and places of business that hosted civil rights organizing were targeted in a campaign of domestic terrorism. The initial response of local law enforcement authorities was not an aggressive search for the bombers. In fact, the Pike County sheriff said to the pastor of a burned church: "You niggers is just bombing one another."[69] Joe Pigott, district attorney in 1969 and in these earlier years as well, recalled national media coverage of the violence: "The first night they talked about church bombings and house burnings in McComb, a town of about 10,000 halfway between Jackson, Miss., and New Orleans, La. The next night they said McComb, Miss. By the third night, they just said McComb. Everybody knew where that was."[70] A visiting journalist described the area as "rolling green country, Klan country, bad country. They warn you about McComb."[71]

The Council of Federated Organizations, or COFO, the cooperative association of groups working in the state that year, took affidavits to document both the violent resistance and local authorities' levels of complicity in that violence.[72] Ora Lee Bryant, a local cafe owner, allowed volunteers to use her home and place of business for meetings and picnics. On July 26, a group of men threw explosives into her yard and fired into her home. She and her husband returned fire, clear evidence that not all black Mississippians practiced nonviolent resistance. When "a local cop whom we know as ['Big John' Sharpling] came up the walk to our house," he "told us to put our guns away."[73] McComb police officers John Sharpling and Eddie Smith, who would still be members of the department during the investigation of the Tina Andrews murder from 1969 to 1971, were later named as defendants, along with the current sheriff and police chief, in a lawsuit filed by McComb residents and other COFO workers in November 1964, seeking an injunction against law enforcement activities that violated their civil rights.[74]

The attack on Bryant's house was not an isolated one. From the late spring through the fall of 1964, COFO workers and local black people were subjected to a range of incidents at the hands of local law enforcement officers, Klansmen, business owners, and unknown parties (the lines among these groups probably overlapped). They were arrested for loitering, trespassing, failing to yield the right of way, reckless driving, having a faulty brake light, stealing electricity, operating businesses without a license, refusing to obey an officer, being a Peeping Tom, illegal possession of alcohol, "criminal syndicalism," "making improper phone calls to whites," and "suspicion," among other charges. They were driven away from local businesses for attempting to use the telephone and for ordering ice cream cones. Others were spat upon, beaten with brass knuckles, and whipped with a leather strap. C. C. Bryant's barber shop was bombed on April 29. On June 22, Bryant's home was bombed; that same evening so were the homes of Freddie Bates and Corrine Andrews. In Pike County, at least seven churches were targets of successful or attempted arson or bombing. On the evening of September 8 alone, four homes (one of a teacher and another of a preacher) and one church were bombed.[75]

Not only black residents felt the wrath of the summer campaign of violence and intimidation. A local white physician, W. T. Mayer, had a cross burned in his yard on August 12, apparently for adding his name to a list published in the newspaper of people who contributed to a fund being raised to rebuild burned black churches. White residents who employed but failed to fire black workers were also subject to violence, as was a white man who was abducted and whipped for "talking too much with Negroes."[76] A local white family, Red and Malva Heffner, and their daughters Carla Heffner and Jan Nave, were hounded from town in 1964 after they invited two white civil rights workers into their home simply to discuss the aims of the work that summer and to present their point of view to the workers. That saga was the subject of a short, grim book by Greenville journalist Hodding Carter, which presents a view of McComb at odds with attempts to read its past as one of a close-knit, welcoming community.[77] It reveals, among other things, the ability of this moment of crisis to fracture lines of white community in McComb.

The Pike County bombings terrorized local African Americans and civil rights workers, but they also greatly alarmed McComb authorities, businessmen, and other broad elements of the white population. Resistance to the civil rights movement, including the creative use of the law, was one thing. This seemed another. Assisted by the F.B.I. and the highway patrol, the sheriff's office and police department found some of those responsible for the bombings. Eleven men were arrested. They ranged in age from the mid-forties to the early twenties. Six of them were Illinois Central Railroad employees. One of them was the son of a prominent local businessman. The charges, of "illegal use of explosives," were serious and carried a possible death penalty under Mississippi law. What authorities found when they made the arrests was equally serious and alarming by anyone's measure. A search of the home of one of the men, Paul Dewey Wilson, charged in the bombings of Alyene Quin and Rev. James Baker, turned up "four high-powered rifles, a pistol of foreign make, thousands of rounds of ammunition, a blackjack, eight wooden clubs, and a set of brass knuckles." Other materials, including a black leatherette hood and apron, goggles, and a hypodermic syringe, hinted at unattractive possibilities. Among Wilson's other possessions were a membership card in the Americans for the Preservation of the White Race, a calling card from Robert Shelton's United Klans of America, and a deputy sheriff's badge.[78]

McComb authorities seemed to have arrested the right men; the bombing campaign stopped. Their fate in court, however, was another matter, and showed that the quest for law and order could be tempered by mercy, or perhaps other considerations. Nine of the eleven men stood trial on October 23. All had initially disclaimed responsibility for the violence, but they pled either guilty or no contest to the charges. They drew either fines (in the case of the three men pleading no contest) or suspended sentences, as the judge said that they were mostly young men just starting out, adding that they had been "provoked" by civil rights activists in the community. F.B.I. director J. Edgar Hoover remarked that it was "scandalous" that the sentences for the nine men were suspended and that they had received probation instead. If one is, like J. Edgar Hoover, shocked at the seeming leniency shown to the McComb bombers by Judge W. H. Watkins, Jr., then consider what might have happened had the cases been strongly contested and gone to trial before a jury of their peers. Stronger evidence in the era resulted in mistrials or acquittals. A prosecutor taking a case about race before a jury in Pike County in those days, as in many other Mississippi counties, took his chances.[79] Judge Watkins did threaten the men with an imposition of their sentences should there be any more bombings in the county. Here, however, is his admonition to the convicted bombers, one in which he explains their situation in a way that made sense to many white Pike County residents:

Now what you have done is to hurt your white friends, your family, and your responsible friends, and it has been to hurt the law. . . . Now, when the law is on your side there's no use and there is no excuse whatever for you doing anything or any act that's contrary to the law, you are both working for the same end, for the same goal, you and the law. . . . But you were not doing it the right way. You should have been cooperating with the law instead of placing your law enforcement officers in jeopardy and in a dangerous situation. We have Civil Defense, we need auxiliary officers to take care of these explosive situations when they arise. . . . I am sure if this situation gets bad enough the sheriff will need auxiliary deputies. Any number of situations might arise where the law enforcement officers need you.[80]

In such an atmosphere, it is little wonder that certain white citizens felt capable of taking the law into their hands and that some members of the police and sheriff's departments could feel that there were higher callings than the letter of the law. Of a 1964 Klan rally at the Pike County fairgrounds, local oilman and die-hard segregationist Emmett Thornhill said that law enforcement officers "haven't bothered us. Besides, a lot of them are members, anyway."[81]

Many people who talked about McComb insisted that matters there were under control or would be if the agitators would simply leave town. In a November 30, 1964, interview on NBC's *Today Show*, Mississippi Governor Paul B. Johnson, Jr., explained: "We have very little trouble in Mississippi . . . we have the lowest crime rate in the entire nation." Asked about the McComb bombers' suspended sentences, Johnson said, "When a circuit judge in Mississippi puts a man on probation, he had better walk a straight line, whether it be a white man, an Indian, a Chinese from our great Mississippi Delta area, a Yugoslav or Chechoslav from the coast." He concluded by assuring the interviewer that black Mississippians were "very, very happy. . . . They want to be left alone."[82] In very many ways, they certainly did, but probably not in the ways that Governor Johnson meant.

The ongoing black interest in registering to vote prefigured changes that would come to the area within a few years. In 1964, approximately four hundred black voters were registered in Pike County. By 1965, that number had risen to two thousand. In Amite County, just to the west, in 1965 some one thousand black voters were registered. In 1964, that number had stood at precisely one, although, as SNCC activist Charles McDew said, "We haven't been able to find him."[83] By the 1970s, black voting had begun to effect changes in McComb city government, to take only one example, changes that continue profoundly to influence public education, economic development, and residential patterns in the city. In recent years, black McComb has enjoyed strong representation on the city board and in other elected local offices, a development that has not set well with many white city residents.[84] As historian Jason Sokol said of the Deep South generally and with some understatement, "A deep resentment toward blacks—if not a condescension or denial of humanity—lasted well beyond the age of civil rights."[85] That story, as much as events of the 1960s, is a chapter in the history of the civil rights movement in the Deep South. McComb remains one of the most understudied centers of the entire civil rights movement. And the story of McComb in the 1970s and 1980s, like that of most towns of the Deep South, remains largely untouched by historians.

By the time of the 1969 murder of Tina Andrews and the trials that would follow in 1971 and 1972, McComb no longer made national news. Civil rights battles now unfolded in the courts and in Justice Department decisions about school desegregation plans and the mechanics of black political participation. By 1970 or so, while many white McComb residents resented the developments of the 1960s, few held any illusions that recent changes in law and black activism would simply go away, as much as they might have liked for that to have happened. McComb in the late 1960s and early 1970s, then, was a city that wished to enjoy order and stability after a decade of challenges that most people in the 1950s, black and white, would scarcely have thought possible. To the extent that it has been studied, McComb's history in the 1960s, like that of Mississippi generally, has been told as a story about race, about black efforts to undermine Jim Crow and violent white resistance to that campaign. But the story of McComb in those years was also a story of social class tensions within the white community. The 1964 bombing campaign worried the political and cultural leadership of the city. It was potentially very bad for business.

Many people in McComb explain that the "best people" in the area organized to fight the rough elements in town. In the midst of that violence, however, said McComb Chamber of Commerce president Robert Brumfield, "a lot of people sat back and enjoyed what was going on."[86] Still, by the end of the summer of 1964, most of white McComb had in fact recoiled against the violence, largely because it seemed out of control and likely to do serious economic damage to the area. On November 17, 1964, the *Enterprise-Journal* published a "Statement of Principles" drafted and circulated by business and civic leaders and signed by well over six hundred people, essentially a who's who of McComb-area doctors, businessmen, and other respected members of the community. The "great majority of our citizens," it read, "believe in law and order and are against violence of any kind." It called for "equal treatment for all citizens under the law" and in a carefully worded passage, said that no one who was a member of any "subversive organization" (in this case, the Ku Klux Klan) should hold elected or appointed office. Decrying extremists "on both sides," the statement ended with a call for dedication to and optimism about Pike County's future. Writing in the New Orleans *Times-Picayune,* reporter Bill Minor called the statement "a national documentary of the American sense of justice and citizenship." Newspaperman and McComb native Mac Gordon later said that the statement was perhaps "the most important document ever presented in McComb."[87] If the statement itself did not end McComb's racial strife (and it did not), it certainly provides evidence that a significant segment of McComb's white population had sickened of the violence practiced by other whites in the county.

This was the Pike County in which Tina Andrews was born, was murdered, and in which two trials failed to convict anyone of that crime. Nothing about the Andrews story would have unfolded the way that it did without McComb's history of race and race relations and the ways that history had shaped the courts, local law enforcement, and people's attitudes toward law and authority. Most people in town, black and white, certainly wished for the bombings and other violence to end. But their diagnosis of the causes and the cure for that violence would have been very different. Black residents of McComb wanted to see things change fundamentally. Whites wanted for things to calm down and go back to the way that they were before, when peace and order, as they saw it, prevailed in the town, and when the police and the sheriff, not night-riding bombers, could keep a handle on matters of race. Former Klan enthusiast Emmitt Thornhill recalled in 1994 that things in McComb were better before "the damn Yankees came in trying to take over. Everybody loved everybody else. Nobody locked their doors."[88] "The Klan," Thornhill had said earlier," had "done a lot of good" in Pike County, "'visiting the sick and helping the needy and screening books,'" meaning "getting sex books out of school libraries."[89] White nostalgia for the alleged good old days of law and order thus occasionally took curious forms in McComb. But Thornhill's reminiscences show how easily white Pike County residents could fail to remember, or perhaps chose not to remember, a time of perceived crisis when tensions among area whites had been high.

The murder of Tina Andrews took place within a context not only of acute racial consciousness in the town, but also a consciousness of potential white working-class unruliness. McComb's business and political leaders could not maintain everything within the city to their liking. But they did wish to convince their fellow white citizens that preserving law and order was essential. Trust the system, they said, much as had Judge Watkins to the 1964 bombers. Despite the turmoil of the mid-1960s, everything in McComb could be calm again, many white residents of the city believed, if they worked to make it so.

2

"The Weirdest Angles
I've Encountered"

Investigating the Murder of Tina Andrews

The person whose body was discovered in the oil field on August 23, 1969, not immediately identified as Tina Andrews, was a homicide victim, with a .38-caliber slug recovered from her right nasal cavity. The bullet had entered her body from a shot to the base of the skull. Another spent bullet was found about twenty feet from the body, and two .38-caliber shells were recovered from the scene. Through August of 1969, and in some ways a good deal longer than that, identification of the remains would prove challenging. "No identification papers or jewelry were found," the local newspaper reported. An area dentist, making an initial examination of the skull, reported that the victim had no dental work that might aid in identification of the body, "although she needed some." Remaining hair on her head allowed the authorities to identify her as white, although her age was uncertain. Some estimates initially put her at eighteen to twenty years of age, although a doctor allowed that she might be younger, perhaps fifteen. She was clad only in short pants ("apparently put on backwards") and a bra, with her panties and a blouse found nearby, about ten feet from the body. Estimates from the skeleton and clothing put her as "rather tall and thin," perhaps five feet, seven inches tall, with a twenty-four inch waist and a thirty-two to thirty-four inch chest.[1]

Photographs of the crime scene taken that August 23 morning show at least ten investigators and other parties at the oil field, most of them clad in the short-sleeved white dress shirts and thin, striped dark neckties one sees in so many other Deep South images from that era.[2] Sammy Keene, a highway patrolman, bends over, peering at Tina Andrews's body, discreetly concealed from the camera here by the couch that had been set upright. A semi-circle of other men, including highway patrolman B. T. Hughes and F.B.I. agent Reesie Timmons, most of them with their hands on their hips, look down at the body, too. Timmons had come to Pike County in 1964, along with as many as twenty-four other agents, when a field office was established in the area to investigate the sharp violence of the place and time. Timmons headed that field office, responsible for eight counties in southwestern Mississippi. He and fellow agent Cy Hoaglund remained in the area when the field office was later reduced in size. Timmons retired in 1979. People's recollections of him say a good deal about the attitude of local whites toward federal authority and outsiders. Joe Pigott, who had worked with Timmons both as district attorney and as circuit judge, said then: "You could always believe what he said. I could depend on what he said to be the truth." Fellow agent Hoaglund recalled: "He was a hard-working professional, a no-nonsense guy." In short, concluded Pigott, Timmons was "a good F.B.I. agent who came here as a Yankee and stayed to be a Southerner." The adjustment was not always easy. "When he first came down here [from New York], Timmons had a hard time understanding the attitude of Southern people . . . it was just so different." But "he got so he could go and talk to members of either race. They knew he was fair." This fair-minded Yankee agent who learned the mysterious ways of southern people was in fact a native of Shiloh, Louisiana, and had lived in that state long enough to graduate from Centenary College there after his World War II service.[3] The definition of outsider-ness in Pike County in that era, then, could seem narrow, and it suggests something about people's lingering sensitivity to local control on matters of law, order, crime, and community.

Area investigators remained uncertain how long the body had lain in the oil field, with some doctors and officers suggesting three weeks; other estimates ran to six weeks. "They hoped the crime lab could come up with more specific information," the newspaper wrote. Beyond the fatal gunshot wound, the body showed additional signs of trauma. District Attorney Joe Pigott said that her jaw was broken. Sheriff Lawson reported that the remains would be sent to the F.B.I. Laboratory in Washington, D.C., for analysis. The area where the body was found, added the sheriff, appeared to have been used as a "lover's lane." Had the victim been sexually assaulted before or after her death? Her panties were not recovered from her body itself and the shorts on the body were backwards, the Jackson newspaper reported. But in those days, there was no mechanism for recovering DNA evidence from her clothing or her physical remains. The deteriorated condition of those remains limited the story that they could tell to investigators, both in Mississippi and beyond.[4]

The coroner's investigation itself also suggests the limits of detective work in the state in that era. Until 1974, when the Mississippi legislature passed the State Medical Examiners Act, elected county coroners investigated cases of "violent or sudden" death, such as that of Tina Andrews. A coroner's jury heard testimony about the probable cause of death from lay and expert witnesses. When an autopsy had been performed, they heard that evidence as well. But the coroner was not necessarily a trained medical professional, as District Attorney Pigott knew, and as he would point out once the case came to trial.[5] Until 1986, in fact, a Mississippi coroner did not have to hold a high school diploma, and anyone who held office then and was a subsequent candidate for reelection continued to be exempt from that educational requirement.[6]

Of the crime scene itself, the oil field in which Tina Andrews was slain should not be imagined as a scene from west Texas or Oklahoma, in which vast derricks are visible from long distances across flat land. Instead, it was the site of a small placement of pumping equipment located amid pine woods and pastures. Only a few minutes' drive from the McComb city limits, it was nevertheless something of a concealed spot. But in other ways, it was a vulnerable place. Anyone doing any killing or anything else there could not count on privacy. If they did their work quickly, perhaps so. But the spot was commonly used, as many adolescents and adults in the area knew, as a site for clandestine physical encounters. While the field itself was relatively shielded from view, then, other people might have arrived at any time to interrupt whatever was happening there.

Given the oil field's frequent use for romance as well as for the dumping of trash, why was the body concealed there above ground and not buried or at least removed to a less detectable site? Perhaps the killer or killers needed to work quickly in order to return to some scene to establish an alibi and thus had no time for a burial. Perhaps they worried that any digging, if indeed they had anything with which to dig, might be interrupted by the arrival of another vehicle. Moving the body may not have seemed a good option. Transporting a bleeding corpse and attempting to find another place to leave it entails many risks. The hasty half-concealment of the body may also suggest that the killing was not planned at all, and that like most things about their actions, other than their having the foresight to bring a gun, the killers were simply improvising. Hiding the body as best as they could and getting away from the scene might have seemed the best option at the time.

Time is generally not the authorities' friend in a murder case, and Pike County lawmen hoped for quick work on the matter. Initially, Pike County officials reported "substantial progress" in the "bizarre murder case." District Attorney Pigott said that "I think that there will be an arrest before the October [1969] term of court. I think that you would be safe in saying that." Just a few days into the investigation, the body still had not been identified, but Pigott also reported "strong evidence in this direction, too."[7] One matter that seemed to have become clearer was the amount of time that the body had lain in the oil field. A study of insects at the site and a pathologist's report suggested that the body had not been there for a month, as initial reports indicated, but rather only a week or perhaps two weeks at the most. In the sweltering Mississippi summer, the body decomposed quickly, probably hastened by the couch under which the remains were concealed, which produced an oven-like effect.

Questions about the identity of the victim, her killer or killers, and the reasons for the murder circulated widely through the area. In early September, District Attorney Pigott acknowledged the speculation that the case had produced. Despite many rumors, cautioned Pigott in early September, and despite his assurances the previous week of quick progress on the case, no arrests had been made. But, continued Pigott, many people, including Sheriff Lawson, highway patrol investigator Donald Butler, and McComb police lieutenant John Sharpling had "worked diligently and interviewed scores of persons" in pursuing leads. "Numerous officers," reported the local newspaper, "have pursued the case around the clock since the body was discovered." Pigott added that the F.B.I. crime lab had completed preliminary analysis of some of the evidence, including the body. "From these preliminary reports," said Pigott, "we feel that we can identify the victim."[8]

It would be more than two and a half weeks before the body was identified. On Friday, September 19, Pigott announced that the remains were those of local girl Tina Marie Andrews. Appearing at the McComb police station at a press conference that also featured Sheriff "Tot" Lawson, Chief of Police Richard Rowley, and police lieutenant John Sharpling, Pigott said that the Andrews family had identified the body based upon "the clothing, the size of the body, the age of the body as determined by the F.B.I. crime lab and other evidence including examination of the teeth." Local authorities had suspected that the remains might be those of Andrews since a few days after their discovery, said Pigott, but he did not specify why the identification had taken so long; when the family had been contacted, questioned about their daughter's disappearance, presented with evidence having to do with the body; or what other role, if any, they had played in the investigation. The family made no public statements about the matter, then or later. In McComb, they had made no appeals to the public for assistance in locating their missing daughter.[9]

Tina Marie Andrews was twelve years old, a student at Otken Elementary School. Born on March 23, 1957, she was the daughter of local couple Fred Paul and Doris Havard Andrews, of 102 Oak Street. Andrews lived and died in a place and an era punctuated by concerns about race and violence. The week that Tina Andrews was born, matters of race were heavy on the minds of McComb people. The local newspaper wrote of a "campaign of hate" directed against southern people. "And the South steadfastly refuses to be the 'whipping boy.'" Also that week, for the first time in many people's memory, if ever in that area, four white men prepared to face trial on rape or kidnapping charges stemming from their assault on a young African American woman east of McComb.[10] Tina had three brothers (another had died very young) and four sisters. Two of the brothers, Freddie and Danny, and one of the sisters, Donna, lived in McComb, with another sister, Winifred, living nearby in Louisiana; the other brother, Ernest, lived in California. The parents had last seen their daughter on the evening of August 13, some ten days before the discovery of the body. Pigott and the other officials asked for public assistance in gathering information about the crime, as they did not have sufficient evidence to make an arrest, or even any strong leads, despite Pigott's earlier assurances that an arrest was imminent. As the murder weapon had been a .38-caliber pistol, Pigott asked that anyone who owned such a weapon or knew of someone who did should report that information to the police. Andrews's family and authorities also announced a reward of $1000 for information leading to the arrest and conviction of her killer or killers. The reward quickly grew, with local businessman and entrepreneur "Uncle Bud" Varnado contributing $250. Authorities had interviewed at that point "upwards of 100 persons," and "numerous bits of evidence have been sent to the FBI lab." Pigott continued: "I think more man-hours have been put in on this case than any other I've been associated with."[11] To that point, however, all those man-hours had yielded little.

The local newspaper included with this story about the identification of the victim a large, over-the-fold photograph of Tina Andrews. It would be the only photograph of Andrews to run in any newspaper at any stage of the story from 1969 through 1972. The source of the photograph was not identified, but it is her fourth-grade school picture.[12] She is dressed in a light-colored blouse, with the collar buttoned at the neck. Her dark hair falls just below her shoulders. Her face, somewhat full and oval, looks no older than her eleven years at the time the picture would have been taken. She wears a slight smile, with her head tilted a bit to the right. Tina Andrews's short life had left practically nothing in the public record to this point, not unusual, given her family's modest circumstances, and also because few average twelve-year-old children have had the opportunity to come to much attention outside their circle of family, friends, and school activities.

Tina's family was not economically or socially prominent in McComb, a fact that would prove consequential to the story that would unfold over the next three years. They had neither the resources nor the influence to press as hard as some other families might have done for a more aggressive or at least a more publicized search for her killer. Her father, Fred P. Andrews, could never quite find his footing or have things break his way. In January 1963, the McComb Fire Department responded to a call at the Andrews's house on Oak Street, to put out a fire that had started in a pan of grease in the kitchen.[13] They were certainly unlucky when it came to matters of fire, as the house was severely damaged in 1968 by a blaze ignited when the gas water heater set fire to brooms and mops in a closet. No one was reported injured in either fire. But the house suffered considerable harm from smoke and water, yet another example of the bad fortune that seemed to dog Fred Andrews.

Tina had a number of cousins in McComb, but she seems not to have been close to them, a matter probably not of her own choosing, but rather of Fred's siblings' decisions not to associate their children with his. A family member later recalled that when she was growing up in McComb, her family insisted to her that she should have nothing to do with Fred Andrews's children, her cousins. Moreover, she was instructed to deny, should anyone ask, that she was related to those Andrews people.[14] One of Fred's siblings, Karey Andrews, was a World War II Navy veteran, as well as a graduate of Southwest Mississippi Junior College. He was many things Fred was not: a successful businessman with children who did well in school. Whatever scruples Karey Andrews might have had about his children associating with his brother Fred's family, that fact did not extend to excluding him from his business arrangements. In 1965, when Karey formed a local business, the Bus Supply Company, Inc., he and Fred were the two incorporators and two of the three members of the board of directors. A member of the extended Andrews family, however, remembers that people thought of Tina's father as "poor, pitiful Fred." The joint venture into the Bus Supply Company, then, seems a sympathetic act from a man who, like others in the family, "had bailed out Fred again and again." Some of his siblings had tried more than once to bring him into business ventures, only to find that for one reason or another, things did not work out very well.[15] A family member insists that during the period that Tina was missing, Fred Andrews made a rare and uncomfortable visit to his brother Karey's house. There, he asked his brother what he should do about Tina. Why did Fred go to his brother rather than to the police? One might naturally wish to confer with family in such a situation. But perhaps also Fred suspected that Karey might somehow be better placed than he to know just what to do.[16]

From her modest home of 1,800 square feet on Oak Street, Tina would have been close to most places of significance to her, including her school and the houses of some of her friends. She would have walked, as did other McComb children of the era, to her places of amusement, including a drive-in restaurant, Mr. Swiss, just a block or so from her house. She would have walked as well the blocks east on Delaware Avenue toward downtown McComb, toward its shopping district and movie theaters. In downtown McComb, one could buy shoes for the family at Vest's, men's clothing at Abdallah's or Nunnery's, children's clothes at Hunt's, or smart women's clothing at the Hollywood Shop, or practically anything one might need at Denman Alford, a department store established in 1900. Away from downtown, budget-conscious shoppers could choose discount stores such as TG&Y, McCrory's, or Gibson's, where Tina Andrews's family had shopped.

In mid-August in Mississippi, just around the time of Tina's death, the black-eyed Susans and Morning Glory vines would still have been in bloom, with summer gardens producing tomatoes, okra, beans, watermelons, and

45

sweet corn. It would not have been time yet for sweet potatoes or turnip and collard greens. Midsummer was the time for revivals among the many Protestant churches represented in Pike County, as it had been for generations. Also in the late summer of 1969, Pike County residents, like other Americans, thrilled at the Apollo moon landing. Fighting in Vietnam continued at a brisk clip, despite President Nixon's vow to bring matters under control. The first American troops were being withdrawn. But still the war hit home. Many area men served in Vietnam, and on July 9, Daniel Sullivan, from Liberty, was killed seven months into his tour of duty.[17] To what degree any of these matters, especially ones of national import, interested Tina Andrews or occupied her time, the record leaves no trace. Like most children in August in Mississippi, she was certainly mainly interested in having fun with what was left of the summer.

There were many ways that a young person might seek amusement on a weeknight in McComb. The school year had not started, so there were no high school football games to attend, although area players were well into their preparation for the season. On August 13, 1969, the last night of Tina Andrews's life, she might have chosen to go to a movie in McComb, if she had the price of admission. At the Ren Drive-In on Highway 98, they had *The Dirty Dozen* and *Grand Prix.* Downtown at the Palace, there was *Mackenna's Gold,* with Gregory Peck and Omar Shariff. And at the State, there was a racy film, an R-rated one, *The Gay Deceivers,* about two men who feign homosexuality to avoid military service ("They Had to Keep Their Hands Off Girls to Keep the Army's Hands Off Them," the poster said). Or she might have stayed home to watch television. In McComb in those days, one could choose from eight television channels, two each from Jackson, New Orleans, and Baton Rouge, and one each from Hattiesburg and Biloxi. The westerns *Gunsmoke* and *Bonanza* were very popular among local viewers, but something like *Rowan & Martin's Laugh-In* would likely have seemed too racy, odd, or political.[18]

There were drive-in restaurants, which always drew a crowd of high-school-age students. Among them was Hollis's on Canal Street near the Greyhound Bus Station that had figured so largely in civil rights-related violence earlier in the decade. During the afternoons, there was the option of shopping at one of the downtown's "dime stores," such as Woolworth's, Morgan and Lindsey's, or McCrory's. That Woolworth's had been the site of what white McComb would have recognized as one of the opening salvos in the civil rights challenge in the town, the 1961 lunch counter sit-in by Hollis Watkins and Curtis Hayes.[19] Patrolman Richard Rowley, by 1969 McComb's chief of police, had arrested both men. All those places were by then legally desegregated, but mainly they still drew white patrons.

As in most small American towns, there was always the possibility of driving around with no particular place to go and looking for something to do or someone to meet. Young people did not have as many automobiles as they would in later decades, but they were available, especially to young working men in their late teens or early twenties. On August 13, Tina decided on the Tiger's Den, probably with no definite plans of where she might eventually wind up. There were a number of places in the town that sold beer, and it seems that Tina, even as a twelve-year-old, had begun to develop an interest in seeing how she could get some for herself. But in important ways, and not simply chronologically, Tina was still a child. A local woman recalls: "I remember seeing her walk down the street, skipping, holding the hem of her dress in her hands. She hummed and sang to herself. She was a sweet girl, but one that didn't have a lot of supervision. But in those days, people did let their children walk around a lot more than they do now."[20] Nothing about that evening of August 13 would have seemed unusual, other than the fact that Tina Andrews never came home. As summer stretched into fall, her family had a child's death to mourn and area authorities had few productive leads about what might have happened to her.

The fall 1969 term of the Pike County Circuit Court was set to open on Monday, October 6, with four cases of homicide and a great number of lesser crimes to consider, but still there were no arrests or further public news on the Tina Andrews case. On Friday, October 3, a warm, cloudy day, Andrews was buried in McComb's Hollywood Cemetery, less than a mile from her house, after an afternoon funeral service at local Hartman Funeral Home. Rev. Timothy Loden, the new pastor at Westgate Baptist Church, officiated. The body had been returned to McComb that Wednesday from the F.B.I. crime lab, which had performed forensic tests on the remains. As was customary, the family placed a notice in the local newspaper thanking friends and family for the "kindness and sympathy shown us in the tragic death of our little daughter, Tina Marie Andrews."[21]

Tina Andrews lived during a period of striking social and cultural change, both in the Deep South and in the nation as a whole.[22] Her life span of twelve years saw a fundamental challenge to Jim Crow in McComb, including the beginnings of black political participation; the perplexities of the war in Vietnam, in which many area young men served, and in which several young men with local connections died; the beginnings of the economic shocks, including inflation, that would mark the 1970s; and the emergence in popular culture, including television, radio, and the movies, of a frankness about sexuality that would have been unacceptable a decade earlier.[23] No twelve-year-old would have had the perspective to appreciate these changes. But such was the context in which the community would have experienced the crime and its aftermath. Many white residents of McComb were worried that things had begun to go badly wrong in the area and in the nation itself in the mid-1960s, and that many matters that had seemed settled—crime, race relations, drug use, and moral values—were now out of control. Historian Whitney Strub rightly points out: "Social and political movements resemble tectonic plate shifts in that seeming sudden catastrophes actually reflect the net effect of long-term incremental change."[24] But living in a period of such obvious changes, most Americans and most McComb residents did not perceive them as incremental. Change seemed to come quickly, and it was largely unwelcome, at least to whites in Pike County. Most of them wished that somehow things could be like they used to be.

People in Pike County, and in the United States as a whole, were not simply imagining in the late 1960s that they were living in an era that was more dangerous than in earlier years. In the late 1950s, the crime rate in the entire United States spiked and would continue to rise through the mid-1970s. The murder rate, too, always one of the most publicized crime figures, increased sharply through these same years. If one uses violent crime as the measure, the country was a less safe place to live during Tina's childhood than it had been in the 1940s and 1950s.[25] In 1969, there were 192 reported murders in Mississippi, with 255 in 1970, and 328 in 1971, a figure that peaked in 1973 with 368 murders in a state with a population of less than 2.3 million people.[26]

Many McComb people believed, as people tend to do, that in the late 1960s and early 1970s they lived in a time of relaxed social standards, and that young people were particularly vulnerable to a culture that seemed out of control. Where had law and order gone? In his remarks to the grand jury that October 1969 term, Judge Gordon Roach denounced lawlessness, permissiveness toward the young, and a general decline in respect for the law, "not confined to the lower brackets." "I have been advised," warned the judge, "that some of our youth in Pike County have tampered with marijuana." The judge blamed too-busy parents and an overindulgence in television as a babysitter. Many people in the town were convinced, as were many other Americans, including President Nixon, that the nation faced a wave of drug use among its children. Against these unwelcome changes, they believed, it was important to support traditional authorities such as churches, schools, and the area police department.[27]

Other storm clouds were on the horizon as well, ones of immediate and particular concern to McComb people. School districts throughout the Deep South were worried that the courts were set to scrap the "all deliberate speed" position on racial desegregation that had allowed foot dragging since the initial *Brown* decisions of 1954 and 1955. The Jim Crow social order, which had seemed so natural and so secure a decade earlier, was clearly falling, at least elements of it, such as the public schools, in which white McComb had been centrally invested. On the matter of the public schools, "never" finally came with the Supreme Court's 1969 decision in *Alexander v. Holmes County Board of Education*. Years of "all deliberate speed" were now ended, as southern school districts prepared for full, immediate racial integration.[28] McComb's public schools, like those in other Mississippi communities, had experimented with "freedom of choice" plans in which black students had attended formerly whites-only schools in the years before 1969. In 1965, in fact, new McComb school superintendent Julian Prince met with civil rights activist Bob Moses to discuss the district's proposed freedom of choice plan. Prince recalled that one of the office secretaries, the wife of a Klansman, went home to report Prince's unorthodox behavior, including "shaking hands with Moses." Local F.B.I. agent Reesie Timmons taught Prince how to check under his hood for explosives before starting his car. Many McComb whites understood that integration would come eventually, and began preparing for it. But white teachers and administrators who participated in those early efforts felt the wrath of other white McComb residents, revealing ways in which white McComb was divided in these years. A young white teacher who had been assigned to work in a black school was spit on by a white woman in downtown McComb. Several other teachers recall acts of shunning or not-so-veiled threats for violating social custom.[29]

Still, when the year 1969 opened, many people in McComb looked forward to the beginning of the 1970s and hoped that the recent years of turmoil were behind them. The local newspaper predicted good economic times ahead, noting that economists forecast "that the boom of the nearby 'seventies' will be even more dynamic and spectacular than the boom of the 'sixties.'" Such would not be the case, in McComb or in the rest of the United States.[30] Taking a careful look at the problems that McComb faced at the end of the sixties decade, an editorial saw "vacant buildings" as the city's most urgent difficulty. Adjustment to a new era in black voting and civil rights did not make that top-ten list, although the newspaper did note that an examination of local Head Start students revealed that some 30 percent of them were infested with worms.[31]

Through the fall of 1969, the investigation into Tina Andrews's murder continued, but there were no breaks in the case. McComb authorities picked up and interrogated several suspects, however, taking two men to Jackson for polygraph tests on November 13. The results of those tests satisfied them that the two men were not involved in Tina Andrews's disappearance or murder. But, said Sheriff Lawson in mid-November, "we are not going to quit."[32] In October, they had taken in Clyde McClanahan, age forty-four, because of a report that "a former convict was carrying a gun in the area." McClanahan was certainly a former convict, having recently been paroled from the state penitentiary where he was serving time for a murder committed on the Gulf Coast. But the police decided that McClanahan had nothing to do with the Andrews case, although they did link him to a recent series of burglaries in the area.[33]

And then for a long time there were no more predictions of forthcoming arrests or very much news at all. Whatever directions the investigation was taking occurred out of the public eye. One year later, there were still no arrests in the case. Charles Dunagin, a reporter for the *Enterprise-Journal* who had covered the story from its beginning, reported a conversation with Sheriff Lawson, who said, very much as he had done a year earlier, "We haven't given up, and we don't intend to give up until we solve it." The investigation had yielded a number of leads, a huge amount of interest in the community, and many rumors. In his conversation with Dunagin, Lawson "disclosed something about the case which hasn't been made public until now: Officers believe they are fairly certain of the illegal use of narcotics by someone connected with the case." Further, said Lawson, during the previous year more than fifteen suspects had been under investigation; not all of them had been cleared. Indeed, during the intense activity of the initial weeks of the investigation, more than one hundred suspects were interviewed, and "officers are known to have driven hundreds of miles to conduct interviews in connection with the investigation." A "veteran state investigator," probably Donald Butler of the highway patrol, commented that "of all the cases that I have worked on, this one has the weirdest angles I've encountered."[34]

What those "weird angles" were, the investigators did not say, but area officials did stress two connected areas that had complicated the investigation: one ultimately significant, the other one less so. The first was the time between the murder and the discovery of the body, leading to the badly deteriorated condition of the remains. The condition of those remains convinced people then and later that they could not be those of a girl who had been missing for ten days. Consequently, much of the investigators' time was initially spent in working to identify the victim. "Rumors, as usual," reported Dunagin, "were rampant after the scantily clad body was found. One concerned a middle-aged McComb man being a prime suspect in the case. He was never charged." Local people were also apparently puzzled by District Attorney Joe Pigott's request that people owning .38-caliber handguns should report those guns to the McComb Police Department. Pigott explained that he was "not naïve enough" to believe that the murderer would report his gun, but rather that the reporting of at least some guns would eliminate those weapons and their owners from the list of suspects. Thus, one year into the investigation, the reward, still standing at more than $2000, had not been claimed, but, reported Dunagin, "they're still working on it—from all angles."[35]

Most murderers are amateurs. Unlike pickpockets, forgers, or car thieves, they rarely repeat their crime often enough to become expert at it. Even so, why would a murderer in Pike County, a place that had its share of murders, have taken Tina Andrews to the oil field, especially if he had not taken her there alone, with the express purpose of killing her? Too many people used the oil field as a place for romantic or sexual encounters. Their work might have been interrupted at any time. Pike County contained many other acres of isolated woods which would have made a much better spot for a successful killing. But many killings, including this one, probably were not premeditated, thus accounting for the abandonment of Tina Andrews's remains as they were later found. If they did not intend to kill Tina, why did at least one of her killers carry a gun, then? A number of people in Pike County carried guns, however, not just ones that intended to commit a crime. An otherwise insignificant arrest in early 1969 gives some gauge of the number of guns one could find in Pike County. Two fifteen-year-old boys stole eleven guns, seven of them from the same home, before practicing with some, keeping some, and dumping a few others in a local pond.[36] Killers also simply make mistakes. In this case, someone apparently left shell casings at the scene, an odd decision which would have required opening the cylinder of the revolver and deliberately dumping the casings on the ground. Another error, it turns out, was allowing a witness to escape the scene.

The investigation of the oil field killing would stretch from late August of 1969 into the early months of 1971, an unusually long period. Over the course of those months, many leads would be considered and discarded. Many of those leads were unproductive, and became so quickly, a pattern that is usual in many murder investigations. Investigators had no murder weapon, no apparent witnesses at that point to anything that Tina Andrews had done that night, and no physical evidence from her remains that would have pointed toward a suspect. No security cameras at any gas station or quick stop would provide images of the victim and her killer, unlike the scenarios one would see in later years on episodes of *Forensic Files* or similar television programs. Despite the investigation, then, a year and more later, the case was growing colder, a matter of real frustration to District Attorney Joe Pigott. But criminal investigations sometimes turn on matters of good fortune as much as they do on good police work, and in early 1971 fortune seemed to hand Joe Pigott information that he needed to break the case.

3
Joe Pigott Receives a Call
Two Indictments and Initial Preparations for a Trial

The day of March 17, 1971, was not a good one for McComb police chief Richard W. Rowley. An experienced man, Rowley had been an officer for over fifteen years and McComb's chief of police since 1967.[1] He had been a member of McComb's police force during eventful years, ones in which they had been the front lines of resistance both to civil rights demonstrations in 1961 and again in 1964, and in the community's efforts to control white resistance to the civil rights movement, a resistance that the local newspaper had called in 1964 a "reign of terrorism." Rowley himself had arrested civil rights demonstrators at the Woolworth's sit-in and the local bus station in 1961. Along with other police officers, he investigated the 1964 summer bombing campaign, leading to the arrests of eleven area white men. From 1961 through 1964, the McComb police also engaged in "harassment arrests" of demonstrators and activists, a practice that by the end of 1964 the police force had largely abandoned. By the end of that year, the local newspaper assured readers, "responsible leadership was in control of the situation," and "law and order, peace and tranquility prevailed."[2]

But, many white McComb residents believed, one could not be too careful. The end of 1964 did not spell an end to efforts to maintain "law and order," often still defined as managing racial matters. As police chief, Rowley continued monitoring civil rights activities. By 1968, some of that activity involved the operation of Head Start centers for early childhood education.[3] Rowley closely cooperated with Mississippi's State Sovereignty Commission, which still did what it could to resist integration. He told the Sovereignty Commission what he saw in McComb, and they provided him advice on how to handle matters. Those Head Start centers seemed much preferable to earlier civil rights work in the area, though, because they "tied up" civil rights workers, who were "so busy making easy money that they are not creating any of the usual dissension at this time."[4] By 1971, work for the police department in McComb was by any measure quieter and less likely to draw national attention than it had been in 1964. The matter that troubled Chief Rowley on March 17, however, had nothing to do with race relations or civil rights. But that fact probably seemed small consolation.

What made Richard Rowley's March 17 so unhappy was the result of a telephone call that District Attorney Joe Pigott had received earlier that year. That call represented a major break in the Andrews investigation, and it led to the most significant piece of state's evidence in the entire case. A woman told him that she knew someone who had been in the oil field with Tina Andrews on the night that she was killed. She recounted specific details about the evening, ones that "only a witness could have known," Pigott told the local newspaper years later. Pigott was convinced that the lead was a sound one, one on which he needed to act. On or about February 9, 1971, Pat Lamkin, a teenage friend of Billie Jo Lambert's, and almost certainly the person who contacted Joe Pigott by telephone, came to Pigott's office and made a statement before him, and later, still in February 1971, she took Billie Jo Lambert with her to him for further discussion of the incident.[5] Lambert then told Pigott her story of what had happened on the evening of August 13, 1969.

Why did the young women contact Pigott, rather than any other area law enforcement official? While district attorneys sometimes receive tips about criminal cases, their role is not primarily investigative. In a typical situation, upon receiving information about an alleged crime for which no arrest had yet occurred, a district attorney's office would refer a caller such as Lamkin to either the police or the sheriff, depending upon the relevant area of jurisdiction. The police or sheriff would then investigate, interview involved parties, gather evidence, and present their report to the district attorney's office for the possible preparation of an indictment. But the information that Pigott received from Lamkin and Lambert made the matter more complicated than a usual Pike County killing. While the two girls probably were not aware of the regular procedural issues involved in an investigation, the story that Lambert told made it clear why she had not wished to go either to the police or the sheriff. The men who had taken her and Tina Andrews to the oil field where Tina's body was later found, said Lambert, were both current members of the McComb Police Department. This alleged involvement of McComb police officers in Tina Andrews's murder provided disturbing indications that the law and order that official McComb hoped now prevailed in the community was not as settled a matter as they hoped. This case had the potential, then, to disrupt a good deal of what prominent white members of the community had worked to reestablish in the years since the troubled mid-1960s.

Members of the McComb Police Department and other area law enforcement agencies had investigated the crime since the discovery of the body. However, Chief Rowley would say in March that the police had "been working with county officers on the case for about two months," a curious statement, unless, of course, Rowley meant something more specific and narrow, such as the investigation having moved in those two months toward an indictment of two of his own men.[6] Joe Pigott moved cautiously, for the story that he had heard promised difficulties ahead. There is no reason that Pigott would have informed Rowley or Lawson of the impending indictments, and there is no evidence that he did. In February 1971, Pigott moved toward his next step, to be taken before a Pike County grand jury.

Pigott and his witness, Billie Jo Lambert, appeared before that Pike County grand jury in March 1971, where she implicated two McComb police officers in the murder. Grand jury testimony and the intentions of a district attorney to seek indictments are secret, in theory at least. Grand juries do not meet in open court. The target of an indictment does not have the right to present evidence or even to attend the proceedings. Did either officer know what was about to happen? Clearly they did, as the two men were on voluntary leave from the McComb Police Department at the time of the indictments. One of them, accompanied by a former girlfriend, appeared at Joe Pigott's office the night before the indictments were handed down in an unsuccessful attempt to establish an alibi.[7]

On March 17, 1971, the grand jury returned indictments against Richard McIntosh and Ted Fleming, for the murder "on or about" August 23, 1969, of Tina Andrews. The charge against both men was not qualified by "first" or "second" degree, but read, in statutory language, that they "did willfully, unlawfully, feloniously and with malice aforethought kill and murder Tina Andrews, a human being."[8] The indictments were returned around noon. Both men appeared at the sheriff's department by 2:30 p.m. that day to turn themselves in to Sheriff Lawson, who placed them in the Pike County Jail in Magnolia.[9] The city of McComb issued a statement: "Because of the action of the grand jury today, police officers Ted Fleming and Richard McIntosh have been suspended from duty." Both the City Board and the police department declined to issue any further statement on the matter, "for fear of prejudicing it."[10]

After the arrests, local reaction to the case sometimes seemed as much about the reputation or character of the police force itself as it did about the act alleged against these two indicted men. In 1971, Chief Rowley's police department, as did departments in most other places, consisted of men who had been on the force for years, as well as some who were newcomers. Ted Fleming was a veteran of the force, while McIntosh was one of those relatively new men. In McComb, veterans such as Fleming had been involved in rough work in the early and mid-1960s, and many of those men were still dreaded by black McComb residents and by some white ones as well. However, the McComb Police Department was no worse than others in the state; when compared with the notoriety earned by lawmen in Jackson, Mississippi, or Neshoba County, for example, it seemed somewhat better.

"Better" was a relative term in Mississippi. In the early 1960s, McComb police had stocked up on tear gas and prepared to purchase helmets and other riot gear for their regular officers in anticipation of serious work. The McComb police auxiliary unit, which had appeared in rudimentary form during World War II, seems to have been revived in force and revised in character in the 1960s as a response to the civil rights movement in the area. In 1964, auxiliary officers were called out to assist during the summer bombing campaign. To at least some of these auxiliary officers, keeping order in the area meant working with a broad array of people who resisted the civil rights movement. In 1964, the auxiliary had been headed by J. Emmett Thornhill, Jr., the son of the man that the Sovereignty Commission itself had called "the wheels behind the fellows that are doing the bombings."[11] Chief Guy and Sheriff Warren had recruited auxiliary deputies from the ranks of the Americans for the Preservation of the White Race, a group of which Guy himself was a member.[12] The F.B.I. later identified a McComb police patrolman as an active member of the Ku Klux Klan, and when police chief George Guy had supplemented his force in 1964 with auxiliary members, some of them too were Klansmen.[13] But for several years now, prominent voices in the community had insisted that McComb was a changed town, one with a fresh respect for law and order and "government by law," not one in which the police or auxiliary forces were engaged in activities that would shake the confidence of "responsible men" in town.[14]

In the immediate period before the meeting of the grand jury, it seems that some of those "responsible men" in town knew that two police officers faced indictment. "Unofficial sources," reported the local newspaper, "said city officials knew the investigation was in progress for several days, but after conferring with county and district authorities took no action against the two officers until the indictment was returned." McIntosh and Fleming knew that indictments were forthcoming because of their voluntary leave from the police department, but that voluntary leave was not publicly announced until the indictments were returned, leading to much speculation about the roles that the officers played in the investigation of the murder and the timetable in which Chief Rowley or Sheriff Lawson became aware that area lawmen were becoming prime suspects in the killing. "Rumors of arrests or indictments," continued the newspaper, "have been rampant. . . . Many of them were grossly exaggerated."[15] Neither subsequent newspaper coverage nor the trials that followed the indictments ever provided clear evidence of what Rowley and Lawson knew and when they knew it.

Readers of the local newspaper learned: "New evidence in the Andrews case was brought to the attention of Dist. Atty. Joe N. Pigott and Sheriff Robert 'Tot' Lawson some two months or perhaps longer ago. The nature of the evidence, it is believed, caused the officials to decide to wait and present it to the grand jury before making a charge." Both Fleming and McIntosh "obviously knew that they were under investigation." Prosecutors wish to play indictments close to the vest. In this case, however, a number of people beyond Joe Pigott's office knew that McIntosh and Fleming were to be indicted, including the men themselves. Clear too was the fact that in the spring of 1971 several people outside the district attorney's office knew that both men had been implicated as suspects in the case.[16] What remains unclear is the precise time and circumstances under which Fleming and McIntosh learned that they were to be indicted.

The names of McIntosh and Fleming obviously were associated with the case before the grand jury met. But Joe Pigott had no indication until early 1971 that the investigation that had seemed stalled in 1970 would eventuate in 1971 in the indictment of two police officers. Pigott had no obvious reason, even if he had the ability to do so, to steer McComb police away from investigating the murder of Tina Andrews in 1969 and 1970. However, in the two trials that followed the indictments, District Attorney Pigott and his successor, Jim Kitchens, would find themselves working as much against the McComb Police Department as with them. Neither district attorney would ever allege a cover-up of the crime by the department, but neither did either man see the police as overly forthcoming with support, either. Police officers in places other than McComb, Mississippi, of course, have a tendency to close ranks and support one of their own. But the difficulties that Pigott and Kitchens would face reveal also the fact that "law and order" might mean different things to different members of the community. For the district attorneys, it meant pursuing a case as strongly as they could no matter the way it might shake confidence in the McComb Police Department. To others in the community, law and order meant supporting the police, no matter what kinds of stories witnesses from undistinguished or disreputable backgrounds might have to tell.

McIntosh and Fleming were arraigned before Circuit Judge J. Gordon Roach on March 19, 1971. Roach was a veteran of the Fourteenth Circuit bench. Like many attorneys involved on both sides of the case, he had held multiple offices in the city and the county. In more than four decades of legal practice, he had been Pike County attorney, city attorney for both McComb and Osyka, and an attorney in private practice. A native of McComb, he graduated from high school there before taking his undergraduate and law degrees at Ole Miss. As was also common for a well-established attorney in the area, he served on local bank boards and worked to establish the new hospital, Southwest Regional Medical Center, in McComb. Long involved in state politics, he managed the successful gubernatorial campaign of Fielding L. Wright in 1947.[17]

Roach had not, however, been judge in the mid-1960s, when he would have sentenced those convicted for their involvement in the civil rights movement and its attendant violence. He had been circuit judge for three years when the 1971 terms of court opened. Governor John Bell Williams had appointed him to the bench in 1968, when W. H. Watkins, in his third term as circuit judge, died at the end of June 1968 at the age of sixty-three. Roach filled the remainder of Watkins's unexpired term, and in 1970 he was easily reelected to the post. Roach would not run again for circuit judge and subsequently reentered private practice in a firm that included his son, John Gordon Roach, Jr.

His portrait, showing a man with a thick wave of gray hair, now hangs in the courthouse in Magnolia.[18] His wife, Kathrine, enjoyed watching her husband on the bench. Area residents remember her as a presence in the courtroom, "knitting as justice was being dispensed."[19] At Roach's death in 1979, the Pike County Courthouse closed during his funeral as an honor to a highly regarded man. That reputation seems well-earned, as his handling of the Andrews case during the 1971 trial would be even-handed by anyone's measure. Still, Roach was one of those Pike County men who had never reconciled himself to the changes that the civil rights movement and the broader cultural shifts of the 1960s had brought to the area. During his time on the bench, he looked at his county and his country and worried that what he saw was largely "turmoil" and "moral decay."[20]

The arraignment itself was well-attended, as were both of the subsequent trials of Richard McIntosh, evidence of the interest the case held for the community. The Jackson, Mississippi, *Clarion-Ledger* reported: "In the courtroom, which was filled almost to capacity, due to the visit to the court by some school students, were the parents and a sister of the Andrews girl."[21] Between the identification of the body and the returning of the indictments, the Andrews family had been publicly silent about the matter. No newspaper ran statements by Tina's parents, nor is there any public record of their reaction to the indictment of two McComb police officers as their daughter's accused killers. The McComb newspaper, while providing ample coverage of the case, was editorially silent about the matter, as it would remain until the end of the trials and well beyond.

Americans periodically worry that they are living of times of danger of child abduction. Tina Andrews had the misfortune not to disappear during one of those times. There were no Amber Alerts in those days, or faces of missing children on milk cartons. There were no cell phones with which a teenage girl could sent texts or photographs or call for assistance, should she find herself in a dangerous situation. During the period between Tina's disappearance and the identification of her body, her family was worried, but hopeful that she would turn up, a stance that led to much speculation about their concern over their child. Nothing suggests that they did not care about her or had washed their hands of her, but rather newspaper coverage suggests that they kept their worries and their inquiries about her largely to themselves or within a narrow circle of family. The case received broad coverage by local media, especially during the trials that followed the indictments. But this was not a case about which the local newspaper ever questioned the speed of the investigation or demanded answers about the outcome of the trials. The town itself, on the other hand, buzzed with speculation about the charges, their accuracy, and whether or not more people were involved in the murder.

Following the indictment, the local newspaper ran front-page photographs of both Fleming and McIntosh. A smiling Ted Fleming appeared in the uniform of the McComb Police Department, while a smiling Richard McIntosh, wearing a casual short-sleeve shirt and sporting a short haircut, looked schoolboyish in a photograph taken several years before the events in question.[22] Fleming, born on April 20, 1934, was thirty-six years old. He had worked in the city as an appliance repairman, operating a business out of his home. He and his younger brother Alton were avid bowlers; both were very good at it. In 1963, Fleming won a trophy for having the highest men's average in his bowling league. In December 1965, he joined the police department as a desk sergeant, according to McComb police chief Richard Rowley. He resigned in May of the following spring to work as an appliance repairman for Sears, Roebuck, but rejoined the force in October 1966, as a patrolman. His time at a patrolman had been largely uneventful, at least in any ways that would have come to public attention.[23]

Along with other members of the police force, he received instruction at the Mississippi Law Enforcement Officers Training Academy, and he participated in basic patrol and investigation work in the city, typical for a member of a small-town police force. He arrested shoplifters, saw to traffic accidents, and helped corral a fugitive wanted by the F.B.I. By the time of his arrest in March 1971, Fleming had gained the rank of lieutenant, earning promotion to that rank in January 1971. He was married to Agnes Bellipani, sister of McComb police officer Bobby Bellipani. When Fleming initially joined the McComb Police Department in 1965, he succeeded his brother-in-law as desk sergeant. McComb was the kind of town where word of mouth or family connections like that were very useful in helping with jobs and other advantages. The Flemings lived on Park Drive in McComb, where the couple had recently built a house. Fleming to this point had lived a quiet life, with nothing in the public record to suggest violence or scandal.[24]

Richard McIntosh, born on December 11, 1946, was twenty-four years old.

He was a 1965 graduate of McComb High School, and classmates remembered him as quiet and unremarkable. Some called him handsome, an appearance that he retained in 1971 and 1972 when he was tried for Tina Andrews's murder. As a child, his life was no more a matter of public record than the lives of other small-town boys. He attended friends' birthday parties, was active in the South McComb Baptist Church, played some basketball and some baseball, batting an enviable .368 in 1962 and winning a spot on the Babe Ruth Farm League All-Star Team. McIntosh even won second place in the boys' division of a yo-yo contest, sponsored by the *Enterprise-Journal,* at one of the local movie theaters, the Palace. He missed out on the $25 savings bond for the first-place winner of that competition, but he did receive a sweater emblem for his skills.[25]

Not a highly talented athlete in high school, he was a manager for the McComb High School football team. McIntosh liked to sing and in high school was a member of a quartet that delivered singing telegrams to fellow classmates on Valentine's Day. His singing talents were also on display to local civic organizations such as the Lions Club and at the state choral festival in Jackson. He was a member of several popular music combos such as were common in those days. One group played a high school "Spring Hop" late in his senior year. After graduation, another group, "The Sunders," played at dances and other teen events in town.[26]

McIntosh's senior year in high school, 1964 to 1965, unfolded amid a year that was remarkable by anyone's standards. McComb people still insist that President Lyndon Johnson had been poised to federalize National Guard troops and place McComb under martial law, an eventuality dreaded by men with guardianship of McComb's commerce and other interests. Other Mississippi cities had perhaps a more notorious reputation than McComb, but few of them in 1971 held a deeper sense of how nearly they had come to chaos. There is no evidence of what McIntosh had thought of these developments. It is likely that he, like most other high school students, had been more concerned with classes, dating, music, and other social activities. In May, Richard McIntosh graduated along with the rest of the McComb High School class of 1965. Because of family finances, one of the state's four-year colleges or universities was not part of his plan. So he remained in McComb for a time.

Years earlier, McIntosh's father, also named Richard McIntosh, had been a dispatcher, a desk sergeant, for the McComb Police Department. The elder

McIntosh, born in McComb, worked for the city for many years, including a job at the water department, before joining the police department. He "gave his duties close and careful attention," remembered the local newspaper. The elder McIntosh was only fifty-three years old when he died in 1958; his fellow police officers were his pallbearers.[27] He had experienced poor health for an extended period, spending time in the Baptist Hospital in Jackson in 1957. In 1958, Richard and Elma McIntosh had six children living at home; they ranged in age from three to fifteen years old. Richard was the third child and the elder of their two sons. In 1966, local radio station WAPF named Elma McIntosh its Mother of the Year, an honor that included an hour-long broadcast in which she was featured, an expenses-paid trip to the Gulf Coast, and many gifts from area merchants.[28] To many people in the community, she was a respectable widow of modest means, raising a large family of young children on her own.

After high school graduation, McIntosh attended Southwest Mississippi Junior College in nearby Summit, but did not finish a degree. Again, family finances were a concern. He also worked in several places and occupations, including Baton Rouge, Louisiana, where he held an off-shore job in the oil industry, and also at Polyflex-M Company, a manufacturer of plastic bags, in Summit. He was a member of the local Mississippi National Guard unit, which ensured that his time in uniform would not involve Vietnam. Never married at the time of his indictment, he lived with his widowed mother on Sedgewick Street in south McComb. Their house was located in White Acres, a low-cost housing development. The development, named for Mississippi governor Hugh White, opened in 1940, replacing run-down company-owned housing built by the McComb Cotton Mill. In a concession to the era's racial imperatives, the northern part of White Acres was open to black residents, while the southern part was reserved for whites.[29]

Richard McIntosh had been a member of the McComb Police Department less than one year when he was indicted, having joined the force on April 15, 1970. It would become a central part of the defense in both trials that he was not a member of the department in August 1969, when Andrews was murdered, and that he had never met fellow officer Ted Fleming before the spring of 1970. He categorically denied, through statements by his defense counsel, that he had any connection with or any knowledge about Tina Andrews or her murder.[30]

Within two days of the March 17 indictment, attorneys for both men began submitting motions to the court.[31] Specifically, B. D. Statham and William Watkins, attorneys for McIntosh, requested bail as well as a hearing on a habeas corpus motion. The purpose of the habeas corpus hearing, a standard feature of a defense, is to compel the state to show why the defendant ought to be held pending the results of the trial. Citing common procedure in Mississippi courts, Judge Roach agreed to hear the motion, but said that during a busy term of court, as this one promised to be, the court could delay such a hearing until the trial was underway. Trial was scheduled to begin for McIntosh on Monday, April 5, 1971.

The best decision that Richard McIntosh made was his choice of an attorney. B. D. Statham was, as the local newspaper put it, a "man of personal and political power" in Pike County. Attorney for the county board of supervisors for over twenty-five years, he was, as board president Sam Alford later said, "one of the best-known board attorneys in the state and was considered by his colleagues as one of the best attorneys in the state." A Navy veteran and a former F.B.I. special agent, Statham was mayor of Magnolia from 1948 to 1952 and a member of the Mississippi State Senate from 1953 to 1955. Active in many county interests, as were many of the leading men involved in the case, Statham was a member of the board of the Southwest Mississippi Bank. A fierce courtroom presence, Statham was regarded as the attorney that one would want were one in serious trouble in Pike County. Richard McIntosh could hardly have found a better advocate than B. D. Statham. Statham was not a large or physically imposing man, but he was one who was used to getting his way in the area.[32]

In his representation of McIntosh in two trials, Statham defended his client precisely as a contemporary law textbook suggested that an attorney must do: "Criminal defense lawyers do not win their cases by arguing reasonable doubt. Effective trial advocacy requires that the attorney's every word, action, and attitude be consistent with the conclusion that his client is innocent."[33] Statham was extremely diligent in preparing his case, searching out weaknesses in opposing witnesses and making sure that his client knew what to expect when taking the witness stand and was prepared to offer crisp, detailed answers. While Statham had an active and successful practice, he did not, like District Attorney Joe Pigott, have the responsibility for building and presenting cases for the State of Mississippi in four counties. The McIntosh case could receive at times his full attention, as well as that of his young partner, William Watkins. That fact would prove a great advantage to Richard McIntosh over the next year.

In the meantime, Ted Fleming's attorney, Wayne Dowdy, filed motions in preparation for the trial of his client, scheduled to begin on April 8, 1971.[34] Dowdy asked the state to produce all physical evidence relating to the charge and indictment, including the autopsy report, photographs from the crime scene, reports from the Mississippi State Crime Laboratory, a list of all potential witnesses, and copies of any statements made by Fleming before his arrest. On the copy of the motion to produce this evidence, filed on March 19, 1971, Dowdy also requested, and then omitted by striking out the request on the typewritten document, a copy of questions to and answers from Fleming while "said defendant was undergoing a lie-detector test or polygraphic examination."[35] Was this an error? Did Fleming in fact submit to a polygraph examination? If so, when and why? In the end, Fleming would never be tried for the murder, so one knows a great deal less about what he might have said than what Richard McIntosh did say in court.

Fleming took the considerable extra expense of retaining a second attorney. One can hire all the attorneys one can afford, of course. While this practice was not unheard of in Pike County, it was not common. Neither, however, was being charged with the murder of a child. Wayne Dowdy, Fleming's lead attorney, was a young man, well-connected in Magnolia, but not an experienced criminal lawyer. His additional attorney, Breed Mounger, Sr., of Tylertown in neighboring Walthall County, most certainly was. Norman Gillis, Jr., a very well-connected McComb lawyer himself, said of Mounger, the "Crafty Red Fox": "Citizens of the area who found themselves in impossible personal predicaments always drove over to Tylertown and hired Breed Mounger. Then they returned to McComb or Magnolia or Brookhaven or Liberty to fetch and sell the family jewels. But what else are earthly goods for? When the chips are down, the things that really count are life, liberty, and staying out of the electric chair."[36]

Mounger had been in practice for decades—since 1932—earning a reputation as formidable as B. D. Statham's, and for the same reasons. He combined an aggressive courtroom presence with vast influence in the area. In his tribute to Mounger, Gillis continued: "Neither the town of Tylertown nor Walthall

County could draw a single official breath without Breed's personal supervision." Like Statham, Mounger had been an attorney for the county's board of supervisors and had represented town and county interests in a number of capacities. In court, "nobody was better at insulting and humiliating the expert witness, or in contradicting and confusing the lay witness."[37]

An accomplished musician, actor, and a licensed pilot to boot, Mounger was an educated man of many interests, and he earned his colleagues' respect, serving as president of the Mississippi Bar Association. In the courtroom before rural juries, however, he could affect a just-folks demeanor, sometimes appearing in an ill-fitting suit and using speech of "someone who had just escaped a piece of Amite County new ground," as a longtime McComb newspaper reporter put it. Even Breed Mounger's reddish-blond hair seemed rumpled. Both he and Statham honed their skills in an era before women jurors, before black jurors, and before "fancy, air-conditioned courtrooms." But "the two attorneys most favored by the area defendant who needed the best he could afford were Breed Mounger of Tylertown and B. D. Statham of Magnolia . . . Individually, either was a formidable rival; together they were a team for the opposition to run and hide from." Neither district attorney in this case ran and hid, but both faced the best the area could offer as criminal defense attorneys.[38]

Both of Fleming's attorneys were thorough, filing motions to obtain all relevant evidence in the state's hands. A further motion on Fleming's behalf sought to compel the state to offer more specific information about the precise date and time of the crime for which Fleming had been indicted.[39] Dowdy anticipated a strategy that McIntosh's attorneys Statham and Watkins would follow in their client's trial: to take advantage of the long period between the murder and the indictment by throwing doubt on the ability of the state to prove basic, specific information about the crime, as well as the identity of the body that the state maintained to be that of Tina Andrews.

Attorneys for both men also focused attention on one particular witness. McIntosh's attorneys, also in a May 19 motion, named a person who would potentially stand as the state's primary witness, Billie Jo Lambert. Statham's motion requested that the court require the state to make Lambert available for "interrogation" and to instruct Lambert to "respond to interrogatories and inquiries" of McIntosh "in her accusation of this defendant." Through both trials in 1971 and 1972, Statham and Watkins worked relentlessly to shake Lambert's story and to undermine her credibility as a witness. Lambert was the only one who could place McIntosh and Fleming in the oil field where Tina Andrews's body was discovered, and indeed she was the only person who would assert that Andrews had even known the men.

Fleming's attorney Wayne Dowdy also prepared to defend his client against the testimony that might be offered by Lambert. In a motion that repeatedly and incorrectly gave the witness's name as "Billy Joe Lambert," Dowdy averred that Lambert "is only fourteen years of age, and because of her tender age, has been more easily influenced by the State and therefore refuses to talk with attorneys for the Defendant Ted Fleming."[40] While Fleming would never stand trial, and thus Dowdy would never have the opportunity to examine Lambert under oath, his reference here to her age previews the double-edged strategy that Statham and Watkins would pursue against Lambert. When it suited their argument at both trials, they would paint Lambert as young, ignorant, and so unreliable that she could not be trusted to remember or know very much of significance. On the other hand, and in the same periods of examination on the witness stand, Statham would attack Lambert as precociously sexual and mature, an experienced, deceptive young woman and a willful, belligerent witness.

Before the trial was scheduled to begin on April 5, several other significant motions and rulings occurred in the case. First, Wayne Dowdy, Fleming's attorney, filed a motion for severance, a request that his client be tried separately from McIntosh.[41] Such a request does not indicate that Dowdy believed his client to be any more or less guilty than McIntosh, but was rather a common strategy in a case where two defendants had been indicted for the same serious crime. That request for severance was granted. Further, on March 26, Judge Roach ruled against McIntosh's habeas corpus motion. Once again, McIntosh's filing the writ and Roach's denial of it are not surprising. As one might expect, McIntosh's defense would through the two trials to come continue to mount a procedurally thorough defense, seeking down to the end to have the charges dismissed before the case went to the jury.

However, through all these various and continued motions, one omission is striking. In his motion denying the habeas corpus writ, Judge Roach indicated that after the March 17 arrest of McIntosh and his arraignment and plea of not guilty on March 19, the court had given the defendant a deadline of March 25 to file a motion for a change of venue, a request to move the trial out of Pike

County. The Pike County Circuit Court file on the case contains no evidence that a change of venue was ever sought. The case attracted massive amounts of area interest and publicity, a circumstance that in some situations might lead a defense attorney to argue that a fair trial in the county was impossible. The case also of course involved the indictment of two current police officers. Was the state concerned that local sympathies might favor those officers? Joe Pigott, the district attorney, knew Pike County very well. He was confident operating in its courts and had argued many times before Judge Roach. At the same time, he had a heavy slate of cases to consider in 1971; arguing for a change of venue would certainly have complicated the McIntosh prosecution, and such a move simply might not have seemed necessary. The defense seemed comfortable with a Pike County trial. Why would they not? The Pike County Courthouse was familiar ground for B. D. Statham. Perhaps no attorney in the area was better known than Statham. Magnolia was his home; he had been mayor. Fundamental matters, including the shaping of the jury, would be in his hands there as they would have been in no other courthouse in the state.

The motion for separation of the cases and the defense efforts to gain access to potential witnesses were all regular and predictable. On Wednesday, March 25, the defense attorneys appeared before Judge Roach. They sought to compel Billie Jo Lambert, Donna Andrews, Pat Lamkin, and Winifred Andrews Mullen to speak with them. All, according to B. D. Statham, had refused to do so. Mullen was a sister of Tina Andrews, as was Donna Andrews. Pat Thomas Lamkin was the girl to whom Lambert had confided her story of what had happened to her and Tina Andrews on the evening of August 13, 1969. As recently as right before court on Wednesday, said Statham, he had attempted to speak with Lambert, whose mother was with her. She refused to talk. "All I am attempting to do," said Statham, "is to find the truth," a statement as much for public consumption as it was a measure of Statham's real intentions or his duty as a defense attorney. Further, said Statham, Donna Andrews, Tina's sister, had told him that Joe Pigott had instructed her that "it would be dangerous and against her best interests" to discuss the case with the defense attorneys. He added that Lambert told him much the same thing.[42]

Wayne Dowdy, appearing as Ted Fleming's attorney, testified to his difficulties in interviewing the state's witnesses. Of the four, he had managed to speak only with Pat Lamkin. After Fleming's arrest, said Dowdy, "I called Miss

Lamkin and asked if I might come to her home and discuss the Tina Andrews murder with her." In that conversation, they did discuss the case and agreed to meet later. However, Dowdy then received a telephone call from "a person identifying herself as Miss Lamkin" who said that the district attorney had advised her not to speak with anyone about the case as it might "endanger" Billie Jo Lambert. Lambert, Lamkin, and Donna Andrews were all teenage girls, unfamiliar with the process unfolding around them and unsure of whom to trust and what precisely they were required to do in this situation, unless instructed by an attorney.[43]

Under cross-examination by Joe Pigott, Dowdy's statements make clear several matters: Dowdy was unaware that the McComb police were involved in the investigation; he had been contacted about the case before the arrests; and Billie Jo Lambert's name was associated with the case before Joe Pigott took Lambert before the grand jury to seek the indictments. The call that Dowdy received reveals some of the understandable confusion about jurisdictional lines in the case, given the varied roles that the attorneys had played. Wayne Dowdy had come to McComb in 1968 to work for Joe Pigott on an unsuccessful election campaign. Dowdy joined Pigott's law firm in February 1969.[44] By 1971, he no longer worked for Pigott. In 1969, at the time of the murder, Dowdy was not a city police judge; in 1971, he was. Pigott asked Dowdy specifically if he were aware that the McComb police, especially John Sharpling, were investigating the case. Dowdy said that he was not.

Dowdy further said that before the indictments, he received a call from a person claiming to have information about the case. That person was clearly seeking to contact someone able to investigate or even to bring charges in the case, as Dowdy had to inform the caller that he was no longer affiliated with Joe Pigott or the district attorney's office. In that call, said Dowdy, "Billie Jo Lambert's name had been mentioned in connection with the murder." Dowdy told the caller instead to contact the sheriff's department, which would have been proper advice, given the logical jurisdiction in the case. Dowdy himself then called the sheriff to tell him about the information that he had received.[45] Dowdy's testimony did not, however, explore what Sheriff Lawson had done with the information. No evidence in fact suggests whether Lawson called Joe Pigott, consulted the police department, or the highway patrol, or indeed whether the name of either McIntosh or Fleming had been mentioned in that call. Nor did Dowdy or anyone else ever say who this caller had been. Given Pat Lamkin's successful effort about this same time to reach Joe Pigott, it is highly likely that she was the caller.

Judge Roach informed the young witnesses that the defense attorneys did have the right to speak with them, but they also had the right to refuse to answer questions. Statham asked Judge Roach to compel the four witnesses to take the stand to answer questions, a request that Roach refused to grant. Finally, Judge Roach instructed all the attorneys that Lambert, then fourteen years old, and Donna Andrews, then fifteen, must have either a parent or guardian present during any questioning.

Clearly, Billie Jo Lambert's name was known, certainly by Wayne Dowdy, and perhaps also by Sheriff Lawson, to be connected with the case before Joe Pigott presented his evidence to the grand jury. Does this fact account for Pigott's alleged advice to Lambert not to discuss the case with anyone because of potential danger to her? The "danger" ought not necessarily to be construed as real physical threats to Lambert and the other potential state's witnesses. Pigott might simply have attempted to stress to the girls the inadvisability of making themselves available to defense counsel. From his point of view, the real danger may have been to the integrity of the case he was attempting to build, heavily dependent as it would be upon the testimony of these girls, especially Lambert.

During the last week of March 1971, McIntosh's defense team filed more motions, these to challenge the constitution of the jury that was to hear the trial, set to begin on April 5. Specifically, the defense argued that the list of jurors that had been drawn for that term of court had been exhausted, and that the efforts of the state to replenish that list of potential jurors had not been done according to statute. The list of potential jurors from the first, third, and fifth supervisors' districts of the county were the ones in question. Judge Gordon Roach had called the county supervisors to the courthouse to replenish the names from the districts to be used for the special panel of jurors for the expected McIntosh and Fleming trials and for other business of the court term. But, argued McIntosh's defense, the list of names had "to be prepared during a legal session of the board and appear on the board's minutes," as the *Enterprise-Journal* reported on April 2.[46]

In the meantime, Judge Roach attempted to draw names to fill the jury for the murder trials from the still-eligible ones from the second and fourth districts of the county. "Speculation was," reported the local newspaper, "that defense attorneys would challenge this list as not being representative of the entire county." Such was the case. In an April 2, 1971, "Motion to Squash Special Venire," McIntosh's attorneys maintained that the jury that had been drawn for the case contained only names from Districts 2 and 4 of Pike County, which contained the cities of McComb and Summit, the largest communities in the county. In those communities, the motion held, "great publicity has been given the case in caption by newspapers [sic], oral and written reports and radio coverage," prejudicing the jury pool against their client. In the remaining districts, 1, 3, and 5, those rural districts, lying "in areas away from the metropolitan areas of Pike County, Mississippi . . . publicity, newspaper coverage, and public sentiment has not concentrated upon the trial of this case."[47] Ted Fleming's attorneys also filed motions on this matter, theirs requesting a continuance of the case because of the exhaustion of the jury pool for that term. In an April 5 reply to the motion of Ted Fleming, Judge Roach found that under the circumstances, the "inability to obtain a special venire facias would deny the defendant a fair and impartial trial," and he ordered the continuance of the case until the October term of court. Judge Roach commented, according to the local newspaper, that "he would have continued it on his own motion even if the defense had not made one."[48] The matter of jury selection, specifically a "special venire" to hear a murder trial, was a feature of Mississippi law that was well known to all parties to this case. Beyond the law was the established informal procedure for selecting the jury that would hear these cases, a process that suggests some advantages that McIntosh obtained by engaging B. D. Statham as his attorney.

Statham was a "shrewd lawyer," as Mississippi Supreme Court justice James Kitchens told me in 2017, and well positioned to take an active part in the selection of the jury pool. The Pike County Board of Supervisors oversaw the drawing of names for jury duty, and Statham, in a manner of speaking, oversaw the Pike County Board of Supervisors; he was their attorney. Kitchens, the district attorney in the second trial of Richard McIntosh, explains the procedure involved in selecting a jury in such a case:

> In a murder case, there would have been a special venire, because you are entitled to a jury just for that one case. But the court term ended, and you couldn't

try things then except during those statutory court terms. The special venire would've been drawn in open court; that was required. The defendant would've been there, his lawyer would've been present, the DA would've been present, the judge and the circuit clerk and the sheriff would've been there. They would draw from the five supervisors' districts, an equal number of jurors from each one. That was done and would be published in the paper. Everybody would know who was summoned for jury duty. . . . B. D. Statham was a clever lawyer. The most powerful lawyer in the county, as far as his ability to win cases, often was the attorney for the Board of Supervisors. The law has changed in the wake of all the shenanigans of the civil rights era where there was a lot of skullduggery going on in juries back then. You couldn't convict anybody for a civil rights crime. Back then the Board of Supervisors, every year, would get an order from the circuit judge saying, "For the ensuing calendar year, I need you to provide the circuit court with x number of jurors, potential jurors. And then I need you to provide me the names of x venire men" they're called. The supervisors were supposed to do that from the voter registration rolls, but they didn't want to sit in there and do that. They would tell the attorney, "You just do that." Or the attorney would say, "Y'all don't have to bother with that, I'll take care of that." So somebody, B. D. Statham or whoever it might be, would go down to voter rolls and pick people he thought would be favorable to him on a jury. This is where the jurors came from. It's really a conflict of interest, but nobody ever complained about it back then because it just had been done that way so long. But he would pick people, number one, that he thought would be favorable to him on a jury. And number two, would not under any circumstance be likely to indict a supervisor for any kind of embezzlement or anything like that the supervisors were notorious for. That's where the veniremen came from. So you've got people that are potentially sympathizers or friends as potential jurors.[49]

The justice system that operated in Pike County by 1971 had changed in many ways since the early 1960s, as Statham and the other attorneys knew. Black people voted and served on juries. White women now served as jurors as well. No one in Mississippi still imagined that the state could "interpose" itself, as some state officials argued in earlier years, overtly to block or undo changes in federal law or otherwise shield them from the civil rights movement. But the system that had been built during the Jim Crow years had not been thoroughly scrapped. As Statham and the other attorneys knew, the jury selection system that Jim Kitchens described to me was extremely malleable in the hands of a skillful person such as B. D. Statham. One of the great ironies of the Tina Andrews case is that such a jury selection system, built to serve Jim Crow imperatives and operating also to protect the interests of powerful and well-favored people such as supervisors, could also operate to shield other interests from a strict accounting of justice. As much as he was able, Statham, a man who made it his business to know Pike County and its eligible jurors, could see that the jury would contain people perhaps inclined to be favorable toward his client.

What other connections might have existed between the older regime in Mississippi and the Andrews trial? In our conversation, Kitchens continued: "There were innuendos that McIntosh was favorably regarded by the Klan. The Klan was a big deal down there back then. There were some devout Klansmen and their descendants are still down there. Most people knew who they were." I told Justice Kitchens that I had never heard a rumor that there was a Klan connection in the Andrews case. Judge Kitchens replied, "Well, it was not necessarily a Klan thing in the sense that it was racially motivated. Of course, it was a white child, but the Klan hierarchy down there didn't want this guy convicted. There were people on the jury from out around Pricedale, which was a hotbed for the Klan, among many. They were thought to have been susceptible of influence by the Klan."[50] By the time of the indictments and the trials, the Ku Klux Klan and similar bands of violent men were no longer active in the ways that they had been just a few years earlier, either in Pike County or anywhere else in Mississippi. F.B.I. investigations, indictments of Klansmen for their activities, and a diminished public taste for overt violence in defense of white supremacy had all combined to render the Klan less potent than it had been half a decade earlier. But the area remained full of men who had been involved in or sympathetic to such activities. Is there a connection with the Tina Andrews murder? Not in any direct sense. Whatever else they might have been, Richard McIntosh and Ted Fleming were not Klansmen. But members of area law enforcement agencies had been, and Klansmen would not have looked upon local lawmen as enemies, but rather as men who had recently stood with them in handling black area residents. The district attorney in this case might have seemed not so much a friend, as Joe Pigott had attempted in 1964 to rein in violence in the county. In this situation, one can imagine in which direction a Klan sympathizer might lean.

Neither McIntosh nor Fleming would spend the summer in the Pike County jail, surely a great relief to them. At this same April hearing, Judge Roach ruled favorably on the request of both defendants for bond, setting it at $25,000 each. Over the previous weekend, however, Ted Fleming had enjoyed a taste of freedom, as one of his attorneys apparently informed the sheriff that bond had already been set. After his attorney posted that bond, the sheriff released Fleming. "He was put back in jail when authorities discovered the error." Both men, the newspaper noted, "are expected to remain on suspension from the police department pending disposition of the cases."[51] So they did. Until the fall of 1971, the local newspaper told its readers literally nothing else about the case. No more motions were filed by any of the attorneys. Neither Joe Pigott nor anyone else released any updates or said anything to suggest that the state was not confident that it had its men in the Tina Andrews case.

The first act of the case of the state of Mississippi versus the two police officers ended on April 9, 1971, as the March term of the Pike County Circuit Court came to a close, "with quite a number of cases being carried over until October," including that of McIntosh and Fleming. Glen Fortenberry, the circuit clerk, said that the court had run out "of both time and jurors to handle all of the 38 indictments returned by the grand jury." The board of supervisors continued its task of filling jury boxes upon which the court would draw in the fall term. All involved parties—defendants Richard McIntosh and Ted Fleming, defense attorneys B. D. Statham, William Watkins, Wayne Dowdy, and Breed Mounger, and District Attorney Joe Pigott and Pike County prosecuting attorney Robert Reeves—would prepare for one of the most anticipated trials in Pike County in a long time.

4

The Summer of 1971
Developments on the Eve of the Trial

District Attorney Joe Ned Pigott, who led the prosecution of Richard McIntosh in the fall of 1971, was not a man afraid of a challenge. He had demonstrated his resourcefulness in fields beyond Pike County, Mississippi. Born in next-door Walthall County in 1925, Pigott graduated from McComb High School at age sixteen. After attending Southwest Mississippi Junior College in nearby Summit, Pigott enrolled at the University of Mississippi, but he did not remain there long. In 1943 at the age of seventeen, he enlisted in the U.S. Army, where he would serve with great distinction during World War II. Earning promotion to sergeant and eventually to first lieutenant, in Europe as a member of the O.S.S. he "parachuted alone numerous times behind enemy lines, gathering intelligence for use in the Allied advance, destroying ancient bridges to thwart Nazi retreats, and escaping from imprisonment by the Nazi SS, all before his 20th birthday. . . . He was the American soldier who ordered a mob in Milan, Italy, which had hung the body of Italian Dictator Benito Mussolini, to cut the body down and disperse."[1] He fought in the Battle of the Bulge, where he suffered severe frostbite. Informed by a medic that both feet should be amputated, Pigott walked away from the medic's tent. "He walked on those same feet and ankles for another seventy years," his son said.[2]

After the war, he returned to the University of Mississippi, earning a bachelor of business administration degree in 1949. Later that same year, he received a degree from the law school there, as did most members of the Mississippi bar. In law school, one of his acquaintances admired a photograph in Pigott's room that showed a "Nazi parade with a Third Reich heavyweight leading the procession astride a horse." Asked where he got the picture, Pigott replied, "I took it."[3] But, as with many men of his generation, the postwar years were not ones in which he talked much about his military service. Instead, he built a legal career. He returned to McComb, first practicing as a member of the prominent firm Cassidy, McLain, and Alford.[4] In 1955 he became the Pike County attorney, serving until 1962. He would also represent the McComb public school district as board attorney (an unpaid position in those days) through the 1960s, during which one of his major pieces of business was dealing with the public schools' earliest moves toward desegregation. Governor Ross Barnett appointed him as district attorney for the Fourteenth Circuit District in 1963. After leaving the district attorney's office in 1972, he returned to private law practice. Elected a circuit court judge in 1974, he served in that capacity from 1975 through his retirement in 1992. "Judge Pigott," recalled an old colleague, "was a very honorable man. His demeanor and his countenance and his personality demanded respect." His son, former U.S. attorney Brad Pigott, remembered, "He loved being a lawyer and a judge."[5]

Audentis fortuna iuvat, the Romans said. In the 1950s and 1960s in Pike County, Joe Pigott might at times have been fortunate, but he was also bold. In 1951, Pigott, as a twenty-six-year-old attorney relatively new to practice, was the court-appointed lawyer for twenty-two-year-old Hattie Lee Barnes, an African American woman charged with the murder of a twenty-three-year-old white man, Lamar Craft, whom she had shot in Pike County.[6] Craft and two of his friends broke into a tavern at which Barnes worked and occasionally slept overnight. Alarmed by the noise of the break-in, Barnes took a .38-caliber pistol and shot Craft dead. Craft was "the son of a prominent Walthall County citizen." His father, Edd Craft, was a candidate for sheriff that year.[7] His brother was the mayor of nearby Tylertown. County officials said that the murder charge was "the only feasible move in the situation." Barnes was jailed "in an undisclosed location," where she was repeatedly interrogated under pre-*Miranda* circumstances. Before she was brought to trial that fall, she herself was shot five times, a clear testimony to the danger in which Barnes found herself and the unpopularity, one might put it with understatement, of a black woman's killing of a white man in southwestern Mississippi.[8]

To Pigott and Charles Gordon, an equally bold reporter for the *Enterprise-Journal,* the murder charge did not seem right; they determined not to see Barnes railroaded. "I thought that the case should be dismissed," Pigott later said.[9] A more likely version of events, he believed, was that Barnes shot Craft in self-defense, fearing that he intended to rape her. Pigott entered a plea of not guilty for Barnes, preparing to defend her in a trial that would be conducted before not only a jury of white men but also a judge, Tom Brady, who was an avowed segregationist and would later become the chief theorist of the Citizens' Councils in Mississippi as the author of *Black Monday,* a denunciation of the *Brown v. Board of Education* decision. But Pigott was resolute. Craft, he argued, "was in the wrong place at the wrong time and had no lawful reason to do what he did." He continued: "I take my oath seriously and have spent the past five weeks preparing to earn the statutory fee of $75 allowable for the services of an appointed attorney." But, Pigott knew, the advocacy of the case of a black woman shooting a prominent white man was not "a very popular thing." Directly confronting what he knew to be Judge Brady's prejudices, he argued in a motion to dismiss the case, "We both know that the law should be applied equally . . . regardless of race." Brady apparently was persuaded, instructing the jury to return a directed verdict of not guilty. In words that certainly surprised many in the courtroom, and in a spirit that would become less common from the Mississippi bench over the next decade, Brady sympathized with the situation in which the African American defendant had found herself. He said: "If the circumstances were reversed and a white lady had defended her bedroom against the intrusion of a black man, we would not be here trying her for murder, but would be consoling her for the horrible experience." In later years, Pigott's wife made copies of his motion to dismiss the case and presented them to their children as a memorial to their father's "commitment to stick up for what's right in the face of adversity."[10]

In 1964, Pigott again demonstrated a commitment to doing what was right, even if it was not popular. During the summer bombing campaign, he was district attorney, but he was also one of those local citizens concerned about the damage the violence was doing to the community's reputation and to the rule of law. Pigott later recalled that he, county attorney Robert Reeves, and Sheriff Warren approached the Chamber of Commerce to ask them to draft a statement condemning the bombings and other violence, if only on the grounds that it was harming the business climate. Insurance companies were dropping coverage on area homes and churches. The Chamber of Commerce refused to speak out. So Pigott and others drafted and circulated a Statement of Principles, advocating the rule of law; it was published later that year in the *Enterprise-Journal.* And that is when Pigott enjoyed good luck. A local woman, having read the Statement, mentioned to her doctor, "I don't know whether they really want to catch these men or not, but there's some people who live next door to me and I see them put these big guns in their cars and go out, and every time they do that, there's a bombing that night." Receiving a tip from the doctor, Pigott and other law enforcement officials met with the woman, organized a stakeout, and arrested some of those bombers. "You like to think it's good law enforcement, good investigation," Pigott said, "but sometimes cases like that turn on good fortune."[11]

The phone call that Joe Pigott received early in 1971 that led to his meeting with Billie Jo Lambert, and then to the indictments of Richard McIntosh and Ted Fleming, was also a piece of good fortune. At the same time, it was a development that demanded both boldness and careful work. Joe Pigott faced the unenviable task of preparing to prosecute two city police officers for the murder of a twelve-year-old girl. Under any circumstances, such a case presented pressures for a district attorney in a small town. Pigott worked constantly with the local police and other area law enforcement officials, whose cooperation was essential in building the cases that he would need to prosecute. Pursuing murder charges against members of the police force would inevitably result in strained relations, to put it mildly. But there were broader considerations and other kinds of pressures as well. The conservative disposition of many white McComb residents meant that a number of them would have perceived the prosecution of a police officer as an attack upon the reputation of the city or upon authority itself. Even if Pigott's office were not deterred by those pressures, he would have been aware of them, connected as he was with McComb's government and business leaders and experienced as he was with the general mood of the community. Neither at the time nor in later years did Joe Pigott say that anyone ever attempted to persuade him not to indict McIntosh and Fleming or not to pursue the prosecutions. Even if they did, he was not deterred. Through the course of the trial, however, Pigott would find himself working against the predetermination of some men in the area not to see any police officer convicted of the murder of Tina Andrews.

Men in elected offices and men with other kinds of power in McComb wished to believe that all there was basically well. They wished to avoid any additional traumas or disruptions of the sort that the community experienced in the early and mid-1960s. As the newspaper editor wrote in the spring before

77

Richard McIntosh's murder trial, the "McComb area has more effective leadership today than at any time in its history. This leadership is in both fields, public and private. It is positive, diversified, and is manifesting enthusiasm over the idea of growth."[12] This McComb leadership had been through difficult years, with the city still working out fundamental details of the post–Jim Crow electoral and educational developments mandated by court rulings and changes in federal law. That same year, the local paper reminded local citizens many times of the importance of maintaining "law and order" in Mississippi, "the first goal of any state." A candidate for justice of the peace agreed: "Law and order. This we must have if we are to survive."[13] In the mid-1960s, many people in Pike County, including Joe Pigott, had believed that law and order meant an end of the bombings and other extralegal violence directed against civil rights activism and black McComb generally. Later in the decade, a respect for law and order also meant in part an acceptance of changes in the legal status of black Mississippians, whether one liked it or not. A number of area civic and business leaders at least understood that the business climate needed calm for further growth and stability, a sense that only became more pronounced as the local and national economies cooled in the early 1970s.

For many other white people in the area, however, a call for law and order meant something else—something more than fostering conditions favorable for economic development. Things had gone badly wrong in the nation and the community in recent years, they believed. The Jim Crow way of life, which they believed was the foundation of social order, had crumbled. Most Americans, write Kevin Kruse and Julian Zelizer in their history of the recent United States, "welcomed the dismantling of the old structures of racial segregation."[14] Most white Pike County residents did not. But in other ways, their reactions to recent history displayed—in common with millions of other Americans—what Kruse and Zelizer characterize as the cultural "fault lines" that the nation experienced in those years. What some Americans saw as liberation, others saw as license and even chaos. What most white Pike County residents saw on television and through other media suggested to them that respect for churches, for hard work, and for basic, common decency was being mocked, perhaps even by some young people in their own community, with their hair styles and tastes in music moving in unfamiliar directions. What happened to the country that they knew? They remembered a time, they said, when people honored tradition, custom, and established authority. What could be done to defend some of the things under assault and even to roll back some of these changes? Supporting people and institutions that represented authority seemed a place to start. In a situation like the Andrews case specifically, a trial of a police officer might seem a trial of the institution of policing itself. Better, some people thought, not to disrupt the operation of a police department which for many local whites was still one of the bulwarks of the law and order that practically everyone agreed in the abstract sense was a very good thing.

In 1970, Judge Gordon Roach, who presided at Richard McIntosh's 1971 trial, addressed the McComb Exchange Club, a men's civic service organization, on the topic of law and order in the country and the local area. That speech reveals some of the ways in which race, policing, and changing times weighed heavily on the minds of prominent Pike County men, and it hints at some of the difficulties Pigott would have in prosecuting McIntosh. Roach told his audience: "Socialistic leadership beginning with the late President Franklin Roosevelt . . . a Marxist, was the beginning of the breakdown in law and order." Decisions by liberal Supreme Court justices further eroded people's belief in the rule of law, he said. Many of those people who had recently advocated civil disobedience, including civil rights leaders, in fact intended "violent overthrow of established government." What was to be done? Throw yourself into support of local law enforcement agencies and the courts, he advised. Do not attempt to avoid jury service, as "Negroes are taking over some of the juries because whites don't want to serve. A white man is going to get the worst of it when there are more Negroes on the juries." Above all, support the local police, "even to the point of using bullets, if necessary."[15] By the last point, Roach seems to have meant to support the police even when *they* use deadly force. At least one wishes to presume that is what he meant. Roach, in fact, worried that his remarks might have been misunderstood, later issuing a statement that he had not meant that citizens should take up arms, but rather that he supported the use of bullets by "constituted police officers or National Guardsmen in enforcing laws and regulations," especially those relating to "recent campus disorders."[16] Roach's comments fell three months before the shootings at Kent State and Jackson State, in which constituted authorities did indeed use bullets against "campus disorders."

At the local level, especially visible in the elections that occurred in the fall of 1970 and those that were anticipated in the spring of 1971, power in the city still seemed in the hands of many of the same men who steered the city through the tumult of the 1960s. Some who had served on the McComb City Board in the mid-1960s were still on the board in the early 1970s. Richard Rowley, a police officer in the mid-1960s, was chief in the early 1970s. Most of the city's main banks and businesses were still run by the same men who had run them a few years earlier. But in other significant ways, the city had moved away from leaders who were in charge in the mid-1960s. In a fall 1970 election, Mayor Gordon Burt was defeated in his reelection bid, while city voters chose not to return former police chief George Guy to that position, choosing instead to retain Richard Rowley.[17] Black voters, more of whom voted for the first time in each election from the late 1960s on, certainly associated both Burt and Guy with the old order in the city, and they voted accordingly. But a number of white voters as well were not pleased with the ways that Burt and Guy had handled the challenges of 1964, from which the city's image still suffered. Some of those white voters wished to strike at the two men who had, they imagined, in some way or another, failed to prevent the crumbling of the old order.

But again, the city's newspaper offered its customary reassurances that some matters were safely in hand: "Our Negro leadership is lending helpful co-operation in many fields of endeavor. This is highly important and is certainly in contrast with many communities that have had the opposite experience." McComb's leaders wished to assure their community and a broader public as well that the bad old days of bombings, unrest, and disorder were the past. As *Enterprise-Journal* editor Oliver Emmerich wrote in the early 1970s: "The story of the Deep South that was and the Deep South that is reveals an enormous contrast," and those changes had come not from "court orders, federal funds, or boycotts," but rather from "the dimensions of good will and understanding."[18] Leave the community alone to work out its own affairs: this was the message, one that the Deep South had sent to the nation for one hundred years. Such a message was not merely rhetoric for outside consumption, though. A broad array of white McComb residents believed, as do people in most communities, that their values and institutions were sound, even as they faced significant threats. Many in McComb wished to believe that the city was just as an ad-miring letter to *Reader's Digest* had characterized it, a town where "people love flowers, trim their lawns, support their schools, obey their laws, attend their churches, love their friends, and welcome visitors."[19] Few wished to believe that police chief Rowley's department employed two men capable of murdering a child.

Despite these hopes that matters could perhaps be set right again, if authority could be bolstered and maintained, the community in which Joe Pigott prepared his prosecution of Richard McIntosh was one that demonstrated considerable lingering uncertainties about how to manage the broader cultural and social changes the previous decade had brought. Pike County showed occasional signs of strong resentment of the ways that stewardship of local matters was being checked or overseen by outsiders, a continuity of resentments that had characterized the area for years. Of the newly integrated public schools, for example, white McComb felt that "the pressure is still on," as Oliver Emmerich put it. "The demands, the confusion, the contradiction, the interference" during the previous school year had "overwhelmed" some towns. But not McComb, which, in Emmerich's telling, was a stable place. Still, "we at the local level are responsible for the dictation by Washington bureaucracy . . . which has repeatedly made mistakes." Emmerich's confident assurances aside, many white people in Pike County, as in other parts of Mississippi, had concluded that withdrawing from the public schools was their only option. Parklane Academy, one of the many segregation academies that had bloomed in the state in the late 1960s and early 1970s, "enrolled 325 students, had received accreditation from the state, and was preparing for physical expansion."[20] As in most other parts of the Deep South, sending one's child to such a private school in this era was a statement not only about one's attitude toward black people, but also about one's fellow whites who would allow their children to go to school with black children.

Whites in the Deep South, including those in McComb, remained sensitive about matters of control and authority. Despite their occasional swipes at outsiders, many of them displayed concerns about the region's reputation. In June 1971, the *Enterprise-Journal* addressed a subject that had long weighed upon white Mississippians: the image of the state nationally. "The state of Mississippi," the paper admitted, "has an evil image . . . this evil image is sorely hurting the best interests of our citizenry." But, the editorial continued, the best strategy was to face the truth. The image had been earned, not just because of civil rights era violence, but also because of the defensive or hostile attitude of state officials and citizens toward national condemnation of that violence. "The state gave the appearance of sanctioning such violence." The positive image of a state, warned the paper, can be tarnished when a state's record "revealed repeated instances of juries leaning to the defense of ones who had committed such crimes."[21] Like most good advice, this editorial probably struck many readers of the newspaper as fine enough in the abstract. But when applied to a specific, local case, such as the murder of Tina Andrews, it proved a good deal harder to apply.

Through the late spring and early summer of 1971, a number of events and decisions unfolded in Pike County that would shape the cases against the two indicted police officers. Several of these decisions involved politics and career changes. Joe Pigott, serving in his ninth year as district attorney, announced that he would not seek reelection. The counties under his watch included Pike, Copiah, Lincoln, and Walthall, a significant chunk of southwestern Mississippi. The forty-five-year-old Pigott's term would run through the October session of the Pike County Circuit Court, in which Fleming and McIntosh would presumably be tried. Why did Pigott choose not to run for reelection? His son explains: "He never told us, but frankly I think he thought he needed to make some more income in private practice. As the first of four, I was to start college in the fall of 1972."[22] Pigott did reenter private practice in 1972. But by 1974, Pigott would run for elective office again, winning a position as judge of the court in which he had led the prosecution of Richard McIntosh in October 1971.

Several other men announced their intentions in advance of that year's campaigns. Robert S. Reeves, Pike County prosecuting attorney, who would assist Pigott in the fall 1971 trial of Richard McIntosh, declared that he would be a candidate to fill the district attorney's office that Pigott planned to vacate in 1972. No one could have anticipated that the change of district attorneys would occur between two trials of McIntosh. Reeves, a 1955 graduate of the University of Mississippi's law school, had long been a practicing attorney in the county. Born in McComb in 1931, Reeves graduated from high school there and went up to Ole Miss for his undergraduate education and his law degree as well. He served in the Marine Corps and would retire after thirty years of service as a full colonel in the Reserves. Associated with his brother, R. B. Reeves, Jr., a state senator in the 1960s and 1970s, in the firm Reeves, Brumfield, and

Reeves, they maintained offices, as did other area attorneys, in both Magnolia and McComb.[23] He married a Magnolia woman, Judee McElwee, in 1961.

Like most attorneys involved in the case, Reeves wore other legal hats as well, representing for over two decades the South Pike school board. He became prosecuting attorney in 1963, appointed to that position by the county board of supervisors after Pigott resigned to accept Governor Ross Barnett's appointment as district attorney. That same year, he won a special election and later a regular election to fill the office. The year 1963 also saw Reeves elected president of the Magnolia Lion's Club, a mark of his comfortable status in the community. By 1971, he had served three terms as Pike County prosecuting attorney, and he would run that fall for Pigott's position as district attorney.[24] His opponents would be Donald B. Patterson and Jim Kitchens. Reeves would lose that race, and Kitchens would become district attorney early in 1972. After the trials of Richard McIntosh, Reeves did not seek reelection as prosecuting attorney, a fact not directly related to the outcome of the case. He spent the rest of the 1970s and the early 1980s in private law practice, and in 1984 he was appointed to the state attorney general's office. He had a respectable reputation in the county as a courtroom attorney and a solid reputation as a man.

Yet another change in political office in 1972 would have consequences for the Andrews case. In the spring of 1971, John Gordon Roach, Jr., became a candidate for Pike County prosecuting attorney, a position that would assist in the handling of the cases against McIntosh and Fleming. Roach was a McComb attorney and former McComb city judge. The thirty-two-year-old Roach was, like many of the attorneys involved in the case, a graduate of McComb High School and the University of Mississippi. The Navy veteran was also a four-year veteran of the bench as the McComb city judge. He was also the son of J. Gordon Roach, the current circuit judge, in whose court the Andrews case was proceeding.[25] As it turned out, then, both the district attorney's office and the county prosecutor's office would be in new hands in 1972. Finally, Pike County sheriff Robert "Tot" Lawson, involved in the Andrews investigation from the beginning, announced that he would run for reelection. Unlike these other men, Lawson clearly liked the job he held, and he would hold onto it, if he could. And he did. Lawson would remain a familiar figure on the Pike County law enforcement scene for many years to come.

One of the most important developments during this busy spring of 1971 involved not a political campaign or another murder, but rather a natural death, that of a McComb police officer. On May 24, 1971, the city learned of the death of police captain John Ira Sharpling, Jr. Only forty years old, "Big John" Sharpling was an eighteen-year veteran of the city's police force. He was a familiar figure to both black and white McComb residents. Sharpling was remembered, then and much later, as a superb football player, the center on the 1948 Big Eight Conference championship team, "probably the biggest man in a high school line in the '40s. . . . He was unmovable."[26] In a team photo, he towers over the other boys. Before McComb High, Sharpling had attended grade school in working-class east McComb, a fact that he made sure voters knew when he ran for police chief in 1970.[27] Sharpling also held a degree from Southwest Mississippi Junior College, not common for law enforcement officers in that time and place. Despite his bulk and his no doubt menacing appearance, Sharpling was a methodical police officer, certainly among the best on the McComb police force, and should not be imagined as a southern caricature. There are no grounds for believing that Sharpling would have protected any of his fellow officers, at least not to the degree of hindering an investigation, should his leads have taken him in their direction.

Still, civil rights activists recalled his enforcement of the old order. References to Sharpling appear in various legal documents filed by and on behalf of black residents of the city seeking relief from denial of their civil rights. There is little doubt that Sharpling, like most other white residents of McComb, did not welcome the changes in the racial order that he saw. In his work on the McComb police force, though, Sharpling did little more than most other Mississippi law enforcement officers of the period, and unlike some of those others, Sharpling was never associated with any of the Klan organizations that operated in the area. It was his job to maintain the sort of public order that most people—at least those with a say in the matter—expected in those years. But more recently, Sharpling had also been one of the chief investigators of the Tina Andrews killing. To this day, local people who recall the Andrews case speculate about the contents of the notes from his inquiries and the role that he might have played had he lived longer. One man remembers: "A police officer told my dad that big John had stayed hard on the case when it was forming up as it did. He had found what really happened and who all was involved. His health was failing and he retired. When this officer found out what big John was sitting on he went to Mrs. Sharpling and ask[ed] for the notes. They could not be found."[28] What "Big John" Sharpling found remains undiscovered. His name seems not to have been mentioned in either trial of Richard McIntosh. His notes, should they still exist, are, like the rest of the police department's files on the Andrews investigation, not public record.

Despite Sharpling's years of service to the McComb Police Department, there is indication that his relations with his chief, Richard Rowley, were not altogether smooth. Whatever the causes of that friction, it suggests tensions within the department and serves also as a reminder that not all of white Mc-Comb operated in lock-step in the period. In the fall of 1970, Sharpling had run unsuccessfully against Rowley for police chief. In that campaign, Sharpling emphasized his recent training in narcotics enforcement and his determination to address a wave of burglaries that had hit the city, both issues that spoke to contemporary concerns about crime and order in the city. But he also pledged to "improve the relations between the police department and the city of Mc-Comb," a testimony to at least Sharpling's awareness that the image of the department remained strained as the city moved into a new decade.[29] McComb voters did not respond favorably to Sharpling's campaign, as least as measured at the polls. He finished third, behind both Chief Rowley and ex-Chief Guy. The following January, Rowley promoted Mike Williams to become his assistant chief of police. One member of the McComb city board voted against that appointment, on the grounds that John Sharpling, as the senior member of the police force, should have received the job. Still, Williams prevailed, with Chief Rowley saying that while seniority was an important consideration, "I also feel that the department must run smoothly in order for the men to work together in harmony."[30]

Maintaining harmony in McComb in 1971, while not as eventful as the period of the mid-1960s, could still represent a challenge. Its residents lived in a period of lingering fallouts from recent years of social reform and cultural changes. Not all of the changes that concerned McComb people involved race. Many people there worried, as did a lot of other Americans, about the younger generation. Those young people were about to have a hand in governance. In the 1971 elections, eighteen-year-olds would be eligible to vote for the first time. Too many of them, people feared, were in the grips of illegal drugs, even some of those who were serving in Vietnam. Nationally, investigative reporter Jack Anderson asserted that drugs accounted for recent American military setbacks: "As thoughtlessly as Esau sold his birthright for a bowl of pottage, young GIs have sold out their country for a sack of marijuana or a few 'caps' of heroin."[31] Closer to home, Pike County sheriff "Tot" Lawson spelled out the dangers of marijuana, which from its initial use "by what we now term minority groups," "had spread like a cancer." Lawson warned area residents that use of "locoweed, giggle-smoke, Mohasky, or Mary Jane" could lead to "anti-social behavior" and "far more deadly drugs." Parents were panicked, he knew, and "rightfully so."[32]

Worries about young people, social breakdown, drug use, and the contemporary music that many older Americans associated with all these developments coalesced in 1971 in the area's reaction to a music festival in McCrea, Louisiana. While concerns about youth culture were as current as the recent headlines, the response to this event suggests that Mississippi residents also viewed the challenges of the present with an eye on their area's particular past. Mississippi officials monitored the festival through the state's Sovereignty Commission, an agency that continued to seek ways to check unwelcomed social change.[33] "Hippie Hoards Await the Word," the local newspaper reported, as Louisiana authorities debated approving final arrangements for the "Celebration of Life" music festival, including logistical challenges to handle a crowd that promised to be far larger than the 23,000-person population of Pointe Coupee Parish. For a time that summer, area people had been unsure where the music festival would land. A Hattiesburg-area farmer, concerned that the young people might come his way, warned: "They better stay off my land. Any hippy that tries to use my place for a toilet is going to wind up in big trouble." Other than a chance to shake their heads again at hippies and changed social mores, what did the music festival mean to the people of Pike County? Local reporter Charles Dunagin explained that "hippies by the hundreds have travelled through the McComb area the past few days, but nobody locally has displayed much excitement about it."[34]

But even a music festival in Louisiana seemed capable of raising echoes of recent, disruptive years. To many area residents, strange young people who seemed out of touch with local customs reminded them of other visitors a few years earlier: "Thus McComb in 1971 is contrasted to 1961 and 1964 when visits by rather strange looking outsiders known as 'freedom riders' and 'COFO work-ers' sparked violence that resounded over the world." Indeed, "time was when a hippie . . . could get his head busted just passing through." Congratulating the city on its better handling of this group of outsiders, Dunagin noted that while there were "some subtle encouragements not to linger too long, there was no police harassment."[35] McComb remained a city with a clear sense of insiders and outsiders, as well as sharp memories of the recent civil rights movement and its consequences, remembered here not as the fruits of local people, but of what used to be called "outside agitators." The Andrews case unfolded in a community that remained socially conservative and suspicious of challenges to local authority.

Also in late June, the community faced an issue that had inflamed tempers in southern communities for decades: attempts of labor to organize local work-ers. Croft Metals, a significant employer in the county, was typical of the post–World War II light industry that had found the South a friendly environment. It was also the sort of business that prominent men throughout the region had worried would be spooked by civil-rights-era violence and bad publicity. Now Croft faced a challenge, and the company mounted a public relations campaign to convince McComb that big labor was a bad thing. Croft's explanation drew upon language of community and interest that was well-established in a na-tional context, but which also had a particularly effective valence in the Deep South, echoing as it did the language of resistance to social change. "For over twelve months now," ran a paid Croft advertisement, "a heavily-financed cam-paign to impose a union on our company has been in progress."[36]

What was the source of the campaign? Grass roots discontent with wages and conditions? No, the threat was from outsiders, in this case "union pro-fessionals from several states," who "have been brought in to cause bewilder-ment and confusion." Now, warned Croft, locals had best not support their efforts, lest Croft join many other "small, independent companies like ours which have been driven to the wall, forced to merge or go out of business." Croft's existence, continued the statement, depended upon the presence in Pike County of conditions that allowed the company "to be free of the restric-tions and harassment generally existing where there are unions." Croft's em-ployees, the majority of them at least, did not agree with this reasoning. On July 1, production workers voted 361 to 286 in favor of a union, in this case the

United Brotherhood of Carpenters and Joiners of America, AFL-CIO. What does the Croft union campaign have to do with the Tina Andrews case? There is no direct connection, and few people in the county would have spoken of the two issues in the same breath. But McComb remained a community in which the public supported authority, order, and stability. Many people in the community worried that challenges to that authority could prove disruptive of forces more fundamental than a factory.[37] But the pro-union vote at Croft again demonstrates fault lines among McComb's white community, ones rooted in social class.

Still, some of the old ghosts of race would not down. By the early 1970s, attempts to call Pike County whites together to defend their way of life no longer worked as they had done even half a decade earlier. Attempts to galvanize the white community along overtly racialist lines could in fact work to point out social class differences among local whites, some of whom embraced such efforts, and others of whom found them an embarrassing or irrelevant relic of bygone times. On July 9, the Ku Klux Klan held a rally near McComb. By the early 1970s, the Klan was no longer the formidable organization that it had been in southwestern Mississippi less than a decade earlier. The rally made no attempt at secrecy; no plans for covert activities apparently were discussed there. Robed Klansmen posed for a photograph for the local newspaper beneath their "well-marked" rally site; "30 uniformed armed guards were performing traffic direction duties." The crowd count varied, with local Klansmen claiming that up to two thousand people attended the rally, while other observers put the number nearer three hundred or four hundred. Still, "an almost 'carnival-like' atmosphere prevailed prior to program time and a large lighted area had been provided for distribution of food." A country band entertained the crowd with their renditions of songs that had become associated with cultural resistance to social change, Merle Haggard's "The Fightin' Side of Me" and "Okie from Muskogee," songs that had immediately made Haggard, as Peter Guralnick puts it, a "symbol of the populist backlash."[38]

Well-known local segregationist Emmett Thornhill, clad not in robes but in a business suit, introduced Klan leader and organizer Robert Shelton, who "spoke at great length on such diverse subjects as segregation, public and private education, welfare and food stamp programs, communism, sex education, and federal aid." The evening continued with a documentary on black urban disorder and concluded with a small child singing while "raffle tickets were drawn to determine the winner of a high-powered rifle." Finally, "a white-robed young woman" set her torch to a diesel-soaked cross "under the light of the full moon," while the crowd sang "The Old Rugged Cross."[39]

Observers of such early 1970s Klan rallies can overreact in two different ways. The first is to see proof that nothing in the South had changed from the 1950s and 1960s. The second is to dismiss them as marginal, clownish sideshows. The significance of this 1971 rally lies somewhere between these two possible judgments. Just a few years earlier, organized Klan and Klan-like groups planned and executed mass waves of bombings and other violence in Pike County. By the early 1970s, those days were gone. Many white Pike County residents rejected that violence, and the great majority of them never had been Klansmen. But the county remained thick with men who had performed that violence and with those who were sympathetic with their aims, if not with their means. Nevertheless, times had changed. So too had the stated aims of the Klan. The language of Robert Shelton at that July 9 rally, with its denunciations of big government, federal interference, and "welfare," demonstrates a convergence of Klan rhetoric and more respectable and more respected regional and indeed national political rhetoric. Did the political right welcome the Klan and Klan sympathizers by taking their language? Or did the Klan adopt the political right's language in an attempt to moderate and modernize? Neither thing happened, at least not in a simple, deliberate, or easily discernable way. The Klan struggled to remain relevant; they wished, as did any organization in the area, to demonstrate that their group stood as useful spokesmen for the real interests of the white people of Pike County. By 1971, no respected public figure in the area admitted any Klan affiliation. Still, Pike County remained a place where the language of social conservatism spoken by Robert Shelton that evening struck a chord.

The Citizens' Council, once another bulwark of the state's resistance to the civil rights movement, struggled as well in these changed times. Founded in the wake of the *Brown* school desegregation decision, the Citizens' Councils were for many years a powerful organization in the state, indeed practically an arm of government. They advocated white supremacy in the region and combined battles against desegregation with a broad denunciation of the communistic influences that they saw driving challenges to the South's Jim Crow order. The Citizens' Councils drew a broad membership from Mississippi's political and economic leaders. They claimed to deplore the lawless tactics of the Klan organizations that spread in the state in the mid-1960s, working instead via a public relations campaign and economic pressure against dissenters from the social order they saw as key to the Mississippi way of life. As journalist Hodding Carter III observed: "The Citizens' Council in fact was often sold as a way to prevent the lower order of whites from taking the initiative in anti-integration movement. It was seen as a way for good people to stop bad people from doing things which would be embarrassing or perhaps even evil."[40] In Pike and Amite Counties, the Citizens' Council drew membership from leading citizens, including McComb's mayor and its prominent attorneys. They met, not surreptitiously as the various Klan organizations typically did, but instead openly at public schools, including McComb High School, where they were addressed by men such as Governor Ross Barnett, and at the Pike County Courthouse.[41] Membership in the organization was something about which men of the era boasted in their campaigns for local office, including judgeships. Into the twenty-first century, some had it listed in their obituaries.[42]

By the middle of the 1960s, the membership and activity of the Pike County Citizens' Council peaked and declined, both in numbers and in the prominence of its members, a pattern apparent in other areas of the state as well. That decline was prompted in part by the failure of the organization to offer white Mississippians effective ways to block desegregation and other civil rights efforts. When public school desegregation became a reality in the late 1960s and early 1970s, some observers wondered if that issue would give the Citizens' Councils fresh life.[43] It did not. By the early 1970s the organization no longer frightened office holders with its power to mobilize voters.[44] What remained of the Citizens' Council, like the Klan, sought to align its message with current social concerns. An advertisement in the local newspaper in 1971 invited voters to question candidates for the upcoming elections on a host of issues: centralization of government, the control of public schools by federal agencies, busing and efforts at racial balance in schools, the protection of private academies, and reflexively, and almost surely with an awareness that the cause on this matter had been lost, the "repeal of the 'Civil Rights' law passed by Congress."[45] A little later, in 1974, the Citizens' Council railed against interracial marriage as represented on the television show "All in the Family," which they characterized as "offensive," "repugnant," and "a serious psychological attack on the white people of this area." By 1975, they attempted, without much success, to organize a white voter registration drive in Pike County.[46] By the 1970s, the Citizens' Council, once a mighty force in Pike County, became one of those relics of the past about which people in the area did not talk much. Red-hot resistance to integration became faintly embarrassing, in some circles at least. But men who had been members of the organization continued to hold other kinds of power and prominence in the community, in the 1970s and for years to come.

Another sign of changed times in Pike County was black candidates for local office, one of them for a seat in the state House of Representatives. "This is the first time," noted the local newspaper, "at least in the past 100 years, that a black man has made a race for this local post." "Normally the race of a candidate would be of no significance in a political contest," asserted the editor, in a line that must have had both black and white readers scratching their heads. But "a change in history is seen here—and a change of history becomes news of interest to the people."[47] For years to come, the race of a candidate would be of significance in local political contests, and it continues to be.

In this atmosphere of sharp cultural challenges and white anxieties over change and authority, the Tina Andrews case made its way into court. The fall term of the Pike County Circuit Court was scheduled to begin on Monday, October 4. District Attorney Joe Pigott noted that the term promised to "be rather active." As was standard practice at the time, the *Enterprise-Journal* published the names of all the prospective jurors from the county that had been summoned for possible service during the term, which included nineteen cases carried over from the spring, as well as four new homicide cases and a number of drug-related offenses. In his charge to the grand jury, Judge J. Gordon Roach noted with satisfaction that "revolutionary forces in the country are on the decline," but he cautioned that diligence was still needed to keep order in his community. His advice included "sterner sentences for those who have no regard for the law and are determined to be criminals," to teach children better manners ("it's not a sin to say yes ma'am or yes sir"), and to stop giving those children everything that they want ("Santa Claus comes every day now"). Too many young people, said Judge Roach, "have little work to do, too much money to spend and automobiles to drive."[48]

Finally, on October 13, 1971, the case against Richard McIntosh and Ted Fleming was "set for call" in the Pike County Circuit Court, meaning that by that date all defense preliminary motions were to be filed and the date for the trial would be set.[49] Both men were free on bond; both remained suspended from the McComb Police Department. The trial for Richard McIntosh was set for October 28. The following week, following standard procedure, the defendants' attorneys filed for and received a special venire panel of seventy-five jurors, from which juries would be drawn to hear both trials.

McIntosh's attorneys also filed one further motion that indicated a strategy that they would pursue at trial. They subpoenaed McComb superintendent of schools Julian D. Prince, requesting that he produce all school records of Tina Andrews and Billie Jo Lambert. Judge Roach ruled favorably on that motion as well.[50] As it would prove, their tactic, along with challenging the state's ability to prove the identity of the body found in the oil field, would be to attack the character as well as the credibility of the two girls allegedly picked up on August 13, 1969 by Fleming and McIntosh. School superintendent Prince and the city of McComb had pressing matters to consider in 1971. The city, along with other Mississippi cities and counties, prepared desegregation plans to comply with recent court mandates that the separate school districts be merged, not with all deliberate speed, but without any further delay. The chafing of white McComb against continuing challenges to their authority to order their affairs as they chose, and indeed against a broader challenge to the legitimacy of their institutions, would prove a key factor in the broader attitudes on display in the court and in the community in 1971 and 1972. As the editor of the McComb newspaper put it, "the McComb School Board decided it was having increasing annoyance and interference from the Department of Health, Education, and Welfare." The city's proposed school reorganization plan would "give local leadership at least a sense of direction and not bureaucratic gobble-de-gook which no one could understand—and which changed from day to day."[51] Many McComb people—white ones, at least—were weary of interference with local authority.

Race and elections weighed on the minds of most of white Pike County, who clearly wondered how much control of local matters would remain with them, and how much they would have to cede to their black neighbors. "With time," Oliver Emmerich assured his readers, "there will be no white bloc and no black bloc. People will simply vote for people and with little consideration for race."[52] Still, Emmerich worried: "There is no question that the blacks have received much pressure to go to the polls Tuesday," he wrote just before the November 1971 elections. "So everyone should plan to vote Tuesday. It seems easy to predict the outcome if the people vote." Emmerich noted that the county consisted of 17,903 whites and 13,827 blacks. "Interesting," he said. "But if too small a fraction of the voters go to the polls Tuesday, anything could happen."[53]

Preparations for the fall 1971 trial of Richard McIntosh unfolded in a county in which white residents searched for a way to articulate their dissatisfaction with changed times. Many of them deeply resented recent challenges to the social order. However they might have defined order or articulated their values, most white people in Pike County believed that the world had changed in ways that were disturbing, and they were determined to do what they could to prevent any more damage to things that they prized. Many white residents were eager to put the bad years of Klan activity and other white criminality, as indeed many of them saw it, in the past and to reestablish that the community was one in which law and order prevailed. A great number of white McComb residents simply did not like disorder or wish any more bad publicity for the town, whatever the source. The murder of Tina Andrews and the subsequent trials for that murder, then, occurred in a community in which the bonds of white community had been stressed and challenged by the determination of black McComb to reject racial oppression and by white disagreement over how best to handle local matters. People of authority and influence "wanted to put on the cloak of law and order and to create the impression that they were running a clean town," a local man told me recently. "There were not going to be any poor white trash whore girls that were going to rock the boat."[54] This desire not to "rock the boat" did not extend so far as to ignore the murder of a twelve-year-old girl. But neither did Andrews's murder occasion the public outrage and demand for the truth, then or later, that it might have done if she had come from a different social background.

5

The *State of Mississippi v. Richard McIntosh*

Opening Salvos

The Pike County Courthouse, located at 200 East Bay Street in Magnolia, Mississippi, is a white, two-story building, with the courtroom on the upper floor. The structure dates from 1882. The original wood-framed building was constructed in 1876, a year after the county seat was moved fourteen miles from Holmesville to Magnolia. That building and all the records it held were consumed in an 1881 fire, not a rare fate for a nineteenth-century southern county courthouse.[1] The courthouse that stands today on East Bay Street was extensively remodeled in 1918 and again in 1965, when the old brick building was entangled in a "stucco or not stucco" controversy. Board of Supervisors attorney B. D. Statham, who would represent Richard McIntosh, was a partisan of stucco, adding that few things were more becoming in a courthouse than "shining white columns and walls." The seventeen windows across the front of the current building are a concession to the Mississippi heat in which much of the court's two terms of work per year were conducted in those days. In the 1965 remodeling, air conditioning was installed, no doubt some relief for anyone entering its doors.[2] That labor was completed in time for Judge W. H. Watkins, Jr., to open the spring 1966 term. The courthouse is not an especially imposing building, unless perhaps one were being tried there for murder, like Richard McIntosh, or one were a fifteen-year-old girl serving as a state's witness in a murder trial, like Billie Jo Lambert.[3]

Compared with McComb, Magnolia was a small community, with a population in 1970 of just under two thousand people.[4] The town was jealous of its role as the seat of county government, which many people were convinced McComb coveted. The distance of ten miles between McComb and Magnolia may sound inconsequential, but for adults in the early 1970s, their sense of

94

distance had been formed in the days when few people had automobiles. Life in these small communities fostered bonds that twenty-first-century observers sometimes fail to appreciate. In this situation, local bonds mattered, especially in the practice of law. Judges and most attorneys knew each other well, had worked with and argued before and against each other in a variety of capacities, and knew that they were likely to continue to do so. The site of the courthouse in Magnolia is also one reason that the civil rights movement of the 1950s and 1960s played out somewhat differently in Pike County than it did in other Mississippi locations. McComb literally did not witness black voters' attempts to register at the courthouse. Over the decades, however, the courthouse in Magnolia meant more to Pike Countians, black and white, than a stage for civil-rights-era drama. It was where one went to pay taxes and conduct other necessary annual business. It was also a place that had witnessed its share of trials for very serious matters, such as the state of Mississippi's case against McIntosh.

Still, if one entered the Pike County Courthouse in 1971, one might have imagined that the civil rights movement had not happened. Judges, attorneys, law enforcement officers, staff and clerks at the courthouse itself: almost every face would have been white, except for those of the black defendants awaiting Pike County justice. Only a few black potential jurors that fall would have indicated changed times. Jury selection for the trial of Richard McIntosh began on the morning of October 28, 1971. McIntosh's attorneys, B. D. Statham and William Watkins, continued to file motions for the continuance of the trial. "The defense based most of its arguments on the unavailability of a witness." All those motions for continuance were denied by Judge Roach; the trial proceeded. "There has been a great deal of speculation," reported the local paper, "about the case for the past two years, but little concrete evidence against the two policemen has been announced by law enforcement officers."[5] Presumably, District Attorney Pigott had saved that evidence for presentation at this trial. Pigott led the prosecution, assisted by Pike County prosecutor Robert S. Reeves. On the day that the jury for the 1971 trial was drawn, the body of another young woman, shot to death, was discovered at a swimming hole in nearby Osyka, "only a few feet from where a young man was killed in an affray" two years earlier. Unlike that of Tina Andrews, however, this young woman's death appeared to be a suicide. Violent death was not rare in southwestern Mis-

sissippi, a circumstance that perhaps explains how the death of one more person, Andrews, coming as she did from an undistinguished background, might
not have shocked the community as much as one might expect. Had the defendant in this trial not been a police officer, the case likely would have drawn less
attention than it did.[6]

This chapter and following chapters focus upon testimony presented by
both the state and the defense in the two trials of Richard McIntosh, as well as
strategies pursued by both legal teams as the trials unfolded. Not only is this
material necessary in understanding how the juries reached their conclusions,
but it also represents the greatest body of information available for understanding what might have happened to Tina Andrews on August 13, 1969. That testimony shows how questions of gender and social class—that of Andrews and
her family and Billie Jo Lambert and hers—were used by McIntosh's defense
team. The words "social class" never appear in the transcript, and defense attorney Statham would certainly have insisted that he was talking about no such
thing, but rather was working instead to challenge the credibility of the state's
main witness. Nor would a juror likely have told you that he or she was hearing
a story about social class or gendered behavior. But that nevertheless is what
it was. The jury heard in part a tale of class and respectability that resonated
with what they had learned to believe well before Tina Andrews lived and died.
Like so much else having to do with this case, many of the factors that shaped
Andrews's life and McIntosh's fate at trial were played out in the open, formed
by the recent history of the county. Other critical influences, products of history as well, such as the attitudes of white jurors about black ones, or the pre-
disposition that some white jurors felt even before they heard the evidence in
court, were not evident in courtroom testimony. However, traces of those features are recoverable in other ways, in part through recollections of surviving
jurors, suggesting major obstacles that the state faced in its efforts to convict
McIntosh.

The testimony offered in the Pike County Courthouse also demonstrates
some of the fundamental difficulties one might have in reconstructing that
night of August 13, 1969, either five decades ago or more recently. Readers today, like the jurors, are faced with flatly contradictory stories. Either the state's
main witness, Billie Jo Lambert, was mistaken about the identity of the two
men who took her and Tina Andrews to the oil field, or she was lying about

some parts of her story. Either the defendant, Richard McIntosh, had no connection whatsoever with the murder of Tina Andrews, or he was lying. But the juries that heard the state's case against McIntosh operated under somewhat different standards than other people who might consider the case. As defense counsel reminded them many times, the juries had to be convinced beyond a reasonable doubt by the evidence presented in court that Richard McIntosh was guilty. McIntosh's defense team ensured that did not happen.

In the first trial of McIntosh, selection of the jury from the special venire panel of seventy-five people took much of the afternoon on Thursday, October 28, 1971. Challenges and questions from prosecution and defense attorneys whittled the pool from seventy-five potential jurors down to twenty-nine before twelve people, with one alternate, were selected. One man was struck from the panel for asserting that it was the job of the defendant to prove his innocence. The selection of the jury took until 5:30 p.m. on Thursday; testimony of witnesses did not begin until the following day. But the questioning of the potential jurors provided clues of what was to come. The defense would spend a great deal of time disputing the identity of the body found in the oil field. Statham suggested as much to the potential jurors, saying that one of the major hurdles for the state would be to establish that the body was in fact that of Tina Andrews.[7]

The prosecution would rely in part upon expert testimony to make that case about the body. District Attorney Pigott asked potential jurors whether the fact that some of the experts, scientists from the F.B.I. lab and the Smithsonian Institute, came from Washington, D.C., would "affect their deliberations," an indication of the sour taste that the word "Washington" had by 1971 left in the mouths of many area white residents. Pigott was aware that the defense would attack the character of the state's major witness, Billie Jo Lambert. Pigott asked potential jurors if the fact that one of the witnesses had a child "out of wedlock" would be a problem for them. He did not at that point, however, mention Lambert's name or offer any further details.

If homicide was not rare in Pike County, the trial of a police officer was. The case drew considerable attention throughout the county, attested by the unusually large crowds in attendance. According to some estimates, nearly 350 people were in the courtroom itself—standing room only—with more spectators in the hallways and outside the courthouse itself. Pigott's opening statement to the jury of eleven men and one woman promised to establish a narrative of the evening of August 13, 1969. Tina Andrews, said Pigott, left her home that night and went to the Tiger's Den, a popular gathering place for McComb's young people. Andrews left there with two other girls, all three of whom, said Pigott, were offered a ride by Ted Fleming and Richard McIntosh. One girl, unidentified, was let out of the car relatively soon, at the corner of Delaware Avenue and James Street. The two men and the two remaining girls then went west of town out Delaware Avenue toward the oil field, but only after the two girls, Lambert and Andrews, had asked to be let out of the car multiple times, a request the men refused. Further, said Pigott, the state would provide evidence that on August 23, 1969, law enforcement officials were called to that oil field after the discovery of human remains, which Pigott said the state would conclusively prove to be those of Tina Andrews.[8] But neither in this opening statement nor anywhere else in the trial could Pigott offer the jury eyewitness testimony that McIntosh had slain Andrews.

Defense attorney Statham's opening statement denied any connection between Andrews and McIntosh, claimed that McIntosh did not know Ted Fleming at the time of the crime, and attacked the credibility and the character of both Andrews and Lambert. One of the state's witnesses, said Statham, speaking of Lambert, was "a young lady of ill repute. She has just given birth to an illegitimate child." Further, said Statham, Andrews herself, the twelve-year-old murder victim, was also "a young lady of ill repute," who was "allowed to go places and do things that were unusual for a girl her age."[9] Statham's choice of words was deliberate, inflammatory, and effective. The term "ill repute" probably would not have been used of a male witness, let alone a male murder victim. There were other words that one might use, especially if the man were black. To contemporary ears, the words "ill repute," when used of a woman, signaled almost exclusively sexual impropriety. Where did one find a prostitute? A house of ill repute. Statham, then, essentially called both girls whores, an assertion that would have been lost on no one in the courtroom. That characterization of the two girls and their worth, advanced by Statham at all stages of the trial, proved a major obstacle to Pigott's prosecution of McIntosh. Some jurors seem to have been convinced that whatever McIntosh might have been doing that evening, Andrews and Lambert were likely involved in things that no respectable girls should have been.

The state began its presentation of witnesses on Friday, October 29, with testimony to establish the nature and provenance of evidence, including the remains. The state's first witness was Mississippi Highway Patrol investigator Donald Butler, who spent much of the morning testifying about the oil field and what he found there. He identified various items that had been placed into evidence, including articles of clothing taken from the body and the crime scene, as well as a number of photographs of the scene itself. The clothing on and near the body, later featured more fully in testimony by one of Andrews's sisters, a witness for the state, included a bra, off-white panties, a pink blouse, and green shorts. Butler's testimony also confirmed earlier reports that the body displayed a bullet hole in the back of the head, as well as a bullet within the nasal cavity.

The body was in an advanced state of decomposition, said Butler, little more than a skeleton. "Many maggots were observed around the skeleton," according to Butler, some of which were sent to the F.B.I. lab to determine by the age of the insects how long the body had lain in the field. Butler also added detail about the handling of the remains after their discovery. Placed in a plastic bag, they were taken first to McComb's Hartman Funeral Home, then to the morgue of Southwest General Hospital for the weekend. On the Monday after the discovery of the body, Andrews's remains were packed and sent along with other evidence to the F.B.I. crime lab.[10]

The defense objected to several elements of Donald Butler's testimony. As Butler was not the first person to arrive on the crime scene, they argued, his testimony should be disregarded, as he could not say whether the body or the scene had been disturbed. Judge Roach overruled that objection. Another piece of evidence that occasioned sparring was a map of the oil field drawn by Butler. The map was admitted, but Statham moved for a mistrial on the grounds that on the map Butler had written "scene of the crime," an assertion that would prejudice the jury. This argument over the map and the caption took place before the judge and not the jury. While Roach declined Statham's motion for a mistrial, he did rule that the words "scene of the crime" should be erased from the map.

Statham also established a line of argument that he would pursue until the end of the trial. The defense would not concede that the body from the oil field was that of Tina Andrews. He told the jury that the body's identification was one of the key weaknesses of the state's case, as indeed it would be should Statham be able to persuade the jury that McIntosh's indictment for the murder of Andrews was based upon a fundamental error such as a misidentification of the remains. As it developed, the jury would spend considerable time listening to the state's attorneys and their expert witnesses speaking to the dental remains and other physical evidence of the body, and to Statham's efforts to discredit those witnesses. Finally Statham told the jury that Richard McIntosh "knows nothing of it [Andrews's murder] and had nothing on earth to do with her." At the conclusion of this first full day's work, Judge Roach sent the sequestered jury back to a local motel for the evening.[11]

Unlike juries a few years earlier in the Pike County Courthouse, the one that decided Richard McIntosh's fate in 1971 did not consist entirely of white men. But if the administration of justice in Pike County was no longer exclusively a matter for white men, it was still largely a business for men only. That fact too would change within a few years, as Pike County juries by the mid-1970s looked more like the demographic makeup of the county. But the 1971 jury consisted of eleven men and only one woman. The jury consisted of the following Pike Countians: Claude Williams, Jr., Clarence A. Speed, Herbert Andrews, Luther Carr, Thomas B. Austin, Harold L. Williams, Clifton McGowan, Mrs. M. V. Harvey, Lamont M. Wilson, J. C. Gardner, Charles E. Brumfield, and F. David Alexander. The alternate juror was Walter Smith. As Statham had ensured through his pretrial motions to Judge Roach, the panel was selected from all five supervisors' districts of Pike County. Brumfield, Gardner, McGowan, and Claude Williams, Jr., came from District One; Andrews and Harvey from District Two; Alexander, Carr, and the alternate, Smith, from District Three; Austin from District Four; and Speed, Harold L. Williams, and Wilson from District Five.[12] Nothing in this distribution suggests a successful attempt to pack the jury in one geographical way or another, although the residency pattern says little about other characteristics or attitudes they might have brought to their service during this trial.

The majority of the jurors, eight, were white, not an especially surprising fact in Pike County in 1971. Among them was the only woman on the jury. Mrs. M. V. Harvey, forty-one, was the wife of a Magnolia physician. Harvey was the foreman of the jury, perhaps a gracious honor to her gender as the only woman juror or instead a concession to her social status.[13] Thomas B. Austin, fifty-three, a McComb businessman, operated Austin Distribution and Central Beverage. He brought Schlitz, Jax, and Heineken beer to area residents. Charles E. Brumfield, forty-seven, was a Navy veteran and a truck driver. Clarence A. Speed, thirty, was a Navy veteran, graduate of Osyka High School, veteran of the National Guard unit in Magnolia, and a member of the U.S. Postal Service. Lamont M. Wilson, thirty-five, was an Army veteran and, like Speed, a member of the U.S. Postal Service. F. David Alexander worked in the car department of the Illinois Central Railroad. Harold L. Williams, thirty-three, was an Air Force veteran who worked in construction.[14]

Four members of the jury were African American men. Herbert Andrews, forty-three, of Magnolia, worked there at the Great American Wirebound Box Company and would eventually do so for thirty-five years. Before his death in 1988, Andrews and his wife saw three of their six children graduate from college; a fourth son was then a current college student. Clifton McGowan, thirty-three, also of Magnolia, was a farmer. He raised cattle and would go on in later years to be active in Democratic politics and a range of other interests in the area. Claude Williams, Jr., thirty-four, was a farmer as well. He ran a fifty-three-acre operation, raising hogs, other livestock, truck crops, and food for the use of his family. J. C. Gardner, thirty-six, lived in the Progress community in southern Pike County.[15]

Of all the features of the trial that indicated changed times in Pike County, black jurors hearing a murder case against a white police officer was the most striking. Publicly, at least, no one in the courtroom objected to the black jurors. Like it or not, white Pike Countians accepted that fact. As registered voters, African Americans could not be excluded *in toto* from the pool of prospective jurors. However, there were ways, peremptory challenges among them, for Mississippi prosecutors to keep specific African Americans off a jury or to limit the number of them on a particular jury.[16] Both District Attorney Pigott and defense attorney Statham recognized that the days of all-white, all-male juries had passed in Pike County. Nothing suggests that either of them attempted to racially stack the jury or would have found any particular advantage in doing so. But African Americans were a minority of the 1971 McIntosh jury. These black jurors themselves surely recognized the significance of their role. For practically all their lives, white law enforcement officers had represented the defense of the old, segregated order. Now these African American men sat weighing the fate of one of those white officers.

Whatever Judge Roach, Statham, and Pigott might have felt about the presence of African American jurors, they conducted the trial without any reference to race. Not all of the white jurors were as accepting of the new order. In a frank, detailed conversation in 2019, one African American juror recounted the dynamics of his service in that trial. Behind the scenes, attitudes about race shaped the jury's work in 1971. Jurors considered the case formally during their deliberations, but they also held conversations during their sequestration, as jurors are instructed not to do, but which they almost always do in any case. That juror, Clifton McGowan, said that several white members of the panel made no secret of their distaste for black jurors: "They wanted to tell us what to do." The sympathies of at least two of those white jurors were clearly with McIntosh from the beginning through the jury's vote. One white juror in particular, recalled McGowan, consistently "talked to us like we were dumb." Another one told McGowan, "I can't vote to convict," no matter what the evidence had shown.[17]

Nothing suggests that the African American jurors deferred to the white majority on the jury. Indeed, Clifton McGowan's recollections insist that they did not. Much had changed in Pike County by the early 1970s, not least some of the habits of deference that many local whites had mistaken for acceptance or contentment with segregation. But still, black juror Herbert Andrews, as a factory laborer, was someone who worked for wages at the pleasure of a white employer, and not an independent farmer on the Lucas Beauchamp model, to draw an example from Faulkner country, a model that seems better to describe Clifton McGowan or Claude Williams, Jr., than the other African American jurors. Whatever these men might have felt about their white peers on the jury, they walked into a place, the Pike County Courthouse, and a system, the administration of Mississippi justice, to which they had surely long felt some ambivalence and alienation. On the one hand, one might imagine a black juror who would not have felt sympathy for the state in its prosecution of Richard McIntosh, knowing as they did that Pike County could be trying an innocent man for a capital crime. On the other hand, and far more likely in this case, few black Pike County residents in 1971 would have had a love for the police department, to put it mildly, given what they knew about the character and reputation of many of those officers in the context of their policing of the black community. And these African American jurors, unlike at least some of their white peers on the jury, listened to what the state and defense had to say and voted as they believed the evidence proved. They seem to have believed that the state of Mississippi had indicted the right man for the murder of Tina Andrews, and they ultimately voted accordingly.[18]

But when these black jurors and the rest of the panel heard the case of Mississippi versus police officer Richard McIntosh that fall of 1971, they did so with uniformed officers of the McComb Police Department standing in the courtroom near the juror's box.[19] Chief Richard Rowley never said publicly why he sent his men there, nor did the judge or either of the state's attorneys openly question the move at the time. The most benign construction of the act is that it was a show of solidarity with the man on trial. More likely, it was an attempt to impress upon the jurors the stakes of the trial: the word of a police officer versus that of outsider experts and members of undistinguished families. The officers' presence invited the jurors—particularly the white ones—to choose whether they were on the side of law and order or not. One can imagine too the impression that the police might have made upon black jurors. The harassment arrests of civil rights demonstrators and the membership of some of those officers in white supremacist organizations might have been one of those features of the area's recent past that had changed by 1971. But Rowley certainly calculated the effect of a rank of armed, uniformed men upon black Pike County residents, one intended to persuade, if not in fact to intimidate. African American juror Clifton McGowan said frankly of the police presence: "The trial was controlled by the police."[20] In later years, District Attorney Joe Pigott's wife said matter-of-factly that the "whole police department lined the walls of the courtroom trying to intimidate the jury."[21]

The trial of Richard McIntosh ran for multiple days. The biracial jury of men and a woman was sequestered during the trial. Unremarkable now, those facts represented relatively new developments in Pike County, ones that the judge who heard the case that fall had been reluctant to accept. The jury ultimately concluded its deliberations in a short time—only a few hours. That fact might seem suspicious. It was not. Mississippi juries had a habit of working quickly. Current Mississippi Supreme Court justice Jim Kitchens, district attorney for Pike County in 1972, and the prosecutor of Richard McIntosh in his 1972 trial, offered during a long conversation in August 2017 recollections of the logistics of jury sequestration and the general habits of Mississippi juries and judges in that era. His comments provide insights into what had changed in Mississippi by the early 1970s, as well as what things had not. The mixed racial and gender composition of the juries in the McIntosh trials was one of those new things. The jury's producing a quick verdict was not new, and was consistent with longer patterns of Mississippi justice.

"The first cases that I tried," said Kitchens,

I was appointed by Judge Roach when I was less than twenty-five years old. I had been out of law school less than a year. He appointed me on two murder cases in Copiah County. I worked them really hard. Joe Pigott was the district attorney. I got acquittals in both cases. We tried both of those cases in one day. These were cases with the death penalty as a possible sentence. We tried one on Tuesday, March 12, 1968, and the other one on Wednesday, March 13, 1968. We tried them both in one day because Judge Roach was horrified at the idea of sequestering a racially mixed jury and a gender mixed jury. He said, "We are going to try these cases today!" The first case, we got through with it way into the night and had to come right back the next morning and try the second case. It didn't take quite as long because it was an easier case . . . self-defense, eye witness saw the other guy shoot first, that kind of thing. But I had been district attorney for two or three years before Judge Roach broke down and sequestered a jury in a murder case. In that particular case, I told him, "Judge, there is no way that we're going to try this case in less than a day. We got it going to multiple days with this case." So he said, "What am I going to do with the jury?" I said, "Judge, I would suggest that we take them down to Brookhaven to the Holiday Inn."[22]

"Multiday trials were rare fifty years ago," Kitchens continued. "It was exceedingly unusual. Mississippi juries historically do not stay out a long time. Before I came on the bench, I had a few that stayed out over the course of a day or two. But, most of the time, two, three hours. . . . I've had them stay out ten minutes when I was district attorney. I've had them just go right out and come right back." The 1971 McIntosh jury's deliberation of a few hours, then, "would've been an average time for a jury to deliberate, especially with people who were predisposed towards acquittal." By 1971 some of the old ways in the Pike County Courthouse had changed. Other habits, rooted in a century or more of broader attitudes about race and gender in the county, were changing more slowly. Judge Roach was now willing to sequester a jury, even though it contained both whites and blacks and a woman along with the men. The McIntosh trial took relatively longer than most other murder trials in Pike County, an indication that the case was as thoroughly pursued as anything else courthouse observers might have seen in many years. This trial would stretch over multiple days, in large part because of the number of witnesses, expert and lay, called by both sides.

After highway patrol investigator Donald Butler left the stand, the next witness was Pike County sheriff Robert "Tot" Lawson. He gave the jury details about the discovery of the body and the initial investigations of the crime. On the morning of August 23, said Lawson, he was in Osyka, Mississippi, some twenty miles south of McComb, nearly on the border of Pike County and the state of Louisiana. There, Lawson received a call notifying him of the discovery of a body in an oil field near McComb. When he arrived, one or two other men were already there, just down the road from the area, which was closed off. Arriving shortly after Lawson were Donald Butler and other law enforcement officials. Also on the scene was McComb physician Edsel Stewart, who conducted a preliminary examination of the remains, which were then taken into town. In McComb, Magnolia dentist Claude Pettey made dental impressions from the skull. All this evidence was then transported to Jackson, from which it was flown to the F.B.I. laboratory in Washington, D.C. Lawson further added that on August 23, when the body was discovered, his office had received no report that Tina Andrews was missing, a statement inconsistent with his remark on August 25, 1969, that "we have only one missing person in the McComb area that it could possibly be."[23] Finally, said Lawson, there was an abandoned house near the scene where the remains were discovered, but it seemingly had no connection with the murder.

The jury also heard expert witnesses, whose testimony about forensic details added a great deal for them to consider, but ultimately little that tied McIntosh either to the crime scene or in any other way to Tina Andrews. Testifying that morning was Frederick Wallace, a special agent for the F.B.I., and a specialist in microscopic analysis of hairs and fibers.[24] At the F.B.I. lab, Wallace had examined the remains received from McComb, including bullets found "under the body." Those bullets had hair on them, which Wallace said had come from a white person. However, continued Wallace, when he compared those hairs with those found on a brush and curlers from Andrews's home that had been sent to him by the Pike County sheriff's department, his conclusion was that those hairs did not match. Wallace also offered testimony on the ballistics tests. Four bullets had been sent to Washington, three recovered from beneath the body and one recovered near the body. The three under the body had all been fired from the same gun; the fourth one could not have been. But those three bullets taken from beneath the body, said Wallace, were in such damaged condition that positively identifying the specific type of weapon from which they were fired was not possible.[25] Wallace's testimony, then, would have done little to alter Statham's contention that the case against his client was built on shaky ground.

The next witness, however, had much to say that might have been persuasive to the jury, so Statham went to work establishing his narrative of an innocent men beset by the word of disreputable people. That witness was the first actually to have known Tina Andrews. Winifred Andrews Mullen, of Baker, Louisiana, about seventy-five miles southwest of McComb, was one of Tina's older sisters.[26] Mullen's testimony served in part to counter defense assertions about the ambiguity of the corpse's identity. She provided a detailed account of her identification of the remains and the clothing recovered from the oil field. The shorts, she said, she had purchased for her own daughter, who had left them at the Andrews house in McComb. She was certain that they were the right ones because they showed several repairs that Mullen had made, including a button that she had sewn back on with a cross stitch. "When I looked at them, I looked at them good and I recognized them," she said. She also identified the bra taken from the scene, "a size 32 B, a Bali Lo brand and heavily padded," reported the local paper.[27]

In his cross-examination of Mullen, Statham expanded the attack on the character and reputation of Tina Andrews that he would develop through the trial. Was she aware, Statham asked, that her sister had missed fifty-seven school days one year and sixty-nine school days another year? Unlike McComb public school superintendent Julian Prince, whose records provided Statham with this information, Mullen was not aware of her sister's poor school attendance. Statham also asked Mullen why her parents had not immediately informed the McComb police or sheriff that Tina had been missing since August 13. "I've lived here before and I would not have called the police either," replied Mullen. On further questioning, she said that she did not "trust the McComb police," showing that distrust of the McComb police was not a simple black or white matter, but also one that was perhaps here complicated by social class, previous experience, or other factors. Countering Statham's assertion that the family did not seem troubled by Tina's disappearance, Mullen insisted that they attempted to locate Tina, placing an announcement and request for information on a Baton Rouge television station, ABC affiliate WBRZ, a station with a significant viewership in the McComb area. But the jury heard the story that Statham wanted to tell: that Tina Andrews was a poorly supervised girl whose family did not seem overly troubled by her behavior or her absence from home.

Also on the first day of the trial, the jury heard substantial testimony on the condition of the remains from two Washington, D.C., area scientists, T. Dale Stewart and Marie U. Nylen. Much of their testimony, including the state's questions and the defense's cross-examination, turned on the age and gender of the remains, a continuing effort to establish that the body in the oil field was that of a girl of Andrews's age. Stewart was a physical anthropologist, long associated with the Smithsonian Institute, one who "probably has seen more skeletons of adolescent girls than anyone else in the world."[28] His testimony was technical, dealing with root ossification as a means of dating teeth and developed or undeveloped epiphyses, or "the bony matter . . . at the end of growing bones."[29] Perhaps worried that the jury would be swayed by a man with impressive credentials and learned knowledge, Statham worked to discount the value of expert testimony itself. Answering a question about the dating of molars, Stewart cited scientific literature published in scholarly journals, a standard practice that Stewart believed underscored the validity of his point. Not so for Statham, who objected to Stewart's testimony "based upon someone else's research, unless he knows of his own knowledge and his own experience." Judge Roach, at least, would not bite. "Experts read and study expert articles. This man is an expert."[30] Noting the skull's broken jaw on the lower left side ("It looked like the result of a severe blow"), Stewart also spoke to the condition of the teeth. "The teeth are the fingerprints of the skeleton," he put it nicely. He was "struck" by the substantial decay present in the teeth. "Three of the first molars were so carious that the whole crown was eaten away." "Unusual," he said, "for a young person of this age to have had no dental attention when the teeth were so badly decayed." Painful, no doubt, and also certainly unfortunate, but perhaps not as unusual as Stewart imagined among poor Mississippians.

The next expert witness was Marie U. Nylen, of the National Institute of Dental Research in Bethesda, Maryland.[31] An odontologist, she was often called upon by the F.B.I. to make forensic examination of dental remains. Jim Kitchens, who as district attorney heard much the same testimony in the 1972 trial of McIntosh, recalled the impression that Nylen made upon him: "She had the most sophisticated photography equipment I'd ever seen. This child had never been to a dentist, which complicated things. But what they were able to do was to take a school day picture of her in which she was smiling, so you can see all her front teeth. Dr. Nylen photographed the photograph, blew it up, and zeroed in on one of the front teeth. She explained that we have calcified places on our teeth that make small flag-like markings. She had the teeth from the skeleton and she found that precise thing [from the photograph] on one of those teeth, and measured it with great precision. She convinced me that this was better than a fingerprint. In addition, she took all of the teeth that she could see and measured the angulation of those teeth. The angulation on those actual teeth was precisely the same as the angulation on the teeth that she could perceive in that photograph. It was extraordinary testimony. That wasn't much of an accomplishment to establish who it was in terms of trying to do justice, but that had to be done before we could do anything else in that case. But the defense—they were good lawyers—they contested everything, as they should have. They contested the identification vigorously."[32]

Statham's cross-examination of Nylen was contentious, marked by a condescension not present in his questioning of Stewart. "Young lady," he asked the woman who had been affiliated with the National Institute of Dental Research since 1949, "do you know that the court is asking you to render an opinion beyond every reasonable doubt?" Many of Statham's questions were punctuated with "Isn't it true?" and "Don't you agree?" and "Now you remember talking with me yesterday, do you not?" and "I just want this young lady to say," a pattern that he had not practiced with Stewart. A non-native English speaker and certainly not as versed as Statham in the language of Mississippi gendered disdain, Nylen nevertheless gave as good as she got, rebuffing Statham's attempts to characterize her work as impressionistic.[33]

Comparing the skull, the teeth, and a photo of Tina Andrews, Nylen concluded: "It is my opinion that they are the one and the same person beyond any reasonable doubt." Statham fixed upon Nylen's wording in her report to the F.B.I. that the evidence "permits" identification of the remains with the photograph. Either suspicious of the standard language of scientific inquiry or simply sensing an opening, Statham asked, "The word permits, what does it mean to you?" "This not being your native tongue and you don't quite understand what permits means, what does reasonable doubt mean?" "I know what reasonable doubt means," rejoined Nylen. District Attorney Pigott had had enough and objected to Statham's leading Nylen into a definition of reasonable doubt. Judge Roach agreed: "The Supreme Court has held that you cannot define a reasonable doubt in law." But Statham persisted. Pigott interjected: "You are supposed to have the common courtesy and professional dignity to wait until the Court rules" (on Pigott's objection). Still, Statham continued: "What did you mean by a degree of certainty?" A frustrated Nylen replied: "I think that question has been objected to." "Well, now you are not the Judge," replied Statham. "If the Judge doesn't want you to say what you meant by a degree of certainty, he'll tell you so." At that point, Judge Roach reminded the court that that is precisely what he said. The exchange shows the obstacles faced in the Circuit Court of Pike County, Mississippi, by a middle-aged woman, a scientist of long experience and considerable expertise. What could younger and less-experienced witnesses do under such questioning?[34]

Next, Claude Pettey, a Magnolia dentist, took the stand. He had examined the remains, taking a dental impression of the skull's top teeth, at McComb's Hartman Funeral Home in August 1969. Again, despite Judge Roach's statements to the court about the constitutional inability of a witness to define "reasonable doubt," Statham pressed Pettey. "Could you state beyond a reasonable doubt" that the examined teeth were those of the same individual whose photograph had been displayed in court? "That is a question I don't know how to answer because I don't know what a reasonable doubt is," replied Pettey. After sparring about the ability of any scientific professional to be without doubt in such a case, Pettey concluded: "Under this circumstance I would be completely satisfied with [a] child of mine that the identification was right." Under cross-examination by assistant prosecutor Robert Reeves, Pettey offered testimony about the decay present in the teeth and the physical manifestations of that decay. "These teeth needed dental attention. Apparently, the body had never had any dental attention. . . . You can certainly assume that they would have a toothache," a fact confirmed in subsequent testimony by Donna Andrews, one of Tina Andrews's sisters.[35]

Donna Andrews was in fact the next witness. Her testimony offered the provenance of the clothing found on the remains, told of the family's efforts to find Tina after her disappearance on August 13, 1969, and through cross-examination by Statham, gave details about the habits of Tina Andrews. Donna Andrews was sixteen years old in 1971, a senior in high school who lived at home with her parents. She was just under two years older than her sister Tina. Donna identified the blouse that was found with the remains because she herself had bought that blouse for Tina. On August 9, 1969, Donna's birthday, just four days before Tina's disappearance, she received a gift of money. She, Tina, and their brother-in-law, Andy Studdard, went to Gibson's, a discount store on Highway 51 South in McComb, and bought clothing, including a blouse, "pink and white . . . low cut in the front and low cut in the back."[36] She also identified a bra, taken from the crime scene, as being very much like one that Tina had owned, part of a gift of clothing received from her sister Winifred Mullen's friend in Baton Rouge, Louisiana.

Through Donna Andrews's testimony, elicited by both the state and the defense, the courtroom also heard what struck many of them as the story of a young girl who seemed to be "on the wrong path," as a local attorney later put it to me.[37] Donna said that she had last seen her sister on Wednesday, August 13, 1969. "I was washing dishes," she recalled, "and Tina said she was going to go to the bathroom, and she went to the bathroom, and my mother came in and asked where she was, and we went and looked in the bathroom, and she had gone; she had slipped out." She was wearing "that pink blouse." That was the last time, Donna said, that anyone in the family had seen Tina.[38]

Statham directed the cross-examination of Donna Andrews. He went quickly to work on the character, reputation, and habits of Tina Andrews and her family. Taking issue with Donna's statement that Tina was a rising fifth-grader, Statham told the court that Tina was a poor student. Using material from Tina's subpoenaed school records, Statham asked Donna: "Did you know that as a matter of fact during the session of 1968–69, that she made 'F' in every course that she was taking?" He continued: "Did you know that as a matter of fact in the session of 1967–1968, she made 'F' on everything but one class, and it was a 'C' on it?" Donna replied that she was not familiar with Tina's grades.[39]

This critical attention to the academic record of a murdered twelve-year-old girl perhaps was Statham's attempt to show the jury that Donna Andrews was not as familiar with her sister as she claimed to be and thus to cloud the effect of Donna's precise testimony about the identification of the clothing that Tina had worn the evening of August 13, as well as Tina's broader pattern of behavior. But he never made that connection for the jury. More likely, Statham wanted instead to impress upon them that Tina Andrews was a girl of low achievements, low promise, and consequently of low value.

Statham then explored Tina's comings and goings from her home on Oak Street, seeking to establish that Tina was a girl under light control. To her best recollection, said Donna, Tina left home that night between 8:00 and 9:00 p.m. Statham wished to show that Tina came and went as she pleased, and that the family did not seem concerned about it. Because she was "accustomed to leaving home like that unannounced," continued Statham, "it really didn't concern anybody . . . this twelve year old little girl was going out at night by herself?" Donna Andrews took issue with that assertion. This line of questioning followed a pattern that would emerge in both trials. When the defense wished to characterize the Andrews family as neglectful or what a jury might have thought of as "trashy," Tina would be a "little girl." But when Tina herself was held up for scrutiny, Tina seemed in the defense's characterization not a "little girl," but a beer-drinking, dive-frequenting, foul-mouthed, precocious young woman.[40]

Well prepared for his interrogation of Donna Andrews, Statham referred to occasions on which Tina had left home for a day or more. While not recalling the specifics for which Statham did not provide dates, details, or his sources of information, Donna testified that Tina's absences were not rare, nor did they occasion panic. Before that evening of August 13, Tina had always come back. Donna could not say whether the family had contacted the police during these earlier absences, but she did tell the jury that the family itself had searched for Tina, precisely what occurred after Tina's August 13, 1969, disappearance.[41]

Donna Andrews's testimony highlights what was to be a problem for the state in making the case against Richard McIntosh. The events of 1969 had occurred over two years before the trial. In response to a question, she said, "I don't remember; it has been two years." She had been a young girl herself, fourteen years old at the time of her sister's disappearance, living in a house with several siblings. Her recollections of some details, such as her sister's clothing, were precise. On other details, such as how many times her sister "slipped out" of the house, how long she remained away from home, where her parents had looked for Tina on earlier occasions, and what Tina did when she left home for the streets of McComb, she was less so. On those matters, Donna did not, nor perhaps could one reasonably expect her to have, precise answers. But Statham's line of questioning was effective in establishing the picture of a household of children's comings and goings and a sort of irresponsibility that some members of the jury would frown upon.

Statham's queries created the impression that the family did not search very hard for this rambling girl, nor did they exhaust the resources for finding her that an average, responsible family would have considered. Why didn't you go out that night to look for her, asked Statham? "Because I couldn't drive, and my mother can't, and my daddy was asleep." Replied Statham: "You all just let her stay out and not knowing where she was, all that night?" "We thought she would come back . . . home," replied Donna, a statement that rings true. "It never occurred to you to go down to the Police Department, and talk to the Chief of Police, or down to the Sheriff's Office, or check with the Patrol, concerning your little sister missing?" "We thought we could find her by ourselves," said Donna. No doubt they believed that they could.[42]

Nothing in the Pike County Circuit Court file on the case, the local newspaper's coverage of the trials, or the existing portion of the trial transcript indicates that Tina Andrews's parents were subpoenaed. Presumably, the parents could have offered a more detailed account of their search for their daughter than her teenage sister did. Probably neither the state nor the defense wished to put the Andrews parents on the stand. Given Statham's questioning of Donna Andrews and Billie Jo Lambert, his questions to the Andrews parents would likely have attempted to highlight their poor parenting skills and served mainly further to sully the reputation of the family of Tina Andrews and Tina herself. Statham told the court that Tina was a girl of ill repute. What did he know about her habits? What did her family know? Whether or not that information would have been relevant, Statham's aggressive defense of McIntosh demonstrated that he had prepared well and would not hesitate to tell the jury of matters that might prove embarrassing to anyone whose reputation he wished to diminish.

During his examination of Donna Andrews and other witnesses, Statham's questioning touched upon contemporary cultural issues in characterizations meant to suggest to the jury that the Andrews family did not share the values of respectable McComb people. In her description of her family's search for Tina, Donna mentioned her older brother Freddie Andrews, twenty-three years old in 1969. "Where was Freddie that night [of August 13, 1969]?" asked Statham. "He wasn't at home," replied Donna. "He didn't come in that night, either, huh? Is he the one with long hair and a beard?" "No sir," said Donna. "He does not have long hair." A seemingly small exchange, but the Pike County courtroom in 1971 heard in Statham's question an implicit criticism of a bearded longhair and a further piece in the story that Statham was building about a disreputable family.[43]

Donna Andrews's testimony also provided the first extended discussion of the Tiger's Den, the place from which Tina and Billie Jo Lambert left directly before allegedly accepting a ride with Fleming and McIntosh. The Tiger's Den was a private club for teenagers, located in downtown McComb. It had operated under that name since the mid-1940s. Organized then under the auspices of the town's Junior Auxiliary, a women's social club, membership was originally for young people in grades seven through twelve or for ages thirteen to nineteen. "Tiger" was a reference to the athletic mascot of the McComb public school teams. Norman Gillis, Jr., son of a pharmacist and well-known McComb resident, who would become a prominent man himself in later years, won a contest in 1944 to name the club. Over the decades, it operated in several locations in downtown McComb, including an early location in the Percy E. Quin Memorial Building on Michigan Avenue. By the 1950s, it moved to the Gillis Drug Store ("Where All the Teenagers Meet") on the corner of State Street. By the late 1960s, however, it was located on the corner of Main Street and Railroad Boulevard, which is the location that Tina Andrews and her friends would have known and frequented.[44] There was nothing sinister about a girl wanting to visit the Tiger's Den and see her friends there. Statham questioned Donna Andrews about the place and its culture. "What did you do at the Tiger's Den?" She replied: "Played records, and danced, and had Cokes." It was not a hangout for adults, in short, unless those adults were interested in meeting teenagers.[45]

Before the defense finished with Donna Andrews, the court heard Statham lead her through questions about the drinking habits of her and her sister, a matter that might seem to speak more to the character of the family than to the question of who murdered Tina Andrews in an oil field. "Do you know whether or not your sister drank beer or not?" Statham asked. "I don't know," Andrews replied. "Have you ever seen her drink beer? Tell the jury now." "I don't remember ever seeing her get it," said Andrews. Statham continued: "Don't you know that on that very night she wanted go down to Pete Wade's to get some beer . . . at twelve years old?" Donna replied: "I have heard Billie Jo Lambert say that; I don't know."[46] Pete Wade was a local businessman who had run a café selling sandwiches and other food on Highway 24 in the Kramertown section of McComb since the 1940s. Originally the Acme Sandwich Shop and Service Station, the establishment was operating by 1949 as "Pete's Place," and would be well-known to a couple of generations of McComb residents as a place to gather for a few beers and listen to local station WAPF's broadcasts of McComb High football games, especially in the 1960s. It was not a place with a hard reputation, but it was no Tiger's Den, and as Statham and the court knew, not a place where a respectable twelve year old girl would go. Once in a while, the atmosphere at Pete's could become rowdy. In August 1971, before Richard McIntosh was tried but recently enough to be on the minds of people in the court that fall, a local teenager had been shot there by a railroad worker after a game of pool went wrong.[47]

Throughout the trial, the habits and character of the Andrews family were set against images of respectability and authority: schools, churches, and the law. Those invocations of authority were bolstered by more than B. D. Statham's words. One of those images of authority was certainly Chief Rowley's armed, uniformed men standing near the jurors. Several people who recall the trial in 1971, including district attorneys Joe Pigott and Jim Kitchens, have described the police presence in the courtroom that October, a matter confirmed by the trial transcript. After a recess, Judge Roach instructed the courtroom: "There are seats out there, so sit down, all of you. That includes you Policemen."[48]

To this point, the state's case aimed mainly to establish the identity of the body found in the oil field. That emphasis was a result of defense efforts to cast doubt on the issue. The amount of expert testimony frankly bored many of the jurors, as it seemed to have little to do with the question of the guilt or innocence of the defendant. Richard McIntosh's defense was effective. His attorneys attacked scientific expertise, largely by clouding the distinction between the "beyond a reasonable doubt" standard under which a jury operates and the more open standards of scientific inquiry. The defense also used the state's witnesses, especially Tina Andrews's sisters, to turn the story before the jury into one about social class and respectability, good parenting and bad, and girls of ill repute who, one could imagine with his line of questioning, might simply have received no more than they deserved at the hands of persons unknown.

6

"A Girl of Ill Repute"

Billie Jo Lambert Testifies

Billie Jo Lambert's conversation earlier in 1971 with District Attorney Joe Pigott was responsible for the indictments of Richard McIntosh and Ted Fleming for the murder of Tina Andrews. She would be the most significant witness in the case, both in her testimony for the state and in her fierce cross-examination by McIntosh's defense attorneys. The trial, both the state and the defense felt, would turn on whether the jury believed her version of the events of August 13, 1969, or whether they believed that of the defense. No witness spent longer in testimony than Lambert. No witness received rougher treatment or had more details of her life revealed. Lambert, along with Tina Andrews herself, seemed at times to be on trial—not Richard McIntosh. Defense attorney B. D. Statham used his cross-examination of Lambert to set the issue before the jury as one of respectability versus the lack of respectability, of lives lived according to local standards of good conduct and parenting and lives that were not. In so doing, Statham's work showed the ways in which white McComb in the early 1970s recognized lines of cleavage in the community based upon social and economic background. Much to Tina Andrews's disadvantage, and to Billie Jo Lambert's as well, McComb often saw matters in terms of social class as well as race.

Born on April 11, 1956, Lambert was thirteen years old in August of 1969.[1] The daughter of Pat Harrison Lambert and George Ann Welch Lambert, Billie Jo was one of eight children, four boys and four girls. By 1969 her parents were divorced, with her father living in Louisiana. In 1969, she, her mother, one of her sisters and two of her brothers lived in McComb. Pat Lambert died in Louisiana on July 11, 1969. During the trial, Billie Jo said that she was uncertain when her father had died, but that she attended his funeral in Louisiana. Whatever the marital status of Pat and George Ann Lambert, Pat was buried in Mc-Comb in Hollywood Cemetery. George Ann, who died in 2003, is buried beside him.[2] Billie Jo's parents were blue-collar people, her mother working hard to support her children. She held jobs at the Holiday Inn, the Kellwood Company, where she was a seamstress, at a local convenience store, and at Dixie Springs Café, where she was a waitress.[3]

Billie Jo Lambert, like Tina Andrews, was an attractive girl. Like Andrews, she seems to have been familiar with the streets and the night life of McComb, and she had an interest in boys. But while jurors saw a photograph of an eleven-year-old Tina Andrews as a central part of the visual evidence introduced in the trial, the Billie Jo Lambert who was on the stand in 1971 and again in 1972 no longer had the appearance of a child. Like most girls her age, she tried to look a little older than she was. But her experiences since 1969 also suggested a girl who had grown up fast and in ways with which a Pike County jury might not have been sympathetic.

Despite her age, Lambert had held various jobs around McComb, including at the two downtown movie theaters and two drive-in restaurants, including Mr. Swiss on Delaware Avenue, near Tina Andrews's home. The Lambert family had moved into town following a fire that destroyed their house in the county. At the time of the 1971 trial, she lived at home and sold Tupperware products. By that time, Lambert had also dropped out of the McComb public schools. She had finished the eighth grade at the McComb High School Skill Center, a vocational school. She left school because she "couldn't concentrate on my school work because I had other things on my mind . . . the incident that I told you about yesterday," meaning the incident of August 13, 1969.[4] The defense spent considerable time on an issue that resonated more strongly in the early 1970s than it would in later years: the fact that she was what was then called an "unwed mother" of a six-week-old baby, whose father's name she did not wish to disclose in court.[5]

Lambert spent hours on the witness stand, her testimony stretching over two days. She took the stand as a state's witness for questioning under District Attorney Joe Pigott. She lived at 310 North Cherry Street, in working-class east McComb.[6] East McComb was literally the other side of the tracks from downtown McComb. People thought of the town as being separated by race, but they thought of east McComb as a place apart as well. A 1968 city directory includes the fact that the community was served by twenty-nine churches, "17 white, 12 colored." In listing opportunities for other wholesome activities in town, the directory notes specifically those available to people in east McComb, namely a gym and a baseball-softball field, a list segregated by geography as well as by race, reflecting much less extensive civic spending for east McComb than for people in other white parts of town.[7] Yet, anecdote suggests that east McComb people generally were hardworking and paid their bills. Some banks considered them good loans, better ones in fact than those made to the city's professionals, who sometimes were not shy about overextending themselves or pulling up stakes after a short time in the area. Indeed, many homes in east McComb carried no mortgage, as workers there pressed themselves to get out from under that obligation.[8] The juries in the Pike County Courthouse in 1971 and 1972 heard little about the diligence of working-class McComb. Instead, they heard a great deal about what they would have thought of as sexual impropriety, poor parenting, and young girls out of control.

On the evening of August 13, 1969, Lambert said, she and Tina Andrews had been at the Tiger's Den. She, Tina, and another girl, whose name she did not know, left there, walked about a block, and sat down on the corner of Railroad Boulevard and Canal Street to talk. Pigott assisted Lambert with the names of the streets and the directions of the compass, because, as Lambert said, "I just know the streets by going on them," a credible statement for a girl who was in 1969 thirteen years old. Lambert told a story that was detailed and chilling. As they sat on the corner, Ted Fleming and Richard McIntosh drove up, asking the girls if they needed a ride. "Tina said that she knew one of them, that he was on the Police Force." To which man was Tina referring? Pigott did not ask her for clarification, but later testimony made it clear that Andrews seemed to know Fleming. "They were supposed to give us a ride home." Throughout her testimony, and under cross-examination by the defense, Lambert never equivocated in her identification of the men as McIntosh and Fleming or in her story of what happened that evening.[9]

After the three girls got in the car, they were driven through downtown, a short distance, and then the car turned west on Delaware Avenue, which would have been toward Tina Andrews's house, but away from east McComb, where Lambert lived. "We stopped on Delaware at a red light, and let this other girl out, to walk home."[10] Of the unknown elements in this case, the identity of the third girl is perhaps the most intriguing. Had she been identified, subpoenaed, and called to testify, she could have added detail about the identity of the men, their automobile, or what was said in that car. Nothing in the existing record speaks conclusively to the identity of the girl. Did Lambert know her and refuse to identify her to investigators or in her later testimony? Perhaps the third girl was someone that Lambert did not know at all, then or later. But McComb was a small town. Did any of the investigators speak with people who might have been at the Tiger's Den that night to ask if anyone saw Lambert and Andrews leave, and with whom? If so, that evidence was never introduced in court. If the state had obtained the identity of the third girl, there is little doubt that she would have been subpoenaed.

Delaware Avenue ran from downtown McComb west until it intersected with Interstate Highway 55. A mixture of commercial and residential properties, the street was highly developed near downtown McComb, but much less so the farther west one went. As the five people proceeded west on Delaware Avenue, the unidentified girl asked to be let out at a red light by the Plantation Chicken restaurant. After the men did that, they continued driving. Tina asked the men to let her out as well on a corner of Delaware Avenue, near the Mr. Swiss drive-in restaurant, located at 1032 Delaware Avenue.[11] The men refused, saying they needed gasoline. "So they rode on down Delaware . . . and they just kept going."[12]

Lambert said that McIntosh drove the car, Ted Fleming sat in the passenger's seat, and she and Andrews were in the back seat, with Andrews sitting behind McIntosh and Lambert behind Fleming. Pigott asked if the driver were present in the courtroom. She identified McIntosh. A person in the courtroom that day recalled that when Lambert took the stand, McIntosh's face "began turning red, and that red rose up from his neck like a thermometer."[13] Any man, however, might be uncomfortable in the presence of a witness accusing him of murder.

Driving out Delaware Avenue on Delaware Avenue Extension, they came onto "a rock road with cattle gaps and all in it." "We turned off to the left and went to a deadend, and they pulled the car up and then backed it." Lambert said that the girls told the men that if they would not take them home, the girls would walk back to town. By the time they got to the parking spot, the girls concluded that the men were not interested in taking them home. "So we got out of the car," said Lambert, "and we took off running."[14]

Two scenarios account for the presence of McIntosh, Fleming, Andrews, and Lambert in the oil field that evening, if indeed Lambert's identification of the men as McIntosh and Fleming is correct, an assertion that McIntosh denied and that the state of Mississippi failed twice to convince a jury of its truth. One is that the two men—one in his twenties and the other in his thirties—saw the two girls, one twelve years old and the other thirteen, as potential sexual partners. Andrews and Lambert both were developing what was called a "reputation," as Statham's unfolding story at the trial took pains to point out. Richard McIntosh, police officer or not, and surely Ted Fleming as well, would have been in a position to know things about the reputations of girls who spent time on the streets of the city and in some of its public establishments. But nothing in Lambert's testimony indicates that either man ever indicated that he knew by name or in any other way the girls to whom they offered the ride that evening.

Another possibility is more sinister. Rumor in McComb has maintained that Andrews and Lambert were sexually active, some of their partners including prominent, older McComb men. In this telling, Andrews and Lambert knew potentially embarrassing information, and either threatened to say what they knew or were believed to be liable to talk. Thus, the trip to the oil field was an errand of attempted intimidation or worse. A member of Tina Andrews's extended family told me matter-of-factly that Tina was sexually involved with older men. "How do you know?" I asked. "That's what everyone said after it happened," she replied, reflecting at least the extent to which the trial and publicity further tarnished the family's reputation. That comment and similar rumors go a long way in explaining Tina Andrews's immediate family's long-term sensitivity about the case and their desire not to talk about it. Another local person took issue with this theory of a broader, sex-inflected conspiracy to silence Tina Andrews, saying that while Andrews might indeed have been sexually active, it would not have been with men of prominence or social standing. "Back in that day, some of those important men downtown kept black women. It was officially hush-hush, but you would see them up on Summit Street. But those men were not involved with twelve- or thirteen-year-old girls. Why would they need to be?"[15]

Lambert herself never breathed a word of any such scenario of silencing or intimidation. Her detailed testimony never recounted much conversation at all between the girls and the two men, nothing that would suggest that the

men took the girls to the oil field on any mission other than one of sexual grat-
ification. The business of the Pike County Circuit Court in 1971 was not concerned with building a deep story of the motives of the men in picking up the
two girls. The job of the state was to convince the jury that Richard McIntosh
had a hand in the events that led to Tina Andrews's body being found in the oil
field; the job of the defense was to cast doubt upon that story. Any version of
the story that supposes that Andrews and Lambert were taken to the oil field
on a mission of intimidation remains unproven and unsupported by credible
evidence.

Lambert's testimony provided the only specific element of the case that
tied McIntosh to the two girls or to physical violence against Andrews. "When
we jumped out of the car and run," she said, "Richard McIntosh caught Tina,
and she called him a son-of-a-bitch. He said that no one called him that and
got away with it, so he hit her, and I took off running." Lambert could not be
certain which arm he had grabbed or upon which side of the face McIntosh had
struck Tina, but she was certain that McIntosh had hit her in the face, a blow
that could have accounted for her broken jaw. That was the last moment that
Lambert saw her friend. She never testified that she heard a gunshot. In fact,
she specifically said that she had not. Nor could she provide details about the
car in which they rode that evening, except that it had four doors, or the way
the two men had been dressed, or other matters that might have added persuasive facts for the jury to consider.[16]

Then, said Lambert, she made her way, alternately walking and running,
from the oil field back into town to Delaware Avenue, and then through town
toward east McComb, crossing the bridge to her house on Cherry Street. Barefooted, casually dressed, and badly shaken by whatever had happened that evening, Lambert returned home to a mother who was upset by a daughter who
had once again come in late. She did not tell her family what had happened,
nor did she consider reporting it to the police. "I didn't know what they would
do if I reported it."[17]

Lambert's testimony included two further elements of the story—one about
a potential threat to her, and another about a subsequent trip to the oil field—
that are intriguing, if undeveloped. At her house later that evening, said Lambert, she heard noises outside her bedroom window. It is possible that those
noises were simply the imagination of a terrified child. However, persuading

her brother-in-law, Richard Wolfe, to investigate, they found a chair "up against my window, my bedroom window." Perhaps the chair was one that Lambert had used in coming and going from her house, if she would even have needed a clandestine way to leave her house. Had the chair been placed against the window by someone who had been with Andrews and Lambert earlier that evening? No testimony, either from Lambert or anyone else, maintained that either McIntosh or Fleming was spotted anywhere near Lambert's home that evening of August 13, 1969. Nor did she report any further incidents of the sort.[18]

Next, Pigott asked Lambert if she ever returned to the oil field. She replied that she had, before the body was discovered, which would have been sometime between August 14 and August 22, 1969, probably toward the latter end of that period. Why had she returned? She went with a friend, Louis Smith, "to talk," while they waited for another friend to finish work. But they left, said Lambert, because when they rolled down the car windows, certainly against the Mississippi August heat, there was "a bad odor out there, so we left." If she and Smith speculated about the source of that odor, she did not say. Why would she have returned to a place where something very bad had happened to her so recently? Habit, perhaps, or to discuss what had happened to Tina Andrews? Lambert was not asked, and she did not say.[19]

Pigott did ask Lambert if she had any further contact with McIntosh after he took her and Andrews to the oil field. She said that the next time she saw him, he was "on Main Street, directing traffic; he was a Police." She had seen him several times in downtown McComb directing traffic. As a police officer, McIntosh would have directed traffic. Whether or not he ever took the girls to the oil field, Lambert almost surely saw him later downtown. But when? In Lambert's initial testimony, she never provided even an approximate date for having seen him in police uniform. Later, however, under cross-examination by Statham, she provided a date apparently of late 1969, when he was not an official member of the department. That date would be seized upon by the defense as evidence of Lambert's unreliability and indeed the shakiness of her entire story. It is possible that her date of late 1969 was an error in her recollection, a particularly unfortunate one for the state. Given the elapsed time between the summer of 1969 and the fall of 1971, a long stretch of time for a girl Lambert's age, perhaps Lambert did not recall correctly the time when she began to see McIntosh in police uniform. Unfortunately for the state's case, the state itself thus offered testimony about a matter—McIntosh's directing traffic in a police uniform—that the defense would take up and be able to contradict.[20]

Lambert also maintained that McIntosh had come to her house "to try to get me to go riding with him, several times" after August 1969. On one of those occasions, "he was drinking beer. And he tried to give me a beer, and I wouldn't take it. And he was, I would say, pretty well looped on beer. And he tried to pull me into the car with him." Lambert would not go. Someone did call the police to report McIntosh's apparently unwelcomed appearance at her house. "He left," she said, "right after they came." Neither Lambert's testimony nor Pigott's questioning established any motivation that McIntosh might have had for contacting Lambert.[21] Nothing in the evidence suggests that anyone at the police department ever followed up on this report or in any way connected this contact of McIntosh with Lambert as having anything to do with the Tina Andrews case.

Perhaps more surprising to the jury and indeed more surprising generally, Lambert said that she had on a subsequent occasion again been in McIntosh's car, which was not, she said, the one that he had driven in 1969. "My sister," she said, meaning Norma Lambert, "wanted a ride out to a friend's house." McIntosh gave her a ride, and Billie Jo came along. Pigott did not ask Lambert why she might have consented to be in the same car with the man who took her and Tina Andrews to the oil field. Nor did the state introduce any other witnesses to corroborate Lambert's assertion of McIntosh's contact with her and her sister. If Lambert's story is true, one might well understand McIntosh's desire to see Lambert, if only to monitor her or perhaps to see what she might say to him about Tina Andrews. But Lambert's willingness to have anything to do with McIntosh remains baffling.[22]

Pigott neared the end of his questioning by asking Lambert to provide more detail of that evening. Had Fleming and McIntosh said anything to the girls on the ride to the oil field or when they arrived at the destination? Fleming, said Lambert, had remarked that "people didn't believe that they would take young girls parking but we could tell them now." How had she and Andrews reacted to that statement? "That was when he stopped and we got out of the car. We had done asked them to take us home about nine times on the way out that little road." She reported no attempts at seduction and no sexual contact between the men and the girls at the scene.[23]

In a brief exchange, Pigott asked Lambert about a matter that he knew the defense would introduce if he did not. She told the court that she was a fifteen-year-old who did not attend school and also the unmarried mother of a six-week-old boy. "And are you keeping the baby?" asked Pigott, a question that seemed more natural in 1971 than it does today. In that time and place, the stigma against unwed mothers, especially teenage ones, was strong, despite its irrelevance to the question of Richard McIntosh's guilt or innocence in the murder of Tina Andrews. Pigott had finished with his witness. It was just after 7:00 p.m., and Lambert had been on the stand less than an hour. But she had established the main lines of her story about the evening of August 13, 1969. She revealed as well some of the weaknesses in her testimony as well as elements of her life that the defense would exploit.[24] Judge Roach adjourned court for the evening, sending the jurors into sequestration at the local Holiday Inn, where the African American jurors would not have been welcomed as guests when the establishment opened in 1961. As the docket of the Pike County Circuit Court puts it, the "jury [was] locked up for the night."[25]

When the trial resumed at 8:30 a.m. on Saturday, October 30, 1971, a Saturday court session being unusual in Pike County, Lambert took the stand for cross-examination. From the opening questions, the defense framed the main issue, "the whole question," as "her integrity of telling the truth."[26] With two brief recesses, Lambert spent more than five hours on the witness stand that Saturday.[27] As one would expect of a seasoned defense attorney, Statham's questioning was sharp. Their exchanges were often contentious. Statham wished to show that Lambert could not tell a believable story about the events of August 13, 1969. More precisely, he attempted to convince the jury that because of Lambert's character and background, she could not be trusted to tell the truth.

Lambert's testimony that Saturday was more detailed than the version she had offered the previous day. Statham began with questions about Lambert's family and background, not unusual, and designed here to showcase the disreputable character of the witness and her family. The questioning also demonstrated Lambert's lack of command of facts, which Statham obviously believed would work to the defense's advantage. Statham asked Lambert when her father had died. "I don't know, exactly," she replied, but then offered "July 11, no, August 11," July 11 being in fact correct. Lambert replied "I don't know" or "I don't remember" to questions about the year of his death, the season of his death, and whether or not she had been in school at the time of his death. Statham exasperatedly said, "Now, young lady, you have been telling the Defense Counsel that you don't know ever since this thing came up, and you refused to talk to anyone except to the State, and you can remember a few things such as the death of your father, can you not?" Lambert replied: "That has nothing to do with the case." Statham scolded her: "I'll decide whether it has anything to do with the case, and not you. Answer the question." The judge instructed her to do so. Again, Lambert replied "I don't know" or "I don't remember" to a series of questions.[28] "In other words," said Statham, "the only thing you remember has to do with Mr. McIntosh and Mr. Fleming here, and you can't remember the other details?" "Is this going to be a broken record the whole time I'm questioning you?" District Attorney Pigott interjected: "We object to arguing with the witness. She answered the questions as he asked them." The judge agreed: "Don't argue with the witness." But Statham said, as much to shape the jury's understanding as anything else: "I'm not going to tolerate this witness saying, I don't know, on everything except something that she wants to know." The judge said rightly, "That will be a matter for the Jury to decide."[29]

Statham then examined Lambert on an issue that Pigott had raised the previous day, the recent birth of her child. His handling of the matter was somewhat rougher than Pigott's. Lambert said that her child was six weeks old. "Can you tell the jury about the time that you became pregnant?" asked Statham, apparently for the benefit of people who were not familiar with the timing of human gestation. "When you was down here at the last term of court," including the meeting of the grand jury, "you were pregnant at that time, weren't you?" "I guess I was," replied Lambert. "There was no guessing about it, was there?" said Statham. "Well, I didn't know at the time that I was." Statham then asked her how many menstrual periods she had missed by the time of the previous court term.[30]

District Attorney Pigott's sense of relevance, and perhaps of decency as well, had had enough. "I think there are some things that are so personal that are absolutely beyond even the cross examination of Mr. Statham." Statham disagreed: "This is very personal, and I'm going to find out about it." Pigott rejoined: "I think it has absolutely nothing to do with this case." Judge Roach agreed to sustain Pigott's objection: "I can't see the relevancy of this." Statham then told the court that he would "forget the period business, Judge." Cutting a very fine distinction indeed, his next question not only continued to pursue the "period business," but also to throw the issue of legal agency onto the fifteen-year-old shoulders of Lambert. "You was pregnant at the time you was down here in March and had Mr. McIntosh and Mr. Fleming indicted, weren't you?" Assistant prosecutor Reeves objected: "She certainly didn't have anyone indicted." On Statham pushed: "Have you instituted any paternity suit for support of this child?" Responding as Statham had hoped, Lambert replied: "I don't understand what you mean."[31]

Finally, Statham challenged Lambert to identify the child's father. Again, the state objected to the relevance of the question. Statham argued that "we want this record to show that the integrity of this witness is at stake, and these questions are quite pertinent." To Statham's thinking, an unwed mother lacked integrity. The judge steered Statham away from this questioning: "You have shown that she has a baby, and that she worked here and yonder, and that she dropped out of school, all these sorts of things. But now as to whether she started a civil proceeding against the father has nothing in the world to do with this case." But B. D. Statham knew better, at least in gauging what a jury would make of his characterization of Lambert.[32]

Statham was an effective attorney. He developed an attack against the credibility of the state's main witness, and that path lay through her character. Whatever objections the state raised, and the judge consistently maintained them, Statham painted Lambert as a person whose word could not be trusted because of her background and her very nature. Statham continued to try to impress upon the jury that Lambert's failure to recall the specifics of her dating history and of which "beer taverns" she had entered and when constituted a fundamental weakness in her testimony and thus in the state's case against McIntosh. Under questioning, Lambert stated that she had begun dating when she was twelve years old, a matter that might not to some observers have been directly relevant to the question of whether or not she and Tina had accepted a ride from the two police officers on August 13, 1969. But it did further the impression that the girls were precocious, if not disreputable. Statham also continued to suggest to the jury that it was Lambert's credibility and Lambert's agency that were central here, not those of the Pike County district attorney's office or the state of Mississippi or Richard McIntosh and Ted Fleming. "I want you to state to this Jury, candidly and honestly, when, as to dates now, you must realize that you have charged a man here with murder, or two men."[33]

The logic of his assertion, or at least the connection between the two clauses of his statement, is puzzling, but the force of the statement upon the jury was clear. If Lambert were not "candid" or "honest" about her dating habits and her comings and goings, then who could believe her testimony against the two men? Again, the state tried to correct Statham. Lambert, objected Pigott, "did not charge anyone with anything . . . she is only a witness to the facts that she knows." As a matter of law, Statham well knew the difference, but he also knew how to manage a jury. He responded: "If her testimony yesterday wasn't a charge, I would like to know what it is."[34]

Lambert seemed to some courtroom observers to bear up well under Statham's questioning. The local newspaper reported that she "was tight-lipped and apparently nervous but was calm and in full control of her emotions."[35] In control and consistent with her story she might have been, but one juror recalled years later that Lambert seemed somehow quite alone in that courtroom and throughout the process, "not treated well at all."[36] Asked to describe her actions on the day of August 13, Lambert replied that she could not recall specific events of the day but was certain that she remembered what happened that night. Statham then raised the issue of the third girl in the car. He asked Lambert if she knew Beverly Henderson. "I do now," said Lambert. In fact, continued Statham, "had not Lambert asked Henderson to say" that she was the third girl allegedly in the car with the men that evening? Lambert twice emphatically denied that she had asked Henderson to come to court to testify that she was the third girl in the car, and said in fact that she had never spoken with Henderson about "this incident," as Statham put it.[37]

This questioning is the first association in the trial of a name with the third girl that Lambert consistently insisted had been in the car with her and Andrews on August 13. A key missing element in both trials would be the lack of testimony from that third girl and indeed the inability of the state to establish that such a third girl even existed. Statham's raising of the issue here attempted to impress upon the jury that Lambert not only was willfully forgetful, but also a person who would manufacture evidence. He did not use the term "suborning perjury," but that is essentially what he asked Lambert if she had done, a charge she flatly denied.

On the evening of August 13, Lambert explained, she and her sister Norma, about two years older than Billie Jo, walked from their house on North Cherry Street to the Tiger's Den, which she described as being located at the corner of Main Street "and that street that runs by the railroad." Statham reminded the court that North Cherry is "over in East McComb, for the benefit of the jury." The clarification, seemingly innocuous, served to remind the jury of Lambert's blue-collar origins. Statham established that Lambert had arrived with her sister, but did not leave with her, nor did Lambert know what time Norma returned home that evening, itself not a shocking detail, but which in Statham's hands managed to sound irresponsible, if not sinister. At the Tiger's Den, she found Tina Andrews and another girl arguing about a boy. To keep the argument from degenerating into a fight, she urged Andrews to come outside. "I asked Tina if she would come walking so that she wouldn't fight that night over something silly, this other girl just came along with us." Lambert, Andrews, and the third girl left the Tiger's Den, walked, talked, and sat down on a curb.[38] "Can you describe this friend?" asked Statham. "No, I can't," replied Lambert. "Now, young lady, I know that you don't think I'm stupid, I hope that you don't," said Statham. "No, I don't think you're stupid," replied Lambert. Why, then, could she not recall anything about the alleged third girl? "I didn't pay no attention to that other girl; I didn't know her, and I wasn't with her." But again, the jury heard Lambert reply "I don't know" to a series of questions from Statham, who continued to point the jury toward gaps in Lambert's memory or knowledge. Statham asked: "Have you made any attempt or effort to locate this other girl since . . . this incident came up?" Lambert replied: "Well, I have looked at places that I went but I didn't go out of my way to look for her." She again insisted that Beverly Henderson was not the third girl, nor had she consulted with Henderson about the incident after Tina's disappearance.[39]

As the three girls sat on the curb, said Lambert, a car drove up and two men inside offered the girls a ride home. "Tina knew the man on the right side of the car to be a policeman, so we got in the car and they were to take us home." "I recognized Richard McIntosh," continued Lambert, as "I had seen him around town, but did not know his name. He was driving." Lambert did not hesitate in identifying both men by name. "How do you know it was Richard McIntosh and Ted Fleming?" asked Statham. Lambert replied: "Because I had seen them before, and I've seen them after then."[40] Lambert did not recognize or could not recall the make or the color of the car, but was certain that it was a four-door automobile, because the men did not have to step out to let the three girls into the back seat. Statham then directed Lambert to look at McIntosh and to say whether or not he looked like he did on that night. Rightly, Lambert replied: "He is a little older. His hair is shorter and his clothing is different." Through hours of cross-examination, Statham pressed Lambert for details of the evening of August 13, 1969, and her actions after that date. Repeatedly, Lambert answered "I don't know" or "I don't remember" to questions about what she wore that evening, what the men wore, what was said, and what she did the day after the incident. But she held to the main lines of her story.[41]

Lambert testified that after the body was discovered in the oil field, she told her mother that she knew the identity of the victim, but that her mother told her to "keep her mouth shut because it was only her word against the word of a policeman." Why, then, asked Statham, had Lambert finally told Pat Lamkin what she knew about the incident? Because, said Lambert, she hoped that if she came forward with what she knew, "she might stop having nightmares if she could talk to someone about it." It was sometime in 1970, said Lambert, that she told Pat Lamkin, "and she was the one that reported it."[42]

Lambert made significant distinctions among Pike County law enforcement authorities, despite Statham's attempts to paint her as ignorant. She specifically did not contact the police or sheriff's departments because she did not trust them, but when Statham asked her about the district or county attorneys or the highway patrol, she said either that she thought that it would not do any good to contact them or that she did not know how to reach them or that she did not think of that possibility. She did not trust the police or the sheriff and his deputies, she said, because she associated Fleming and perhaps McIntosh with what she knew of local law enforcement. Statham, however, intended to make Lambert's silence that evening seem suspicious—as if no reasonable person would fail to avail herself of all these resources, unless of course the whole story were a fabrication.

Why, asked Statham, had Lambert not asked anyone for help that evening or told anyone what had happened? Along Delaware Avenue, he reminded the jury, there were many places where a girl in Lambert's situation might have sought help. What about the Holiday Inn motel, asked Statham? Or service stations? Or restaurants? Why had Lambert not walked into any of those places to ask for assistance? Did you not believe, asked Statham, that anyone in any of those places would have helped you? "I wasn't interested in what was open. . . . I was interested in getting home." Why, he continued, would she not have flagged down a car to ask for a ride home, if her feet and ankle were injured, as she had said? In a well-considered response, Lambert said: "I had done got one ride out to a place that wasn't my home, and I didn't want to get another one."[43]

What had happened at home? Her mother, her sister, and her brother-in-law were awake, but Lambert could not recall what time she arrived. While they were concerned about her and wondered why she did not call them for a ride home, she did not share with them details of the evening, a fact that Statham wished for the jury to see as literally incredible. But according to Lambert's own testimony, she had no idea that Tina Andrews had been killed. What she knew was that she and a friend had been picked up by two men, at least one of whom was connected with the McComb Police Department, men who had soon expressed a wish to "go parking" with them. She escaped that dilemma the best way she could and made her way home to a household clearly impatient with Lambert's comings and goings. Many girls in her position would have wished only to avoid any more trouble. Why, Statham continued, had Lambert not told her story of what had happened until the next year? "I had been telling my mother and my aunt and all that I knew who it was, but they told me to shut my mouth, because I could get in trouble by saying I knew who it was, and they didn't think that I did. . . . They didn't want to listen to me."[44]

Billie Jo Lambert's story was consistent. She was a fifteen-year-old girl, facing one of the most formidable criminal defense attorneys in that part of the state. But while B. D. Statham was able to show that there were many matters about which Lambert did not know, she was adamant about one thing: she did not trust law enforcement authorities in Pike County. On the evening of August 13, 1969, asked Statham, why did you not report what had happened to the police department? "Was I supposed to go up to the Police Station and report it when [Fleming] was a Police himself?" Then why not report it to the sheriff's department, countered Statham? "For the simple reason," replied Lambert, "that they are all with the law, and if the law would lie and say that they was going to take us home and didn't, well, what good would it do to report [it]?"[45]

As she neared the end of her testimony, Statham's attack on Lambert's character ramped up. His job as a defense attorney was to pick holes in her story or otherwise to convince jurors that they should not believe her. But his path to that goal was through questions that painted Lambert as a tramp and a thief. Without objection, Statham asked Lambert about unspecific incidents with no apparent connection to the Tina Andrews murder. One of those occasions involved Lambert's mother returning home to discover a boy or boys exiting the house through Lambert's bedroom window. "Do you remember when your mother came in and a hasty retreat was made?" "A what?" replied Lambert. Statham expanded his question with a salacious-sounding scene. "Do you remember when your mother came in," and a boy was there, "and you didn't know she was coming in, and she found you all later out in the bushes there at your house?" "That never happened," replied Lambert. But the jury certainly heard the story.[46]

Throughout these lines of questioning, which amounted to constructing a story of Lambert as a trampy, disreputable girl, the defense demonstrated a level of preparation and indeed a ruthlessness that the state, for whatever reasons, did not match. Certainly the attacks on Lambert scored points with the jury, whose ability to discern what was relevant and what was not was not sufficiently guided here by the state. Whatever they might have concluded about Richard McIntosh's involvement with Tina Andrews, they heard details about Lambert that could not but have lowered her in their estimation.

Statham continued to try to persuade the jury that no one could have witnessed what Lambert did and keep it a secret for so long. Pike County was a community of churchgoers, and Statham raised the question of Lambert's faith. After the body was discovered, he asked, "did you go and confide that information even with your preacher, or do you go to church?" In small-town Mississippi in that era, one could hardly have asked a more potentially awkward question than the latter one. "I go to church," Lambert insisted, but she also said that she confided in no one, a statement consistent not only with what Lambert had previously said, but also with the apparent facts of the story: a young girl, with what she truly believed to be few options, had chosen to keep quiet as long as she was able. Statham here, though, had framed the question

131

so as to have Lambert insist that she did not trust her preacher, again an admission that would not have sat well with the jury.[47]

Statham also informed the jury that Pat Lamkin, to whom Lambert had confided about the incident, was living with the Andrews family, was pregnant, and that her husband and she were separated. He also returned to a subject Joe Pigott had raised in earlier questioning: Lambert's statement that she had returned to the oil field site with a boy sometime in August 1969 before the body was found. In Statham's line of questioning, he added details that made that return trip seem tawdry. The boy was from east McComb; he was in high school; they had met at the Tiger's Den. And "what was you all going out there for, to play tiddlywinks, or what?" asked Statham. "Just to talk," Lambert replied. "And that's all you intended to do?" continued Statham.[48]

Statham ended his cross-examination of Lambert, and thus her time on the witness stand, by implying that she had come forward with her story hoping for the cash reward that had been offered for information about the crime. Indeed, he implied that she might have seen or heard details of the crime from local media coverage and then hatched the idea of coming forward with what she allegedly knew. Lambert denied that she had concocted any story. Statham also suggested that the entire Lambert clan, and some of the Andrews family as well, had fallen over each other quarreling over shares of the potential reward, a line of questioning that not only further painted a picture of dysfunctional families but also suggested that any stories coming from any of them were motivated by a desire for money rather than being the truth about what had happened to Tina Andrews.

Statham tried one more line of questioning to persuade the jury that Lambert's entire story was unreliable. Had she no confidence in anyone in Pike County? Not the police, the sheriff, the prosecutors, the newspaper reporter who covered the story? Not her school principal, her preacher, her family, or the Andrews family? Perhaps she had no confidence in them because she knew that they would not believe her because she had a reputation as a liar and a thief. Those in her family that she tried to tell did not believe her, Lambert admitted. "Why is it that people don't want to believe you?" he asked. "Do you have a reputation of not telling the truth?" "No, I don't, not that I know of," Lambert replied. "Have you ever been accused of being dishonest and not telling the truth? Do you remember stealing six dollars from the little Ferguson girl?" an assertion unconnected with any previous testimony, one that Lambert denied, and one that prompted an objection from Joe Pigott. Statham insisted that the questioning led to the heart of the larger question of her credibility. Judge Roach finally ruled: "That's not a proper inquiry of the character of anyone . . . the fact that someone had been accused of something doesn't necessarily make it so." The objection of the state was sustained, but the jury was left with the impression that Statham wished to make.[49]

The state's final witness was Jimmie Nell Lambert Wolfe, of Baker, Louisiana. She was Billie Jo's older sister, and she had been living with the Lamberts in August 1969. She explained that on the night of August 13, 1969, Billie Jo had returned home, barefooted and with injured feet, exhausted, and frightened, but that she had not told what had happened that evening. "She was scared to death, extremely nervous, and she couldn't sleep that night. She thought somebody had followed her home."[50] In sharp cross-examination, Statham questioned Wolfe's ability to recall some details of that evening, but not others, and tried again to impress upon the jury how odd it was that a family would allow Billie Jo to come and go in that fashion without pressing her for information about what she had been up to. "Now did you all grill her on why she had been out there [past Delaware Avenue], or did you have any interest in finding out why she was in this shape?" "You notice things," remarked Statham, "that would be convenient for you to find strange one and a half to two years later, but you seem to forget [other] things." Later, said Wolfe, her sister told her, after the body in the oil field was discovered, that she knew who it was. She had not, however, used Tina Andrews's name. Did you do anything or make any further inquiries or inform the police? No, said Wolfe. Statham suggested that perhaps Wolfe simply did not believe her sister. "I guess I believed her," said Wolfe, but the information was too vague, she said, to take to the police. With that testimony and cross-examination, the state rested its case against Richard McIntosh.

Girls who come and go from home at will and without supervision; girls who have no respect for the city and county law enforcement authorities and who in fact regard them with contempt and suspicion; girls who ride around and park with boys; girls who become pregnant by these boys, who either do or do not marry them and who often simply disappear from their lives; families that violate basic canons of what the Pike County jurors would have believed about sexual propriety and common decency. This was the story that B. D. Statham told about Tina Andrews, Billie Jo Lambert, and their families. It was a scorched-earth defense that gave no quarter to the age of either girl.

It was also a defense that showed no regard for Lambert's or Andrews's status as white southern women. For long as there had been Jim Crow in the South and violence to support it, one of the main justifications of that system was the need to protect the honor of white women. Critics had long pointed out the baseness of the contention that only potential lynching tempered the appetites of black men for white women, insisting that violence done in the name of white women served largely as an excuse to maintain white male supremacy. Still, on most occasions white southerners, including people in Pike County, would have insisted that they held (white) women in particular regard. In the words of their Brookhaven neighbor, Judge Thomas Brady, who had on earlier occasions presided in the Pike County Courthouse, the "loveliest and the purest of God's creatures, the nearest thing to an angelic being that treads this terrestrial ball is a well-bred, cultured Southern white woman or her blue-eyed, golden-haired little girl."[51] Unfortunately for them, neither Tina Andrews nor Billie Jo Lambert were blue-eyed or golden-haired. Instead, they were blue-collar, or at least their families were. And as B. D. Statham had taken great pains to tell the jury, Andrews and Lambert were not well-bred, cultured women. Instead, they were marginal, economically and socially. It was precisely the kind of defense that Richard McIntosh needed. And apparently it worked.

Joe Pigott, Pike County District
Attorney in the 1971 trial. Photograph
courtesy of Linda P. Robinson.

Jim Kitchens, Pike County District
Attorney in the 1972 trial. Photograph
courtesy of James W. Kitchens.

B. D. Statham, defense attorney for Richard McIntosh. Photograph courtesy of *Enterprise-Journal*.

McComb Police Lt. Ted Fleming, arrested for but never convicted of the murder of Tina Andrews. Photograph courtesy of *Enterprise-Journal*.

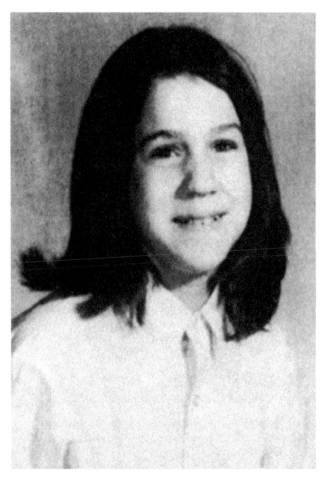

Tina Marie Andrews (1957–1969), school photo, used as evidence in 1971 and 1972 trials. Photograph courtesy of *Enterprise-Journal*.

Richard McIntosh, tried twice for the murder of Tina Andrews. Photograph courtesy of *Enterprise-Journal*.

Oil field crime scene in August 1969, with McComb-area law enforcement authorities viewing the couch under which Tina Andrews's remains were concealed. Photograph courtesy of *Enterprise-Journal*.

Pike County Courthouse, Magnolia, Mississippi, location of the two trials of Richard McIntosh for the murder of Tina Andrews. Photographed in 2019, courtesy of Carroll Case.

Grave of Tina Marie Andrews and her parents, Hollywood
Cemetery, McComb, Mississippi. Photographed in 2019,
courtesy of Carroll Case.

Oak Street, McComb, Mississippi, home of Tina Andrews in 1969.
Photographed in 2019, courtesy of Carroll Case.

North Cherry Street, McComb, Mississippi, home of Billie Jo Lambert in 1969.
Photographed in 2019, courtesy of Carroll Case.

Corner of Railroad Boulevard and Canal Street, McComb, Mississippi, where Andrews and Lambert accepted the ride that took them to the oil field. Photographed in 2019, courtesy of Carroll Case.

Oil field outside McComb, Mississippi, where Tina Andrews's remains were discovered in 1969. Photographed in 2019, courtesy of Carroll Case.

Downtown McComb, Mississippi, location of police station in 1969.
Photographed in 2019, courtesy of Carroll Case.

Corner of Main Street and Railroad Boulevard, McComb, Mississippi, location of the Tiger's Den in 1969. Photographed in 2019, courtesy of Carroll Case.

7

The *State of Mississippi v. Richard McIntosh*
The Defense Makes Its Case

Richard McIntosh received his money's worth from his attorneys. During their questioning of Billie Jo Lambert, Statham and Watkins challenged her at every turn, explaining to the jury that she was a disreputable person who told an implausible story. At every stage of the case, especially during their presentation of McIntosh's defense, his attorneys proved themselves not only well-prepared, but skillful in the selection and presentation of their own witnesses. They told of a respectable young man who was at most a victim of mistaken identity. Statham and Watkins also showed themselves, in their handling of Lambert, willing to stretch the boundaries not only of good taste but also of what an observer might regard as fair play. Ultimately, however, not all jurors viewed matters the defense's way, but not enough of them disagreed with it to win the state's case against McIntosh. McIntosh's defense was not only effective, but also revealed how social class dynamics operated among Pike Countians. Other matters involving the jury, ones that also shaped the decision that they reached, reveal as well how law enforcement and other forms of power worked in Pike County. Those latter factors, perhaps more than anything presented at trial by either side, wrought the verdict in the first trial of Richard McIntosh.

Before the defense began its presentation, all four attorneys—Statham, Watkins, Pigott, and Reeves—met in Judge Roach's chambers to hear yet another defense motion to dismiss the case. Statham called for a directed verdict and dismissal of charges against his client. The state, he maintained, had not established corpus delicti (concrete evidence that a crime had been committed), had not proved that Andrews died by violent means, and had not made a sufficient connection between his client and Andrews. At the most, said

Statham, the state's evidence asserted that McIntosh had struck Andrews on the jaw, appropriately a charge of assault and battery, not murder.[1]

Judge Roach ruled against the defense. He was convinced that expert testimony had established that the remains from the oil field were those of Tina Andrews. Still, he said, "this case gives me a great deal of concern. It certainly is not the strongest case I have seen because it is principally circumstantial evidence." The jury did not hear those words, but all attorneys present were aware that no witness and no other evidence connected McIntosh (or Fleming) with the murder itself. While the evidence of the "causal connection" between Andrews and the defendant was indeed circumstantial, Roach continued, it remained the case that testimony did contend that McIntosh and Fleming were the last people seen with Andrews prior to her death. Thus, the trial would continue.[2]

B. D. Statham began with witnesses whose testimony attempted flatly to contradict elements of Billie Jo Lambert's story. The defense worked first to establish that contrary to Lambert's testimony, McIntosh could not have directed downtown traffic in late 1969 because he was not employed by the McComb Police Department until the spring of 1970. Thomas J. Haffey, McComb city clerk, testified that city records showed that McIntosh was hired by the city on March 1, 1970. He was not, then, a city policeman "during that critical period of August 1969 until Christmas time 1969," as Statham put it, that is, during the period from the murder of Tina Andrews through the time when Lambert had allegedly seen him directing traffic in downtown McComb. But was McIntosh possibly an auxiliary police officer? Haffey testified he had no records of the employment of auxiliary officers, but that they wore uniforms, directed traffic, and performed other police duties. In short, asked the state on cross-examination, would there be any way for the general public to tell the difference between a regular officer and an auxiliary officer? Haffey admitted that there really was not. But he had no conclusive evidence one way or another about McIntosh's possible status as an auxiliary officer. Neither did the state. No one would ever prove whether or not McIntosh had been an auxiliary officer. But neither did anything presented contradict Lambert's testimony that she had in fact seen McIntosh directing traffic in McComb, despite her apparent confusion about dates.[3]

The defense contested the identity of the body, as it would do to the end of the trial, calling Pike County coroner Joseph P. Kennedy as a witness. Unlike many Mississippi coroners, whose formal qualifications for office did not then require even a high school diploma, Kennedy did have some relevant training in the handling of bodies. He was a mortician, with experience in embalming and funeral directing at a local establishment. In Kennedy's judgment, the body found in the oil field could not have been that of a girl missing for approximately ten days because of the remains' level of decomposition. However, the state challenged the testimony of Kennedy on the grounds that the coroner was, whatever else his skills, not an expert on human decomposition. On cross-examination, Joe Pigott demonstrated that in Mississippi a coroner did not establish a cause of death, a task instead for a coroner's jury of six people; that Kennedy was a former employee of the McComb Police Department; that he had never in his four and a half years as coroner been called to testify as to the time or date of a person's death; and that he had no training in pathology. In short, said Pigott, Kennedy was "a very nice man and a very competent man to preside over a coroner's jury," but not someone who could offer expert testimony on the decomposition of human remains. Judge Roach agreed.[4]

Testimony had stretched into early Saturday evening, but the defense had scarcely begun to present its case. So the court adjourned for the remainder of the weekend. While Judge Roach appreciated that the jury would not want to be sequestered for two more nights, "the Court is the Court, and that is all there is to it."[5] Before sending the jury back to McComb and to the Holiday Inn, Judge Roach advised them simply to "take it in stride . . . I know you will because you are good men and women." He also advised them, in instructions typical for sequestration, not to read about the case in the newspaper or to talk among themselves about the case or to let anyone else talk with them about it. Some jurors heeded the judge's instructions. But others did not and spent some of their time at the motel that weekend discussing the case, including their impressions of the weight of the evidence presented to that point. More than one juror seems to have been determined not to vote guilty, even before hearing the bulk of the defense testimony.[6]

With the resumption of court on Monday morning, the defense and the state met again in Judge Roach's chambers. The defense motioned to allow Julian Prince, the McComb public school superintendent, to testify about the contents of Tina Andrews's school record; the defense dropped its attempt to have Billie Jo Lambert's school records entered as evidence. The state objected, with Pigott arguing that the materials were not public records and Robert Reeves adding that they were "remote." "Tina Andrews is not on trial," added Pigott. The jury heard none of these arguments, but they offer insight into the defense's strategy and the attitude of the court itself by this point of the trial. The records were essential, argued Statham, in demonstrating a key point he wished the jury to understand: that Tina Andrews was "a little girl" who had "habits of disappearing" during which her family did not know where she was and did not seem interested in looking for her. He also wished for more specific testimony to show how poor her grades were. In short, Statham wished more detail to craft his story about social class, respectability, and family irresponsibility to the jury.[7]

Pigott maintained that these records amounted to "an attempt to assault the deceased's character and reputation," which is of course precisely what they were. As a point of law, he said, the records should be considered inadmissible. Statham continued to raise the possibility that someone who disappeared as much as Tina Andrews did might not even be the body found in the oil field, a suggestion that Judge Roach seemed impatient on hearing it yet again. "I have let the defendant go far afield in the questioning of witnesses in regard to Tina Andrews' absence at various times, and possibly should not have done so," admitted Judge Roach. But the judge, like the state's attorneys, failed to see the relevance of the records, except perhaps to demonstrate that Tina Andrews "was dumb or what-have-you. It has no connection with the . . . alleged crime that was committed." And so Superintendent Prince was not allowed to testify.[8]

That fact actually did not matter very much, because Statham had already presented this information to the jury via questions he had asked Donna Andrews, Tina's sister, while she was on the stand. The jury would certainly, in the absence of specific instructions, have failed to understand a distinction between Prince's testimony not being allowed and Donna Andrews's being allowed. Had the state wished to prevent Tina's school attendance and records from being part of the story that the jury was allowed to consider, they missed that opportunity when they failed to object to Statham's line of questioning of Donna Andrews.

Statham also introduced an expert witness to once more dispute the identity of the body. Forrest G. Bratley, a Jackson pathologist, through extensive testimony and cross-examination, said that the body found on August 23, 1969, could not be that of a person who was alive on August 13. The state of decomposition was too great for that to be possible, he said. Bratley had a good deal of experience with human remains and had in fact served as an expert witness in a number of other trials. In this case, however, he had never examined the body itself, and his testimony was based only upon his examination of photographs of the remains. Pigott and Bratley spent a good deal of time that day discussing the life cycle of flies, temperature, and humidity in a Mississippi August, and other related matters. Some of these discussions occurred with the jury outside the courtroom, as Pigott and Statham argued over the framing of questions and the type of testimony that a jury could properly hear. In the end, the jury did hear Bratley's opinion. And again, they heard Statham attempt to raise a nagging doubt of whether the man who was on trial was even accused of the right crime.[9]

The Pike County Circuit Court's term that fall was busy; this trial occurred among the examination of other crimes, large and small. During a noon recess, Judge Roach sentenced two men who had been convicted of the possession and sale of marijuana. Despite misgivings, Judge Roach gave both men, ages eighteen and nineteen, suspended sentences of two years, along with five years of probation. "I have just about reached the end of my rope," said the judge, "and it won't be long before a first offender finds himself in Parchman." "He told the youths to get a haircut, go to church every Sunday, and to be in bed by 10 each evening," advice that speaks to his diagnosis, one that many members of the community would have agreed with, about the basic causes of youth crime and delinquency in the area.[10]

But the main business occupying Judge Roach that day was the trial of Richard McIntosh. Other than McIntosh himself, the key defense witness was Dorothy Marie Nettles, McIntosh's former girlfriend. The contrast between her story and Lambert's could hardly have been starker. Her testimony placed her with McIntosh on every evening of the week of August 10, 1969, bolstering the defense claim that McIntosh was nowhere near Andrews and the other girls that evening of August 13. Nettles's relationship with McIntosh was incredibly fortunate in its timing. She had met him only in July 1969, but the couple had become extremely serious, leading to their spending so much time together. They had "planned to be married." But the relationship cooled as quickly as it had begun. By fall of 1969, things between Nettles and McIntosh were over.

Luckily for McIntosh, many memories remained, ones that would provide an alibi for the twenty-five-year-old defendant at precisely the time during which someone else, if that alibi is true, had given the girls a ride to the oil field and murdered one of them.[11]

While Statham had been diligent in researching and attacking the character and credibility of both Lambert and Andrews, the state apparently had no luck in digging as effectively into the background of Nettles to see whether she might be the kind of person who could tell such a convenient story about a fervid, whirlwind romance without its being true. Perhaps she was telling the truth and was a young woman who was apparently as wholesome as the defense had argued that Billie Jo Lambert was not. Whatever the case, the state ultimately had nothing fundamentally to contradict Nettles's story about McIntosh's whereabouts on the evening of August 13, 1969.

At the time of her appearance in court, Nettles lived in McComb at the Hillside Trailer Court. In 1969, she had lived in the city as well, at 528 Edgar Street, about a block off Broadway Street in downtown McComb. The distance from her house to the oil field where Tina Andrews was murdered—or from that oil field back to her house—was thus about the same distance and time as a drive from the Tiger's Den to Delaware Avenue Extension and out to the oil field, or there and back. Nettles was a long-distance operator for South Central Bell, the telephone company. In July 1969, she had met McIntosh at the Mr. Swiss Drive-In, coincidentally very near Tina Andrews's home.

Nettles, whose memories of events from over two years before the trial were extremely precise and extraordinarily convenient for McIntosh, maintained that on the evening of August 9, she and McIntosh's sister went to Louisiana to pick up McIntosh and McIntosh's sister's husband. McIntosh worked offshore in the oil business and had not yet joined the McComb Police Department. What of the following days, especially the evening of August 13, when Tina Andrews had last been seen alive? Despite working a split shift from 11:00 a.m. to 3:00 p.m. and again from 7:00 p.m. to 10:00 p.m., she had been with McIntosh every day between the shifts and again after her work ended until "about 1 in the morning."[12] Such a timetable, one might note, did leave McIntosh free to do whatever he chose for a portion of each evening, including that of August 13. Further, testified Nettles, McIntosh, a member of the Mississippi National Guard, had been sent out of town on August 17, when Hurricane Camille struck the Mississippi Gulf Coast. Finally, said Nettles, McIntosh started a new job that same eventful week, at Polyflex, a manufacturing concern in nearby Summit.[13]

When compared to the testimony offered by Billie Jo Lambert, Nettles's was extremely clear on days and times. On August 10, for instance, McIntosh arrived home about "5:30 or 6:00." Later that evening, his sister had to be taken to the emergency room. Nettles recalled not only the name of the physician that the sister saw, but also the amount of time they spent at the hospital: "We were down there for thirty to forty-five minutes." Again unlike Lambert, she remembered precisely not only the days she had worked during the week of August 10, 1969, but also the times of her shifts, which allowed her to place McIntosh with her for very specific blocks of time. The defense also established that Nettles and McIntosh enjoyed very wholesome time together, with lots of card playing, watching television with his mother, or occasionally "riding around." If they ever stopped at one of the Pike County establishments that served beer or if they ever parked in a secluded spot for romantic time together, Nettles did not mention it, nor did the defense ask such questions of her. Over the state's objection, Nettles was asked and answered the question of whether during the week of August 10, 1969, McIntosh seemed at all unusual. "He always seemed like the same Richard McIntosh to me," she replied, a remarkable astuteness of judgment about a person that she had known only a matter of weeks and would stop dating within a matter of weeks after that fateful period.[14]

On cross-examination, Pigott not only attempted to shake Nettles's story, but also to explain to the jury why Nettles might have come to be a witness with such specific recollection. "You are very interested in helping Richard McIntosh, aren't you?" asked Pigott. "Yes, I am," answered Nettles, no doubt honestly. Pigott established that on March 16, 1971, the day before the grand jury met and the indictments of McIntosh and Fleming were handed down, Richard McIntosh brought or at least accompanied Dorothy Nettles to Joe Pigott's office. Here Nettles's recollection of specific days and times failed her, but Pigott told the jury that they arrived at his office around 5:30 p.m. to offer Pigott a very specific alibi for McIntosh for the evening of August 10, 1969. They had both been under the mistaken impression that Sunday, August 10, rather than Wednesday, August 13, was the date for which McIntosh's whereabouts needed explaining. Obviously, then, Pigott believed that Nettles's alibi for McIntosh was constructed at McIntosh's request to fit the needs of the occasion. He was not able, however, to catch Nettles in any flat contradictions of fact during her testimony or to produce other witnesses who could have blasted that alibi. Before excusing Nettles, Pigott asked her about two men, neither of whose names had been mentioned in court to that point. He asked Nettles if she knew Michael Howell or Rollin Copelan. She said that she knew "of them" through McIntosh. Both names would be mentioned again by Pigott when he questioned McIntosh. All three men figured in a story that Pigott knew, but was unable to introduce as evidence.[15]

The defense's main witness was Richard McIntosh himself. He took the stand on the afternoon of Monday, November 1. His attorneys ensured that in every way he made a favorable impression upon the jury. McIntosh was neatly groomed, with his hair cut over his ears and above the collar of the dress shirt that he wore. Dressed for his appearance in "gray slacks, blue blazer, blue shirt, and striped tie," the "soft-spoken" McIntosh made an attractive package. People who were present in the court that day recall that McIntosh and both his attorneys, especially William Watkins, were handsome, well-dressed, and eminently respectable-looking men.[16]

Point by point, McIntosh's testimony refuted the story told by Billie Jo Lambert. Yes, of course he was a McComb police officer, he said, but he had not joined the force until March 10, 1970, so he could not have been seen by Lambert directing traffic downtown around Christmas of 1969. No, he had never been a member of the police auxiliary, so no one would have reasonably identified him as a member of the department in that year. Further, he could not have been performing police duties in any case in the winter of 1969, as his ankle was in a cast from November 1969 through January 1970. On all these matters, McIntosh had at his command very specific information, again unlike Lambert. Had he been under suspension from the police department at any time? Yes, said McIntosh, from the time of the grand jury's indictment. But had he been on voluntary leave from the department? He had been, of course, but he did not say that here, and Statham did not ask.[17]

McIntosh's personal story was also different from Lambert's. Until his indictment, he had been a member in good standing of the National Guard, a matter that would have commanded the respect of the jury, given the high regard placed upon military service by Mississippians, then and later. He was also a longtime churchgoer, a member of the South McComb Baptist Church, "practically all my life," he said. Fundamentally, then, McIntosh was quite similar to many members of the jury before which he sat: a white man, native of the area, with military service to his credit, with a churched background, nothing, it seemed, of public record to impugn his character, and coming from a financially modest but respectable household. A widow's son, McIntosh seemed to defend himself against an accuser of much more disreputable character and background.

As for his alleged acquaintance with Ted Fleming, he did not know him, had never associated with him, and had never been in a car with him prior to his first day of employment with the McComb Police Department. "Ted Fleming and I did not know each other in 1969," he said positively. In August 1969 did McIntosh know either Billie Jo Lambert or Tina Andrews? No, he did not. As later testimony would show, Statham had reasons for asking specifically about the August 1969 date of McIntosh's acquaintance with Lambert, rather than asking generally if he knew Lambert. So, then, on August 13, 1969, Statham asked his client, did he and Ted Fleming pick up three girls at the corner of Railroad Avenue and Canal Street? In a curiously qualified answer, McIntosh said, "On that particular occasion I did not pick any young girls up." He also denied that he had ever been to the oil field site that Lambert described.[18]

McIntosh's testimony did indicate that he had gone to Billie Jo Lambert's house after the disappearance of Tina Andrews—more than once, in fact, and on at least one occasion that visit resulted in McIntosh and a friend of his riding around in his car with two teenage girls, almost certainly both under the age of eighteen. Both those visits occurred after he began work as a police officer. How did he meet Lambert? "I had seen her around town." Initially, he did not know her personally, but he "had seen her uptown, along the streets." But when precisely did he meet her? Here, McIntosh's sharp memory for detail became fuzzy. "I don't recall the exact month, or even the time of year." But on one occasion, in the company of his friend Wayne Spillman, with whom he had attended Southwest Mississippi Junior College, McIntosh found himself on North Cherry Street, where the Lamberts lived. He and Spillman "had no particular place in mind to go," and how they made their way to Cherry Street he did not recall. In front of the Lambert house on that occasion, there were "young kids" out there. "Just why we stopped, I do not know."[19]

Some of the girls, including Norma Lambert, Billie Jo's sister, asked the men to take them riding around, which the men did. He knew the "kids," said McIntosh, by sight if not by name, and had talked with them both on and off duty. "They knew me as Richard McIntosh, policeman." What he had talked with them about, either in an official or unofficial capacity, McIntosh did not say. He and his friend took Norma and her friend riding around at the girls' request, both of those girls certainly being in their early teens. After a time, the men took the girls home, again at their request. The jury thus heard from McIntosh's own testimony a story similar to the one that Lambert told. McIntosh and a friend went riding around with no particular place to go, as the old tune of thwarted lust by Chuck Berry, also a man with a taste for underage girls, puts it. People who knew McIntosh in the 1960s remember that he enjoyed young women, teenage girls in particular. There is nothing surprising about a young man being attracted to young women, of course, but that interest of his clearly continued beyond McIntosh's high school years, when it became more problematic and his opportunity to seek girls out at high school dances and other events became more difficult, or at least more likely to draw attention.

McIntosh's association with underage girls is not merely a matter of rumor. Later that same year of 1970, according to McIntosh, Lambert herself, or a person saying that she was Lambert, called him, asking him to come to her house on North Cherry Street. Here, McIntosh's recollection of dates was a little sharper. The weather was cool, perhaps the fall or early winter. And it was certainly a Wednesday night, as that was always McIntosh's night off. The telephone call came around midnight. "I do not recall the exact conversation, but she never did get around to exactly why she had called me over there, and I still don't know why she called me over there."[20] He pulled up to the curb in front of her house, and Lambert came out to his car. He slid to the passenger's side, and Lambert took a seat behind the wheel. The encounter was not lengthy— perhaps ten or fifteen minutes—before it was interrupted by the arrival of a McComb police patrol car. Upon the arrival of the patrol car, said McIntosh, Lambert exited his car, "without saying anything," and walked back into her house. McIntosh's fellow patrolman who arrived at the scene told him that he had received a call about an off-duty patrolman "being over on Cherry Street," and that he had been dispatched to investigate the call.[21]

At the time of his admitted 1970 visit to the Lambert house, the Tina Andrews case was slightly more than a year old and still under active investigation. But Lambert herself had made no overtures to Joe Pigott or other law enforcement authorities. She had, according to her own testimony, discussed elements of the story of August 13, 1969, with family and friends. If McIntosh had in fact known Lambert earlier, say in 1969, then his visit to her house in 1970 was bold. Why risk such a visit, unless one's caution were outweighed by the need to know what Lambert might say? But McIntosh categorically denied that he knew Lambert in 1969. The most innocent construction that one can put on the visit is that McIntosh, a man with an admitted interest in the company of teenage girls, received a call from one and wished to see what a brief midnight drive might yield. After all, from his house on Sedgewick Street, he could have covered the less than two miles distance to North Cherry Street in just a few minutes. What did they discuss during the brief period that Lambert sat in McIntosh's car? He claimed not to remember, an astounding gap in his recollection, given both the apparent significance of such a visit and McIntosh's own sharp memories of many other matters.

Why would the defense have chosen to have McIntosh tell this story, containing as it does elements that raise echoes of August 1969? In part, of course, because Lambert had testified that McIntosh had been to her house, so the matter would seem to need attention from the defense. Perhaps Statham wished to show that Lambert was not frightened of Richard McIntosh. Otherwise, why would she have summoned him to her house? The testimony about Lambert's call to McIntosh also let the jury hear once again the story of Lambert as an unsupervised, perhaps promiscuous girl. McIntosh was positive, he said, that the visit to her house was the only time that he had "ever been in the company of Miss Lambert." And while his memory failed him on other particulars of the conversation, he was certain that on that occasion, Tina Andrews's name and fate had not come up.[22]

When asked more generally by Statham if he knew anything about Tina Andrews or her fate, McIntosh stated categorically: "I do not have any idea as to exactly what happened; I don't know any of the facts other than what has been published in the newspaper about the particular incident and the finding of a body." Nor, McIntosh said, did he know any members of the Andrews family at all, other than Tina's brother Freddie. "A lot of people knew Freddie," McIntosh said, "and expressed different," a characterization cut off by an objection from

Pigott. Statham concluded his examination of McIntosh by having him state again categorically that he had never picked up Andrews, Lambert, and a third girl, had never taken them to the oil field, had never struck Tina Andrews, had nothing whatsoever to do with her death, and indeed did not "know anything relative to the death of Tina Andrews."[23]

After a brief recess, the state began its cross-examination of McIntosh. That cross-examination, led entirely by Joe Pigott, was extremely brief when compared with the time that B. D. Statham had spent cross-examining Lambert, the state's main witness. Pigott, unlike Statham, had no revelations about character or reputation with which to shake the jury's confidence in McIntosh's story. In this trial, and also in the subsequent 1972 trial, the state was limited both by the types of evidence that it held, as well as by well-established legal principles governing relevance and admissibility. Much of the case against McIntosh was circumstantial. Other than Lambert's testimony, the state had little to connect McIntosh with Tina Andrews. Indeed, it was probably not clear to the jury why Pigott asked McIntosh some of the things that he did. If some of Pigott's questions were intended to lead into productive lines of inquiry, they were not or could not be developed. But Joe Pigott knew more than he was able to use in court.

First, Pigott asked McIntosh whether in March 1969 he had lived in Baton Rouge, Louisiana, at an address on East Roosevelt Street. He believed that he had, McIntosh said. Pigott asked McIntosh with whom he had lived. With Rollin Copelan and Mike Howell, McIntosh replied; they were two young men from the McComb area, although neither Pigott nor McIntosh identified them or said anything further about them. Pigott had asked Dorothy Nettles, McIntosh's ex-girlfriend, if she knew those two men during his cross-examination of her earlier in the day. Even if the jury could not see what Pigott was trying to get at with those questions, McIntosh no doubt did. Pigott had information about McIntosh's activities in Baton Rouge that contain numerous parallels to the Tina Andrews case. But it was information that was not admissible, a fact that both Pigott and McIntosh's defense team well knew.

On March 21, 1969, less than five months before twelve-year-old Tina Andrews was murdered, a fifteen-year-old girl in Baton Rouge reported that she had been raped. Two men, Copelan and Howell, were arrested for aggravated rape. McIntosh was arrested for accessory after the fact of aggravated rape. Before a Baton Rouge judge at a bail hearing, the girl testified that after Copelan and Howell raped her, she dressed and attempted to leave a bedroom of the house in which the men lived, at which point McIntosh grabbed her. Other testimony and subsequent charges suggest that McIntosh had sex with her as well. The testimony in that Baton Rouge courtroom contained other parallels to the Andrews case, specifically those of publicly shaming a teenage girl and questioning her reputation. The defense attorney, Ossie B. Brown, reduced the alleged victim to tears by insisting that she detail "how and when she resisted the advances" of the men. He further asked her why she would have consented to "date" Howell, a married man, and produced half a dozen young men in court, asking them to stand while the fifteen-year-old was questioned about whether she had ever had sex with them.[24] In September, when the case was set to come to trial, the district attorney's office was forced to request a continuance, as the fifteen-year-old victim could not be located when the sheriff's deputies attempted to serve her a subpoena. Over the summer, the district attorney had modified the charges against the three men, from aggravated rape (or accessory, in McIntosh's case) to the lesser offense of "carnal knowledge of a juvenile." In January 1970, the witness again did not appear for the trial. The district attorney and the defense attorney agreed to a motion for indefinite postponement of the charges against Copelan, Howell, and McIntosh. The charges were "passed without date." Only a fresh motion and hearing could have carried the case forward again. That never happened. So, then, Joe Pigott was left with nothing about a conviction or a pending indictment in a rape or carnal knowledge case to give the Pike County jury in 1971.[25] In leading with the question, Pigott attempted to rattle McIntosh by showing him he knew something of his secrets. But the jury likely would not have known what to have made of this exchange. No judge or defense attorney would have allowed Pigott to flesh out this story in court.[26]

Perhaps other people in the courthouse knew the Baton Rouge story of Richard McIntosh's arrest in 1969. The Baton Rouge newspapers covered it, as they also covered the story of McIntosh's arrest in 1971 and the trial that fall. In those 1971 stories, both the *State-Times* and the *Advocate* referred consistently to the 1969 case.[27] In the initial coverage of McIntosh's 1971 arrest, fully half the stories told in detail of the East Baton Rouge Parish arrest on "accessory after the fact of aggravated rape" and the amended charge of "carnal knowledge" of a teenage girl. Not only would readers of those stories have learned that McIntosh had been charged with sex with a "juvenile" in Baton Rouge, but also that he and Ted Fleming were both reported to have been administered polygraph tests in connection with the Tina Andrews killing. If so, those tests were never introduced as evidence or otherwise mentioned in either of his trials.[28] But it is likely that most people in court that day did not know of the 1969 arrest, at least not from accounts in the Baton Rouge papers. If Pike County people took a Louisiana newspaper, it was almost surely a New Orleans paper instead.

Pigott then asked McIntosh about an automobile, specifically if he had owned a white four-door 1963 Pontiac Catalina in 1969. Yes, McIntosh replied. What was Pigott's point? Lambert testified that the three girls accepted a ride in a four-door automobile that was not a police vehicle. But she could remember nothing about the car, not even the color. Did Pigott expect the jury to conclude that McIntosh's was the vehicle to which Lambert's testimony referred? If so, the jury may have been puzzled by the relevance of McIntosh's ownership of this car.

During this cross-examination, Pigott asked McIntosh if he owned or had owned guns. McIntosh replied that he had owned at least three, including two .38-caliber pistols, the type of weapon used to kill Tina Andrews, although Pigott never made that point directly. Currently, said McIntosh, he owned only a .357. What had happened to the .38-caliber pistols, asked Pigott? McIntosh replied that he had sold one of the .38s to a friend, Jack Parker, but denied that he had made attempts to get the weapon back from Parker. But he did say that he had asked Parker if he still had the gun or knew where it was. There was nothing rare in a Mississippi man's owning handguns. Pike County was thick with them. It is doubtful that the jury would have raised an eyebrow at a police officer and a National Guardsman fond of weapons.[29]

One of the few questions that might have raised a troubling issue was Pigott's suggestion that McIntosh could have been involved in the investigation of Tina Andrews's murder. But McIntosh denied that he had, at least in any "active" way. Pigott offered little solid evidence to contradict him. Yes, McIntosh admitted, he had seen some "pictures," perhaps of the crime scene, that "the late John Sharpling had taken, he showed them to me." But that was it. Only on one other occasion had he participated in the investigation. On patrol,

McIntosh and fellow officer Mike Williams were asked by Sheriff Lawson to "check or find out" about a man, whose name McIntosh could not remember, but who perhaps had lived in east McComb; he might have had some involvement with the case.[30] But Pigott knew, as did McIntosh, that the McComb Police Department had been involved in the investigation of the case from the beginning. There would have been no reason for Chief Rowley or anyone else to have steered McIntosh away from looking into a tip about the case, of which there had been many.

Pigott also asked if McIntosh and Ted Fleming had questioned a man who came to the McComb police station purportedly with information about Andrews's murder. That man, "Ecshol Harvey," probably the court reporter's mistake in hearing the name "Esco Harvey," a McComb resident, was taken outside the police station into a car by Fleming and McIntosh and questioned privately, Pigott said. Esco Harvey, a native of Tylertown in Walthall County, was forty years old in 1970, an Air Force veteran and a longtime resident of McComb. McIntosh denied that incident had occurred. More precisely, he said that he did not "remember that incident." Pigott offered the jury no more information than his question and McIntosh's categorical denial. If Harvey had indeed come to the police station, that would not have been unusual. During murder investigations, authorities commonly receive tips, a great many of which lead nowhere. But Fleming and McIntosh taking the man aside for private questioning would have been unusual and in the circumstances, highly improper. But without anything else to offer the jury, Pigott could suggest but not prove impropriety.[31]

Pigott then led McIntosh through a long description of the road that led from Delaware Avenue Extension to the oil field site where the body was found. Emphasizing details such as the presence of two cattle gaps on the oil field road and the distance of two-tenths of a mile from the main road to the oil field clearing, all that Pigott could elicit from McIntosh was his statement that he was now familiar with that information, presumably from previous testimony. McIntosh said that he knew the area as a "favorite parking place of a lot of the teenagers." He did not recall ever in recent years having refused to drive out to that particular spot. Pigott concluded by asking McIntosh if he ever used "reload cartridges" in any weapon that he owned. McIntosh replied that the McComb Police Department occasionally used such ammunition for practice. Was Pigott's question related to information contained in a ballistics report on the rounds taken from the crime scene? Again, if that was the case, the jury would have had to presume such a connection.[32]

With those questions, Joe Pigott and the state of Mississippi were finished with Richard McIntosh. Compared with B. D. Statham's long, contentious questioning of Billie Jo Lambert, Pigott's time with McIntosh elicited no seeming contradictions, no inability to recall important elements of his story, and nothing that damaged McIntosh's character or reputation. No member of the jury could have concluded that the state had found out McIntosh in any lie. If the state had very much on Richard McIntosh, other than Billie Jo Lambert's testimony, the jury did not hear it.

Statham then took McIntosh for a brief "redirect examination," offering the jury alternative explanations for evidence that Pigott had introduced. Was there anything significant about McIntosh's familiarity with the oil field site, as Pigott had established? Not at all, Statham suggested. McIntosh was a life-long resident of the area, familiar with many places in and near the city. The reloaded ammunition that McIntosh had testified was used by the McComb police for practice? Until he joined the department in the spring of 1970, said McIntosh, he had no access to such ammunition. Statham had McIntosh say again to the jury that he did not recall ever in 1969 or 1970 refusing to go with anyone to the oil field site. With that, McIntosh was excused.[33]

To the end of the trial, the defense attempted to tell the jury that Tina Andrews was a girl of poor character. To that end, Statham called Ronnie Reed, a young man who had worked at the Tiger's Den when Tina was a patron. The defense asked him to describe Tina's activities at the place, which included Tina's writing foul language on the walls. "I had to get onto her about that," said Reed. "Then her brother came in later, and he got onto Tina for being down there." Pigott objected to the relevance of this testimony. Judge Roach ordered the jury out to consider whether Reed's testimony should be allowed. But the jury had heard an addition to the story of Tina Andrews the unruly girl that Statham had built since his opening statement.

Outside the presence of the jury, Reed said that on one occasion Tina left the Tiger's Den (whether it was August 13, 1969, no one got a chance to establish) with a young man whose current whereabouts Reed did not know; he believed him to be in the state prison "on dope charges." Statham very much wanted the jury to hear more of this material, he said. He wished to show that Andrews kept company with a boy "of notorious character." That she was in the Tiger's Den writing foul words on the wall would show them "the type of girl she was." The state maintained, and Judge Roach concurred, that Reed's inability to recall specific dates and other concrete matters rendered the testimony inadmissible.[34]

The defense concluded by presenting four character witnesses for McIntosh. These witnesses were Benjamin Leon Empson, a pharmacist for whom he worked in high school; David Millican, pastor of South McComb Baptist Church, of which McIntosh was a member; Alice Mercier, a local woman who had known McIntosh for eighteen years; and H. W. Magee, Jr., McIntosh's National Guard company commander. All testified that McIntosh had a good, peaceful reputation in the community. This choice of witnesses reiterated McIntosh's status as a churchgoer and a National Guardsman, factors that contrasted with information the jury had learned about the Lambert and Andrews families, and ones calculated to make a good impression upon these jurors.[35]

The state called two rebuttal witnesses after McIntosh's testimony and cross-examination. One of them, Tina Andrews's sister Donna, was called to offer information about the collection of Tina's hairbrushes and curlers after her death. The state wished to reassure the jury that the identity of the body was certain. Pigott intended to connect Donna's answers with information from F.B.I. laboratory reports. However, Statham saw that her testimony was not qualified as rebuttal, as the defense expert witnesses had not presented information about Tina Andrews's hair as a means for identifying the remains. Donna's testimony consisted of precisely seventeen words, twelve of which were "Yes, Sir," in response to Pigott's questions. Judge Roach agreed with the defense that Donna's testimony was not allowable under rules governing rebuttal witnesses. If Pigott thought that Statham would fail to notice the issue, he was mistaken. If this was one of the best pieces of rebuttal testimony that the state could muster, then the state had little left to present.[36]

The last witness did offer two intriguing elements, one of which appeared flatly to contradict McIntosh. The state's witness was Jack Parker, a lifelong resident of McComb, a member of the National Guard, and by McIntosh's own earlier testimony, a man that knew McIntosh very well. Under frequent objection by Statham, Pigott led Parker through questions about the oil field site.

Parker's remarks about McIntosh's feelings for the oil field presented a story that is suggestive, if not conclusive as evidence in court or ultimately persuasive to the jury. Parker said that on one occasion he and McIntosh had been on a double date, and that Parker had driven the couples out to the well-known parking spot. Parker believed this date had occurred after the disappearance of Tina Andrews. But, said Parker, as they approached the area, McIntosh "said let's go somewhere else." McIntosh's distaste for the rendezvous point may have stemmed from several causes. If McIntosh had been there before under unpleasant circumstances, one can understand his reluctance to return.

Pigott also asked Parker if McIntosh had ever given him a pistol. Yes, said Parker, McIntosh had given him a .38-caliber RG, as "a gift of friendship." The gun was "foreign-made," noted Pigott. The .38-caliber RG was indeed foreign-made, a product of the Rohm Gesellschaft company. Firearms aficionados may recall that John Hickley, Jr., used a RG-14 revolver in his assassination attempt on President Ronald Reagan. But before the Gun Control Act of 1968, passed in reaction to the political assassinations of the 1960s, practically anyone could order firearms via mail order from advertisements in a great number of magazines. Here, as with other lines of questioning by Pigott, the jury heard nothing that connected this specific kind of weapon, let alone this weapon itself, with the murder of Tina Andrews.[37]

As it had been throughout the trial, Statham's cross-examination of the witness was effective, demonstrating that Parker's command of dates was shaky. He also appeared to catch Parker in what a layperson might call a lie. Parker could not recall the year of the double date that he had described, or whether or not McIntosh had been a police officer at the time. Who was Parker's date that evening, asked Statham? Parker did not wish to say. Statham insisted, saying that he might like to call her as a witness. Parker then said that he could not recall her name. Incredulous, Statham pressed him for the date's name. "Just a few seconds ago you knew, but now you have forgot: Is that your testimony?" Reluctantly, Parker admitted that the date was his wife, a woman to whom he was no longer married. Parker's puzzling attempt to evade Statham's questions could not have done much favorably to impress the jury. What about that gun, asked Statham? Parker no longer had that gun, he said. It was, to his knowledge, now in Walker, Louisiana. Had anyone previously asked about the gun or attempted to examine it? Parker did not know, but certainly not while it was in his possession. Parker added that he had only known for an hour or so that he would be called to testify, which might account for his ragged and probably unpersuasive use as a state's witness.[38]

In his chambers, Judge Roach listened to one more appeal by the defense for a directed verdict of not guilty. Statham said that there was sufficient doubt that his client had had anything at all to do with Tina Andrews's death or anything that might have caused her death. The state argued that the case was sound and ought to be turned over to the jury. Judge Roach agreed, but not before noting that "the weakest point in this case is the causal connection between this defendant having committed this crime by killing this deceased."[39]

The jury began deliberations at 5:17 p.m., and they returned to the courtroom at 6:53 p.m., telling the judge that "we have gone over the evidence, and we cannot reach a decision." Judge Roach ordered them to continue. At 9:28 p.m., the jury returned again. Mrs. Marvin V. Harvey, the foreman, told the judge that they could not reach a verdict. Eight ballots had been taken, with no clear result. Judge Roach polled each member of the jury, asking if they might be able to reach a verdict, if they were to continue. The consensus was that they could not. One juror, Thomas B. Austin, told the judge: "We're all split up." Richard McIntosh's 1971 trial for the murder of Tina Andrews ended with the jury unable to reach a verdict. After four hours of deliberation, they were deadlocked. Roach declared a mistrial, and the jury was dismissed. McIntosh remained free on bond.[40]

Why did the jury deadlock? One reason simply might have been that the state was unable to prove its case beyond a reasonable doubt. Statham worked mightily to convince the jury that there were many reasonable doubts that McIntosh had murdered Andrews. McIntosh testified that he had known neither Andrews nor Lambert in 1969, nor did he know Ted Fleming until McIntosh joined the McComb police force in March 1970. He had an alibi for the evening of the murder. Dorothy Nettles, testifying for the defense, said that she had dated McIntosh at the time and that she spent the evening of August 13, 1969, with him. Perhaps that testimony, despite anything that Billie Jo Lambert or Joe Pigott had to say, proved persuasive. But other factors seem to have been at work as the jury pondered Richard McIntosh's fate. A key element seems to have been the long period that the jury was sequestered and what happened during that weekend of sequestration.

Along with the identity of the defendant as a police officer, there were other reasons that the trial seemed unusual to Pike County observers, including the jurors themselves. They were sequestered for four nights, a long period for the time and place. It was especially uncommon for a jury to be held over on a Sunday, the "first time in the memory of many local court observers." No court in Mississippi held Sunday sessions. Some of these jurors chafed at the time away from family and other priorities. This was the Deep South, where football was king. The Saturday court proceedings interfered with the plans of many people in the courtroom to drive to Jackson to attend the football doubleheader in Memorial Stadium. The judge, some of the attorneys, and several of the jurors held tickets to those games, and they were sorely disappointed not to be able to use them. The fans missed a thriller in the first of the two games, as the Ole Miss Rebels, a three-touchdown underdog, ran out to a 21–0 lead over the LSU Tigers and held on for a 24–22 victory in front of a sellout crowd.[41] The nightcap was less of a contest, with Alabama plastering Mississippi State 41–10.

The long weekend allowed the jurors time to do more than ponder football. Over the years in Pike County, several rumors have circulated concerning irregularities in the jury's operation. Some people remain convinced that the jury was fixed—that one member of the jury was placed or was pressured to ensure a vote for acquittal. One can hear that a member of the jury was pulled from the courtroom and taken into the hall during the trial, ostensibly to discuss a "business emergency," but actually to have pressure applied to ensure a hung jury. The second of these rumors is easier to dispel than the first. No juror was pulled from the courtroom during the trial. No one who was present in the courtroom has ever said so. No newspaper reported it, and it would have seemed a very unusual event indeed. One cannot imagine District Attorney Joe Pigott, Prosecutor Bobby Reeves, or Judge Gordon Roach consenting to a juror's being removed for a private conversation and then returned to the panel. But both of these rumors, as it turns out, have some basis in fact. Those matters, as well as the vote of the jury that led to the mistrial, can be confirmed by a surviving witness willing to speak on the record.

There is no official record of the jury's deliberations, and thus no precise tally how the jury was "all split up," as Thomas B. Austin put it. The local newspaper reported that "unofficial rumor put it at seven for conviction, three for acquittal, and two undecided. Another unofficial report had the vote at eight for conviction, two for acquittal, and two undecided."[42] The newspaper's sources seem to have been informed, and according to recent statements by a juror, reflect fairly closely how the jury ultimately voted. In the spring of 2019, Clifton McGowan offered an account of the jury's work that fall, including events during their sequestration at the Holiday Inn in McComb. His memories, sharp after nearly half a century, suggest that District Attorney Pigott and County Prosecutor Reeves worked against a deck that was more stacked than they knew. McGowan's story reveals how matters of race, social class, and influence in the community operated during this trial. The racial matters are perhaps the least surprising of the elements. McGowan was one of four African American jurors, all men. He recalls the resentment that some of the white jurors felt at the presence of black jurors, and he remembers that some of them, one or two in particular, felt that the black jurors should be swayed by the whites. The African American jurors were not, as it turns out, when it came to voting. In the end, McGowan recalls, the vote was locked with two jurors, both white men, adamant for acquittal, with no prospects of changing their votes.[43]

One of those two men, Lamont Wilson, a postal worker from Chatawa in southern Pike County, told McGowan over the weekend at the Holiday Inn that the evidence presented by the state had in fact seemed compelling. "They proved it," he said, "but I can't vote to convict." Remarks by Wilson to McGowan further suggest that Wilson felt pressure from another white juror to hold out for acquittal of McIntosh. The Holiday Inn featured a great deal of activity that weekend other than jurors conducting officially prohibited conversations among themselves about the case in progress. Some of that activity helps to explain why Wilson might not have felt himself able to vote for conviction. The entire second floor of the Holiday Inn was reserved for the jury. Court bailiffs were present to ensure that the jurors stayed put and that no one attempted to interfere with them. Those bailiffs did not do either of those things, at least not for all of the jurors. From the balcony of that second floor of the Holiday Inn, McGowan was able to observe Sheriff "Tot" Lawson arrive on two evenings of the jury's sequestration. Feeling no need for subtlety, Lawson drove his official, marked vehicle. One juror, Thomas B. Austin, left his room, sat in Lawson's car for lengthy conversation, and then returned to his room. In this case, Pike County rumor was half-right. A juror had been removed for conversation—not from the courtroom itself, but rather from the motel. The conversations between Lawson and Austin seem to have been in the nature of consultation, rather than pressure or intimidation. On that score, then, Pike County rumor falls short in explaining what happened to hang the jury in the case. No one needed to be coerced in this case. It was simply the sort of thing that Lawson and Austin understood needed to be discussed and handled properly.[44]

A bold man, McGowan confronted the bailiffs at the motel, asking why Austin had been allowed to leave, when no one else had that opportunity. "It's about his business," he was told. In one sense, of course, it was. While Austin was a prominent area businessman, it is highly unlikely that Tot Lawson needed to bring Austin pressing news of the beer distribution industry on two evenings during the trial. Instead, the remark about business suggests a manner of thinking that was long held in Pike County: that a white man's activities were "business" that a black man like McGowan had no call to question. But McGowan was not easily satisfied. In the courthouse, McGowan asked Sheriff Lawson why he had allowed Austin to leave the motel and hold conversations with him. Again, McGowan was told that the conversations had to do with Austin's business. The fact that a black man openly questioned Lawson about his conduct as sheriff must have seemed to Lawson one of those signs of changed times in Pike County. A few years earlier, there would have been no black jurors, and in earlier years, few black men in the area would have so directly challenged a sheriff without the real possibility of retaliation.[45]

What was at stake for Thomas Austin in Richard McIntosh's trial? In 1971, Austin was a prominent, influential man. McComb had treated Austin well; he felt a proprietary interest in his hometown's stability and reputation. A 1938 graduate of McComb High School, he was one of the oldest members of the jury. During World War II, Austin trained as a cadet with the Army Air Corps, although the war ended before he saw overseas action; three of his brothers served in various branches of the armed forces. In one of the indications of the small social world of McComb, in 1944 he and future district attorney Pigott were ushers at Pigott's brother's wedding. In August 1946, he married Emily Schneider, a local schoolteacher. They remained in McComb, where he worked for Kramer Services, a local business firm with a variety of interests, including cotton warehousing, hotel and restaurant management, and beer distribution. By the late 1940s, Mrs. Emily Austin was becoming a fixture of McComb's active round of women's clubs and organizations, and would remain so for decades, a testimony to the couple's comfortable status. In their home on Kentucky Avenue, she hosted club meetings attended by wives of the established and powerful. The young couple were on their way up in McComb.[46]

Thomas Austin as well was on the move socially and professionally in the late 1940s and 1950s. He, like his wife, was a joiner, with membership in social service organizations such as the Exchange Club, one example of the sense of commitment he was beginning to stake out in McComb. In 1949, however, his business interests prompted a move to Jackson, although his wife stayed behind with her family to finish out the school year. Soon joining her husband in Jackson, Emily Austin threw herself into the social swim there as well, "becoming known in bridge, cooking, and sewing circles in the Capitol City." By 1953, however, the couple were back in McComb, living on Burke Street. Mrs. Austin resumed her local club activities without missing a beat. Austin's work with Kramer Services had given him a taste for the beer business. He returned to McComb as the owner of the Jax Distributing Company, which handled the New Orleans product ("always smooth and satisfying") loved by many area residents. Over the next twenty years, Austin would expand his beer empire, and he would do very well indeed with it, soon winning regional and national recognition for his booming sale of Jax and Schlitz. In 1957 he was elected president of the Mississippi Malt Beverage Association. His Catholic faith might have set him apart in some ways from his peers, but that religion's tolerant attitude toward alcohol did not present the impediment to his work that membership in a Southern Baptist congregation would have done. The beer business carried no social stigma for Austin or his family. The wife of the First Baptist Church minister was often a guest in his home for one of Mrs. Austin's many club meetings.[47]

In the 1960s, Thomas Austin continued to rise in McComb. He and his family moved into an impressive 2,600-square-feet brown brick ranch house of the type very popular in that era, located at 212 Oak Street. In one of the many coincidences in this story, that house was located one block from Fred Andrews's home, a short walk but an immense economic and social distance. One measure of Austin's increasing influence was his 1969 election to the board of the First Federal Savings and Loan Association, on which he served with District Attorney Joe Pigott and Mayor John Thompson, among others. In

1970 he ran unopposed for a seat on the McComb City Democratic Executive Committee. The beer business continued to thrive, as Austin spun off an associated concern, Central Beverage, to handle malt liquor products as well as the import Heineken. In 1971, he was elected to the board of directors of Mechanics Bank. On the eve of his 1971 jury service, Thomas Austin was a man of property and standing, a member of the Lion's Club, the McComb Chamber of Commerce, the Brookhaven-Lincoln County Chamber of Commerce, the Mississippi Economic Council, the Knights of Columbus, and the parish council of his church, St. Alphonsus.[48] He had a great deal invested, literally and figuratively, in McComb—in its status, business climate, and also in the effective operation of its law enforcement. He was precisely the sort of man who would have understood that things that he prized would not be well served by damage to the reputation of the McComb Police Department and by extension, the city.

There is no evidence of a quid pro quo in Austin's refusal to vote to convict McIntosh or in Sheriff "Tot" Lawson's conversations with Austin at the Holiday Inn. There would not need to have been. Lawson understood gratitude; Austin understood responsibility. Over the years, the business of a sheriff and a beer distributor would have intersected in multiple ways. Sheriffs in Mississippi in those days wore several hats. They were their county's chief peace officer, and were in charge of the county jail. But they were also tax collectors; they did well for themselves in that capacity. As the local paper reported, because of their ability to keep a percentage of all taxes they collected, "many [sheriffs] make more money than the governor."[49] Establishments that wished to sell the beer that Austin distributed required permits; they also needed what both Austin and Lawson would have understood to be reasonable policing, which might not always have been the same thing as adherence to the strict letter of the law.

When the grand jury indicted Ted Fleming and Richard McIntosh, Lawson had no choice but to take them into custody and put them in his jail. No doubt he hated having to do that to his fellow law enforcement officers. His department and Chief Richard Rowley's police department worked together smoothly and not always with a strict demarcation of jurisdiction, which was fine with Lawson, not the sort of man to complain when someone took some of the burden of his labors from his shoulders. Lawson's bailiffs at the Holiday Inn, too, would have understood. If the sheriff wished to speak with a juror, who were they to say no? The specifics of Austin's conversations with Lawson outside the Holiday Inn; the particular reasons Lawson had for trusting him; Austin's strong will that Richard McIntosh should not be convicted of the murder of Tina Andrews, even before he had heard all the evidence presented in the trial; all the precise reasons for all of those things are matters that Lawson and Austin took to the grave. At his death in 2011, Austin's obituary noted that he "was interested in his community." No doubt he was.[50]

The day after McIntosh's mistrial, November 2, 1971, was also election day in Pike County and the rest of Mississippi. Voter turnout was unusually heavy, with the most-watched race pitting Democrat William Waller against Independent Charles Evers for governor. Evers, mayor of Fayette, brother of slain civil rights leader Medgar Evers, was the first major African American candidate for state office since Reconstruction. Waller was elected in what is widely regarded as the first campaign by a white gubernatorial candidate to reach out to black voters. White Pike County voters could scan the next day's headlines to be reassured that Evers had been defeated "three to one," that the election had seen "Blacks Defeated in Amite" County, and that the election had witnessed "Most Black Candidates Defeated."[51] But still, a majority of black Mississippians were registered to vote and were beginning to win local and county-level posts. By the early 1970s, notes historian James Cobb, "major gains in black political influence were too obvious to deny."[52]

The trial for the murder of Tina Andrews occurred in a county in which violence by black and white residents occurred with regularity. One should not presume local people were accepting of it, however. Many believed it was a testimony to the continued breakdown of law and order in the state and the nation. The October 5 grand jury that preceded the term of court in which Richard McIntosh was tried returned indictments against twenty-five people, including a murder charge against twenty-three-year-old Eddie Allen and a manslaughter charge against nineteen-year-old Ronald Aubrey Hammons. Allen was represented by John Gordon Roach, Jr., the judge's son, and Hammons was represented by B. D. Statham and William Watkins. Also indicted for murder that term was Shirley Mae James, who had killed her husband. All three pled not guilty. In the Allen case, the state got their man, as he agreed to plead guilty to a reduced charge of manslaughter for the July 4 stabbing at a barbeque establishment south of McComb; Judge Roach sentenced him to seven years in the penitentiary. Hammons also escaped the full brunt of his charges, as his attorneys and the prosecutor agreed to a guilty plea to a reduced charge of simple assault, a misdemeanor, for his shotgun killing of a twenty-two-year-old man at Percy Quin State Park. He received a $1000 fine plus a six-month sentence in county jail; the sentence was suspended. Shirley Mae James as well pled guilty to a reduced charge of manslaughter, receiving a $2000 fine and a fifteen-year prison sentence, which the judge again suspended. She had shot her husband, Jesse Napoleon James, after he returned from a 2:00 a.m. trip to get some barbeque. She hailed people she heard in her yard, and not receiving a reply, opened fire with a .22 rifle; one of her shots struck her husband in the head. The state, then, went three for three in these other indictments (two for two on the barbeque-related charges), but only after negotiating plea deals, something that apparently never was seriously considered in the case of Richard McIntosh or Ted Fleming.[53]

In Pike County in those days, then, it was not unusual for a person to be charged with murder and then to negotiate a plea on a lesser charge and to escape prison time entirely. Nothing suggests that the jury that heard the case against Richard McIntosh took murder lightly. In the end, most of them voted that Joe Pigott and Bobby Reeves had proved the case beyond a reasonable doubt. But not all of them. Two of the jurors would not be moved. There is no indication that Pigott or Judge Roach ever learned of the irregular activities at the Holiday Inn during the jury's sequestration. There is no indication that McIntosh or his defense attorneys knew of those events, either. But in the fall of 1971, the state of Mississippi was not yet finished with either Richard McIntosh or Ted Fleming. Both men would wait until the next term of court in 1972 to learn their fate. But both men and their attorneys, having seen how one trial had gone, might have liked their odds.

8

The *State of Mississippi v. Richard McIntosh*

The 1972 Trial

Between the November 1971 mistrial of Richard McIntosh and his retrial in the spring of 1972 there were no announced legal developments in the Tina Andrews case. No one came forward to Pike County authorities with new information that would prove consequential. McIntosh's attorneys worked to hone their strategy, preparing a more elaborate defense for this second round. McIntosh and Fleming, both still free on bond, remained in Pike County. Outgoing district attorney Joe Pigott briefed incoming district attorney Jim Kitchens on the case, one among several pieces of business that Kitchens would inherit. A great advantage that McIntosh enjoyed in his second trial is that both Kitchens and county prosecuting attorney John Gordon Roach, Jr., were new to the case in 1972; both of his attorneys were not. The case and some of its particulars were familiar to many people in Pike County, including the men and women who would form the jury for this next trial.

Given the result of the first trial, one might wonder if the state should have sought a change of venue for the second one. Pike County had all winter to speculate on the case. Many people in the potential jury pool heard details of the case and read or listened to the evidence that both sides had presented in 1971. Some had reached conclusions about McIntosh's involvement in the murder of Tina Andrews. There is no evidence that the state seriously considered such a motion. Perhaps Kitchens, a district attorney new to his position and eager to get to work on a number of cases, might have hesitated to try to move the case. His task was nevertheless complicated by his having inherited the case in mid-stream. He and John Gordon Roach, Jr. had a vast amount of work to do in a short time, far more than the defense team. The Tina Andrews case did not occur in isolation, but was only one case, albeit a highly visible one, that came to the desk of a busy, underassisted, and new district attorney.

All the principal characters in the story waited through the winter for the second act to begin. The Tina Andrews murder remained a topic of great interest and continued speculation in Pike County, easily the most significant local story of the year, the *Enterprise-Journal* reported in an end-of-the-year retrospective.[1] But by late spring of 1972, that story would be finished, so far as the local newspaper and more important, the legal system of the state of Mississippi were concerned. Richard McIntosh and Ted Fleming would be free men, both of them able to begin putting their lives and reputations back together as best as they could. It was a resolution of which McComb police chief Richard Rowley said he was "real proud."[2]

No one else would ever be arrested for the murder of Tina Andrews. Local law enforcement authorities seem never to have carried their work beyond the evidence that they had collected by 1971. Some people in the community, including the writers for the local newspaper, moved on to fresher news and more pressing developments. Some other people, however, including Billie Jo Lambert and the family of Tina Andrews, were left to conclude that in Pike County, Mississippi, one could get away with murder. That work of forgetting by the broader community was greatly enabled by the story presented by the defense in this second trial. The jury heard that some lives and some families in the area mattered less than others because of their social background. What really mattered, the defense sought to show, was the restoration of order, the defense of local institutions, and the principles of respectability. That is not of course how the defense would have explained matters, however. They would have maintained that the state offered no compelling evidence to convict Richard McIntosh of murder. For many reasons, that is how the jury viewed the matter.

In the winter of 1971, the family of Tina Andrews mourned their daughter. She had been buried in McComb's Hollywood Cemetery in 1969, but her repose, like her death, was accompanied by violence and publicity. Within weeks of the November mistrial of McIntosh, her grave was desecrated. Some person or persons, never identified, smashed a photograph of Andrews affixed to her tombstone. Over the weekend of November 19, 1971, said Sheriff Lawson, the Andrews family reported that someone, apparently using "a hammer or a pick," had destroyed the photograph. No other graves seemed to have been damaged. In a note that rang consistently through events from 1969 to 1971, the family chose not to report the damage to the McComb police, even though the act occurred within the city.[3] What resentment or hatred prompted the act? Why in the fall of 1971, rather than at some earlier time? Whatever the motives, whether revenge, frustration, or intimidation, or whoever the grave desecrator, the message the family received was that even in death, malign acts would attend the memory of Tina Andrews.

Several significant matters occurred between the trials. Joe Pigott finished his service as district attorney, as did Robert Reeves as county prosecutor. Jim Kitchens and John Gordon Roach, Jr., assumed those offices in 1972.[4] Both new men needed quickly to familiarize themselves with the McIntosh case that they would presumably try again, and to prepare themselves as well for a potential trial of Ted Fleming. There were also eighty new cases that they would present to the March 1972 grand jury. Defense counsel for both McIntosh and Fleming remained unchanged. The defense had the advantage of having heard what the state had to offer, and appeared successfully once to have countered it. If the state had anything new to present, rules of evidence ensured that the defense would know it. But the state did not.

Jim Kitchens had run successfully for district attorney in 1971, defeating two other candidates. Like many other Mississippians, Kitchens was concerned about matters of law and order: "Our country is plagued by a steady and consistent rise in crime."[5] His background and the nature of the office in that period suggest some of the difficulties that he would face in attempting to convict Richard McIntosh. Kitchens ran in part on a platform promising to devote himself full time to his job. District attorneys in Mississippi then had the option of retaining a private practice while in office. Kitchens said he would not do that; his opponents in the 1971 election had not made that promise. Even on the job full time, though, Kitchens, like Joe Pigott before him, was responsible for cases in four counties, one of which, Lincoln, had a town, Brookhaven, as large as McComb. In each of these counties, the district attorney was assisted only by one elected county prosecutor, which ensured a very heavy caseload. "No Man Can Serve Two Masters," Kitchens' campaign materials counseled, a reference to his decision to go full-time on the district attorney's office.[6] But the district attorney in fact served many masters in his four counties, with few hands to help him in the investigation and preparation of the many criminal cases that would cross his desk. "There were no assistant district attorneys at all then," recalled Kitchens, "and the county prosecutor . . . was a part time position."[7]

Kitchens, tall, lean, and angular in those days, with deep eyes and tight-set lips that could broaden into a winning smile, was an experienced criminal lawyer, albeit one with fewer years of experience than B. D. Statham. Kitchens took well to campaigns and elections. He was and would remain appealing to voters, but over the years maintained a reputation above local partisanship. He was a 1964 graduate of the University of Southern Mississippi, one detail that set him apart from most of the Pike County attorneys and judges, who had spent their undergraduate years in Oxford rather than Hattiesburg. Kitchens did head to Ole Miss for his law degree, which he earned in 1967. After four years in private practice, he won election as district attorney in 1971, a position he held through reelections in 1975 and 1979, after which he reentered private practice. In 2008, he won election to the state's Supreme Court, defeating a sitting justice. Kitchens defended that seat in 2016.[8]

In 1972 he lived in Crystal Springs in Copiah County, where he was born, over sixty miles from the courthouse in Magnolia. This fact too presented a potential complication for Kitchens, or at least a circumstance that set him apart from the previous district attorney, Pigott, as well as the attorneys he would face in court that spring. In the run-off election for district attorney between Kitchens and Pike County prosecuting attorney Robert S. Reeves in 1971, Kitchens carried his home county of Copiah by a very wide margin, and he also won a narrow contest in Copiah's southern neighbor, Lincoln County. But Reeves defeated Kitchens in lightly populated Walthall County, just to the west of Pike County, and in Pike itself, home to both McComb and Magnolia, Reeves won over 70 percent of the vote. Still, Kitchens' large margin in Copiah proved the difference in winning the post for him. He ran unopposed in the fall election, as did many local and county Democratic candidates in those days. Kitchens was not a member of the insider group of Magnolia attorneys, nor had he cultivated years of working relationships with the police and sheriff's departments. Pike County had welcomed relative outsiders, such as Fleming's attorney Wayne Dowdy, into the area's legal fold, but Kitchens was literally new to the job and relatively less known in the area than McIntosh's defense counsel in the spring of 1972.[9]

Kitchens and other area attorneys prepared for the spring 1972 term of the Pike County Circuit Court, with the docket potentially a heavy one, especially on criminal cases. Among the eighty new cases likely to be presented to the grand jury were three homicides and a "good number" of drug cases. The most-anticipated case was the retrial of Richard McIntosh, with the possibility of Ted Fleming being tried that spring as well. In March, just before the term opened, neither Kitchens nor Roach would say whether or not McIntosh's case was one they intended to present to the grand jury, but that was in fact their plan.[10]

The spring court term opened on March 20, 1972, with Judge Roach offering his traditional charge to the grand jury. In the judge's estimation, the main challenges facing the area were an increase in drug abuse and burglary. As he had done through his years on the bench, Judge Roach warned the grand jurors that the county and the nation faced a rising tide of crime, one that stemmed from a decline in morality. Young people, he said, represented a particular challenge. "We live in an age which has a space age mentality," he counseled, "and a dark age spirituality." What should the citizens of Pike County do? "Rally around the officers," he insisted.[11] Such a diagnosis and a recommendation could have been heard in small-town courthouses throughout the United States in 1972. Many Americans did believe that they were living in an era of increasing criminality and a lack of respect for law and order. President Nixon and Attorney General John Mitchell had said much the same thing for several years.

Before his 1968 election, in fact, Nixon lamented that despite its "freedom and material abundance," the nation had become "among the most lawless and violent in the history of the free peoples."[12] He concluded: "Far from being a great society, ours is becoming a lawless society." A recent biographer of Nixon argues that the call for law and order "was a legitimate issue—and a euphemism," not one aimed solely at white southerners. Political strategist Kevin Phillips said that the principal issue in the 1968 election was the "law and order/Negro socio-economic revolution syndrome." Nixon's adviser Bob Haldeman gauged his boss's thoughts on the matter: "RN has emotional access to lower middle class white—not fair [to call them] racist—but concerned re crime & violence, law & order." They were concerned, as the crime rate had spiked in the 1960s. Apparently they did see that Nixon understood. To Deep South white voters, George Wallace understood as well, and many Americans worried that if politicians like Nixon would not offer proposals to sooth these anxieties, then someone like Wallace would.[13]

In Pike County, these concerns about law and order and the "Negro socio-economic revolution syndrome," as Kevin Phillips put it, were inflected through years of local social change. A longtime resident of McComb told me: "A lot of people here were worried that the changes in civil rights laws and black people's attitudes would lead to a lot more crime. People would say that a lot of black people felt like they had a license to steal anything that wasn't nailed down."[14] Such attitudes were as old as the South itself. Without a proper respect for the law, many whites believed, chaos would overwhelm order. Traditionally, chaos and order were explicitly color-coded. In some ways, particularly in voting and elections, the old ways no longer held. But at an almost visceral level, support for the law by local whites stood as a proxy for support of many traditional ways that people in the county had long felt were under assault. There is no reason that the grand jurors would have listened to Judge Roach's remarks about "supporting the officers" and thought immediately of the cases against Ted Fleming and Richard McIntosh. But there is every reason to believe that very many people in the county, including a good number of those grand jurors, retained a strong respect for the law and order that officers such as the two indicted men were supposed to represent.

By March 29, Judge Roach scheduled McIntosh's trial for the now-open spring term; the case of Ted Fleming was set for call as well.[15] April 3, 1972, the day that McIntosh's second trial was to begin, was an eventful day in Pike County for other reasons as well. In McComb, a long-anticipated parade in honor of the city's centennial celebration was held, despite literal and figurative storm clouds. Rain was predicted; so was the Ku Klux Klan. The Klan applied for a permit to march in the parade, but certainly to the relief of many people in the city, black and white, their application had been submitted after the deadline and was denied. However, the Klan enlisted the assistance of the American Civil Liberties Union, which announced their intention to file a writ of mandamus in the Pike County Circuit Court to allow a contingent of mounted Klansmen into the parade. The writ was denied, but some members of the Klan attended the parade, apparently hoping to participate anyway. However, McComb police arrested two Klansmen, both of them on concealed weapons charges. One man was spotted by the police with a pistol tucked into the bib of his overalls.[16] The continued, albeit attenuated, presence of the Ku Klux Klan in Pike County indicates at least two things. First, many area white people had not reconciled themselves to the changes that had occurred in the last decade. The city's resistance to the Klan presence in the centennial parade also reflects the discomfort that McComb civic and business leaders had with the Klan, which seemed a relic of the bad old days of bombings and out-of-control white resistance both to area blacks and to accepted forms of authority.

The official marking of the McComb centennial also witnessed a farewell and a scandal associated with one of the city's downtown landmarks, the McColgan Hotel. Established in 1889, the McColgan was by the early 1970s the oldest business operation in McComb. "The McColgan Hotel, with its once famous Palm Room," remembered the newspaper editor, "long has been a part of the life of this community." Located on Front and Main Streets, the hotel housed offices for several other businesses, including the Western Union service. The McColgan was in decline physically, and perhaps in other ways as well, by 1972. In a preview of the restructuring of downtown McComb that would occur in the 1970s, the McColgan closed on the same day that McIntosh's trial opened. Urban renewal, one of the watchwords of the era, had reached McComb.[17]

The previous week, the McColgan had figured in an "explosive" burglary trial in Pike County Circuit Court. Judge Roach presided over this trial; the prosecution was handled by the new district attorney, Jim Kitchens. Testimony "made public evidence of a professional prostitution operation in McComb and hinted at a rift between law enforcement agencies in the community."[18] The trial involved Noel Francis Hines, also known as Paul St. John, accused of burglarizing Gillis Drug Store on February 1, 1972. Dr. M. V. Harvey, whose practice was located in the McColgan (and whose wife had been the foreman of the 1971 McIntosh jury), reported to police that six vials of a painkilling drug had been taken from his office.[19] Hines, a twenty-seven-year-old native of nearby Franklin County, was arrested on February 16 by highway patrol investigator Donald Butler. Hines was a man with a considerable criminal record, having served time in Georgia as well as in Louisiana's Angola prison for breaking and entering and car theft. At the time of his arrest, said Sheriff Lawson, Hines had only been out of prison in Georgia for a month and was currently wanted in Baton Rouge, Louisiana, on charges of forgery and car theft. In this case, too, he was accused of taking a car, a 1964 Chevrolet, from behind the McColgan Hotel, where he had been staying.

The cast involved in the McColgan burglary case were many of the same ones who figured in one or both of the trials of Richard McIntosh: Judge J. Gordon Roach, highway patrol investigator Donald Butler, Sheriff "Tot" Lawson, District Attorney Jim Kitchens, police chief Richard Rowley, Pike County prosecuting attorney John Gordon Roach, Jr., who thus argued the state's case before his father the judge, and former district attorney Joe Pigott, this time serving as a court-appointed defense attorney for Hines. The state's efforts to convict Hines resulted in a mistrial after an hour of jury deliberation. Still, District Attorney Kitchens was determined to clean up this species of organized vice in the county. He maintained: "Sworn uncontradicted testimony in circuit court of this county has proven that professional prostitutes have been operating in the McColgan Hotel for a long period of time. Sheriff Robert Lawson and I have told parties involved, in no uncertain terms, that this activity must come to an immediate halt."[20]

Mrs. Eve Holifield of Laurel, Mississippi, provided evidence of "this activity," as Kitchens put it, in testimony that must have been as interesting as anything else heard in the courthouse that term. "When asked her profession by Kitchens, the flaming redhead replied without hesitation, 'I'm a professional prostitute,' and added that has been the purpose of her visits to McComb." Her trade had brought her to the McColgan for stretches of a week or so somewhere between fifteen and twenty times over the previous two years. She further testified that the McComb police had never given her trouble about her work. Indeed, she was not acquainted in an official capacity with any members of the police force.[21]

Holifield told the court that two nights before the burglary, she had been "instructed" to go to Noel Francis Hines's room, where he told her of his plans to "rip off" a drug store. Holifield further testified that after the burglary, Hines had come to her room to display drugs, watches, and other "loot" from his work. Testimony about the investigation of the crime does indeed suggest a "rift," as the local newspaper described it, between law enforcement agencies in the area. Police chief Richard Rowley said that one of his men, Captain Eddie W. Smith, had been primarily responsible for investigating the crime. He said too that Holifield had been interviewed and tape-recorded at the McComb police headquarters. But his version of the story suggests that one of the main areas of police interest was the role of the highway patrol and the sheriff's department in the investigation of the crime, specifically their interrogation of Holifield.[22]

Highway patrol investigator Donald Butler told the court that indeed he and Deputy Sheriff Jimmy Carruth had interviewed Holifield in her room at the McColgan, asking her for information about the burglary. Shortly after that interview, said Butler, police chief Rowley called Butler's commanding officer, after which Butler was removed from the case. Rowley apparently worried that Butler was investigating not only the burglary but also the McComb police, which Butler's testimony denied. While the state did not get their man in this trial, what the case does provide is evidence of organized sexual vice in McComb, the involvement of a downtown business, and a "hint," as the town's newspaper put it, that McComb law enforcement officials were not all on the same page in seeking to stamp out this vice. It also suggests some of the obstacles a district attorney might face if he needed the cooperation of the police department, especially in working a case that might involve their own members.[23]

The McColgan Hotel is remembered to this day, at least by McCombites of a certain age. Charles Dunagin, a veteran reporter for the *Enterprise-Journal*, recalled that when he moved into the place when he came to town in 1963, it had an unsavory reputation, of which he was unaware. When he told people where he was staying, "they would make no comment and look away." In Dunagin's memory, the shady women there were "ladies of the evening from New Orleans who were shuttled in and out of the McColgan by their handlers."[24] Jim Kitchens recalled, "This burglar, who was not from down there, ended up with one of these prostitutes at the McColgan Hotel. She was an informant for Donald Butler, and she told him this guy had all these rings, watches, and things. It turned out that this woman, though she was a prostitute, she was a credible prostitute. Maybe that's not an inconsistency we can get past, but she had information on a bunch of police officers in McComb. They were letting that whorehouse up there operate because of favors that they were getting from these women."[25]

The McColgan burglary trial at the end of March had been Kitchens' first major case before the Pike County Circuit Court. The April trial of Richard McIntosh would be his next one. Judge Gordon Roach, however, would not

181

preside over that trial. Suffering from an infected tooth as well as from general exhaustion, Roach was advised by his physician not to be on the bench for the remainder of the spring term. In his place would be Judge Darwin Maples of Lucedale, a small town in George County, approximately 125 miles from Magnolia. Roach requested that Maples take his place, which he did officially in an order signed on April 3, 1972, the day the case was set down for trial. As they had done the previous fall, William Watkins and B. D. Statham, still McIntosh's attorneys, filed a successful, standard motion for a jury to be drawn from a special venire list.[26] In the meantime, Sheriff Lawson and his deputies delivered subpoenas to witnesses for both the state and the defense. Some of them were the same people who would present much the same evidence that they had done in the previous trial. Others, called mainly for the defense, were new, and they added considerable detail and complexity to the story that Statham and Watkins told.[27]

After jury selection, which took most of Monday, April 3, McIntosh's second trial began hearing witnesses on April 4. The jury consisted of Wendell H. Alford, Ernest Hughes, Jessie Mae Nunnery, Thomas Earl Moore, J. J. Carter, Howard Jenkins, Ernest Matthews, Mrs. T. R. Quinn, Katie Browning, Harold E. Morgan, B. C. Hayman, and Ralph L. Reeves; Gary N. Travis was the alternate. As in the first trial, the jury consisted of both men and women, black and white, but in terms of both race and gender, white men were represented in proportions greater than their share of the county's population.[28] In 1971, however, there were four African American jurors; this time there were five. In 1971, one woman served; this time there were three. On paper, at least, it no way appeared to be a jury predisposed to acquitting a man accused of murdering a child. Indeed, if one were a betting person, one might have looked at the gender and racial composition of that jury and imagined another hung jury and another mistrial. But such was not to be the case.

Who were the jurors in the second trial of Richard McIntosh?[29] Wendell H. Alford, thirty-seven, operated a press at MacMillen Bloedel in Magnolia, a manufacturer of corrugated boxes, among other materials, and was a National Guardsman. Ralph L. Reeves, sixty, the owner of Reeves Well and Pump Service, had been a McComb city selectman from 1966–70. Reeves was also a graduate of Mississippi College and a prominent local Baptist. B. C. Hayman, forty-nine, of McComb, a highly decorated World War II veteran of the Army

Air Corps, worked for South Central Bell, the regional telephone service company. Thomas Earl Moore, thirty-six, an Air Force veteran, with service in the Korean War, was a salesman at Parker Auto Parts on South Broadway in McComb. Harold E. Morgan, forty-two, a state highway department employee, came from Pricedale in rural northeastern Pike County, where he had previously run unsuccessfully for trustee on the county school board. Ernest W. Hughes, fifty-nine, of rural Pike County, was a farmer. All of these men were white. Mrs. T. R. Quinn, a middle-aged white woman from Osyka, was the only white woman on the jury.[30]

Five of the jurors were African American. Jessie Mae Nunnery, forty-three, of Magnolia, worked there at Beacham Memorial Hospital. Howard Jenkins had run unsuccessfully in 1971 as a candidate for constable in District Five of Pike County. Ernest Matthews, fifty, of McComb, a U.S. Army veteran of World War II, worked for the Great Southern Wirebound Box Company in Magnolia. Katie Browning, a schoolteacher living near Fernwood, had long been active in black community affairs and would serve for many years as a poll watcher and election worker. J. J. Carter, forty-six, of Magnolia, a successful farmer and later a Pike County Library Board trustee, was the twelfth juror.[31]

As did the jury in 1971, this panel represented a much closer cross-section of the community than one would have seen on a Pike County jury a decade earlier. In yet another indication of changed times, the local newspaper never identified the jurors by race. Only a few years earlier, it would have been almost impossible to find a Mississippi newspaper that did not identify local people by race. In no obvious way does this jury suggest a group with an interest in exonerating a police officer because of his status. But as in 1971, B. D. Statham, as attorney for the board of supervisors, enjoyed a good deal of latitude in shaping the jury to his liking. He knew many of the people from whom the jury was drawn. Jim Kitchens, a relative newcomer to the area, did not, at least not nearly as well.

The jury, also as in the 1971 trial, consisted of people from all areas of Pike County. Most of them were working people, a term they would have embraced, as "working class" was not a term much used by area people. The African American jurors certainly did not think in terms of supporting the police for authority's sake or of restoring the old days. Perhaps the fact that the case involved white people only would have removed some pressure from black jurors; if either Tina Andrews or her alleged killers had been black, the story would likely have unfolded in much different ways, not least in the consideration of the seating of the jury. Pike County, Mississippi, in 1972 was socially and culturally conservative in some measure. Black and white county residents believed many of the same things about family, hard work, and sexual propriety, all matters which Statham had stressed mightily in the 1971 trial and would again in 1972.

Several people who had not testified but who had been summoned in 1971 were again issued subpoenas in 1972, some of them for Richard McIntosh's trial and some for Ted Fleming's potential trial. One was Pat Lamkin, the friend to whom Billie Jo Lambert gave her account of what happened on August 13, 1969. She did not testify in the first trial, nor would she in this one. Another was Beverly Henderson, whom Statham had asserted that Billie Jo Lambert was trying to convince to claim to be the third girl who accepted a ride outside the Tiger's Den. Henderson, like Lamkin, did not testify in either trial. A new name among the potential witnesses was George Kratzschmar, the father of Billie Jo Lambert's child, whose identity she had refused to reveal in court in 1971. Some of these witnesses were called for the defense, others for the state. Once again, Tina Andrews's parents were not summoned by either side.[32]

Many of the witnesses and much of the testimony in 1972, especially that of the state's case, was similar to that presented at the 1971 trial, not surprising, given the lack of new developments in the months between the trials.[33] As in 1971, highway patrol investigator Donald Butler was the state's first witness. Butler began with testimony about his 1969 investigation of the case. He answered state's questions about photographs and physical evidence, and underwent cross-examination by defense counsel. Another repeat witness from 1971 was Dr. T. Dale Stewart of the Department of Physical Anthropology of the Smithsonian Institute. As he had done in the fall, Stewart offered expert testimony on the human remains, essentially a skeleton, recovered from the oil field. But the state had learned from the great efforts the defense expended in the first trial to cast doubt on the body's identity. In part, the defense had argued that the condition of the remains could not represent those of a body that had been in the oil field only ten days. This time, Stewart expanded his remarks on the rate of deterioration of human bodies. In Stewart's judgment, the heat and humidity of the Mississippi August, amplified by the recent hurricane-influenced weather, accelerated the decomposition rate, making it well possible that the body had lain in the oil field for ten days or so. Dr. Marie Nylen testified again for the state, presenting her conclusions about the identity of the body, based upon forensic dental testing. Another state's witness testifying about the condition of the remains and efforts to gain evidence from them was F.B.I. agent Frederick Wallace, of the bureau's crime lab. He explained to the jury various forensic examinations made on the body.[34]

The early part of the trial was, according to the local newspaper, "for the most part a replay" of the previous trial, with "no new witnesses or significant evidence being presented by either side."[35] Neither the state nor the defense, however, saw the matter as *pro forma*. As in 1971, the trial stretched over four days, a long period for a Pike County murder trial. The testimony on both sides was as detailed and the cross-examination by Statham just as aggressive and contentious as it had been in 1971. Lambert remained consistent in her story, as did McIntosh in his. In theory, at least, all this material was new to these jurors. But by 1972, it would have been difficult for anyone living in the area not to be familiar with the broad outlines of the case, the people involved, and perhaps even some of the evidence that had been presented in 1971. A man who served on the 1972 jury later remarked, "Of course I knew all about it. I read the paper. Everybody talked about it. And everybody had an opinion about whether or not he did it. I did, too. You couldn't have found anybody in Pike County who didn't."[36] But jurors' preconceptions based upon their impressions of the previous trial could have cut either way and did not necessarily favor either the state or the defense. Other factors, including new evidence and testimony presented by the defense, seem to have shaped the outcome of this trial.

The jury heard several possible scenarios—one of them quite bizarre—that might have accounted for Tina Andrews's fate. The defense crafted this story through cross-examination of the state's witnesses as well as the testimony of its own witnesses. This evidence, which had not been presented at the first trial, served the defense well by introducing a far more complicated story than the one heard by the 1971 jury. That additional complexity, with its possible if not altogether probable alternatives, proved a factor in persuading the jury that whatever had happened to Tina Andrews, Richard McIntosh might not have been responsible. Some of this new information included two reports by highway patrol investigator Donald Butler. Butler was one of the first investigators on the scene. In the previous fall's trial, his map of the oil field occasioned contention between state and defense over his labeling of the area as the "scene of the crime." But in 1972, Butler's reports, introduced as evidence during Statham's cross-examination of Butler, revealed the wider role he played in searching for the murderer of Tina Andrews. Both of his reports offered the jury scenarios of men seeking the company of young girls, and the names of those men did not include McIntosh or Fleming. Both reports appeared to suggest that men other than the two indicted police officers could have been responsible for Andrews's death. Such alternative possibilities were precisely the kind of information that might introduce a reasonable doubt into the minds of jurors. The introduction of those reports by the defense represents one of the wisest moves made by Statham and Watkins.[37]

Butler's first report detailed his investigation of Norman Stietenroth, a fifty-seven-year-old McComb resident who operated the Western Union office, above which he lived with his son, Charles. The office and residence were located in downtown McComb between the Gillis Drug Store and the Tiger's Den. Butler said that on August 26, 1969, several days after the remains were found, but significantly before the identification of those remains was announced on September 19, Stietenroth called the Andrews residence, spoke with Tina Andrews's teenage sister Donna, attempting to arrange a meeting with her. What did Stietenroth wish to discuss with Donna? She did apparently agree to see him, but did not show up. Instead, on this occasion her family did contact law enforcement officers to tell them what had happened, and the meeting place was "staked out," with Donald Butler following a surely disappointed Stietenroth back to the Western Union office.[38]

There, Butler observed Stietenroth confront his son, Charles, who was in his early thirties. Charles died in 1970, considerably before the indictment and trials. He was physically handicapped, using a wheelchair. Norman, according to the report, struck his son, cursed him vigorously, and blamed him for the botched meeting with Donna Andrews. In an incredible exchange, according to Butler's testimony, Norman threatened his son, saying that "Tina would be #1, Donna #2, and you, you flat-footed son-of-a-bitch, will be #3," adding, "I am going to kill you." Stietenroth told his son that "the stupid officers could not find out anything . . . he and Tina were just beginning to make out when she slapped him and he cracked her across the jaw." Apparently not a man easily deterred, Stietenroth made another attempt to meet with Donna Andrews. Finally, said Butler, Norman Stietenroth was taken to Jackson for a lie detector test, but because of his "upset condition," the "correct test could not be taken."[39]

The remarks, if they were correctly heard and reported, are profoundly interesting. They also help to explain why some people in Pike County have been convinced that the murder involved a much broader array of characters than McIntosh and Fleming. But this report of Butler's raises more questions than it answers. What was Stietenroth's source of information about the exchange between the officers and Tina Andrews? Were "the officers" McIntosh and Fleming? McIntosh, the defense had taken pains to establish, was not an officer in 1969. What were the officers supposed to find out? Stietenroth's frustration suggests that "the stupid officers" were on an errand, either their own or another's, at least in part to interrogate either Andrews or Lambert. The nature of the exchange between Norman and Charles suggests a person (the father) discussing a matter with a person (the son) who is conversant with the events. Or a rant delivered to a person who is not familiar with them but is rather a convenient target for venting. Or perhaps something in between.

It is difficult to know what degree of credence to give to these reported remarks. What stake did Stietenroth have in his amateur investigation of Tina and Donna Andrews? Why would anyone delegate to him the responsibility of contacting Donna Andrews? What could Donna have known about that evening or other things her sister had done or knew about? Nothing in Lambert's testimony suggested that the men who took her and Tina Andrews to the oil field were trying to "find out anything" from them, other than what kind of physical satisfaction they might enjoy. In Lambert's testimony, no one in the car was positioned to "make out," with the men in the front seat and the girls in the back until the car stopped. If Stietenroth's source for this information was correct, it suggests a deeper motive for the men who gave the girls a ride that evening, and certainly also the involvement, one way or another, of other people, either before or after August 13, 1969. But no other evidence, introduced by either the state or the defense, suggested any involvement of Stietenroth in the murder.

Why would the defense introduce Butler's reports into evidence? They suggested to the jury that people other than McIntosh and Fleming had been investigated. But anyone who had discussed the case or read the newspaper knew that many suspects had been questioned. Butler's account of Stietenroth's remarks hardly clears McIntosh or contradicts Lambert's testimony. It seems in fact to support Lambert's contention that "officers" were involved in the matter. But the introduction of Stietenroth into the story, especially his reported threats to kill several people, complicated the state's task of convincing the jury that the identity of Andrews's killer was clear.

Norman Stietenroth was not subpoenaed by either the state or the defense. He did not testify at either trial. He died in 1979, remembered in McComb as an odd character, a man who stood in front of his place of business repeatedly tossing a hammer into the air and catching it. Another longtime McComb resident reports that Stietenroth also practiced his tossing and catching skills with a small hatchet. His work with that instrument was less skillful than with a hammer, as Stietenroth one day missed his catch, with the hatchet striking his head a sharp blow. Stietenroth's obituary describes him only as a "retired accountant" and a Presbyterian.[40]

Did Norman Stietenroth have any association with Tina Andrews? A contemporary McComb woman maintains that he did, but not in any way that would implicate him in her murder. In downtown McComb, in a building next to the Palace Theater on Main Street, was a small shop on the corner of Front and Main, operated by "Snowball" Whittington, a local insurance agent. The shop, open late, sold hamburgers, sodas, and other snacks. One evening, sitting on stools next to each other were Tina and Stietenroth, an odd sight, given the discrepancy in age and the late hour. They were clearly together, talking and laughing. On her shoulder Tina carried a small sling purse. When opened, the purse revealed a considerable amount of money, more than a girl Tina's age might be expected to carry. Sue Williams, now in her seventies, was then in her twenties. She knew Stietenroth, at least by sight and reputation, but she did not know the girl with him that evening. "I couldn't believe that a girl that age would be down here late—that her parents would allow it." And with Stietenroth? "He gave me the heebie-jeebies, and I was old." The girl with Stietenroth looked to Williams very much like a "little girl," a term that Mississippians use generally to describe a female of tender years. Williams says she thought little more of the encounter until later in the summer of 1969, when the newspaper published a photograph of Tina Andrews after her remains were identified.

Williams then told her sister, "That's her! That's the girl who was at Snowball's with Stietenroth."[41]

The story says nothing about Richard McIntosh or Ted Fleming, and does not indicate that Stietenroth was the source of the money in Tina's handbag. But it does suggest that she was familiar with the company of older men, that she had income from some source, and that as the defense had demonstrated, kept late hours for a twelve-year-old. But the jury heard none of this information, nor would it have done anything to strengthen the state's case against McIntosh. Quite the contrary. But whatever one might remember or think about Norman Stietenroth, it seems extraordinarily unlikely that he gave anyone a ride to an oil field or murdered anyone there.

The second of Donald Butler's reports, also entered into evidence for the first time in the 1972 trial, dated from August 1969 as well. It detailed the interview of Butler and Sheriff Lawson with Vernon E. Steele. This report described events of August 12, 1969, the day before Tina Andrews was last seen alive. Steele and Gerald Felder, a man from Summit, another small town in Pike County, riding in Felder's car, picked up Tina and Donna Andrews at the Tiger's Den. A third man, Ray Fortenberry, "said to have been Donna's boyfriend," was also with them. "After trying to find a girl for Felder, Felder took the group to Steele's auto and left them." Then, "Fortenberry, Steele, and the two girls went to a house out from Fernwood," another small Pike County community. Billie Jo Lambert's name was not associated with the incident, nor was there any assertion that either of the men killed Tina Andrews. But the report did further the impression Statham sought to make upon the jury: that Tina Andrews was a girl who had a habit not only of frequenting the Tiger's Den, but also of accepting rides with older men.[42] With such a girl, Statham implied, who knows what might have happened to her?

During testimony, Ray Fortenberry said that he and Vernon Steele had in fact been with Tina and Donna Andrews on the night of August 12 and into the morning hours of August 13. However, when District Attorney Kitchens asked Fortenberry if he had ever used marijuana or LSD, Fortenberry pled the Fifth Amendment to avoid answering the question. The tale of Felder and Fortenberry and their interest in the Andrews girls was suggestive and somewhat salacious. It offered nothing to connect Richard McIntosh or Ted Fleming with the death of Tina Andrews. As such, it precisely served the defense's strategy. After presenting twelve witnesses, the state rested its case at 4:30 p.m. on Wednesday. The defense prepared to call their witnesses.[43]

Statham called police chief Richard Rowley, who testified that McIntosh had not been with the department in 1969, either regular or auxiliary. The question of whether McIntosh was an auxiliary officer in 1969 was a loose end of sorts in the first trial that Statham determined to tie up. In McComb, men did move from auxiliary police service to the regular force. Bobby Bellipanni, Ted Fleming's brother-in-law and one of the first law enforcement men on the scene in 1969, was one example.[44] Into the twenty-first century, retired McComb police officers were used as an auxiliary or reserve force. Wearing a police uniform, they could also be hired as security officers, leading to concerns about liability or ambiguity, as potentially confusing later as it might have been to a teenage girl decades earlier. Taking the witness for cross-examination, Kitchens asked Rowley if he had ordered uniformed McComb policemen to appear in court in the 1971 trial to support their former colleague. Rowley admitted that he had. Before this trial, Kitchens had moved to ensure that there would not be a repeat of the performance. But the state still had no evidence to show that McIntosh had ever been a reserve officer.[45]

Once again, McIntosh's ex-girlfriend Dorothy Nettles proved a fortunate defense witness. Nettles testified that she and McIntosh dated very heavily for several months in the summer of 1969, including the days surrounding the disappearance of Tina Andrews. McIntosh had been with her every night of the week in question. In preparation for this trial, the state subpoenaed utility records of Nettles' Edgar Street house from 1968 through 1970 to confirm her residency there. But as in the 1971 trial, the state presented nothing to discredit her testimony. Thus, McIntosh's main alibi for the evening of August 13, 1969, seemed to stand.[46]

Taking no chances, the defense introduced new witnesses and a new element of the story to cast doubt upon Lambert's contention that McIntosh and Fleming had taken her and Andrews to the oil field. The defense called three witnesses to vouch for Ted Fleming on the evening of August 13. One of those witnesses was Fleming's wife, one was his brother, and the other was at the time a fellow McComb police officer. All were people who might know of Fleming's activities on that evening; all might also have some stake in supporting Fleming. Bobby Williams, by then a former McComb police officer, testified that he had been partnered with Fleming on the night of August 13 and had taken Fleming home about 9:45 p.m. Both Fleming's wife, Agnes, and his brother, Alton, stated that Fleming had arrived at Alton's house about twenty minutes after Ted Fleming's shift ended. Fleming and his wife then took his brother's children home with them, where, according to Mrs. Fleming, they remained for the rest of the evening.[47] Why would the testimony about the location of Ted Fleming on that evening have been deemed relevant in a trial of Richard McIntosh? One certainly understands why the defense would wish to have it heard. It produced an alibi for one of the men that Lambert claimed to have picked up the girls that night. It thus gave the jury further reason to doubt Lambert's identification of the men, as well as her ability generally to recall or tell the truth.[48]

The defense presented character witnesses for McIntosh. These were the same people who had testified the previous fall: Alice Mercier, H. W. Magee, Jr., Leon Empson, and Rev. David Millican. At no point in either trial did the state produce witnesses, either directly or indirectly, to vouch for the character of either Tina Andrews or Billie Jo Lambert. As a formal matter, a state's witness is not in a position to be supported by character witnesses. Nor is a murder victim. But that legal distinction might have been lost on the jury, who heard little other than damning references to the character of both girls and their families, in contrast to the very good things they heard about the character of Richard McIntosh.[49]

The state had rested its case on Wednesday. After five hours of work, the defense concluded matters on Thursday. The lot of Richard McIntosh was then in the hands of the jury. The trial had lasted for four days. The jury heard testimony from twenty-five witnesses. In its instructions from the state, the jury was given several options when weighing McIntosh's fate. They were to consider the question of both his guilt and his punishment should they find him guilty. Mississippi was a state that believed in capital punishment, so that was a possibility. So too was a life sentence in Parchman, the state penitentiary. Or they could, if they found him guilty, but were unable to reach a choice of punishment, allow the court then to sentence him to life imprisonment. They were also given the option of a verdict of manslaughter. Under Mississippi law, manslaughter was a killing "done in the heat of passion, without malice and without any premeditation."[50] The jury was also instructed that an eyewitness was not necessary for a conviction, and that the "crime charged here may be proven by circumstances," which is precisely the sort of story that the state's evidence had to tell the jury.

The defense also presented instructions to the jury, reminding them that McIntosh was not required at any point to demonstrate his innocence, and that "suppositions, conjectures, or even probabilities" were not sufficient to reach a guilty verdict. The defense also told the jury, and here of course Statham and Watkins hoped that the jury would think of their handling of Billie Jo Lambert, that if a witness had made different or conflicting statements about a point of testimony, or if a witness's "intelligence" or "manner while upon the stand" failed to satisfy them, then they could distrust or discount that entire testimony. Such instructions were not unique to this trial, but they spoke directly to the ways in which the defense had framed the testimony and the character of Billie Jo Lambert.[51]

The nine men and three women deliberated for two and a half hours on Thursday, April 6, before returning a verdict. The foreman of the jury, my great-uncle Ralph Reeves, printed a note, which was handed to Judge Maples. It read: "We, the Jury, Find the Defendent [sic] Not Guilty." With that, McIntosh finally was free of the legal hand of the state of Mississippi. McIntosh "took the verdict of the jury with a release of emotion, which his attorney, B. D. Statham, said was a combination of 'joy and gratitude.'" Statham noted that for McIntosh, "the past year has been a traumatic experience, with a loss of friends and prestige, but McIntosh will start from here rebuilding his life."[52]

Experiencing one criminal trial for murder is a wrenching, consuming ordeal. Experiencing two, as did McIntosh, is a fate no one wishes to undergo. It would also have been extraordinarily expensive. The firm of Statham and Watkins invested not only a great deal of time in court but also in investigatory work prior to the trial. Their services did not come cheap. Richard McIntosh, a man of modest means, living with his widowed mother on a city police patrolman's salary (which was not paid during his suspension from the police force), was much more fortunate than the average person in his situation in being able to retain the services of his attorneys. There was no legal defense fund for McIntosh, at least not a formal one. If anyone stepped forward, grateful perhaps for the opportunity to defray the costs, and they were considerable, of the defense of one of McComb's thin blue line, that person chose to remain anonymous.

Judge Gordon Roach was back on the bench on the morning of Friday, April 7. If anyone from either the state or the defense thought the return of Judge Roach at this point in the trial was problematic, the record does not show it. District Attorney Jim Kitchens concluded that if the state could not convict Richard McIntosh in two trials, then its odds of convicting Ted Fleming were slim. Then and later, attorneys on both sides believed that the state had much the better case against McIntosh than against Fleming. Kitchens presented the court a motion of *nolle prosequi*, a decision to dismiss charges against Fleming. Judge Roach received the nol-pros motion from Kitchens, and there the legal matter against both men ended.[53]

What convinced the jury to return the not guilty verdict? By the standards of the place and time, the length of deliberation was not unusually quick, but compared with the difficulties that the 1971 jury had in reaching a verdict, it is striking. In 1971, a majority of jurors voted for conviction. This time the matter was never close, except perhaps to a full acquittal on the first ballot. Was the state's case weaker than it had been in 1971? The testimony itself was much the same, almost verbatim through stretches of it. McIntosh was crisp, clear, and positive in his answers, as he very well might be, well prepared both by his defense counsel and by his experience in answering similar questions the previous fall. To this jury, it seems to have appeared that McIntosh had nothing to do with the crime, other than in the story presented in Billie Jo Lambert's testimony. There were no other witnesses who could establish a connection between McIntosh and Tina Andrews, and no physical evidence such as a murder weapon or blood stains in his car, for instance, that tied him either to Andrews or the crime scene. In short, the jury had to decide whether they believed Lambert or McIntosh. B. D. Statham had done much to convince them that Lambert simply did not have a believable story and that the state had not proved its case beyond a reasonable doubt.

Statham's work as a defense attorney in both trials was everything that a defendant such as McIntosh could hope for. Experienced, aggressive, and well-prepared, he attacked Billie Jo Lambert and her character, apparently with devastating effect. He also worked steadily to undermine the impact of the expert testimony that the state had to take such pains to present, largely because of the lingering doubts about the identity of the body from the oil field. Statham cannily played against the jury's suspicions of outsiders and experts. In his questioning of one of the dental experts, he mispronounced the word "incisor" by using a short i in the second syllable. Why? To show the jury that he too was a bit baffled by these scientists with their obtuse notions that flew in the face of democratic common sense and plain ways.[54]

One member of the 1972 jury later told a relative: "We had the right man," meaning that in the eyes of this juror, at least, the man on trial was responsible for the crime. But, continued that juror, "they didn't prove it."[55] Remarks from surviving jurors—made both on and off the record—suggest that the men and women who deliberated McIntosh's fate heard a story about which some of them had already formed an opinion; not all of those opinions held that McIntosh was innocent. Some people in Pike County, then and later, some who were on the jury and some who were not, believed that the right man was on trial for the crime. But the state simply could not offer a compelling reason to convict McIntosh. The unanimous verdict of not guilty, reached in about two hours, meant literally that the jury did not find that the state had proved McIntosh's guilt beyond a reasonable doubt. A polished defense offered them a story that did not allow them to convict McIntosh based upon the evidence offered, when that evidence was largely the testimony of Billie Jo Lambert, a witness whose character and reputation had been sullied through Statham's effective work. No conspiracy to fix this jury was involved or was necessary.

The state could not present a witness who saw anyone slay Tina Andrews. The state's main witness, Lambert, presented a detailed story about the circumstances that led the two girls to the oil field and the identities of the men who took them there. But as in 1971, the defense was able to cast doubt upon a number of elements of Lambert's story. Most significant, perhaps, was the defense's ability to provide testimony that placed both McIntosh and Fleming somewhere other than downtown McComb and a location off Delaware Avenue Extension on the evening of August 13, 1969. Another major weakness that the defense attacked was the time that it had taken Lambert to come to McComb authorities with her story. What difference would it have made to the investigation and to the state's case if Lambert had come forward more quickly? It is difficult to say what additional evidence that might have yielded.

As it stood, the defense effectively attacked both the gaps in Lambert's memory and her reasons for keeping silent for so long.

A principal job of both the defense and the state is to tell a persuasive story to a jury. Perhaps the jury was skeptical why, despite Lambert's continued protestations, someone who had seen such a thing would not trust Pike County authorities and institutions. The jury consisted in part of men and women who did not wish to believe that a fundamental institution like the McComb Police Department was corrupted with murderers. Some might have felt that on some level, a girl like Tina Andrews might have received no more than she deserved. As a McComb woman told me recently: "When this happened, Tina was just twelve years old. People in town didn't know who she was. But they did know about her family, and they judged her based on what they thought they knew about them. They thought her family was trashy, and they thought that she was, too, and so they didn't care about her."[56] Other jurors, the black jurors, probably were less inclined toward respect for the McComb police. But they heard the same evidence that the white jurors did. None were ultimately persuaded that the state had made its case, at least beyond a reasonable doubt.

As in 1971, the courthouse in Magnolia was overcrowded with observers. But for those who did not wish to drive to the courthouse in Magnolia, what did they learn of the case? Compared with the 1971 trial, the coverage of the 1972 trial in the local newspaper is spare. In 1971, the paper published many columns of detailed summary of testimony. In 1972, it did not. Also conspicuous is the absence in 1972 of any photographs of anyone associated with the trial. Other than a picture of the new district attorney and the new prosecutor just before the court term began, one saw no photograph of Tina Andrews or Richard McIntosh or the oil field. Billie Jo Lambert's photograph never appeared at any point in either trial. The paper in 1972, however, did feature many photographs of bewhiskered men and costumed locals celebrating the city's centennial. Many editorial columns by Oliver Emmerich celebrated the positive and the upbeat about the city. There is evidence that some people—at least the ones editing the *Enterprise-Journal*—were tired of Tina Andrews by 1972. When the newspaper compiled a list of the top area stories of 1972, the celebration of the city's centennial was "the news story of 1972." Also high on the list were urban renewal, that year's elections, ambulance service problems, "and way down in ninth place was more about the Andrews murder case."[57]

The verdict excited no public expressions of outrage or even of strong disappointment, with no calls to seek new evidence or a better understanding of what had happened to Tina Andrews. Privately, reaction was mixed, with many people certain that justice had not been done. Some people, then and later, believed that McIntosh and Fleming were not guilty of any crime, as they both were not by the measure of Mississippi justice. How did Tina Andrews's family react to this second disappointment in finding someone to punish for the death of their child? As they had done throughout the entire case, they kept their reactions to themselves.

The circumstances of the 1972 acquittal help allay several long-standing rumors about the case. A deliberation of two and a half hours, with no evidence of the jury asking for clarification of any points of law, suggests that they did not have undue difficulty reaching their conclusion. But neither was it so quick a verdict that one might suspect a too-light consideration of the matter, a habit that Mississippi juries in other times and places had practiced. The presence in the courtroom of Judge Darwin Maples from Lucedale seems not to have made any difference in the 1972 outcome. Maples made no rulings that were significantly different than the ones made by Roach in 1971. Neither judge, in fact, was inordinately involved or conspicuously intrusive, certainly not in any partisan fashion. But what Judge Maples's presence does preclude is the telling of the story as one about the collusion of Pike County authorities to cover up a police crime or some broader pattern of criminal activity. Mississippi was indeed a small place, especially in the days when white men still held a near-monopoly on positions of authority. But Darwin Maples was not a Pike County man.

A Navy veteran and a graduate of the University of Mississippi School of Law, Maples served two terms in the Mississippi House of Representatives in the 1950s. Like the other attorneys involved in the two trials, Maples had held a number of local and county offices, typical for a well-respected small-town attorney, then and later in Mississippi. He served as prosecutor for his native George County and also represented the Board of Supervisors there. In 1972, Maples was a ten-year veteran of the bench, serving as Circuit Judge for George, Greene, and Jackson Counties, a tier of counties in extreme southeastern Mississippi that included very lightly populated areas as well as the larger Gulf Coast cities of Pascagoula and Moss Point. He would go on to serve three decades in that position, retiring as one of the senior judges in the state. His tenure was marked by a number of innovative measures, including restitution programs as well as instituting pay for the public defender position. He heard cases in the 1960s involving Ku Klux Klan violence in the area and earned a reputation as a well-respected presence on the bench. In the 1972 trial in Pike County, neither the state nor the defense could have found much to complain about in the selection of Judge Maples to hear the case.[58] As an outsider in Pike County, Maples had no particular stake in the outcome of this trial.

Considered within the context of other cases that were tried in the Pike County Circuit Court in 1971 and 1972, some matters about the case against Richard McIntosh are unusual, while others are not. The indictments against McIntosh and Ted Fleming were among thirty-four returned on March 17, 1971, a large number for a Pike County grand jury in those days. If one studies the large, folio-sized pages on which the Pike County Circuit Court docket was written, one fact is striking. Compared with any of the other indictments returned that day, the case of the state of Mississippi versus Richard McIntosh and Ted Fleming was remarkably more active, measured in terms of docket entries, than any other. In the matter of Francis Noel Hines, the McColgan burglary case tried in early 1972 by district attorney Jim Kitchens, the docket entries, from indictment through motions to produce through the recording of a hung jury, occupy twenty-five lines. McIntosh and Fleming's cases, on the other hand, had to be carried over to later pages several times, ultimately consuming ninety lines. But of course the Andrews murder case was complex, with defense attorneys filing motions for two defendants from March 1971 into the second trial in April 1972.[59]

The March 1972 court term featured three murder charges, not counting the pending cases against McIntosh and Fleming. More than twenty cases had been carried over from the fall's term, giving new men Kitchens and Roach a good deal to handle. Murder charges were brought against Michael Zackery, represented by Statham and Watkins; Wade Washington, also represented by Statham and Watkins; and Roosevelt Wells, represented by a court-appointed attorney. All three men pled not guilty. Zackery withdrew his guilty plea on the murder charge, a Christmas Eve slaying of William Ross. A guilty plea to a manslaughter charge instead netted him a $1,000 fine and a ten-year prison sentence, suspended. Washington's case was not resolved that term, as Statham and Watkins entered a successful motion to have Washington taken to Whitfield, the state mental hospital, when a bed should become available, to have him assessed for mental competency to stand trial. Back in Pike County for the October term of court, Washington too pled guilty to a manslaughter charge; his three-year sentence at Parchman was not suspended. Wells was the unluckiest of the bunch. He too swapped his not guilty plea on the murder charge for a guilty plea on manslaughter. But his attorney could not keep Judge Roach from sentencing Wells to ten years in prison, not suspended. One of the continued cases, that of Thelma Addison on charges of murder, also ended with a guilty plea for manslaughter and another ten-year sentence, suspended. In Pike County, Mississippi, in 1971 and 1972, it was not strictly speaking easy to enter court and get off scot-free with murder. But it was certainly possible to kill someone, whether a relative, an acquaintance, or a relative stranger, and spend no time in prison.[60]

Plea deals, reduced charges, and suspended sentences often rouse public ire. But prosecutors and defense attorneys alike will tell you that such is the way that business is done in most parts of the country, not just in Pike County, Mississippi. These reduced pleas suggest nothing so much as a court with a very heavy docket and an eagerness to keep matters moving. Some of the pleas for reduced charges also suggest an older element of Mississippi justice: in cases where both the killer and the victim were African American, closing the official books on a case might have seemed more important than exacting the full penalty of the law. Why no plea deal for McIntosh? The state and the defense believed they could get what they wanted at trial rather than through a plea bargain. The defense in this case was correct.

The two trials of Richard McIntosh for the murder of Tina Andrews took place within an eventful period of reckoning and remembrance in the city and the county, even if people would not have thought deliberately about the trial in those terms. In McComb, the community celebrated the city's centennial, an event that allowed white McComb to think about a distant past, rather than a more recent one that had seen such sharp challenges to the Jim Crow order. The city continued to tout itself as a place of great opportunity. At the beginning of 1972, editor Oliver Emmerich again reminded *Enterprise-Journal* readers, as he had done for many, many years, that "it's a privilege to live in the McComb Area, and our goal should be to make it an even greater privilege than ever before."[61]

Much had changed in the city in the late 1960s and early 1970s, not least of which was the collapse of the longtime white southern effort to stem challenges to Jim Crow and to assert that black people in the community were content with their lot. By the 1970s, that fiction was impossible to maintain. But much had not changed in McComb. Despite economic rough times and the fact that black political participation had definitely come, power in McComb remained largely in the hands of the sort of people who had held it since the town's founding. Old names and old families held their positions and their authority, especially in the ways that really matter: the power to transmit inherited wealth over time and the power to signal broader kinds of authority and values. Many of these men of influence did not wish to see two McComb police officers convicted of murder. That would have been bad for the image of McComb. Not perhaps as bad as things had seemed in 1964, but still a step in the wrong direction. There is also no doubt that some of those same people resented and despised Tina Andrews and her family, and Billie Jo Lambert as well, for having put them in this position. But those people did not constitute the juries in the trials of Richard McIntosh. Other Pike County people did. And they did not convict McIntosh.

Broad elements of the white community remained committed to local institutions as the only practicable way to sustain matters of common good: ensuring economic stability, navigating the end of many aspects of racial segregation and the preservation of some others, and reasserting their belief in a basic commonality of white interests. The verdicts in the Tina Andrews trials were in some measure a statement in support of law and order. In 1964, many white McComb residents believed, both outside agitators and blue-collar Klansmen had disrupted an equilibrium that had served the area well for many decades. While black and white residents defined justice in different ways, practically no one in the area regretted the end of bombings and vigilantism. The verdicts in the trials were in no explicit sense a rebuke of the white working class for their activities in the 1960s. Indeed, it was an occasion for a broad spectrum of Pike County—white Pike County, at least, as represented on the juries—to reassert its basic support of the county's law enforcement agencies, courts, and shared values about respectability and gendered behavior. The story of the 1970s in the city would be the fracturing of a white sense of community, one that had been built in large part upon perceived shared interests defined against those of the black population. With the end of that possibility, at least in the ways that it had been defined since the era of Reconstruction, came a retreat into the class-insulated, resource-determined enclaves of a pattern that was emerging not only in the American South, but also in many other parts of the United States. But when Tina Andrews was murdered, that part of the story was yet to unfold.

The grim conclusion that one must reach at the end of the two trials of Richard McIntosh is that in Pike County, Mississippi, someone got away with the murder of Tina Andrews. Twice juries there were asked by the state to believe that McIntosh was guilty of that murder, and twice those juries failed to convict him. One of the great ironies of this tale as a southern story is that black residents of Pike County knew that sometimes things like this happened. They knew that law enforcement officials did not always get the bad guy, and that indeed sometimes they were the bad guy. They knew that not everyone arrested was guilty, and that sometimes people were guilty, but went unpunished. They had seen that no great conspiracy was required for the state either to get or not to get its man when someone was murdered. That was simply a fact of life in Pike County, Mississippi.

9

After the Trials

The Fates of People and the City

Driving on Interstate Highway 55, about an hour and a half south of Jackson one takes exit 18 to reach downtown McComb. Just off the exit and heading east, it is easy to retrace the route down Delaware Avenue that Billie Jo Lambert walked toward her Cherry Street home on the night of August 13, 1969. Near the interstate, Delaware Avenue is thick with fast food restaurants, convenience stores, and strip malls, busier and more brilliantly lighted than the street Lambert and her friend Tina Andrews knew fifty years ago. Much has changed, on Delaware Avenue and in other parts of McComb, too. The Mr. Swiss Drive-In is long gone, as is Plantation Chicken. So is Pete's Place, where Tina might have looked for beer and older companionship. The Tiger's Den has not operated in decades, although the building still exists, along with the street-level stairs down which one walked to enter the establishment. Many landmarks and other features associated with this story, however, remain much as they were fifty years ago, or at least recognizable. The Andrews home on Oak Street still stands, as do those of the Lamberts and the Flemings. So do some of the same dynamics and divisions of race and social class that shaped the trials of 1971 and 1972. The fates of the people who figured in those trials demonstrate many things: fortune and chance, the power of good and bad decisions to form lives. But those fates also show the continuities in the McComb story between the institutions that had been built before Andrews was born, that were challenged during the years she lived, and that continue to exercise power over the city and Andrews's memory to this day.

Coming off that exit to McComb, a turn west still takes one onto Delaware Avenue Extension, and from there to the oil field where Tina Andrews's body was found. The pattern of roads has changed. You cannot drive as directly there now as could two men with two girls in 1969. In the clearing where the body and the couch lay is oil field equipment of recent vintage. Compared with photographs of the 1969 crime scene, the spot is recognizable, but only if you know what happened there five decades ago. On a warm Pike County August evening, such as the one on which I walked the site in 2018, it remains isolated, dark, and silent, except for the sound of cicadas.

After the two trials were over and the case dropped as a formal matter by the state of Mississippi, the name of Tina Andrews did not appear for a long time in the McComb newspaper. Those references came much later, in years well after the early 1970s, mainly upon the retirement of someone who had figured prominently in the trial or investigations of 1969 to 1972. In a 2005 retrospective honoring his long career in the law as well as his distinguished World War II military service, former district attorney and retired circuit judge Joe Pigott said of the Andrews murder, "If I were ever going to write a book, I'd write a book about that case."[1] Pigott never wrote that book. But in his remarks to the reporter, he spoke frankly about substantial matters of the case that had been seriously contested at the trials in 1971 and 1972. His remarks demonstrate, among other things, the ability of a man of his influence, position, and enviable record to say what he liked after a long career.

Pigott explained that three girls who had been enjoying an evening at the Tiger's Den were approached by two men who offered them a ride. Both men were police officers. "They trusted them and got in." Pigott continued: "When the car pulled up to the intersection of Delaware Avenue and James Street, one of the women got out and walked to her home down the block. The others stayed in the car, and travelled to an isolated dirt road leading to an oil well just west of town." In the reporter's account of Pigott's remarks, a significant detail is added, one that is not supported by testimony at either trial: "The girl [Lambert] saw the men shoot Andrews." "Two years later," the story continues, "Pigott received a phone call from someone who claimed to know a woman who witnessed Andrews' killing. The woman recounted details that only a witness could have known."

Pigott's remarks suggest no ambiguity about the fate of Tina Andrews that evening in 1969 or the identity of the men who took her to her death. So why was he not able to win a conviction in 1971? "First of all, we had to prove who [the two men were], and that was not easy." Pigott's comments suggest as well some of the pressures under which he and his successor, Jim Kitchens, operated. "When a district attorney fingers police officers in a killing, it can lead to rocky working relationships." His wife added, "Everything went against him." Without giving her name, Pigott praised Billie Jo Lambert: "Man, she made a fantastic witness." The reporter continued, "Defense attorneys cross-examined Pigott's star witness for three days, but she never budged." Pigott concluded, "There were several suspects, but it turned out that it couldn't have been any of them," leaving no doubt in the reader's mind that Pigott believed that he had the right men, but simply could not win a conviction. The *Enterprise-Journal* contained a significant error, one that speaks to the ways in which the case was sometimes remembered in the community. "One of the officers pleaded guilty, and the other's case ended in a hung jury, he said," a conclusion that must have been a reporter's error in hearing Pigott's remarks. In the newspaper's next issue was a correction, telling readers that neither man had been convicted.[2] Similarly, in a 1992 article on the occasion of Judge Pigott's resignation from the bench, the newspaper noted the case in almost the same words: "Two Mc-Comb police officers were indicted for the killing. One officer pleaded guilty and the other's trial ended in a hung jury."[3] For that story, no correction was ever issued.

Of the men and women who played central roles in the story that unfolded from 1969 through 1972, some died relatively young; others are still living as of the year 2019. Some stayed in Pike County; others moved away. Some became more prominent than they were in the early 1970s; others all but disappeared. But one fact remains: no one was ever convicted for the killing of Tina Andrews. A McComb man told me recently, "A lot of people in town just wanted to forget about the Tina Andrews case. Or maybe it's better to say that they didn't have to try very hard to forget it. Tina and her family were not people you thought about a lot, if they weren't your family. And even if they were, a lot of people in McComb didn't want to think about them any more than they had to."[4]

With the acquittal of Richard McIntosh in April 1972 and the *nolle prosequi* entered by District Attorney Jim Kitchens in the case of Ted Fleming, the Pike County Circuit Court and the legal system of Mississippi were finished with the men. Both McIntosh and Fleming were free immediately to resume their lives. And so they did. Because of his acquittal, McIntosh could never be tried again on the same charges. Fleming, on the other hand, might have been tried again, as the charges were dismissed without prejudice, a legal distinction that meant that a future Pike County district attorney might have reopened the case. But none ever did.

Neither McIntosh nor Fleming ever again wore the uniform of the McComb Police Department. A matter not addressed through their year-long suspension was whether it was a paid or unpaid suspension, and more specifically, whether a lifting of the suspension would result not only in the men's reinstatement to the police department, but also in their being paid back salary. The McComb City Board met shortly after the end of the April 1972 trial. While the board's session was private, "the consensus of the board seemed to be that the two officers should not be reinstated; that, even though cleared in the courts, the charges and publicity surrounding them damaged their effectiveness as officers." Should they receive back pay? The board deferred that decision "for further study and research."[5] There is no evidence whether or not the attorneys for Fleming and McIntosh were part of these discussions, or indeed if the men retained legal counsel for any purposes after the April acquittal of McIntosh and the dismissal of charges against Fleming. In a recent conversation, one of Fleming's attorneys said that with the legal charges dropped in April 1972, his representation of Fleming was over.[6]

In a decision that surely featured much interesting off-the-record conversation, the McComb City Board on April 25, 1972, voted to offer the men 50 percent of their salaries for a year in exchange for their signing an agreement not to seek further claims against the city. That same day, the city's Retirement and Disability Board agreed to reimburse the men all that they had paid into the retirement fund. The McComb City Board's 50 percent proposal was formally made by P. A. Deere, the head of the police committee. It was seconded by the chairman of the finance committee, Herbert Wilmesherr, and unanimously approved by board members Jewel D. Conerly, Harvey Vest, Philip Brady, and Cliff White. In language that was boilerplate, but which nevertheless rings true here, the board's formal resolution held that the settlement was merited by "the immediate and temporary, as well as the permanent, health, safety, finances and public safety and convenience."[7] Mayor John S. Thompson approved the resolution. Given the dismissal of the legal charges against both men, why did they accept the city's offer and not seek to return to their jobs as police officers? Why, at the least, did they not seek back pay for the period of their suspension? City Attorney W. A. Wiltshire said that "legally there is a question, but probably they are entitled to some compensation. The law is not clear in such cases, and despite considerable research, no concrete precedents were found."[8]

Ted Fleming agreed almost immediately to the city's offer. "He said that while he would like to return to police work, he realized the handicap that the publicity and rumors surrounding the charges would place upon himself and his fellow officers." Instead, said Fleming, he planned to enter the refrigeration business.[9] Eventually, Fleming did just that, opening Southwest Refrigeration and Air Conditioning, advertising twenty years of experience in the field.[10] Before that venture, however, Fleming tried his hand at fried chicken; he and his wife took over an established restaurant, "Tom & Til's Fried Chicken," offering patrons "the same good fried chicken . . . nothing changed but the location!"[11] Fleming, having never stood trial in the Andrews case, worked diligently over the years to live in McComb as if no legal entanglement had ever befallen him.

Richard McIntosh was not as quick as Fleming to accept the city's offer, telling the newspaper that he "preferred not to make a statement until receiving official notification from the city about the offer." Just after his acquittal, he worked for an area automobile dealership, Sam Owen's Chevrolet, in Magnolia. With his legal affairs settled, McIntosh had significant personal news. In early May 1972, he announced his engagement to Kathy Gay Hess of Liberty, Mississippi, some twenty-five miles west of McComb in neighboring Amite County. Theirs was a very short engagement; the couple were married at the Liberty Baptist Church on May 20. A graduate of the University of Southern Mississippi, the new Mrs. McIntosh planned to teach in the McComb public schools.[12]

Pike County dealt with a final piece of business stemming from the McIntosh trials: the cost of the preparation of a 1971 trial transcript. A transcript and two copies had been made, all to aid the prosecution team of Kitchens and Roach in preparing the case for the 1972 term. The Jackson-based court reporter, Ed Mills, billed the city $900, a sum that some members of the board of supervisors felt was inordinately high. The board announced that they would "investigate further" before tendering payment.[13] Other than that loose end, the county and the city seem then to have marked down the matter of McIntosh, Fleming, and Tina Andrews as a closed account.

In the years immediately following the trials, the biggest story in McComb involved neither a murder nor a police scandal, but rather a storm. On January 10, 1975, the city was struck by an intense tornado. Entering the town from the southwest, the tornado cut a path approximately two blocks wide and thirty-eight blocks long. The city's downtown business district was spared, but other business and many residential areas were hit hard, including a "black government housing project," as a contemporary account put it. Four people in the McComb area were killed. The toll could have been worse, as the storm struck North Pike Elementary School. "Here, indeed, was evidence of the Lord's mighty protection, for even though there were injuries, there were no deaths."[14] McComb dug out. Local businessman Thomas Austin, juror in the 1971 McIntosh trial, coordinated distribution of donated financial relief, serving as president of the McComb–Southwest Mississippi Tornado Relief Fund. Elvis Presley held a benefit concert in Jackson for the residents of Pike County and other areas of the state damaged by the storms. Later, in gratitude for the King's help, the city renamed a stretch of state Highway 98 running through south McComb as Elvis Presley Boulevard.[15]

But if McComb people were grateful for the King's help, as well as for that of the Lord, some white residents remained suspicious of other authorities. Why was federal disaster aid slow in coming? "That old familiar feeling of paranoia felt by Mississippians toward the federal government returned and once again we wondered if the federal government was going to 'punish' us for misuse of funds in other areas by tornado victims and use us as a 'whipping post' as it sometimes seems they have been doing since Civil War days. . . . Were we paranoid thinking we weren't getting the needed help because we were who we were? Mississippians who have long been living in the experimental state for new amendments which ten years after we began compliance, other Americans living in the northeastern part of the United States were just beginning to fight not to comply with?"[16] In McComb in 1975, even the response to a devastating tornado, at least the response from this observer, demonstrated still-simmering resentment toward the previous decade's social changes and the "amendments" the national government wrought in the life of the Deep South.

By the late 1970s, one of the things that had changed in McComb was the pattern of teenage recreation and romance that Tina Andrews, Billie Jo Lambert, and their acquaintances, younger and older, had known. A high school student observed that the "typical Saturday night for a McComb teenager is to get a tank of gas, take off for McDonalds, speed down Delaware, through Sonic, down Delaware again, through Burger King, and back up Delaware again." Fast food restaurant franchises hit McComb in the 1970s, as in many small Mississippi towns. What of downtown, including places such as the Tiger's Den and Gillis Drug Store, that had been an integral part of the social lives of young McComb people—the white ones, at least? The downtown area had been reshaped into what many had hoped would be an outdoor, pedestrian-friendly mall. But many people found, as did the above high school student, that the closing off of key downtown streets to automobile traffic "made it more difficult and certainly more inaccessible to shop in downtown McComb." Downtown was no longer the social or economic center of the city. By the 1980s, young people knew of the Tiger's Den only as a nickname for the home venues for the McComb High School sports teams.[17] And the old cruising and parking habits? The March 3, 1978, issue of the *Enterprise-Journal*, devoted heavily to the views of young people on McComb, published a half-page photograph of a dirt road leading through pine woods to an oil field site. A newspaper staffer, one with either a very wicked sense of the significance of the scene in the Tina Andrews case, or perhaps not, wrote: "This lane off Smithdale Road probably won't mean much to today's teens who dominate the Delaware scene. Oil wells use to be prime areas for young sweethearts to park for socializing, especially on weekends."[18]

What of changes in racial matters in town since the mid-1960s, particularly public school integration? One student observed, in comments that could have been made of most Mississippi towns then and for years to come: "In many aspects the students are as far apart as they were before. We go to school together, but outside of school, we never do anything together." Homecoming week represented a partial exception, when "blacks and whites work together for the benefit of their team and class." But at the end of homecoming week, "the blacks have their homecoming dance and the whites have theirs. Many people like this way of doing things and want no change."[19]

Through these years of Pike County's adjustment to economic and social changes, one thing remained consistent. Ted Fleming did not disappear from the community. Nor did he ever behave publicly as if he had anything to hide or for which he should feel ashamed. While he could have faced a fresh criminal prosecution for Tina Andrews's murder, Fleming never seemed to act like it. Three years after the dismissal of the charges against him, Fleming still had a taste for law enforcement. In late winter 1975, "Teddy J. 'Ted' Fleming, McComb businessman," filed to run for Pike County constable in the third district.[20] Voters were not persuaded, with Fleming finishing a distant third place among three candidates.[21]

Fleming retained the friendship and indeed the respect of some people in McComb. In 1975, he was vice president of the McComb Evening Lion's Club, a men's service organization. By 1976, he took over management of McComb Bowl, in the Plaza Shopping Center. In 1979, he chaired the bowling group for the local March of Dimes Sports Festival. That same year he ran again for constable. His campaign advertisement in this unsuccessful second bid promised a man who believed in "close cooperation between all law enforcement personnel," the pattern followed by the sheriff's department and the police department in Pike County between 1969 and 1971.[22] Only a reader with a particular sense of irony would note that Fleming also promised "firm but moderate treatment for our youth." The results were again not favorable, with Fleming finishing third of five candidates in the August primary.[23] A man with no quit in him, especially on this score, he tried again for constable in 1984, when he promised "a man with experience" and vowed to make the area "a better and safer place to live and to raise our children."[24] He lost that race, too.

Fleming never moved from McComb after the trials of Richard McIntosh. His wife, the former Agnes Bellipanni, was a member of the small but significant Catholic minority in McComb, a longtime parishioner of St. Alphonsus Catholic Church on Delaware Avenue. Fleming had been married previously. In 1960, he sued his wife Idelle Charlene Fleming, then living in Gurnee, Illinois, for divorce.[25] Married in Illinois in 1953, they returned to McComb, where Fleming had previously lived, in 1954. No children were born during their seven-year marriage, which seems to have been an unhappy one, but it is also a matter that has nothing to do with the trouble in which Fleming found himself in 1971. Later that same year of 1960, he married Agnes Bellipanni, to whom he remained married until his death forty-four years later. She survived him by less than three years. If she wondered about his involvement in the Tina Andrews case, she kept those questions close to her heart. People in the community who remember "Sister," as she was called, say that she did not talk about the matter, and very few people indeed ever asked her about it.[26]

Ted Fleming very occasionally had official contact with his former police colleagues and with the Pike County justice system. In 1989, his house on Georgia Avenue was burglarized. Thieves made off with electronics equipment, including a Bearcat scanner, with which he could have listened to the police work that he enjoyed and clearly missed.[27] Years later, the police again came to his house, this time when his ten-year-old Lincoln Continental automobile caught fire. Unlike Richard McIntosh, Ted Fleming did return to face a jury in the Pike County Courthouse. This time he was a plaintiff, not a defendant, as he might have been in 1971 or 1972. In 1987, he successfully sued the McDonald's restaurant on Delaware Avenue for injuries received during the 1984 McComb Christmas parade when he fell over one of their portable signs and hurt his leg. His wife Agnes testified on his behalf. The jury deliberated for two hours, about as long as it had done in McIntosh's second trial, in 1972, before deciding in Fleming's favor and awarding him $3,500 in damages, a small sum compared with the bonanzas Mississippi juries would become famous for awarding injury victims in the next decade.[28]

One can watch Fleming age in photographs in the local paper. He was the kind of man who seems always to have smiled in the presence of a camera, although no one remembers him as handsome, as they did McIntosh, his former partner-in-indictment. He appears as manager of the bowling alley, and with his wife witnessing his son Chad sign a scholarship offer to play tennis at Southwest Mississippi Community College. His health began to go downhill a bit in the late 1990s, but he rallied and still enjoyed bowling when he felt like it. He did that often, right down to his death in 2004. Fleming was remembered with respect by area bowlers, who inducted him into the Pike County Bowling Association's Memorial Hall of Fame in 2010. The taste for bowling also passed to the next Fleming generation; that same year his son Chad rolled a perfect 300 game.[29] Ted Fleming's name appeared many dozens of times in the local newspaper in the years after 1972, but with the exception of his unsuccessful campaigns for constable, and one or two other instances, always to give the news of his latest bowling activities, as a player or manager, and never in connection with his 1971 arrest for Tina Andrews's murder. But despite his longtime residence in McComb and indeed prominence of a sort in the community, his obituary was not printed in that newspaper.

In the years after Richard McIntosh's acquittal of murder charges in 1972, his life followed a different pattern than that of Fleming, one less visible and more wandering. A McComb woman said, "After the trial, it's like Richard just dropped off the face of the earth. You never heard of him again."[30] So it would appear to many McComb people. Unlike Fleming, McIntosh did not run for public office, operate a business in the city, sue any local business for an injury received there, or spend the rest of his life in McComb. McIntosh did remain in the area for several years after his acquittal, certainly into the mid-1970s. Within a few years, however, McIntosh left McComb, living out of state in various places, including Arizona and North Carolina.[31] His mother, Elma Evans McIntosh, continued to live in Pike County, but not in McComb. She moved to Summit, just a few miles north of town, where she died in 1987. Six children survived her, including Richard, who was living then in Prescott, Arizona. Other McIntosh family members stayed in the area. They were what locals would have called working people. His sister Reba trained as a secretary at Southwest Mississippi Junior College and took a job at the local Kellwood Company.[32]

But they all left the old family house on Sedgewick in the public housing development of White Acres, another McComb place that changed in the 1970s. When McIntosh's name comes up these days, one is often told that he grew up in White Acres, a fact that several people mentioned to me as if it would reveal something fundamental about the man. McComb people, like many other Americans, often talk about social class without using the term. "Living in White Acres" would not have been thought of in the 1950s and 1960s as "living in public housing" in the sense that white Mississippians now think of it, but public housing indeed it was. But "White Acres" did not carry the same disapproving judgment about behavior and values that invocations of "east McComb" did, where Billie Jo Lambert and her family lived. "White Acres" signaled modest means—people "who worked hard, but who didn't have a lot of money," a local woman told me, "but not trashy." "But trashy? That's what a lot of people thought about east McComb. Now that was considered the wrong side of the tracks."[33] These days in McComb, "White Acres" carries a different valence for several reasons, including the fact that for the last few decades, White Acres has been almost exclusively black.

Richard McIntosh eventually returned to the area, but not to McComb, or even to Pike County. Apparently family interests brought him back to southwestern Mississippi. But not for a while, certainly not in the 1970s. By 1979,

Richard and Kathy Hess McIntosh had started a family, with a four-year-old son, Richard Wesley, and a new baby boy, Kyle, born in Lumberton, North Carolina, when the couple lived in Fair Bluff.[34] Through the 1980s, McIntosh lived quietly, it appears, in several states before finally returning to Mississippi, this time to Amite County, just west of Pike County. By 1990, McIntosh sang in a wedding at his old church, South McComb Baptist, in October of that year; his son Wes served as an usher. By 1992, the year his mother-in-law died, he lived in Liberty, where he has remained. His son Wes would graduate from Amite School Center in Liberty, and he would, like his father, attend the community college in Summit. He took a job in Baton Rouge, again like his father, and in 1999 married a girl he had met there; presumably Richard and Kathy would then have grandchildren to look forward to.[35]

In recent years, Richard McIntosh has remained at Liberty. He has lived a life out of the public eye—much as he prefers it, one imagines. Nothing that he might have done since 1972 has brought him before the courts or into the public record in an unfavorable light, short of occasional newspaper stories mentioning the murder of Tina Andrews; his name, however, has not appeared in those stories. In the last decade, he has worked construction, even helping to install playground equipment at his old church, South McComb Baptist.[36] In 2015, McIntosh, along with other members of the McComb High School class of 1965, participated in "five days of fun with friends" at his fiftieth class reunion. A smiling, bearded McIntosh appears in a color photograph in the local newspaper with several dozen of his classmates, with a number of whom he retains ties of friendship and acquaintance.[37] But why should he not? In the eyes of the state of Mississippi, he was found not guilty of the murder of Tina Andrews.

Tina Andrews's family remembered their child. In 1999, a paid advertisement appeared in the *Enterprise-Journal*, "In Loving Memory of Tina Marie Andrews, 3/23/57–8/13/69." Featuring a photo other than the school picture that had appeared in the newspaper decades earlier, this one showed a younger child, who faced the camera directly and wore a sweet expression. The memorial continued: "30 years have passed since she was taken from us. Our grief and sorrow still remain. Sadly missed and never forgotten, Mother, Sisters & Brothers."[38] In the 1970s and following years, all the remaining Andrews family left McComb; some of them would eventually return. Fred and Doris Andrews stayed on Oak Street for a short time after the trials, but that situation would not last long. By 1973, Fred Andrews was a delinquent payer of his property taxes in Pike County. In 1974, he seemingly had moved out of the Oak Street house, and was being sued ("whose Post Office Box and Street Address after diligent search is unknown") in the Pike County Chancery Court by the Bank of McComb, likely for his mortgage or another loan.[39]

Their adult children had already moved from McComb, many of them out of state. In 1983, Tina's brother Freddie, then living at a Louisiana address, was convicted in McComb City Court of a drunk-driving charge.[40] As a young man, Freddie was certainly something of what Richard McIntosh and B. D. Statham tried to tell the court in 1971: known to local law enforcement as a young man who might be headed toward unfortunate things. But the presentation Freddie made to McComb was not necessarily an indication of bad character, but rather perhaps the persona of a defiant young man reacting against many difficulties at home as well as public slights about his family's reputation and status. Freddie Andrews was not forever the teenager who was on a path to trouble in McComb. He grew up, moved away, and made a life for himself, an opportunity that his little sister never had. One of his cousins remembered learning of Freddie's death years later only by reading his obituary in the New Orleans *Times-Picayune*. Freddie, a man whose alleged reputation both Statham and Watkins had attempted to make an issue in the trials, died of cancer in Lucedale, Mississippi, where his mother had been born, in 2014. Fred Paul Andrews, Jr., the last surviving son of Fred and Doris, was sixty-eight.[41]

Fred Andrews, the father of the family, was a World War II veteran, having served in the Marine Corps. He was a working man, or tried to be. Like much of his family, he spent time in Louisiana, working in Baton Rouge for Gulf States Fabricators, manufacturer of steel tanks, bins, piping, and plate work. But he returned to Pike County, where he had been born in 1914, and died at Southwest Mississippi Regional Medical Center in 1984, after a long illness. As with his daughter Tina, his funeral services were held at Hartman Funeral Home. His was a life marked by sorrow and disappointment and not by much of what his family and neighbors would have termed material success.[42] As is usually the case, Fred Andrews's relative failures likely seemed keener because of his relatives' successes. Of his brother, and occasional business partner, Karey, people in McComb said, "Everything he touched turned to gold. It wasn't like that for Fred."[43]

Tina's mother, Doris Havard Andrews, died in 2002, while living in Denham Springs, Louisiana, about seventy-five miles southwest of McComb. At her death, four of Doris Andrews's daughters were living in Louisiana, one in River Ridge, and three there in Denham Springs, including Donna and Winifred, both of whom had testified in Pike County Circuit Court during the trials. Along with Tina and a girl, Eunice Pauline Andrews, who had died very young, two of Doris' sons, Danny Walton Andrews and Michael Perry Andrews, had predeceased her, as had her husband Fred. Fred and Doris Andrews are buried in McComb's Hollywood Cemetery, next to their daughter Tina.[44] McComb was not a place where any of the Andrews family experienced much respect or regard from the community. One can understand why Tina's siblings left the area. But they chose or followed their parents' wishes in choosing to put them to rest there.

Some of the attorneys who represented one side or the other in the case went on to long and successful careers. Others did not. By every measure, B. D. Statham's professional career was rewarding: Navy veteran, F.B.I. agent, mayor of Magnolia, state senator, and perhaps the most sought-after defense attorney in his part of the state. But he lived only three more years after winning the acquittal of Richard McIntosh. He died in Magnolia on July 10, 1975. He was, the McComb newspaper noted, the "unfortunate victim of a malignancy." Statham was an attorney worth paying simply to watch in action, as long as you did not face him as an adversary, as did Billie Jo Lambert. Richard McIntosh, so far as one can tell, owed his freedom to Statham's effective counsel. One hopes that he paid his respects to Statham in one fashion or another. The legal establishment of Pike County did, as the flag flew at half-staff at the courthouse in Statham's honor. One of his pallbearers was Sheriff "Tot" Lawson. Statham was only sixty years old.[45]

The life of William Franklin Watkins, Statham's young partner and associate in the 1971 and 1972 trials, did not bear out the promise of his youth. A man with deep roots in the area, ones of which he was proud, Watkins was born in McComb in 1942 and grew up in Summit. He graduated from McComb High School and Millsaps College. Watkins attended graduate school in German at the University of Mississippi, where he earned his law degree. At all stages an excellent student, he retained throughout his life a range of intellectual interests, particularly literature and theater. In 1968, he married Jean Maitre, a New Orleans native and fellow Ole Miss graduate. The young couple moved to Magnolia, where he joined Statham in the newly renamed firm of Statham and Watkins. By 1974, the couple had two daughters.[46] Busy with legal work and social activities, William Watkins seemed to be well on his way to a successful career and fruitful life.

Unlike many of his contemporaries in the 1970s who found the Republican Party a congenial home, Watkins was and remained a Democrat, serving as party chairman for Pike County in the 1970s. He succeeded his former partner, B. D. Statham, as attorney for the Board of Supervisors, serving seven years before being replaced in 1982 as a result of "personal differences between himself and several board members." His law firm continued to operate as Statham and Watkins, even as another attorney, Keith Starrett, became his partner. He handled his share of cases in the Pike County Circuit Court. Joe Pigott had replaced Gordon Roach as judge; other attorneys from Watkins's earliest days of practice remained familiar faces in that courthouse as well. Other matters did not go as well for Watkins. After Statham's early death, their law firm, by 1978 called Statham, Watkins, Starrett, and Mitchell, did not match its earlier pattern of success. Watkins never developed the formidable reputation of Statham, but few attorneys in the area did. In other ways, Watkins foundered, personally and professionally. By the end of the decade, he and his wife divorced. He remarried in 1981, this time to Magnolia native Lynn Lampton.[47]

Watkins tried his hand in the area's oil and gas business, founding Estrellita Oil while continuing to practice law. By the late 1980s and early 1990s, he enjoyed poor luck in business deals, leading to loan defaults and eventually his filing bankruptcy. Things became worse for Watkins; he later faced various federal fraud charges.[48] In March 1991, he pled guilty to two counts stemming from a Louisiana indictment and three from a Mississippi indictment, charges that he had falsified land title records to receive bank loans. Later that same year, he was disbarred from the practice of law by the state of Mississippi. He also developed a reputation in Pike County for decisions marred by financial exigencies and drinking. Naturally, Watkins maintained that allegations of financial impropriety were greatly exaggerated. "The examinations made over a twelve-year period," said Watkins, "revealed irregularities on four relatively minor loans." His financial records had been combed, he said, only because of the efforts "of a couple of people here in our community." But a Mississippi Supreme Court justice who heard the disbarment proceedings disagreed, saying: "Here was an attorney desperate for money, and who did not care who got hurt, as long as it was not himself."[49]

Once a young man of talent, Watkins might have been marked for a long career in local legal practice or perhaps even in politics. But that was not to be. The fallout from his legal and financial troubles continued through the 1990s and indeed after Watkins's death. As of 2019, his estate is still defending claims brought against his failed oil company.[50] Watkins died in 2008 at the relatively young age of sixty-five. He is recalled in McComb as a bright and able man, one of charm and refinement, one with whom it was pleasant to socialize, but perhaps one best to steer clear of in financial dealings.[51] "Of all the lawyers involved in the case," a local man remembers, "he was the smartest. Not necessarily the best lawyer, but overall the smartest man." Not every Mississippi attorney's obituary speaks of the person's love for Rilke and Goethe, writers Watkins enjoyed reading in German.[52]

Highway patrol investigator Donald Butler, involved in the Andrews case from the discovery of the body through both trials, enjoyed a storied career, both before and after his testimony in the Pike County Courthouse. Butler knew southwest Mississippi intimately. Born on a farm near Liberty in Amite County, the son of a sheriff's deputy, he spent forty-seven years in law enforcement. An excellent football player at Liberty High School and later at Southwest Mississippi Junior College, Butler was then and later a man of formidable, indeed intimidating stature. He weighed two hundred pounds in his prep football days in an era when that would have made a standard size for an NFL player.[53] After service in the Marine Corps, Butler joined the state highway patrol, beginning as a dispatcher in 1962 and by 1964 moving into an active role as an investigator, with study in 1966 at the F.B.I.'s National Police Academy. He was a superb pistol marksman, a skill that would serve him well over the years. The local newspaper ran a photograph of Butler with F.B.I. director J. Edgar Hoover presenting him a certificate for his perfect score on an F.B.I. marksman's shooting range.[54] In the mid- and late 1960s, Butler worked a variety of cases, including robberies and other violent crime, and also observed and investigated incidents arising from civil rights activism in southwestern Mississippi. By the end of the decade, his work involved close cooperation with many of the principal figures in the Andrews case, including District Attorney Joe Pigott and Sheriff "Tot" Lawson.[55]

By 1980, Butler had risen to the post of chief of the southern division of the Mississippi Highway Patrol. In that year, Governor William Winter named him chief of the Mississippi Highway Patrol, where he dealt with the continued desegregation of the patrol. In 1984, Butler became head of the state's Bureau of Narcotics, a position he held until 1988.[56] At the end of his career, Butler returned to his roots in southwestern Mississippi, first working as a consultant for Sheriff "Tot" Lawson's Pike County department and then in Amite County, where he served as chief sheriff's deputy for five years.[57] His sheriff, Gene McClendon, said that Butler was "as good in law enforcement as anybody in the country or in the state." After the election of a new sheriff in 1999, Butler retired from that position. But he was not finished with law enforcement. In 2004 he returned to the Mississippi Bureau of Narcotics, this time as the deputy director.[58] It was there in Amite County that he died in 2009 at age seventy-three, "still on the job," as the local paper put it.[59]

Butler demanded professionalism from those who worked with him. "A lot of this sorriness lies with us," he said upon surveying some of his fellow troopers upon taking the chief position in 1980. "We hire them, put a badge on them—then go to court and wonder why they didn't read the defendant his rights."[60] But Butler was more than an administrator. He went undercover in prison to expose corruption at Parchman, extracted a confession from a Klansman to break an infamous civil rights-era slaying, and tracked down mobsters.[61] Of all the men profiled in this book, Donald Butler would make the most intriguing subject for a movie. Jim Kitchens, who also enjoyed an enviable career, respected Butler's tenacity and integrity so much that he hired him as an investigator for his law firm when he returned to private practice.[62] Was Butler a "dangerous man," as someone in McComb told me? In some ways, yes, indeed. Butler was a man you would want on your side, and no one you would wish to cross.

Sheriff Robert "Tot" Lawson had a storied career, too, albeit for different reasons than Butler. Lawson lived to a ripe old age, dying at home in Magnolia on June 12, 2011, at age eighty-eight. A fixture on the Pike County scene for decades, he served as town marshal of Magnolia for nearly two decades beginning in the late 1940s. Lawson lived into a new era in Mississippi law enforcement, one in which sheriffs were allowed to serve consecutive terms in office. Elected sheriff in 1966, he went on to serve five terms, winning reelection in 1968, 1972, and 1976. In 1980 he chose not to run, but clearly still had the itch to be sheriff. Voters sent him back into office after the 1988 election. He left office in 1990 after an abbreviated term. Lawson attempted a comeback in 1992, but Pike County voters chose the incumbent over Lawson by a wide margin. After that, he was elected police chief of Magnolia, serving multiple terms. At his death, colleagues remembered Lawson at his best. Joe Pigott, with whom Lawson had worked during Pigott's many years as district attorney and circuit judge, said of him: "He was a good law enforcement officer and did his best to keep Magnolia a safe place," certainly a fair but restrained statement.[63] The current sheriff in 2019, Mark Shepherd, added: "Tot was a legendary law enforcement officer. Tot was around for many years," again both accurate appraisals, the careful kind of thing one would wish to say of the dead.

Lawson's last years as sheriff were clouded by scandal, which led to his resignation in January 1990. One difficulty seemed to be his inability to run that office on a strictly accounted budget. Another stemmed from the condition of the Pike County jail. But the most troubling issues involved two claims by prisoners in 1989 that they had been arrested and then released from jail in order to "set up other people to commit crimes while lawmen lay in wait to arrest them." One man, Ricky Stovall, filed a federal lawsuit against Lawson and one of his deputies, Dick Wilson, claiming not only that he had been arrested and jailed simply to pressure him into setting up a burglary, but also that in the process of making an arrest in that burglary, Deputy Wilson had shot him.[64] Jailhouse lawsuits are notorious, frequent, and not always the best indication of what really happened. But these suits seem to have been something other than nuisance suits. Lawson consistently denied their allegations, claiming that his resignation was prompted by health concerns and perhaps to a degree by the distraction of the lawsuits, but mainly, he said, by the poor condition of the jail, from which he feared another lawsuit.

"He has had a colorful career," reported the local paper in 1990. Indeed he had. The scandals of the late 1980s were not Lawson's first. In 1978, a Pike County grand jury "looked into what were termed 'questionable' purchasing procedures."[65] He survived those questions, but was indicted in 1979 for two misdemeanor counts of neglect of duty, stemming from his allegedly having released seven inmates from custody by mistake. Nothing if not durable, Lawson won acquittal on those charges. But the 1989 and 1990 allegations were too much to handle. Lawson tried to defend himself, but he was labeled by one local man as a "two-time quitter," and the man further noted that Ricky Stovall, who had sued Lawson and was also a man who had compiled an estimable record of minor criminal offenses, was "still carrying birdshot around in his back and backside."[66] In short, Tot Lawson was something of a scoundrel and also the kind of Mississippi sheriff who would have enjoyed referring to himself as a lawman. A longtime McComb resident told me, in words that ought to stand as Lawson's epitaph, "he was a good old boy, and they loved him."[67]

Compared with Lawson's career, that of McComb police chief Richard Rowley featured less drama, fewer elections, and no indictments. Rowley served as police chief until 1975, when he retired after twenty years of service with the department.[68] Future police chiefs would be appointed by the city board, rather than elected, as Rowley had been, a development that one can read in different ways. A move away from elections could reflect a belief that the people themselves might not be the best judges of a law enforcement professional. But such a move might also be seen as taking a democratic process away from an electorate that had been expanded in ways with which local people of power and influence were not pleased.

Before joining the police department, Rowley worked for ten years for the Illinois Central Railroad. After his retirement from the police department, he took a job in the maintenance department at the Southwest Mississippi Regional Medical Center, the local hospital, where his duties included not only keeping up the physical plant but also supervising hospital security.[69] Rowley ran for city selectman in 1976, but he failed to win. He continued to live in McComb, where he died in June 1989.[70] He served as a transitional police chief in McComb, one whose career spanned the years from the department's participation in massive resistance to the civil rights movement to their understanding that law enforcement in the area had entered a new era, like it or not. Rowley never in later years made public comment about the fact that two of his police officers had been arrested for murdering a child.

In the 1970s, Billie Jo Lambert was largely absent from the public eye. Like many people of modest standing, Lambert has left relatively fewer traces than those of the lawyers and judges of whom she saw so much in the early 1970s. By 1978, she seems not to have lived in the area, as a Baton Rouge attorney placed an advertisement in the local newspaper asking anyone who knew the whereabouts of Billie Jo Lambert Bordelon to contact him.[71] But the city of McComb was a place to which she returned, for work and for family reasons. Hollywood Cemetery became the resting place for many people involved one way or another in the Tina Andrews case. Billie Jo Lambert's parents, Pat and George Ann, are buried there. So is her brother Charles and her sister Jimmie Nell Lambert Wolfe, who testified in the Pike County Courthouse and who died in 2016. So too is her son, Robert Alex Lambert, an infant at the time of Richard McIntosh's first trial in 1971.[72]

Alex Lambert's life demonstrates how sharp violence and frustrations with the courts and broader legal system continued to mark the lives of many working-class Pike County residents. On February 24, 1996, the twenty-four-year-old Lambert was shot to death outside a Texaco gasoline station on Pearl River Avenue in east McComb, a short walk from the North Cherry Street house where Billie Jo Lambert lived in 1969. A thirty-three-year-old man was arrested on the scene. McComb police investigators admitted that "details were sketchy," but said that apparently a fistfight in the parking lot had escalated, with Joseph Slaughter shooting Lambert. Slaughter was married to a woman who previously had been married to Lambert; that woman was the daughter of Pat Lamkin, the woman with whom Billie Jo Lambert had gone to District Attorney Joe Pigott's office with the story of what had happened in the oil field on the night of August 13, 1969.[73]

By 1996, Billie Jo Lambert no longer lived on Cherry Street or anywhere else in McComb, and she was no longer Billie Jo Lambert, but rather Billie Jo Bordelon. Married for years to James Bordelon, Billie Jo lived in Liberty, to the west of McComb in Amite County. One of her neighbors in Liberty was and continues to be Richard McIntosh. One year later, in February 1997, Bordelon filed a $30 million civil law suit in Pike County Circuit Court against Joseph Slaughter and his employer, Lott Furniture Company of McComb. Seeking $15 million each from the two parties for the wrongful death of her son Alex, Bordelon's suit claimed that Slaughter's employer knew of his "dangerous and violent propensity" and that the killing had occurred during his hours of employment. Slaughter was by that time serving a sentence in Parchman penitentiary.[74]

Other than as a party to issues arising from matters of estate and those arising from the murder of her son, Bordelon has, certainly much to her relief, avoided contact with the courts of Pike County, Mississippi. She has lived and worked in Amite and Pike Counties for years. Like many other people, Billie Bordelon created a Facebook page, one to which she rarely posts. But her profile picture features a youthful Bordelon, in a photograph probably taken in the late 1970s or early 1980s. On the left of the photograph, partially cropped out, one sees the face of a small child, probably Alex, her ill-fated son.[75]

A visitor to downtown McComb these days can hardly realize how much those few blocks were central to the community in the late 1960s. City Hall is still there, along with a few banks and some attorneys' offices, but the department stores, movie theaters, drug stores, and other features that made downtown vibrant are largely shuttered. A few formerly major buildings are literally falling down. There is little pedestrian traffic, and practically none of the shoppers that would have been so prominent in the 1950s and 1960s. McComb has struggled to find an identity marketable to tourists. Unlike Natchez and Vicksburg, there are no Civil War–era homes or battlefields. Unlike the Delta, tourists from around the world do not make pilgrimages to sites associated with blues musicians. There has been some attempt to create buzz with a festival celebrating the city's railroad heritage and another recognizing the music of native son Bo Diddley, one of the area's many African Americans who left the county for greener pastures in the North.[76] But compared with many of its neighbors, especially nearby Brookhaven, McComb has struggled not only with cultural matters but also with uneven economic development, crime, and other matters rooted in the Jim Crow years.

Other parts of the city, including the former black business district on Summit Street, are not what they were in earlier decades. A Mississippi Blues Trail marker tells one that racial integration in McComb spelled the end of Summit Street as a "thriving African American business district." Commerce "began to decline when much of the African American trade dispersed to other parts of town."[77] These days on Summit Street, a number of businesses feature signs cautioning patrons not to loiter or to carry firearms into the establishment. To-day's businesses give little evidence of what the place once represented to black

McComb. One can get a haircut, buy package liquor, go to a club, or attend church, but that is about it. Summit Street now intersects with what seems inevitable in an economically depressed area of a small Mississippi town, Martin Luther King, Jr. Drive.

On a recent trip to McComb, a friend, a native of Michigan, came with me to Summit Street. "Sometimes," he observed, "it's hard to believe that the civil rights movement here happened at all." However, one can take either a guided or a driving tour of the civil rights history of McComb.[78] The former Freedom House on Wall Street is now a vacant lot. Burgland Senior High School, the site of the 1961 student walk-out, is now Higgins Middle School. Alyene "Mama" Quin's house still stands, as does that of C. C. Bryant. So does the former Greyhound Bus Station; the guide for the driving tour reminds us that even after integration, many black patrons still continued to use the former "black side" of the station. One can see McComb City Hall and recall the kneel-ins and arrests that occurred there, as well as the policies enacted inside the building. In the city hall today, a visitor might have a chance to speak with McComb's mayor, Quordiniah Lockley, an African American man elected in 2018. For the first time in McComb's history, the city board now has a black majority.[79]

The trains, so central to the city's history, still roll through downtown McComb, although not nearly so often as in the old days. Amtrak has long provided the only passenger service in the area, as it has to other Americans. Two Amtrak trains a day pass through on their way between Chicago and New Orleans. These days, riding the train is more an act of nostalgia or pleasure than it is a matter of basic transportation, as it would have been many decades ago. Across the street from the current Amtrak station is the former location of the Tiger's Den. Walk a few blocks further down South Railroad Avenue from the corner of Railroad and Canal, where three girls met two men in 1969, and one reaches the Kramertown section of McComb, named for an old city father and shaper of the community. There in 1969 a person could have found beer and places to meet drinking-age companions. Entering the area now, one sees a sign boasting of the "Kramertown National Historic District," a purely local assertion, not one corroborated by a state-issued marker. Without that sign, one could be excused for not recognizing the historical significance of this area of a few square blocks.

The building that housed Kramertown Hardware still stands, a business I visited with my grandfather in the 1970s. There is also The Icehouse, a bar and still later an event center, but at one point no doubt an ice house. A sign on the front advertises it as "Southwest Mississippi's Premier Night Spot." I remember it as well, and at least a few times in the early 1980s I would have been there, drinking beer and looking for the sort of adventures that took teenagers into this area a decade or two earlier. The Icehouse figures today on the McComb police blotter and in many white McComb residents' tales about black crime in the city.

In Magnolia, the downtown area of a few blocks is surrounded with late nineteenth-century houses, some of which were once beautiful and some that still are. The business district, once vital, is now, like McComb's, much diminished when compared with earlier decades. There today are the offices of a small but lively newspaper, lawyers' offices, and a few cafes and dollar stores. Outside the Pike County Courthouse, which continues to do a brisk business, especially with divorces and drug-related offenses, there is no memorial to the Civil War dead. Instead, there is a recent monument to area men who died in twentieth-century conflicts, from World War I through Vietnam, a testimony in part to the reach of the military draft into the smallest American communities, but also to the area's devotion to military service. There is also a recent memorial to the "Pike County Public Safety Officers Who Gave Their Lives to Protect and Serve the Community." On that marker are twelve names.

In the circuit clerk's office is a composite photograph of the Pike County bar in 1998. Many of the men whose names appear in this book were still active then: Pigott, Dowdy, Roach, and Reeves among them. The Pike County Courthouse was remodeled again in 1974; the court term ended abruptly in October when Judge Gordon Roach sustained a defense objection that the court, then being held in the Magnolia Community Center, was not legally constituted.[80] Over the last years, since Richard McIntosh has made his home in Amite County, there has been no reason for him ever to return to the Pike County Courthouse, whether to pay taxes, renew the plates for his vehicles, or to report for jury duty.

The Tina Andrews case has remained a matter of local interest, some of that interest intense, over the last decades. Members of Andrews's family have shown little public interest in the case, most of them seeming simply to want the matter to rest. In this sense, it is very much unlike civil rights–era murders, about which many families wish to, and are encouraged to, tell their stories and even to seek delayed justice. As a matter of criminal law for the courts of Pike County, the matter is closed. The most direct route for any fresh prosecution in the case was blocked in 2004 with the death of Ted Fleming. An acquitted Richard McIntosh has had no reason to anticipate any further trouble from the state of Mississippi about what happened to Tina Andrews in 1969.

In the last decade, those people who remember Tina Andrews have periodically left notes on her grave marker in McComb's Hollywood Cemetery, as well as memorials on various internet sites. In 2011, one person wrote on Facebook: "Many years later, you have friends who you don't even know. You have not been forgotten. I will make sure that you have new flowers on your grave on Saturday, the 42nd anniversary of your death. Left by Anonymous on 10 Aug 2011."[81] The clearing in the oil field where Tina Andrews died is perhaps thirty yards by thirty yards. People in the Deep South enjoy measuring things in terms of acreage or football fields. Where she was murdered and where her body was found is closer in size to a football field's two end zones than to the rest of the field itself. The clearing is surrounded by loblolly pine, sweetgum, and hickory, a typical mix for an area in this part of the state that has been cleared and allowed to regenerate. There is active equipment on the site, a natural gas gathering system, maintained by Denbury Onshore, LLC. Denbury's signs warn one not to trespass on the site. Because this is private land, there are no memorials here, makeshift or otherwise, to mark the place where Tina Andrews died.

10

Searching for Tina Andrews
Conversations and Rumors, but No Smoking Guns

McComb is my hometown. In the summer of 2016, I received a message from a relative, a longtime resident of the city. "What do you know about Tina Andrews?" she asked. "Very little," I replied, reminding her that I was only four when Andrews was murdered. Growing up in McComb, I lived on Delaware Avenue, the street down which Tina Andrews walked many times, including the night of August 13, 1969. That same night, Billie Jo Lambert would almost certainly have walked past my house as she made her way home to Cherry Street. Those are matters of coincidence, ones that I discovered only after beginning work on this story. No one in my family, within my hearing at least, ever mentioned the case. However, my grandmother operated a beauty shop on Delaware Avenue. Many words were likely spoken about the matter among the women there between 1969 and 1972. There are other coincidences as well. Two close relatives were members of the McComb High School class of 1965, along with Richard McIntosh. A great-uncle, long dead, was foreman of the 1972 jury that heard McIntosh's second trial.

Writing this book, I heard a great deal about the case from many people. In Pike County, a rich oral tradition, in some quarters at least, has kept green the memory of Tina Andrews. One person's oral tradition, however, is another person's gossip. From the beginning of my search to learn what happened to Andrews, one primary task was to decide what was true and what was not, what could be documented and what could not, and what could be written and what could not. Some people who were involved in the matter one way or another refused to speak with me.[1] Many others were generous with their recollections of Tina Andrews, the other principal characters in this story, and the people and forces that shaped McComb. All of those stories, however, were remembered through nearly a half-century, during which memories, as they do, form and adapt, and come to serve many purposes.

Despite efforts to confine this account to precisely what the public record could reveal about the case and its context, a darker story came regularly to my attention. In the summer of 2018, I spoke with a McComb woman who remembers Tina Andrews, as well as a number of other people connected with the matter. "This town has hidden the truth of her death, and that is a shame," she told me. "Lots of elite people were involved and old money, too. The town was bought. A lot of that old money is gone now, but back then, a lot of men could make things happen with just a phone call or two."[2] Elite is a matter of perspective, and old money is a relative term in McComb, a city less than one hundred years old when Andrews was murdered. But still, the possibility of something more sinister seemed too insistent to ignore. McComb certainly was a town, like many other places, in which well-placed men could indeed "make things happen" with a phone call or a few remarks on the sidewalk after church or over a friendly game of cards.

First, the rumors. One of the fullest publicly available sources of information on the Andrews case is Facebook's Pike County Cold Cases page, launched in 2011. From the beginning, the Andrews story attracted a great deal of attention from local people and former residents, who posted many recollections of the matter and stories of what they had been told over the years. Some of that information is to some degree informed, but much is not. One development reported on that page is subject to confirmation. Within weeks of the page's launch, on the anniversary of Tina Andrews's death, someone left a note on her grave: "Tina, At long last someone is speaking out for you. RIP." The posted photograph shows a single pink rose at the base of her grave marker. The page itself seems to have driven that anniversary remembrance of Andrews. People wrote that they would visit her grave that day; some of them clearly did. By late afternoon, another visitor had left a small potted plant, with a stylized butterfly and tiny house included in the arrangement, all in bright pastel colors, something a young girl would have liked. By evening, more people had come, leaving an assortment of stuffed animals, including teddy bears and a rabbit, and a small pink plush pillow upon which rested strands of colorful plastic beads and a cross. On the photo of this anniversary commemoration posted to the Facebook page, one comment read: "I think that Tina has evolved into 'belonging' to each of us."[3]

An African American woman, a school friend of Tina's, remembered her in comments posted to that page. During the "freedom of choice" period before the full racial integration of the McComb schools, black families could send their children to a "white" school, where the reception they met was at best cool. "Tina was a very pretty girl," she recalled, "who had these eyes that glimmered (beautiful) but was often sad and angry looking, even as a kid, I saw so much hurt behind them, especially when she was trying to be tough. Tina was my friend in school, yes in '69,' Tina and I were friends. You see Tina and I had something in common, a lot of the kids didn't like us and wouldn't play with us. For Tina, it was because she was considered 'poor white trash' and well I'll leave it to your imagination what I was called." "Tina," the woman continued, "was dealt a really bad hand in life." Of the rumors of Tina's being involved with older men? "As to the reference of her being sexually active with men, as it may be true . . . I think that the act was forced upon her, long before the day of her death."

The last comment speaks to one of the most persistent but difficult rumors associated with the writing of this book: implications or assertions that Tina Andrews was sexually active or that her activity had something to do with her murder. This is one element of the story that has left no trace in publicly available records. But still, people had things to tell me that spoke to these rumors. If this then is in part the story of a twelve-year-old girl who had sex with older men, can that story be told? I do not ask whether the story should be told as a matter of common decency. Rather, can such a story be recovered? There are no arrest records to attest to the matter. No one who was sexually involved with a child and still living would be stupid enough to confirm that fact. As a matter of historical reconstruction, one is left with rumor. Did Tina Andrews's family know or suspect anything of the kind to be happening? A member of Andrews's extended family told me Tina was a girl who found older men who were willing to give her money and she did what they wanted in order to get it. What about Tina's murder and the trials? "The police were involved, so they covered it up. The family and a lot of people in town wanted justice, but they didn't get it because of who these guys were."[4] As with all fifty-year-old memories, especially recollections of "what people said," these should be weighed very carefully. They at least confirm that Tina Andrews lived in a town where her own extended family thought that she was indeed some of the very things that B. D. Statham suggested that she and Billie Jo Lambert were—girls with a "reputation."

One would have to be naïve to believe that a girl of twelve might not do whatever she believed was necessary to get the things she wanted, whether they were material things or what she believed to be attention or affection. It is possible that Andrews was a girl abused by men who took advantage of her. "Abuse" would be the proper term, as she was twelve years old, a child, incapable of consent to any sexual contact that might have occurred. Anyone who is in a direct position to know anything about any of these scenarios is either dead or silent. And that, so far as this story is concerned, is where that matter must rest.

During my work on this book, I was fortunate not to have to rely upon rumor. Many people connected with the case spoke with me candidly and at length. One of the most helpful of them was Jim Kitchens, the district attorney in the 1972 trial of Richard McIntosh. In August 2017, I interviewed Justice James W. Kitchens in his chambers in the Mississippi Supreme Court Building on Congress Street in Jackson. A month earlier, I had written Justice Kitchens, asking if he would talk with me about the Tina Andrews murder. He is the only man still living of the original two judges, two district attorneys, and two defense attorneys for Richard McIntosh. A week after my letter, I received a reply from Kitchens, in which he said that he remembered well "the broad outlines of the case" and invited me to call his secretary to arrange an interview on my next trip to Mississippi.[5]

On many matters, Kitchens was specific and frank. Like Billie Jo Lambert herself, he did not have confidence in Pike County–area law enforcement agencies, other than the F.B.I. field office, of which Lambert was almost certainly unaware. Like Lambert, Kitchens seemed certain, as a former prosecutor would be, that the state had the right man on trial in 1971 and 1972. Without making excuses for himself, Kitchens recalled in detail the fundamental challenges the state faced in prosecuting Richard McIntosh.

Why, I asked Kitchens, had Lambert taken so long to come forward with her story? He replied: "A kid like that was probably afraid of two policemen. She, rightly, may have assumed that 'Who're they going to believe, me or them?'"

227

Kitchens continued: "What probably made this thing go south for McIntosh and Fleming was when one of them struck her on the jaw, and they realized they'd broken her jaw. There wasn't any way to explain that. That was going to be found out. That was probably the thing that cost her her life. If she'd just said, 'These two guys took me out and made me have sex with them,' they probably would've had plausible deniability in some regard for that. But they couldn't explain a kid with a broken jaw. She probably made a lot of noise when that happened, too. They probably killed her knowing it made her be quiet."[6]

I asked Kitchens about Lambert's reliability and the degree to which an attorney considers whether or not a witness is telling the truth, as distinct from the matter of whether or not she makes a good witness. "You always evaluate your witnesses. It's the same as in any other human endeavor. You try to identify your weaknesses and your strengths and try to minimize your weaknesses as best you can. In the later years of my practice, I would've spent more time with a witness like that, putting her through practice examinations and things like that that I don't think I did then. But nevertheless, no matter what you did, a lawyer like B. D. Statham still would've known that this is a teenager that was drinking beer, still would've known that her reputation was tarnished and even today a lawyer would try to exploit that to the greatest extent possible. If I was getting ready to prosecute that case now, I think that I would know more about what her weaknesses were. I would've made it my business to find out more about it. I would have filed a motion *in limine,* asking that the judge not allow the defense to go into whether this child ever had a beer or not because it really wasn't relevant to the issues before the court. I probably could get that kept out." Kitchens is correct that a great weakness in both trials for the state was the relatively unprepared presentation of Lambert as well as the wide latitude Statham was given to introduce stories about her character and reputation, ones that changes in attitudes and court procedure in the state would not allow so easily today. "She was on the stand for hours," I reminded Kitchens. "Oh, yes," he replied, "Statham was a relentless, almost vicious, lawyer."

Kitchens remains very attentive to the matter of the murder weapon, the .38-caliber revolver. "That British stuff, particularly British war surplus material, was plentiful then. The Klan was notorious about having that kind of stuff and were known for having a bunch of these Webley revolvers. So that was another sort of a thin Klan connection in the case. She was shot with a Webley.

I came to learn, to my horror as a district attorney, that a lot of policemen carried a second gun that they called a drop gun. If they shot somebody that was unarmed, they'd drop that second gun down there and I thought at the time, well, that [Webley] could've been his drop gun. I didn't argue that because I didn't have any evidence of it. But it was not unusual. I bet you there's Webleys buried in the ground all over Pike County." Kitchens spoke with surprising frankness about his difficulties with Pike County law enforcement. "At that time, there was corruption in McComb. I couldn't trust the chief of police, and I couldn't trust the sheriff down there. The police department in McComb was pretty rotten. It was not a good outfit at that time."

Was a transcript of the 1972 trial ever made? Kitchens thinks not. "To my knowledge," he said, "there was no transcript made of the second trial. Most people think that transcripts always follow a trial but, as you probably know, unless the case is appealed, there's really not much need to make a transcript. Though occasionally, some interested party will just hire the court reporter to make a transcript from his or her notes." If some interested party did in fact order a transcript of the 1972 trial, it still has not come to light. The Pike County circuit clerk's office holds a small file of perhaps two hundred documents on the case from the indictments through the acquittal of McIntosh and the dismissal of charges against Fleming. The file is thin: defense motions, the judge's replies to those motions, and subpoenas to witnesses. There are no copies of crime scene photographs, a coroner's jury report, a death certificate, any record of the evidence that had been entered before the grand jury, any copies of receipts or notes on other physical evidence in the case, including the clothing that Tina Andrews wore or the bullet that was taken from her head. There are no copies of expert witnesses' reports, notes of police or F.B.I. investigations of the crime, or any records of any interviews with either the defendants or other potential or actual witnesses in the case. Nor are there copies of the transcripts of either trial, at least one of which certainly does exist. One would not expect to find all of this material in a court file on the case, or on any case, frankly. But in many places, at least some of it would have been retained somewhere in the court's files. In Pike County, it was not. In most jurisdictions, some of these specific records would not properly have been kept in a courthouse file at all. They would have been held in the district attorney's office. In Pike County, for various reasons, they are not, at least not anymore.

What has become of the rest of the records in the case of the *State of Mississippi v. Richard McIntosh*? Justice Kitchens explained how the nature of the district attorney's office in the early 1970s, broadly accepted contemporary record-keeping practices, and the nature of the men who held the district attorney's office all have led to the absence of materials from the case. "I once had a file on this case, of course. It was as good a file as you could have had on the case. I'm meticulous about files and I had really good files on pretty much everything to the extent that you could with the poor-quality law enforcement we had in a lot of places then. But I thought long and hard about those files and I wanted to keep them because I thought that a lot of them would have had some historical value. I had all the newspaper clippings about all the cases and everything in those files. Plus all the police reports, all my notes, my trial notes, and, in some cases, transcripts. But I thought, you know, these files were created at public expense, and I don't have a right to [keep them myself]."

"We were in this murky time when DAs had historically been practicing attorneys and they considered the DA's job as just part of their law practice. But I was a full-time DA, and I thought, this is really state property. The Archives and History Department wasn't nearly as interested in public records then as they are now. And so, I let [Kitchens' successor Dunn Lampton] keep all those files. It's a small office down there, and five or six years or more later, there was some file that I wanted to look at for some reason. I was trying to refresh my memory about it, something in an old case in the DA's office. I called him and said, 'Dunn, I need to come down there and look at an old file. When would be convenient for you for me to do that?' or something or other. He said, 'Oh, I won't have that file.' I said, 'Yes, you do, it's there with all the files.' They were consecutively numbered by year and had the name of the county on the tab on there. He said, 'Oh man, I threw those things away. I couldn't keep all those. I didn't have anywhere to store them.' And those things are just gone. There's not any kind of retention policy in the state now about DA's records. They're pretty much ad lib to do anything they want to with them. People will take things, deputy clerks, lawyers that are in there browsing around." The evidence from the Tina Andrews case—her clothing, the photographs from the crime scene, even the slug taken from her skull—went somewhere. It is grim to imagine that anyone regarded any of it as a trophy or an appropriate souvenir. If anyone has any of it still, he has not bragged about it, in public at least.

Finally, Justice Kitchens told me: "It was a shaky case, it really was. I don't say that to console myself. I regret losing the case because I was convinced the guy was guilty, and Judge Pigott was. He and I talked about it some before and after, but, it's just, you know, some of them slip through the cracks and that'll be it. Maybe if I had been more experienced, older, I might have done a better job on it." Jim Kitchens' remarks are not only frank, but also generous in shouldering responsibility for not winning a conviction in the case. But given the obstacles faced by the state, it is by no means clear that any district attorney could have persuaded a jury of Richard McIntosh's guilt.

Just before I left his chambers, Justice Kitchens added: "Judge Pigott was asked by somebody one day, who he wanted to talk to first when he got to Heaven. And he said Tina Marie Andrews: I want her to tell me exactly what happened out there that night. He never lost his interest or his curiosity about that case. When I left the DA's office, there were unsolved murder cases in every one of my counties. And this is one of them. This didn't happen while I was DA, but I was responsible for the case. I wished a lot of times I could have another shot at that case." Once the Andrews case reached the district attorney's office in Pike County, both Joe Pigott and Jim Kitchens did the best that they could with the materials that they had. Fortune failed Tina Andrews, and Billie Jo Lambert as well, long before two men were indicted for the murder in 1971.

Some of the questions that I believed that I had come to Jackson to ask Justice Kitchens I never asked. I never directly asked him if he was surprised or disappointed in himself for not winning the case, although he said as much. Or if he had made mistakes in preparing his case, although on that matter as well, he explained what an older, more experienced version of himself might have done differently. Or if he felt that the jury had been fixed. Or if he felt that anyone in the community had otherwise attempted to interfere with or had interfered with the investigation or the prosecution of the case. Or if McIntosh and Fleming had, in his opinion, murdered Andrews at the behest of men who were worried that Andrews had knowledge of crimes that those men did not wish to be revealed. In the end, though, Justice Kitchens told me a great deal, particularly about the ways in which a system of law enforcement and justice that had been formed in the Jim Crow era influenced the course of the Tina Andrews investigation and trials.

The other district attorney in the case, Joe Pigott, died in 2015, well before

I began writing this book. In the summer of 2017, I contacted Pigott's son Brad, a former U.S. attorney for the Southern District of Mississippi, now in private practice in Jackson. I asked if his father ever drafted the book that he had spoken of writing about his prominent cases. His father had not, Brad Pigott told me. Over lunch at Hal & Mal's, a city landmark, he shared recollections of his father's involvement in the Andrews case, about which his father had spoken over the years, as well as of other Pike County legal matters, including his father's work in the summer of 1964, which had helped break the wave of bombings in McComb. Brad Pigott, an attorney with his own distinguished record of going after civil rights–era cold cases, is convinced that in 1971 the recent racial history of McComb was a central factor in the case breaking the way that it did for the state.[7] Would a jury that was more racially representative of Pike County, he wondered, have been so quick to acquit a police officer, given what black residents knew of the police? Pigott confirmed that the case had gnawed at his father over the years. After our catfish lunch, we drove back to Pigott's law office, located just across the street from a Jackson public elementary school, long named for President Jefferson Davis and then in the process of being renamed for President Barack Obama. There in the conference room, Pigott presented to me the single most important extant source of information on the case: an original copy of the transcript of the 1971 trial of Richard McIntosh. Bookmarks in the document suggest that his father had consulted it over the years, making notes on matters such as road measurements and cattle gaps, testimony to the degree to which the case had indeed remained on Judge Pigott's mind.

In the summers of 2017 and 2018, I spent much time with Mississippi lawyers. In Magnolia, I visited Dee Bates, current district attorney for the Fourteenth District, thus the successor to Joe Pigott and Jim Kitchens. In the summer of 2017, I arrived at Bates's office unannounced. He received me cordially, showing immediate familiarity with the Andrews case. Bates said that "people have asked about the case over the years. People have wondered if any charges still could be filed." Ted Fleming's death in 2004 ended that possibility, for Fleming, at least. Because Fleming's case in 1972 had been "nol prossed," it was dismissed without prejudice, Bates told me; it could have been reopened and a new indictment sought. There is no evidence that possibility was ever seriously considered. What about the many years that had elapsed? Specifically, what of Fleming's possible contention that his constitutional right to a speedy trial might have been violated? One irony of Mississippi justice in recent decades has been the relaxation of speedy trial protection. State officials, willing to seek justice in decades-old civil rights–era crimes, have been generous in allowing prosecutors to pursue just such old cases. Federal authorities as well have shown periodic interest in these old cases, too, depending upon the priorities of the current attorney general. But Ted Fleming never faced that fate.

Bates seemed enthusiastic about my interest in the case, saying that he too had long been intrigued by the matter, personally if not professionally. An earnest, solidly built man in his forties, Bates is too young to have living memories of the case. Still, he knew of or knows people involved in the matter, including Richard McIntosh. Bates told me that his office has no materials whatsoever on the case, because he had looked for them and inquired about them from his immediate predecessors. He encouraged my inquiries, giving me the names of a few people who might offer more information. An area highway patrol investigator, based in nearby Brookhaven, has in fact made recent inquiries both to Bates's office and to Justice Jim Kitchens about the possibility of reopening the Tina Andrews case. My two inquiries to that investigator have gone unanswered. I qualified both of my queries to that investigator with a statement that I did not wish to interfere in any case he thought might be reopened. Still, it seems highly unlikely that Dee Bates will ever find sufficient legal grounds for reopening the matter of Tina Andrews.

Like many people in the area's legal community, Bates holds great respect for Judge Joe Pigott. On a return visit of mine to Magnolia in 2018, Bates seemed concerned that I might suggest that the prosecution in 1971 had not been vigorous, an impression that I did not intend to make. "Judge Pigott was a World War II hero, a good lawyer, and a good man," he said, facts that are without dispute.[8] Bates pointed to the older house in Magnolia that is his district attorney's office. "It's a lot easier to tear down than to build up," he said, but whether the remark applied only to a district attorney's work or also to a historian's, he did not say. I gave him a copy of the 1971 transcript, which he seemed pleased to have. I also told him that Jim Kitchens had specifically said that his successor, Dunn Lampton, had discarded Andrews's trial materials, a contention that Bates respectfully contested. As we stood in the yard outside the Pike County district attorney's Magnolia office, a sudden Mississippi summer shower began to fall, abbreviating a meeting that was less full than our first one had been. Still, Bates has remained one of those people in Pike County who believes that the Tina Andrews story represents a case in which full justice was never delivered.

On Tuesday, May 22, 2018, the day after my second conversation with Bates, I met with Wayne Dowdy, one of Ted Fleming's defense attorneys. I had written Dowdy earlier in the summer. He called me, inviting me to come see him when I was in town, a characteristically cordial Mississippi practice. His law offices, Dowdy, Cochram, and Watt, on Cherry Street in Magnolia, are just across the street from the Pike County Courthouse. Dowdy, seventy-four, has had a full, varied business and political career in county, state, and national politics. His office is filled with photographs and memorabilia, including, among this faithful Democrat's treasures, a framed, signed note from Ronald Reagan. A Georgia native, Dowdy graduated from Jackson's Millsaps College in 1965. Unlike many contemporaries before the Mississippi bar, Dowdy did not hold a degree from the University of Mississippi's law school, but rather from the Mississippi College School of Law, known at his graduation in 1968 as the Jackson School of Law. In addition to his legal career, Dowdy long maintained interests in broadcasting; he was at one time involved in the ownership or management of radio stations in five different states. Mayor of McComb from 1978 to 1981, Dowdy ran successfully as a Democrat in a 1981 special election to fill a U.S. House of Representatives seat vacated by the scandal-prone Jon Hinson. He defended that seat by narrow margins in 1982 and 1984 and more comfortably in 1986. In 1988 he ran unsuccessfully against Republican U.S. Representative Trent Lott for one of Mississippi's U.S. Senate seats. Dowdy ran for office again in the 1991 Democratic gubernatorial primary, but was not successful. In many other ways, Dowdy's career has been very satisfying.[9]

He came to McComb to work for Joe Pigott on Pigott's unsuccessful 1968 campaign for Congress. In early 1969, the twenty-five-year-old Dowdy joined Pigott's law firm.[10] The two men remained close over the years. When Dowdy became a U.S. Congressman, one of Pigott's sons worked in his Washington office and another son managed one of his reelection campaigns.[11] "Judge Pigott was an excellent attorney," he told me. Dowdy was a young man in 1971 when the indictments in the Andrews case were handed down. He was also a McComb Municipal Court judge, a step in the cursus honorum of local and

county offices that more than one other attorney involved in the case had occupied. The city judgeship was not then an elected office, but one appointed by
the city board. The position came open in 1969 when John Gordon Roach, Jr.,
Jim Kitchens' assistant in the 1972 trial of McIntosh, decided to run for county
prosecutor. Dowdy and William Watkins, B. D. Statham's partner, were con-
tenders to replace Roach. Dowdy, somewhat to his surprise, given his youth
and his lack of deep Pike County roots, was selected for the position, a fact that
Dowdy attributes to "resentment of B. D. Statham and the Magnolia clique."
At the time of his appointment, Dowdy had lived in the area less than a year
and as the local paper reported, had only "registered to vote last week."[12] Later,
also like Joe Pigott, he represented McComb as the school board's attorney.
Like B. D. Statham, he enjoyed a long run as the attorney for the county board
of supervisors. Dowdy also served in recent years as McComb's city attorney, a
tenure that came to an end in 2018, when Dowdy and three other McComb city
officials, namely the police chief, the municipal court judge, and the city prosecutor, were fired. An area newspaper reported, "The upheaval follows turnover
in city elections." Indeed it did, as the four fired officials were white, with the
decisions to replace officials in several of the cases coming along a four-to-two
vote of the city board, with the four being black and the two being white.[13]

In our hour-and-a-half conversation, Dowdy was gracious but guarded.
While he said nothing to discourage my interest in the Tina Andrews murder,
neither did he recommend my pursuit of the topic. Unlike Jim Kitchens, he
did not ask me to record our conversation. Dowdy of course remembered the
case. As Ted Fleming's attorney, he had attended both the 1971 and the 1972
trials. But he never argued the case in the Pike County Circuit Court. Unlike
Joe Pigott or Jim Kitchens, then, Dowdy seems not to have spent the time that
those men did in revisiting details of the matter, which is not striking, given
also his long and active legal and political career. In a brief meeting the previous evening, Dowdy had asked if I had seen the county court file. When I told
him that it contained mostly defense motions and orders to Sheriff Lawson to
deliver subpoenas, he said that most of those motions would have been made
by B. D. Statham. Many were, but a number had also been made by the firm of
Guy and Dowdy, under Dowdy's signature. He also expressed surprise that the
courthouse did not have copies of the trial transcripts. But then again, there
has been no particular reason in the last decades for Dowdy to have needed to

consult a trial transcript, as his involvement with the case ended in 1972, as did everyone else's, with the dismissal of charges against his client Ted Fleming.[14]

A careful attorney and prudent man, Dowdy said nothing to indicate that he believed either Fleming or McIntosh had anything to do with the murder of Tina Andrews. More than once, in fact, Dowdy said that a chief weakness of the state's case was a failure to positively identify Fleming as being one of the men who had taken Andrews to the oil field. This of course is not borne out by Billie Jo Lambert's consistent assertions that Fleming was one of the two men in the car that evening, but it is understandable as a statement by a man who was prepared to defend Ted Fleming in the early 1970s. The state did not of course appear to have convinced the jury of the soundness of Lambert's testimony. Jim Kitchens, prosecutor in 1972, also recalled: "Nobody among the prosecutors that dealt with this case, nobody thought they had a very strong case against Fleming. They thought the better case was against McIntosh and, in both instances, the case was entirely circumstantial."[15] Other prosecutors in the case, including Joe Pigott and Robert Reeves, clearly did feel that the state had a stronger case against McIntosh than it did against Fleming. Given these statements, it becomes clearer why the state of Mississippi chose McIntosh as the first of the two men to try.

Dowdy did remember the evening in 1971 that Ted Fleming came to his house seeking legal representation. He did not recall positively if Fleming's wife Agnes came with him. "Judge," Fleming said to Dowdy, "I've been indicted." But Agnes was, said Dowdy, "devastated" by the indictment. As the wife of a police officer accused of murdering a child, no doubt she was. Fleming's family, suggested Dowdy, was "well-connected," especially his in-laws, the Bellipanis; Agnes's brother Bobby Bellipani was a McComb police officer as well, a man who had been on the scene when Tina Andrews's body was discovered in 1969. Dowdy recalled that his own wife seemed shocked when she learned the purpose of Fleming's visit that evening, which is no surprise, given the degree of publicity and speculation that had attached to the case in the area by 1971. Still, said Dowdy, "I always believed Ted was innocent."[16]

Dowdy well remembered other principal figures in the case. He had high praise for the skills and toughness of then highway patrol investigator Donald Butler. "If I were going to be dropped behind enemy lines and had to pick one man to go with me, that man would be Donald Butler." He then told me a story about Butler's superb marksmanship, a story that involved Butler's shooting a suspect dead. Dowdy further suggested that both Sheriff "Tot" Lawson and Joe Pigott were close to Butler, a characterization that seems to apply to almost all of the men who played principal roles in the investigation and the trials. Of B. D. Statham, Dowdy said, "He was a great defense attorney . . . the best in the area." His praise of Sheriff Robert "Tot" Lawson was not quite as high. Dowdy recalled that Statham had a good deal of influence over Lawson, which is no doubt true, given only Statham's longtime role as attorney for the county's board of supervisors. He suggested, cautiously, that Lawson was not as diligent or capable an investigator as Donald Butler, which, of course, can also be interpreted as consistent with Dowdy's high praise of Butler. His further suggestion was that Butler did a great deal of the footwork, in this case and others, on which local law enforcement authorities, including Lawson, would rely. Dowdy also confirmed the suggestion made to me by Jim Kitchens that as board attorney, B. D. Statham had a large role in the selection of the jury pool that would be used in this case and in other cases.[17]

Continuing his recollections of Statham, Dowdy said that the defense attorney's considerable reputation had led Dowdy to imagine that Statham would be a large, imposing man. He was not. Instead, Statham was a slight man, with a habit of hitching up his pants constantly, almost a nervous fidget, whenever he came into a room.[18] Like other men involved in the case, including his young partner William Watkins, Statham's personal life was complicated, involving a divorce and the long-term, out-of-state care of a special needs child; but none of those matters seem particularly to bear on this story. Statham was extremely well connected and powerful in the county, and he was able to use that power aboveboard and in ways that never attached any cloud or scandal to his public reputation. With power that could be used openly, why operate in any other fashion? Whatever one may think of Statham's work as a cross-examiner of Billie Jo Lambert or Tina Andrews's sisters, he did nothing in either trial that went beyond the bounds of the law or of what one might wish for if Statham were one's defense counsel.

Dowdy expressed some surprise when I reminded him of the ages of Andrews and Lambert. "Twelve?" he said, perhaps testimony to the degree that Statham's rough work had created an impression of girls older than their years. He asked me if Lambert were still in the area. I said that indeed she was. He asked if I had talked with her. I said that I had not, did not offer that I had her telephone number on the legal pad in my hand. I remarked that Statham had conducted an aggressive defense, even subpoenaing the school records of Tina Andrews and Billie Jo Lambert. Dowdy registered clear surprise. "Joe Pigott allowed that?" he said. Of course Dowdy was correct. Pigott had not allowed the records to be formally introduced at trial, even though Statham was able to make effective use of that material in his cross-examination of Tina's sister Donna.[19]

Finally, Dowdy asked me to keep him informed of anything that I might write about the case; I agreed. I mentioned that a great deal of rumor had long attached itself to the case, a fact that he seemed to acknowledge but did not amplify. I explained that I was not interested in writing about unsupported rumor. Dowdy characterized the writing about unsupported rumor as libel, which I took as nothing more than a statement of fact from a seasoned attorney. I left with thanks to Dowdy for his time, and also with the impression that he had told me what he could of the matter and his involvement with it. I also felt that he would not be hesitant to tell people that he had talked with someone interested in the Tina Andrews murder case. He did as much the previous afternoon in his office when I arranged to meet him. He and his secretary were setting up soft drinks and ice for a local political gathering. He introduced me to an elderly man by telling him my name, my father's name, and that I was there about the Andrews murder. The reaction from that man registered at least surprise.[20]

The next month, in June 2018, I wrote to John Gordon Roach, Jr., county prosecutor in the 1972 trial, the man who had assisted Jim Kitchens. Roach's law firm stands just across the street from McComb City Hall, and Roach is still listed on the firm's shingle as a member "of counsel" of the firm. But in recent years, Roach has faced a multitude of health problems. I received from him a gracious e-mail reply, telling me that the state of his health made it too difficult for him to speak with me. He had words of praise for Jim Kitchens, and he said that Kitchens, the district attorney, would have been responsible for the main lines of strategy and the conduct of the state's case in the trial itself.[21] With that exchange of e-mails with Roach, I had very nearly exhausted all my Mississippi lawyers, and I then turned my attention to a search for records that might still be held in Mississippi or elsewhere.

What that search revealed is that many official records that might speak to the case no longer exist, or if they do exist, they are not available for public inspection or via other channels short of a court order. On the morning of May 23, 2018, I spoke with a woman in the legal division of the Mississippi Department of Public Safety (MDPS). I asked her assistance in locating any records, including reports written by highway patrol investigator Donald Butler, pertaining to the case. Her online search yielded no returns for Richard McIntosh or Tina Andrews. Her belief was that the agency does not generally hold records from cases dating from that period. In some cases, she said, records are not held beyond a period of seven years, although, depending upon the type of case, records could still exist. She suggested, not very hopefully, that I check with the Mississippi Department of Archives and History, which, as it turns out, holds nothing in the way of MDPS criminal investigation records.

I followed up with a letter on June 20, 2018, to the Mississippi Department of Public Safety, requesting access to the two 1969 investigation reports of Donald Butler. A week later, I received a reply. Under the Mississippi Public Records Act, Mississippi Bureau of Investigation reports are exempt from disclosure. The person answering my letter did suggest that I might contact the Pike County Circuit Court, as they might have records "relevant to your inquiry."[22] I also attempted to obtain Federal Bureau of Investigation records relating to the case, whether reports of the area office or results of forensic examinations made in the F.B.I. laboratories in the Washington, D.C., area. The result of my Freedom of Information Act request was a letter informing me that "records which may have been responsive to your request were destroyed on December 1, 1994," perhaps reflecting a twenty-five-year practice of records retention.[23] In the case of the *State of Mississippi v. Richard McIntosh*, then, some official records no longer exist, others may or may not exist, but are essentially unavailable to a researcher, and others have simply disappeared.

With the search for official records seeming to have come to an end, I turned my attention to people in Pike County who might be able to tell me more about Tina Andrews. All of them were directly connected in one way or another with principal figures in the case. Many of them have retained a strong interest in the case over the years; others have not. Some of them spoke with me openly. Others spoke with me guardedly, or not at all. One McComb resident who has spent years considering the Andrews case is Carroll Case, a retired banker and also a writer and artist of considerable talent. Following a telephone conversation, Case invited me into his home to talk over the Tina Andrews murder. He spent much of a morning in June 2018 driving me around the city, pointing out the locations of the Lambert, Andrews, and Fleming houses, as well as the former location of the Tiger's Den and the block along which Lambert, Andrews, and the still-unidentified third girl walked before allegedly being picked up by McIntosh and Fleming. Case and I retraced the route that they would have taken out Delaware Avenue to the oil field where Andrews was found.[24]

Case, like many McComb residents, has strong beliefs about Andrews's killers and their motivations, as well as about the role that other forces in the community played in the unfolding of the investigation and trials. He generously shared his thoughts with me over a long conversation and in subsequent telephone calls and other communications, but throughout our talks, he made it clear that he did not wish to dictate the lines of my argument in this book, nor has he. Case had long been considering writing his own book on the Andrews case. Previously, he had spent years researching and writing a book on another chapter of southwestern Mississippi history. That book, *The Slaughter,* part historical research and part imaginative recreation, explores a long-rumored massacre of black soldiers during World War II at a southwest Mississippi military facility. The book's conclusions were categorically denied by the Defense Department, but have attracted attention from many black Mississippians, who are aware that governmental denials of atrocities against black people cannot always be taken at face value.[25]

In 1998, following the publication of that book, Case said in an interview with the *Enterprise-Journal* that he planned next to write about the Tina Andrews murder.[26] After that article appeared, Case received a telephone call from Karey Andrews, Tina Andrews's uncle. Andrews asked to meet with Case, not at his house, but rather at a private location. They met at the local mall, on a bench in front of the bookstore. Andrews firmly warned Case that attempting to write a book on the Tina Andrews case could be dangerous. "This goes deeper than you think it goes," warned Andrews. Case does remain well convinced that the matter goes deep into the heart of corruption in Pike County.[27]

For a time, Case made inquiries into the matter. Case's friend George Kratzschmar is the father of Billie Jo Lambert's son Alex, who was an infant at the time of the 1971 trial. He gave Lambert's contact information to Case, who attempted to reach her to discuss the murder. He did speak with her, sometime around the year 2000. She then worked at the Dollar Tree, a retail discount store in McComb. In an initial telephone conversation at her workplace, she told him that she could not talk about the case. In a follow-up call, Case asked again to talk, and still she was hesitant. In a third call, Lambert said, "I'm not supposed to be talking with you, but I'm going to, if you'll come out to where I live." "Come by yourself," she told him. "I'm scared." "I went out to her house," Case told me, "a little house off a country road. She couldn't talk to me for looking out the window." Case did not tape the conversation, but recalls it with clarity. One reason for her hesitation to talk, said Case, was her abiding fear of Ted Fleming and Richard McIntosh.[28]

Lambert told Case a story of the evening of August 13, 1969, that was in every way consistent with the testimony that she had given in both trials. She did not hedge or qualify on her identification of the two men as those who had picked up the three girls outside the Tiger's Den. She said that after the men refused to drop off Tina at the corner near her house, the girls began whispering in the back seat. "We knew exactly what was going to happen." "If it had been somebody else, it might have been a difference. But we did not want them." When she returned home that evening, she tried to tell her mother, but her mother, exasperated by her daughter's conduct, did not want to hear. Once Tina Andrews's photograph appeared in the local newspaper, however, her mother asked her if she knew Tina. "That's what I was trying to tell you about," she told her mother. "I was with Tina that night."[29]

Some years after the trials, probably in the late 1990s, Case spoke with William Watkins, B. D. Statham's partner and the co-defense counsel in both trials. Watkins had kept a scrapbook of the case. Case asked Watkins: "I know that there is a matter of attorney-client privilege here. So I'm going to try to ask the question in a way that you can answer. Do you think that after the 1972 trial that the sheriff's department or the police department should have continued to search for the real killer of Tina Andrews?" After a brief pause, Watkins replied: "No." Case also gave me a copy of a brief film, "Trains," that he created over a decade ago. It is a speculative and impressionist work in which he imagines a young woman seeking vengeance against a man whom she believes responsible for Tina Andrews's death. The film alludes to injustices and conspiracies in the case. "I wanted to stick it to the legal system," Case told me, "because I know how corrupt and crooked it was." Case was also profoundly disturbed by a common reaction that he received when people learned of his interest in the case. Why bring that up now, they asked? That happened a long time ago.[30]

Case sees the missing transcripts and lack of other evidence from the trial as an indication that the record has been deliberately scrubbed. While that is not impossible, the lack of evidence is also consistent with the record-keeping practices that were standard for the era not only in Pike County but in other Mississippi counties, too. Mississippi counties have wide discretion in deciding which records to keep and which to discard, as Justice Jim Kitchens' experiences point out. That decision often comes down to storage space. Many people have access to court records, including evidence, and it is not rare for materials of interest simply to walk out of a courthouse with no record of who had the material and when.

An account in the local newspaper in July 2018 describes conditions in the Pike County Courthouse basement, where generations of records are kept. "It's a wreck," the local tax collector said. "The labyrinthine basement," the story continues, "contains hundreds of musty old record books—but also boxes of papers, bound copies of old newspapers in no particular order, discarded computers, furniture, even Christmas decorations." It was time for a good house-cleaning, local officials decided. "It's become a dumping ground for unwanted material." The county needs a policy, they announced, "regulating use of records in the basement."[31] It is no surprise, given this description, that people looking for records that might throw light on the Tina Andrews case have been disappointed.

In a case such as the *State of Mississippi v. Richard McIntosh*, a case that resulted in an acquittal of the defendant, some custodian of records may have concluded that there seemed no reason to retain material that would not be needed in a future trial or an appeal. But what of a potential trial of Ted Fleming? A thorough and careful system, either that of the circuit court or the district attorney's office, might have kept those records and that evidence in hopes that something new might turn up that could offer a chance for a reopening of the case. But they did not. Even so, a Pike County district attorney might not have wished to put Billie Jo Lambert through a third trial. No one who prosecuted the case thought that the state's case against Fleming was as strong as the one against McIntosh. With no new evidence, there seems to have been no reasonable hope of winning a conviction against Fleming.

People sometimes imagine that southerners, particularly white southerners, are careful custodians of their past, a people who forget nothing and who hold antiquities and other relics in their attics. Such is not the case now generally, if it ever was. Like many other institutions in southwestern Mississippi, the Pike County Coroner's Office is not the most diligent keeper of records. But they are not, after all, a historical archive. In recent years, the coroner operated out of an office at the Southwest Mississippi Regional Medical Center. The Pike County Courthouse holds no coroners' records. And neither, apparently, does the coroner's office itself hold records on the Tina Andrews case, an investigation that occurred half a century ago.

In the summer of 2018, I made one last trip to Mississippi to tie down what I could about the case. Billie Jo Lambert Bordelon still lives in Amite County. I decided to contact her. A friend provided me with two possible telephone numbers for her. Neither worked. I found a third; it too had been disconnected. I thought hard about the matter before I began driving toward Liberty, about fifteen minutes west of McComb. Amite County feels very rural, even by Mississippi standards. If one expects southern self-conscious quaint, it is not to be found there. On a Wednesday afternoon in July, I drove past the Bordelon house twice, reluctant initially to stop because of the reception I feared, and also, I hope, out of hesitation to disturb a woman whose life ought to have purchased at least some relief from unexpected strangers at her door asking about painful events of half a century ago. But still I stopped. Their dog barked at me, but it was not menacing, nor was it either chained to a tree or running loose, facts which might disappoint people expecting that kind of southern story. It was a quiet road, with a mixture of small, modest houses fronting the road and others set deeper into larger acreage.

On my second knock upon the door, James Bordelon answered. Bordelon, Billie Jo's husband, a man with deep, sad-looking eyes, received me more cordially than most other men would have done in the circumstances. I explained why I was there: not to ask for anything, but rather to deliver a message. I told him that I had written this book, and wanted his wife to know about it before it appeared. I also said that I would welcome a chance to talk with her. I left my telephone number. If Billie Jo Bordelon was home during this conversation, I did not know it. He said that she might call me, but his manner of delivery did not suggest to expect it. I promised him that I would not bother either one of them again, and I have not. So far no call or other communication has come from Billie Jo Bordelon, and there I have let the matter rest.

Having driven to Liberty, it seemed fitting to see where Richard McIntosh lives. His address, available as a matter of public record, is about fifteen miles from the Bordelon house, but not along a route that would cause either of them to drive past the other's place unless that choice were very deliberate. My wife suggested that if McIntosh were not home, I might leave my card and a note stating my business, advice that I ignored. Richard McIntosh certainly has as much right as anyone else in Amite County, Mississippi, to order an unwelcomed stranger off his porch and insist that he not set foot on his property again. But that is not what happened. I knocked on his door, and no one answered. On a return trip the next day, no one answered then, either. After I left Mississippi, I regretted not having tried harder to speak with Richard McIntosh, who is, after all, one of the few remaining principal characters in this story.

The trials of Richard McIntosh occurred almost half a century ago. Not very many of the twenty-four jurors who heard those cases are still living. Bennie Hayman, or B. C. Hayman, as his name appeared in the list of jurors in the newspaper in 1972, is ninety-five. I called him one July morning in 2018, explaining my interest in the case. Because personal connections still count for a lot in a town like McComb, I told him who I was. He said that he had bought a lot of groceries from my grandfather and remembered him well. Mr. Hayman invited me to his house in north McComb, where we spent two and a half hours discussing the case and other local matters, including the fact that his late wife had been one of my kindergarten teachers.[32] A man with a keen memory for detail, Mr. Hayman told me the origins of the goat that was our companion at Miss Mattie and Miss Sybil's kindergarten.

He remembered many details of his service on that 1972 jury. A woman sitting next to him in the jury box sported an unusually large diamond ring, he said. He asked her at one point please to hold the ring a little lower, or he might not be able to hear anything that the lawyers were saying. The jury did not have difficulty reaching a verdict, he recalled. On an initial poll, only one man voted for a guilty charge. But that man seemed confused about the matter, said Hayman, and after further discussion, changed his vote to not guilty, producing a unanimous verdict for acquittal. In his memory, which is sharp, no one unduly pressured that lone guilty vote; or if he felt pressured, he quickly acquiesced. In any case, the matter was done much more quickly than it had been in 1971. Both girls had bad reputations, he offered, a judgment shaped not by any previous knowledge of either girl or her family, but rather from the testimony and B. D. Statham's effective efforts at shaping the jury's understanding of the matter. He had a daughter, he said, and what Billie Jo Lambert described of both girls' habits seemed hard to believe. The jury heard a lot about both girls, Hayman recalled, and what they heard of them was not good.[33]

The jury was sequestered, Hayman recalled. At their motel, they received the local newspaper in the evenings, but everything related to the trial had been cut out. One evening, as the jury was led out of the courthouse, his neighbor Charlie Gordon, a reporter for the *Enterprise-Journal,* shouted to him through the crowd for some reaction to what was happening in the courtroom. The jurors were transported in a small bus, and police had to push back the crowds to allow them to reach the vehicle. The courtroom itself was crowded, with people standing there and in the halls and even outside the building. Murder trials were not unusual in Pike County, but ones involving a police officer attracted greater attention. I asked Hayman if Tina Andrews's parents were in the courtroom. If they were, he said, they were not conspicuous, and he did not know them by sight. What he knew of the case in 1972 was nothing more than he had read in the newspaper, he said, and it had not overly captured his attention.[34]

The jury on which he served, as we have noted, consisted of men and women, black and white, relatively recent innovations in Pike County. Indeed, when the jury was drawn, another juror commented to him that it was not "an all-white outfit." Hayman said several times that the central fact leading to the acquittal, in his estimation, was the state's inability to make a solid case for conviction, one beyond a reasonable doubt. Time and again, B. D. Statham advised them that if they had "any doubt," the only choice was acquittal. He remembered too the great specificity of the jury's instructions, and he recalled the effect that their emphasis on "any reasonable doubt" had upon deliberations. He remembered too the great amount of expert testimony, much of it by people "brought down from Washington." It was tedious, he said, and "boring," and many jurors were not interested in it. McIntosh, on the other hand, was "very precise." "He had a very straight story." Lambert's story was just not as sharp or believable as that of McIntosh, he told me, in large part because Statham "blew holes in her story" and pointed out how many things she just could not remember. Just as important, perhaps, Statham did not "paint a very pretty picture" of who those girls were and the kinds of things they had been doing.[35]

Hayman served in Europe during World War II and experienced harrowing times as a German prisoner of war. A nose gunner on a B-26 bomber, Hayman flew sixteen missions and was shot down during a raid on an oil refinery. Held in a prison camp in Romania, one of Hayman's tasks was to bury German dead brought frozen in boxcars from the battlefields of Stalingrad. He came back to McComb, married, and raised a family. He still meets friends for coffee, these days at a Burger King rather than at the kind of café one would have found in McComb decades ago. Near the end of our conversation, Hayman grew silent for a moment and then said, "I killed two men during the war. I shot down others, and that didn't bother me as much. But I killed two men face to face. They had shot me, and I had to do it. But I think about it every night. Whoever did that to Tina Andrews has to think about it every night, too, and has to live with it." "If she had been a Roosevelt or somebody with money, it might have been different." Hayman did not explain just how things might have been different, but his comment does suggest ways that the case was shaped by factors that were determined by the time the jury heard the evidence.[36]

Bennie Hayman's recollections of the trial and its aftermath also suggest that not everyone in McComb was obsessed by the case or saw it as unfinished business. When the trial was over, he says, few people asked him about it. "My parents never even asked me about the trial." He and other members of the jury in 1972 were not naïve, nor were they pressured or manipulated into delivering the verdict that they did. They heard the evidence. They might have suspected that the state was somehow close to the truth in the case that they presented. But they had no physical evidence, he remembers, no witnesses other than Lambert and all those scientific experts, none of whom tied the defendant to the remains or the crime scene, and in the end, a great amount of what he described, certainly shaped by B. D. Statham's presentation of the case, as "hearsay."[37]

Later, said Hayman, the "scuttlebutt" was that they had tried the wrong man. But Hayman presented that recollection just as an interesting fact, not as an assertion that anything wrong had been done in the trial of which he was a part. Hayman's recollections suggest that for many people on the jury, they were presented not with the duty to solve a mystery, but rather with the task simply of listening to the evidence presented and attempting to decide whether or not the state had made its case. To twelve men and women in the Pike County Circuit Court in the spring of 1972, the state had not. Their time deliberating was no shorter than was common in local courts in those days. At the end of our conversation, I asked Hayman why he thought that the McComb police had been so involved in the investigation of the murder. He replied: "I don't know why the police were involved. Seems like it should have been the sheriff and the constables—that is interesting." Nearly half a century later, Hayman's recollection of Statham's work in the courtroom remains vivid. "He was a bulldog," said Hayman. "He talked so much that his voice became hoarse during the trial."[38]

In downtown McComb along Railroad Avenue these days, one would never know that the Tiger's Den was once a popular place to go, just as one might not imagine that the old train cars on display and the still-operating Amtrak station once represented a major economic and cultural force in the county. On a late July afternoon in 2018, I watched a young man unloading a boxed appliance in front of McComb Electric, one of the few active businesses in that block of Railroad Avenue. As are very many young people in the area, he was friendly, asking if he could help me. He told me that the railroad shops across the street had once been formidable; he pointed me in the direction of the former locations of manufacturing concerns in town. When I asked if he had heard of the Tiger's Den, though, about half a block from his father's business, he said that he had not, but that he would ask his father about it, if I wished.

Practically across the street from the old location of the Tiger's Den, I spoke with a McComb woman who worked at Mr. Swiss, the popular drive-in restaurant near the Andrews house on Oak Street. She recalled Tina and her sister: "I remember selling them ice cream. She was a pretty girl. I told her and her sister to go home. They shouldn't be staying out that late." She remembered the murder and its aftermath: "She was found under a couch . . . out there in that oil field. It was an awful thing. No one deserves that." "There are still a lot of murders down here . . . a lot of people are afraid to talk . . . they know things, but they are afraid to talk to the police." Her judgment of the McComb police is shared by many other African Americans of her age.[39]

Just west of the I-55 intersection with Delaware Avenue Extension, as if one were driving toward the oil field, one sees to the left Oliver Emmerich Drive, named for the longtime editor of the *Enterprise-Journal*. Follow that road, and one arrives at the offices of the newspaper, which, like many other local businesses, is no longer located in downtown McComb. I visited their office to ask if they might have original photographs that had run in the newspaper between 1969 and 1972, especially of the crime scene in 1969. I hoped that an original photograph might help me identify other men who had been there when Tina Andrews's body was discovered. I did not mention the specific photographs that I was looking for, but was told that they would not have anything that old. Fifty years ago sometimes seems a very long time in McComb. The newspaper has long been run digitally. That visit to the newspaper office marked another instance, then, of McComb not saving its past, if only because of space limitations and a sense that the importance of the moment had passed.

Finished with McComb, I drove again toward Magnolia. Like other small towns in the area, Magnolia lies off an exit from Interstate 55. Ten miles south of the Magnolia exit, one hits the Louisiana state line. Life in Pike County has long been flavored by its proximity to Louisiana. Many people here are fans of Louisiana State University football and Louisiana food, and in earlier decades, of the liquor that was freely and legally available there, unlike the case in long legally dry Mississippi. Evidences of Louisiana ways were present in a gas station and convenience store where I stopped, a mile or so from the heart of the old downtown, still the seat of county government. At the convenience store, they sell LeBlanc's hot Louisiana boudin, an excellent type of sausage, often eaten right in the car, washed down with a can of beer, for which convenience stores gladly furnish a brown paper "sleeve," which fools no one. Also for sale were quails' eggs, pigs' feet, and pickled eggs from vast jars, and at the cash register, a basket of bootlegged DVDs, including copies of still-in-the-theater titles such as *Ready Player One*. As one enters the town of Magnolia, the official sign advertises it as the seat of county government of Pike County, the place with the most industry per capita of any county in Mississippi, an assertion qualified enough perhaps to be true.

Mississippi county courthouses are not archives maintained to serve the idle curiosity of a historian. During my visit to Magnolia, I asked to see the courtroom. But court was not in session and the court administrator left strict written orders, a copy of which a deputy showed me, forbidding access to the courtroom when it was not in use. Apologetic but firm, the deputy could not let me see the scene where Richard McIntosh had been tried twice. Not wishing to interrupt the deputy's lunch any further, I apologized for bothering him. In the Pike County Courthouse Annex, now the home of the Pike County Chancery Court, I asked an African American deputy if the site had in fact once been that of the Pike County jail. "It sure was," he said, "but that was a long time ago." If one were unfortunate enough to be the subject of an indictment handed down by a grand jury in the court that is now next door, an indictment that was turned over to the sheriff with a warrant for arrest, then this was the jail to which one would have been brought, surely a dolorous place in those days. Both Richard McIntosh and Ted Fleming were held there until they posted bond. I mentioned the broad outlines of the story that I was here to research, and when I said the words "oil field," he immediately knew precisely what I meant. He recalled a female victim, and reading about the case in the newspaper. I asked him too about the jurisdiction question. He said that it might have been the case that the police were the first to respond to the call about the body, in which case their involvement was entirely appropriate. But, he suggested, in similar situations, the police would then have turned the matter over to the sheriff's department for investigation. When I told him that was not what had happened in this case, he reflected for a moment and said, "In those days the police here had a habit of doing what they wanted to do," a matter-of-fact statement that is surely supported by events of the era.

Finished with Mississippi, I headed north in my rental car. Back in Missouri, where I have lived for longer than I care to remember, Mississippi was still very much on my mind. So I wrote letters and made phone calls. I attempted to contact Donna Andrews, Tina's sister and a prominent trial witness. As did most of her family, she moved away from McComb in the years after the trials. She lives now in Louisiana. I wrote to her, but she never responded. I never considered driving to her home, not that far from Pike County, to attempt to speak with her in person.

In August 2018, I contacted a cousin of Tina Andrews, also a native of Mc-

Comb, but for many years an out-of-state resident. I asked her to speak with me about the case and to tell me what she remembered about Fred Andrews and his family. She did so, but only on the condition that neither her name nor any identifying details be used in this book. Her recollections of Tina were of a child who had little supervision, other than that of her sisters Donna and Winifred, with the latter a "mother hen" who did her best to take care of her siblings. Older brother "Sonny" was "polite and charismatic," a big brother who tried to watch out for his younger siblings. Fred seemed unable to do anything with either the children or their mother. The families of Fred Andrews and his siblings were not close. "We never even went to their house, but maybe Fred brought the kids over here a few times." She does not recall Fred Andrews and his children attending family reunions. As for Tina? "I'm not sure how often I even saw her. I'm not even sure that she would have recognized me if she'd seen me walking down the street. But I do remember her. By the time she was twelve, she looked a whole lot older than that." Over the years after Tina's death, the cousins, and there were many, in that Fred was one of eight siblings, did not keep up with Fred's children, even to the point of being sure where they were living or indeed if they were alive.

Tina Andrews's death certificate stands as another small mystery in this story. Mississippi issued death certificates—beginning later than many other states, but they certainly did so by the late 1960s. Generally those death certificates, even in the case of a homicide victim, are a matter of public record. The State of Mississippi is more reticent than some other states about releasing those death certificates, however. Typically, one has to be a family member or somehow legally involved with the deceased person to request that record. After fifty years, some of those barriers are relaxed. But not in the case of Tina Andrews. If one telephones the Mississippi State Department of Health's Vital Statistics Office, one will be told, after a couple of transfers and some time on hold, that Tina Andrews's death certificate is sealed by family request. What does that certificate say, and why was it sealed? Death certificates contain no assertion about the killer of a homicide victim. Nor do they contain graphic physical descriptions of the sort that one might find in a coroner's report. What did the family wish to protect or to shield from public view? Perhaps the answer is simple: sealing the death certificate was one of the few steps left that they could take to guard the family's privacy after a searing and disappointing quest for justice.

I visit McComb whenever I can, but never as often as I wish. On every trip to the city, I drive down Delaware Avenue and turn south toward Hollywood Cemetery. There I visit the graves of the grandparents with whom I lived in the late 1960s and early 1970s, those of my other grandparents, and that of my father as well. Not too far from my father's plot is the place where Tina Andrews and her parents are buried. When I visited that grave in May 2017, one of the two vases built into their marker was lined with pages from a 2015 issue of the *Enterprise-Journal*. The vases held what appeared to be recently placed arrangements of artificial flowers, a remembrance for a family whose lives were hard ones, with many sorrows to bear.

CONCLUSION

What Happened to Tina Andrews?

Who killed Tina Andrews, and why? By this point, readers may reasonably expect an answer to those questions. Unfortunately, neither one admits of a clear response, especially the latter. If one believes Billie Jo Lambert's testimony, and twice a Pike County jury did not, at least beyond a reasonable doubt, the answer to the first question may seem somewhat the clearer of the two. But that is not saying a good deal, and it certainly says nothing definitive. The story that I have offered does not prove anything that Joe Pigott and Jim Kitchens could not. No long-silent witnesses have come forward. No other fresh evidence has turned up, certainly none that would have made a difference in the trials of 1971 and 1972. So far as the state of Mississippi is concerned, then, Tina Andrews met her death at the hands of persons who remain unknown, or at least unconvicted.

What of the motive for her killing? In neither trial did the district attorney concern himself with providing a motive. A successful prosecution does not require that the state establish motive, a fact that may surprise some aficionados of crime fiction. Intent is a separate matter. It speaks in part to whether an act was deliberate or accidental, and it can mark the difference between a charge of murder and one of manslaughter, among other things. Some trials do feature discussions of a defendant's motives. If one kills a terminally ill spouse at her request and to relieve her of pain, for instance, one's attorney may wish to show the jury that compassion was the motive for the killing and thus convince them that an otherwise seemingly unfathomable act makes sense in the context of the larger narrative that they are telling. But still, one is being tried for murder, motive or not. However, Joe Pigott and Jim Kitchens did not offer the jurors an explanation of why Tina Andrews was murdered. In a story such as this one, the motive is perhaps as intriguing to the reader as the identity of the killer or killers. Well before either trial, in March 1971, the Baton Rouge newspapers twice reported a potential motive for Andrews's murder that is present in no other account. A source in Magnolia told a reporter that Andrews "came upon the policemen and a female in compromising circumstances and for this reason she was allegedly killed."[1] Such an account makes sense of a sort, but it is not supported by any other evidence and is likely an early example of the kind of rumor that surrounded the case from the beginning. It also of course does not explain why Tina Andrews was in the oil field in the first place.

For all the detail about the evening of August 13, 1969, that Billie Jo Lambert recalled and to which she testified in court in 1971 and 1972, she never explained why she thought Tina Andrews had been killed. As a matter of testimony in a murder trial, that sort of speculation would not have been directly relevant, perhaps, but as we have seen, less relevant material was presented in one fashion or another to the jury. But Lambert was not there when Tina was killed, and to this day she has not said—publicly, at least—why she believes that it was done. If one believes her testimony about the identity of the people in that oil field on that August night, only three other people might shed light on that question; two of them are dead.

It requires no great imaginative leap to know why two men took two girls to that oil field, a well-known make-out spot. It is no real puzzle why two girls would have resisted unwelcomed advances. But why was Tina Andrews murdered? The man who killed her might have regretted doing it, or having to do it, as perhaps he thought of it. That regret may not have been immediate, but likely it came in time, at least as the investigation into the case broadened. Few people kill so cavalierly that they do not seek to avoid detection and punishment. A great many instances of assault or rape or abduction do in fact turn into cases of murder or manslaughter in the blink of an eye, as the victim's resistance to those acts produces anger or injuries that lead to a situation different than the one that the person who thought he or she was in control of the matter envisioned. Had Tina's jaw not been broken, as Justice Jim Kitchens suggested, it is possible that she would have returned home with a story to tell or not to tell, as she saw fit. But she did not.

Tina Andrews's life and death, and the search for her killer or killers, were shaped not only by her decisions and those of many adults she knew, but also by matters of chance, primarily her social class and gender, and matters of history, principally that of McComb's violent support over the years for Jim Crow. On almost all those scores, she was quite unlucky in that place and time. But Richard McIntosh and Ted Fleming, considering the period only after they were indicted, enjoyed great good fortune, the most significant piece of which was their foresight to have been born white men. Had a black man been on trial for Tina Andrews's murder, a defense attorney such as B. D. Statham might have been much more circumspect about his characterization of Andrews and Lambert as "girls of ill repute." In such a scenario, prevailing attitudes about race might have shielded the two girls from some of the kinds of criticism that they received. By the year 1971, two black men—had those two been black men—would not have been carried from the Pike County jail and lynched for allegedly murdering a white girl. But many people in Pike County could remember when that sort of thing had been done in Mississippi. One did not have to be very old, either. In 1959 in Poplarville, about eighty miles southeast of McComb, Mack Charles Parker, accused of raping a pregnant white woman, was taken from his cell, beaten, and shot; his body was dumped in the Pearl River.[2] Short of that kind of lynching, there were still by 1971, and surely in later decades, too, ways in which a white girl like Lambert could have proved a believable witness before a Pike County jury should the defendant have been African American. But he was not.

Still, what might the trials have looked like if the defendant had been a black man? A fictional analogue is suggestive. With no offense intended toward any of the attorneys who represented either side in 1971 and 1972, none was Atticus Finch.[3] Despite Finch's skills and character, however, that lawyer, in his much-beloved incarnation in the novel and film To Kill A Mockingbird, shows us the difficulty of persuading a jury to take a black man's word over a white woman's, especially when matters of sexuality are involved, even when the white woman comes from less than a sterling background, social or otherwise. But Richard McIntosh was no Tom Robinson, either. Unlike Atticus Finch's client, he did not need to be. In his attempt to win acquittal of his client, B. D. Statham felt no need for Hail Mary courtroom tricks, such as demonstrating to the jury an arm lamed, an arm that could not have inflicted harm upon a white woman's body. There was no need either, as author Harper Lee felt obliged to do with Tom Robinson, to present McIntosh as a sexually benign or even neutered being. The juries in the Pike County Courthouse heard that McIntosh kept heavy company with his girlfriend, and that he rode around with under-age girls. But those facts did not prove taints on his character that caused them fundamentally to doubt his testimony. Of course the case that was tried in 1971 and 1972 did not involve fictional attorneys or a case of a white woman's word against a black man's, and so there the usefulness of the comparison with Harper Lee's creation runs out. Matters of race and comparisons with famous novels and films aside, Richard McIntosh was very lucky on another score: in the state of Mississippi, as in the rest of the United States of America, men have been sent to death row on far less compelling evidence than the juries heard in the Pike County Courthouse.

In Pike County over the decades, one of the principal factors that has led to misunderstandings about the legal fates of Richard McIntosh and Ted Fleming is people's misconceptions about what courts of law can and cannot do. Generations of movies, television shows, and crime novels have led people to expect surprise witnesses, sleights of hand with evidence presentation, and other moments of high drama. Some people too expect that people who seem guilty of a crime should be punished for it. But procedures that govern what prosecutors can do are well-defined, sometimes arcane and sometimes prosaic, and often frustrating or even incomprehensible to people without legal train-ing. Further, in several basic ways, criminal prosecutions in Mississippi were different in 1971 and 1972 than they would be in later years. "That was in the days before the advent of pretrial discovery in criminal cases," explained Jim Kitchens. "And motion practice was not nearly as extensive as it is now in the preliminary aspects of a prosecution."[4] In Mississippi, as in other states, the broadening of pretrial discovery prevented both sides of a case from surprising each other in court with evidence. Even so, this case presented nothing that turned on a particularly contested piece of physical evidence (other than the identity of the body itself) or an unexpected witness. Perhaps most important, it was much less common in those days to shield a witness, especially one of Billie Jo Lambert's gender and social class, from attacks on her character and reputation. Ultimately, then, the state's case amounted to one person's word against another's. The juries' verdicts mean—if only in a formal legal sense— that the state did not prove its case beyond a reasonable doubt.

Still, to a layperson's eye, there are questions worth asking about the kinds of evidence that was presented or that might have been. Richard McIntosh claimed that he did not know Ted Fleming in 1969. Under oath in 1971, McIntosh said, "Ted Fleming and I did not know each other during 1969. I met Ted Fleming the day that I went to work for the Police Department, in McComb, in 1970."[5] Statham asked, "Had you ever, prior to that time, associated with Ted Fleming? Had Ted Fleming ever been in your car with you prior to March 10, 1970?" "No sir, I did not," answered McIntosh without equivocation. Such testimony left an opportunity for the state. Had they been able to produce a single witness to contradict McIntosh, to show that he had in fact known or been associated with Fleming in any way prior to March 10, 1970, the jury might have been persuaded that McIntosh was also lying about other, more fundamental matters. But the state could not produce such a witness. No one seems to have come forward in later years to maintain anything different. Statham, careful attorney that he was, however, would never have framed the question in that way if he knew that the state could produce a witness to contradict his client.

Further, the defense subpoenaed Tina Andrews's school records, and Statham informed the court that Tina was a poor student, failing classes in the fourth grade. Why it matters that Tina was not a good student, except as part of Statham's broader strategy of painting the girls as people of little worth, it is difficult to see. The jury did not, however, hear anything about Richard McIntosh's school records, either at McComb High School or from his brief, recent attendance at Southwest Mississippi Junior College in nearby Summit. Nor did they hear about his performance evaluations from the various places that he had worked. It is of course possible that this material would have painted McIntosh in a favorable light. Indeed, the jury did hear from defense-introduced character witnesses for McIntosh who spoke briefly but positively to these issues. Ultimately, Statham failed to have Tina Andrews's school records admitted as official evidence, but he was able to tell the jury about those matters, especially in his questioning of Tina's sister Donna. Whether or not they might have revealed anything potentially damaging, McIntosh's records from school and work, however, appear not to have been subpoenaed or used by the state.

The case of Tina Andrews involves multiple lines of story and many types of information, unfolded over the course of decades. The first layer consists of fact, matters that we can know with comfortable certainty. In August 1969, human remains were found in an oil field off Schmidt Road in McComb, Mississippi. Those remains were identified—conclusively, one can say—as those of twelve-year-old Tina Marie Andrews. The law enforcement authorities of Pike County—the sheriff's department and the police department—conducted an investigation, assisted by the Mississippi Highway Patrol. Nearly a year and a half later, two indictments were returned against two men who were then members of the McComb Police Department. One of those officers was tried twice, with a mistrial and then an acquittal. Following immediately upon that acquittal, charges against the second police officer were dropped, without prejudice. He was never indicted again or tried.

The second layer of information still extant and from which one can build a story with reasonable confidence, albeit confidence tempered by caution, involves statements made by people materially involved in the case: for instance, statements made during trial, as reflected in the partial transcript that does remain of the 1971 trial of Richard McIntosh. Other reliable and verifiable information can be drawn from contemporary published accounts of the case in the local newspaper and in much shorter, derivative coverage in other Mississippi and Louisiana newspapers. Still other useful information can be gathered from statements made over the years by people who were involved in the case: Joe Pigott, for example, and more recently, Jim Kitchens, as well as surviving jurors. Beyond that information, we are left largely with speculation and questions.

What can we ultimately say about the reasons that the state of Mississippi failed to obtain a conviction? One weakness in the state's case, and indeed one of the most significant missing elements of the entire story, was the failure to identify the third girl who was allegedly in the car with the other four people before they proceeded to the oil field. Had that girl been identified, and had she testified, then perhaps Billie Jo Lambert's story would have seemed more credible. Lambert herself consistently said in testimony that she did not know the name of the other girl. If that was the case, then the state's locating her was no easy task. Short of wholesale interviews with anyone who might have been in the Tiger's Den that night, and there is no evidence such an attempt was made, how could she have been identified? It is possible, of course, that the name of the third girl did emerge during the investigation and that it might have been known to the state or the defense or to both. In the 1971 trial, attorney B. D. Statham asked Lambert if she had asked Beverly Henderson "to come down here and be a witness for the State, and testify that she was with you and Tina the night that you state that these two men picked you up." Lambert denied that she had asked Henderson to come to court to offer testimony. But Statham never asked Lambert directly if Henderson was the third girl in the car. Lambert did say that she did not know if Henderson was in the Tiger's Den that evening, which is not precisely the same thing as saying whether or not Henderson was outside the Tiger's Den or in the car with the other four people.[6]

Was there truly a third girl sitting on the corner of Railroad and Canal with Andrews and Lambert? Lambert always insisted so. Consider the extra layer of complication that the third girl's presence presented to the events that unfolded on August 13, 1969. Two men pull up to that corner. They see three girls, apparently together. Do they know any of the girls, by reputation, at least? If their intention was to find each of them a sexual partner for the evening, why would two men need three girls? If the men knew specifically that Tina and Billie Jo were the girls that they wanted, either for physical pleasure or some other errand, did they pick up the third girl simply because there was not a graceful way to leave her and take the other two? If the two men picked up the girls with the intention of taking only Tina and Billie Jo to the oil field, how could they have known that there would be an opportunity to rid themselves of the third girl before they left McComb? According to Lambert, the men offered the girls a ride home. From the time the girls stepped into the car, they drove away from east McComb, where Billie Jo lived. Although Lambert never said so in court, and it might have seemed too trivial a matter to mention, or it too might have been one of those things that she simply did not remember, the simplest solution is that the third girl told the men, either directly or in response to a question, that she lived on James, a street two blocks east of Oak, where Tina lived. However, had the third girl lived on Oak with Tina, or on some street well out of the direction they apparently intended to head, their plans, either well thought out or quickly improvised, would have been less easily accomplished.

If the third girl was a minor, and she almost certainly was, did she ever speak to her mother, as Billie Jo Lambert did, about the ride she received that evening from two men? Perhaps not that evening, as there would have seemed no special reason to explain to her family how she had made her way from downtown back to her house on James Street. After she learned the fate of Tina

Andrews? It is surely possible as well that if she ever did breathe a word of what happened on August 13, a ride that would have seemed innocuous at the time, that her mother, like Lambert's, might well have advised her to be quiet about it. And so there was no third girl to serve as a state's witness.

In both trials, the defense showed that the state had no witness to Tina Andrews's murder. The most the state could offer was Lambert's account of what had happened apparently sometime on the evening of Andrews's death. Lambert testified that Richard McIntosh struck Tina on the face, a blow that likely broke her jaw. There in the darkness of the oil field, at what point did any of them know how badly she was hurt? Several people, including former district attorney Jim Kitchens, maintain that was the fateful moment, the realization that led one or both men to decide to silence Tina in the face of an undeniable complication. A question to which there is no clear answer is the time at which Tina was shot. It is certainly possible that Tina began to scream after she was injured. If so, would the men have waited to shoot her, so long that Billie Jo Lambert could not have heard a gunshot? The .38-caliber round would have been shot out of a revolver, so using a silencer, as people generally do on television, was out of the question. Fictional killers often have the foresight or luck to have available a pillow or similar object to muffle the sound of a shot. In the oil field, they probably did not. Absent any attempts to conceal the sound of the shot, one could probably have heard that shot from close to a mile away. But the woods in the area, and the sounds of traffic from the interstate highway or Delaware Avenue might have interfered with Billie Jo Lambert's ability to hear it. And as she testified, she was terrified, confused, and interested mainly in getting home, all of which might have affected her perceptions and memories of the event.

One possibility is that Tina Andrews was not shot immediately after her injury. A punch to the face, delivered by a fit young man to the face of a twelve-year-old girl, one delivered with sufficient force to break her jaw, could easily have knocked her unconscious. It probably would have produced a concussion, had Tina lived to experience it. In that case, the gunshot to the head might not have been delivered to a struggling girl, but rather execution-style, to an unconscious child lying face down on the ground in an oil field clearing. Such details as bullet trajectory were not introduced as evidence in either trial and frankly do not matter much except in one's reconstruction of the scene of the crime.

Still, one might be allowed to imagine that in her last moments, Tina Andrews was spared the realization of a .38-caliber revolver being placed to her head. We also do not know precisely what else might have happened to Tina before or after she died. The initial newspaper report on the crime scene tells us that her body "was clad in shorts and a brassiere. Panties and a blouse were found about ten feet from the body."[7] Several scenarios could account for why she was found wearing shorts but no panties. To imagine any of those possibilities is deeply disturbing. But the state of Mississippi had no first-hand knowledge of these last moments, and we are left, then, with speculation about what might have been.

The involvement of the McComb Police Department in the investigation of the case remains another puzzling element of the story. Why were the police involved at all? The body was discovered at a location clearly outside the city limits. In Pike County, the investigation of a crime in that location would seem to fall within the jurisdiction of the sheriff's department, not the police department. The Mississippi Highway Patrol would reasonably be involved in the case, as their statutory authority grants that agency jurisdiction anywhere within the state. The F.B.I. as well might be interested in the case, especially given the recent history of McComb. One possibility is that Sheriff Lawson himself asked for assistance from the police department. He had a reputation for relying on the assistance of other law enforcement authorities in the area. Pike County authorities did cooperate regularly on the investigations of many matters. In the early winter of 1972, for example, a missing child in rural Pike County brought out the police department, the sheriff's department, a highway patrol investigator (the very active Donald Butler), and even the game warden.[8]

But through two trials under two different district attorneys, no one seemed overly concerned that the McComb Police Department had investigated the murder. Whether or not the involvement of McComb police was jurisdictionally irregular or in this specific case problematic, such cooperation of the sheriff's and police departments was not rare, as the investigations of many other cases in this era makes clear. Indeed, in the late 1960s, the city purchased new radio equipment for the police department so the police and sheriff's department could maintain close contact. Another possible reason for the involvement of the police department is simply that McComb was a small town.

Members of the two departments cooperated in ways that seemed convenient, often without worrying very much about whose official jurisdiction was whose.

There is no direct evidence that either McIntosh or Fleming were considered suspects in the case before Billie Jo Lambert, aided by Pat Lamkin, took her story to the district attorney. One nagging question does remain, however. At the time of the indictments, both men were on voluntary leave from the department, the timing of which and the specific reasons for which were never publicly stated. With the police department actively involved in the investigation from the beginning, it seems improbable that members of the police force, McIntosh and Fleming included, would not have been in a position to learn a good deal about what law enforcement agencies in the area knew and did not know about the matter. Early in the investigation, however, there would have been no apparent need to keep these details from any members of the McComb Police Department. By the time that the case reached District Attorney Joe Pigott's office, the police department knew what they knew, and there was nothing that Pigott could do about that fact.

In the Pike County Courthouse, Billie Jo Lambert faced not only formidable barriers of social class, but of gender as well. In almost every way that mattered, Pike County in 1971 and 1972 was still run by white men. The police force, the sheriff's department, the district attorney and the prosecutor, the judges, the local doctors and dentists who examined Tina Andrews's remains, the majority of the juries in both trials: all were men, and with the exception of a few jurors, all were white men. It seemed natural (to white people, at least) in a place like Pike County for that to be the case. Black voices had emerged successfully to challenge the right of whites exclusively to govern McComb, but for the most part, the white, male foundation still held. A young woman from an undistinguished social background would have felt herself to be, as she indeed was, very much at a disadvantage in this atmosphere.

In two trials, the juries heard a story of white working-class life lived on the margins of respectability. The defense argued in effect that Lambert's lack of respectability shook her credibility as a witness. The jury weighed whether or not Lambert's version of the events of August 13, 1969, was believable. But they were also listening to another story as well. The trial was in some measure about the telling of lives—those of the Lambert and Andrews families. The story that emerged failed to connect positively with the audience, at least in ways that would make them sympathetic to Lambert and Andrews. It failed to make them say "I know" and "I understand." Instead, what they heard seemed not altogether alien, but rather close enough to allow them to act as expert judges not only of the evidence presented, but also of the value of lives that would produce such evidence. At many turns, they could ask themselves questions such as these: Who lets their children roam like that? Who doesn't know the date of her father's death? Who doesn't follow her little sister's school attendance and academic record? Who has a family that is afraid of the law? Paradoxically, a jury in that time and place would have expected such a story to emerge from the lives of black families. With white ones, however, it seems that the proximity, at least in terms of race, produced a visceral recoil that worked to the defense's advantage. The sense of respectability and of the need to guard it would have been strong among the working people that dominated the juries in both trials.

Neither of the district attorneys, Joe Pigott and Jim Kitchens, did anything other than to argue the case as vigorously as they could, given the witnesses that they were able to call. Pigott and Kitchens were effective attorneys, both of whom were experienced in criminal law. The judges in the two trials ran an effective courtroom, ruling more often favorably on the state's motions than on those of the defense. If the state can be faulted for anything in the trials, it is the lack of preparation of Billie Jo Lambert. In similar trials, both then and later, an essential witness such as Lambert would have been thoroughly primed by the state to face what they would have anticipated as the main lines of attack by the defense. But the state could not compel Billie Jo Lambert to offer a story more detailed than she could remember. The state could not paint Lambert as anything other than what she was: a fifteen-year-old unwed mother who had waited a long time to come forward with her story, a story that was not in its main lines corroborated by that of any other witness.

Some people in Pike County continue to remember the story of Tina Andrews through the same class-inflected lens that B. D. Statham used to such good effect in both trials. What kind of people would not move heaven and earth to find a missing daughter? Who would not have marched into the police department to demand answers when a child failed to come home at night? Who would let a child of that age come and go without more supervision?

And who does not teach a child of that age not to get into a car with strangers? To frame those questions in that way is to suggest that the Andrews family or Tina herself is in some measure to blame for her fate or at least the failure to discover what happened to her. In *The Road to Wigan Pier*, his study of conditions in working-class northern England during the Great Depression, George Orwell offers a useful corrective to these notions. Observing a young woman, greatly aged by care and drudgery, kneeling outside her house in the cold to unclog a drain, Orwell writes: her face "wore, for the second in which I saw it, the most desolate, hopeless expression I have ever seen. It struck me then that we are mistaken when we say that 'It isn't the same for them as it would be for us,' and that people bred in the slums can imagine nothing but the slums. For what I saw in her face was not the ignorant suffering of an animal. She knew well enough what was happening to her—understood as well as I did how dreadful a destiny it was to be kneeling there in the bitter cold, on the slimy stones of a slum backyard, poking a stick up a foul drain-pipe."[9] Substitute "working class" or "white trash" or "those people" for slum-dwellers, and we get close to understanding what Tina Andrews's parents suffered, even if they were unable to do very much about it.

A consideration of social class in Pike County does make it possible to imagine a scenario that might have presented Pigott and Kitchens with a much stronger case, one that they surely might have won. There were many families (white ones, certainly) in McComb that felt that law enforcement officials were not elements to be feared, but rather allies or even men over whom they had some leverage. If Billie Jo Lambert had come from such a family, she would still have been terrified by what had happened to her, but she might have told her story to her family and had it received sympathetically and with a sense of outrage. Had the police or the sheriff or the district attorney received a call that evening, demanding action, there were families in town that could have ensured that something would have been done. What would that "something" have looked like? A quicker identification of the alleged killers; a search for and examination of their automobile; a thorough and exacting search for the third girl; and a near-immediate examination of Tina Andrews's remains, perhaps. It is impossible to say what evidence that search might have yielded, and that is also what did not happen here.

In two trials, the state of Mississippi—more specifically, two juries of his peers in the Pike County Circuit Court—failed to find Richard McIntosh guilty of the murder of Tina Andrews. The jury did not, as a matter of fact, declare him innocent, nor did a Pike County jury have the option of returning a verdict of "not proven" or some other, more nuanced option between "guilty" and "not guilty." Has McIntosh, then, earned the right to be left alone? To ask this question is to suggest some of the ways that the history of race in Mississippi shaped both the events of 1969 to 1972 as well as the ways that they have been remembered. Had Tina Andrews been an African American child, this story would fit neatly within familiar stories of the era. Few people these days suggest that verdicts of courts in Mississippi in that era that touch upon matters of race should be considered the last word on the matter. The investigation, retelling, and reopening of race-inflected cases from those decades remains one of the most significant and visible stories about Mississippi and the Deep South, kept fresh by historians, newspaper reporters, and law school professors and students. In those situations, even to suggest that these things happened a long time ago or to assert that some matters of the past are better left alone seems to betray an ignorance of the way that things worked in Mississippi.

To ask if Richard McIntosh has some right to privacy is not to suggest that he has a responsibility to speak with a historian who is writing a book about the Tina Andrews case. The answer to that question seems obvious. What, though, of Billie Jo Lambert Bordelon or the surviving members of Tina Andrews's family? Does the historian's desire for a story outweigh their considerations of privacy or reticence or even fear? To put the question more abstractly, what debt does the past owe to the present? Perhaps the present owes to the past our not using it simply as a platform from which to declare our moral superiority. If we do that, we deserve whatever we receive in future years. But it seems no injustice to McComb's recent past or to any of the people involved in the case to argue that Tina Andrews's killer or killers were never convicted of any crime because in part of who Tina Andrews was.

Why has the story of Tina Andrews to this point been an untold one, except through Pike County memory and speculation? The history of race in Mississippi seems to yield at least some suggestions. Unlike many other unsolved murders from Mississippi in the twentieth century, this one has no overt connection to the history and regime of racial controls that so obsessed the state then and historians of the state more recently. Thus, no reporter and no historian has identified the Tina Andrews case as one that cries out for retelling or solving, in the manner of other civil rights–era murder cases. In recent decades, historians of Mississippi, its state institutions, most newspapers, and indeed many politicians have tried honestly to face the state's troubled past. The state flag continues to rankle many people, black and white. Currently, none of the state's public universities fly that flag; neither do many towns and cities. But in other ways, people like to point out, the state has come a long way. Commemorative sites and physical markers honor the work of the many local people who battled against a racially segregated society. The newly opened and spectacular museum in Jackson devoted to the state's civil rights movement is perhaps the most obvious of these efforts. But speaking out now against those days and practices exacts very little toll—nothing, one might fairly say, in comparison with that faced by people in the decades before the 1970s. The state remembers Emmett Till, Medgar Evers, and James Cheney, Andrew Goodman, and Michael Schwerner. Those acts of memory are especially appropriate, given the state's active work in their oppression and indeed in part in their deaths.

In the last decade, the F.B.I. and other law enforcement agencies have sought fresh evidence on a number of civil rights–era murders, mostly from the 1950s and 1960s. In 2006, the Jackson Division, which covered the state of Mississippi, solicited leads and other information on forty-three slayings, including one each in McComb, Brookhaven, and Liberty. Very recently, the Justice Department announced that it would reopen the investigation of the Emmett Till slaying, one in which the two confessed murderers are very long dead, and a case about which practically no one does not know that a profound wrong was done not only by the killers, but by the state of Mississippi as well.[10]

Tina Andrews does not fit neatly into satisfying tales of racial reconciliation or the honoring of martyrs. At the time of her death, many in the community thought that Tina Andrews simply did not matter very much because of her social background. The Jackson *Clarion-Ledger* and its investigative reporters have apparently found nothing of interest in the story of her life and death. Because her story does not satisfy any contemporary need for apology or facing facts, as some of these men and women have seen in other Mississippi stories, it has largely remained, as a local reporter wrote in 1982, "obscured by time, silence, and the curtains drawn by history."[11] "That's the way the erasure of the past tends to work," wrote Paul Hendrickson in his superlative study of Mississippi lawmen, "by selective memory and willed amnesia and the wearing away of time."[12]

Tina Andrews's story will fail to provide readers with closure. People enjoy stories with closure, ones in which matters ultimately make sense. In stories of crime, readers prefer to see miscreants brought to justice, or failing that, to know precisely why justice failed. Some people, of course, prefer stories in which the outlaw wins. In southern stories, the answer to miscarriages of justice is often a racist system, or one corrupted in some other way. Tina Andrews's murder does not provide that kind of story, although it does feature a system that was shaped by race and in which various kinds of influence and indeed corruption operated. But as much as we might like to see it, at least as the central element of a satisfying story, there was no broad conspiracy involved in protecting the killer or killers. There is no evidence that Tina Andrews was taken to the oil field that night to be executed in order to ensure her silence about scandalous matters of which she knew. What of other conspiracies? Prominent people in the town wished to see the two police officers acquitted and might even have helped to arrange legal counsel for them. Certainly the rest of the police department supported their colleagues, and their presence in force at the first trial suggests as much. It is impossible to credit any version of events in which Joe Pigott or Jim Kitchens failed to prosecute the case vigorously in order to protect anyone's reputation. The two district attorneys did the best that they could with a case that simply might not have been winnable. Did business interests in McComb exercise a good deal of control over local matters? Of course. Did they fix two juries to protect a police officer? Not in any simple way involving bribery or intimidation.

Nothing like the complete story of the murder of Tina Andrews will ever be known. Viewers of television shows like *Forensic Files* expect neat twists in which fragments of evidence result in convictions of killers. But that will never happen in this case. If one believes the story that Billie Jo Lambert told in court in 1971 and 1972, four people were in the oil field on August 13, 1969. Two of those people, Tina Andrews and Ted Fleming, are dead. Lambert and Richard McIntosh have very different and irreconcilable accounts of what happened that night. It is very unlikely at this point that either of those two people will change their account. If any witnesses to any part of the events on that night have any further information to offer, they have never come forward to tell of it.

The year 2019 marked the fiftieth anniversary of the death of Tina Andrews. The passage of time has silenced many people who might have known significant things about her or about her murder. Time has allowed those who remember the case to tell and retell the story, sometimes conflating it with what they believe they remember about other events in the community in those years. The Tina Andrews story tells us a lot about the demons that people in McComb have feared over the last decades: sexual depravity by prominent men; the control of the city by powerful, monied interests who could make people rise and fall financially and in other ways at their bidding; and children lost to sex and drugs, children who were not being raised as more respectable people's parents raised them.

The slim facts of Tina Andrews's life and what little we can say for certain about her death can scarcely bear the weight of so much story. That is why she has been enlisted in other causes. To call for justice or even vengeance on her behalf can become a powerful, satisfying way to rail against one's own enemies. Over the last decades in Pike County, those enemies have sometimes been associated with very specific community grudges or disappointments or failures. Her story has also been called upon to distill broader anxieties into manageable form, attached to a figure who can become both something more and something less than she was from 1957 to 1969. Few of us are comfortable admitting the degree to which we wish to exact revenge upon the things we hate or fear, if only because it is not pleasant to acknowledge how much the idea consumes us, especially if we cannot realize those wishes. But perhaps we feel better calling for someone's head when we do it on behalf of another, especially a dead child.

Tina Marie Andrews, born in McComb, Mississippi, in 1957, was not dealt a particularly favorable hand of cards with which to play. What we can know of her twelve years suggests that near the end of her life she seemed not to be on a path that might lead to good things. There is no way we can know what her life would have been like. She did not have that chance, either. Because of the actions of people never convicted by the state of Mississippi, she lies in a graveyard beside the bodies of her parents, in that sense at least at rest.

Notes

Introduction

1. This reconstruction of events of August 13, 1969, is drawn largely from testimony given in *State of Mississippi v. Richard McIntosh*, Pike County Circuit Court Case #11,468; partial copy of trial transcript in author's possession. Other information about that evening, along with the description of the town of McComb, comes from contemporary coverage in Louisiana and Mississippi newspapers, primarily from that of the McComb daily newspaper, the *Enterprise-Journal*, as well as from interviews cited below.

2. The "new" Otken Elementary School, which Tina Andrews attended, now serves grades one through three. It is located at 401 Montana Avenue. The distance from Tina Andrews's house at 102 Oak Street to the school was just under half a mile, a walk of approximately ten minutes. According to a plaque in the school, Otken Elementary was built in 1958 and 1959 and dedicated and opened in the latter year.

3. *Enterprise-Journal*, July 9, 1969. On the repeal of Mississippi's compulsory school attendance law, see Charles C. Bolton, *William F. Winter and the New Mississippi: A Biography* (Jackson: University Press of Mississippi, 2013), 101. On the broader context of Mississippi public education in this period, see Bolton, *The Hardest Deal of All: The Battle over School Integration in Mississippi, 1870–1980* (Jackson: University Press of Mississippi, 2005). Former McComb public school superintendent Julian Prince's memoir contains much detail on the integration of the McComb schools and on the efforts of white and black parents to make public education work in the town. See Julian D. Prince, *Balancing the Scales: A Turbulent Age of Mississippi History during School Integration* (n.p.: St. Luke's Writers' Press, 2018).

4. Interview with Carroll Case, July 24, 2018; interview with Emily Sue Williams, July 24, 2018.

5. For the location of downtown McComb businesses, see *McComb and Magnolia, Mississippi City Directory, Including Fernwood and Summit* (Richmond, VA: R. L. Polk, 1969). See also South Central Bell, *McComb Telephone Directory, 1968*. A memoir of McComb that includes detailed description of the downtown in the 1950s and 1960s is Mac Gordon, *Hometown: A Remembrance* (Magnolia, MS: Magnolia Gazette Publishing Company, 2011).

6. Joyce Carol Oates, "Where Are You Going, Where Have You Been?" (1966). An authorized electronic version of the text is available at: *https://celestialtimepiece.com/2015/01/21/where-are-you -going-where-have-you-been/*. The opening sentences of this Introduction offer a modest nod toward Oates's story.

7. The Tiger's Den had operated since the mid-1940s in several locations in downtown Mc-Comb. Over the years the name or at least the spelling of the name varied slightly, given in the local newspaper as the Tiger Den, the Tigers Den, and sometimes the Tiger's Den. See *Enterprise-Journal*, May 20, 1944; March 17, 1969; and September 27, 1966.

8. For a chart of that year's top popular music, see https://www.americanradiohistory.com /hd2/IDX-Business/Music/Archive-Billboard-IDX/IDX/60s/1969/Billboard%201969–12–27-OCR -Page-0017.pdf.

9. Interview with Emily Sue Williams, July 24, 2018.

10. For McComb's weather data for August 13, 1969, see http://www.wunderground.am/history /airport/KMCB/1969/8/13/DailyHistory.html?req_city=Osyka&req_state=MS&req_statename =&reqdb.zip=39657&reqdb.magic=1&reqdb.wmo=99999.

11. Construction of Interstate Highway 55 had begun in Mississippi in 1957 and was finally completed in 1973. By the mid-1960s, however, much of Mississippi, including the McComb area, was served by the new highway. See https://www.interstate-guide.com/i-055.html; http://www .ajfroggie.com/roads/msroutes/i055.htm. The area of the highway between Summit and Magnolia (McComb being located between those two towns) opened in 1961; *Enterprise-Journal*, August 31, 1961.

12. Philip D. Hearn, *Hurricane Camille: Monster Storm of the Gulf Coast* (Jackson: University Press of Mississippi, 2004); Mark M. Smith, *Camille, 1969: Histories of a Hurricane* (Athens: University of Georgia Press, 2011). For Camille's impact on the McComb area, see *Enterprise-Journal*, August 18, 1969. The city received high winds and heavy rainfall, but no significant damage.

13. *Enterprise-Journal*, August 25, 1969; Pike County Mississippi Cold Case Facebook Page; https://www.facebook.com/Pike-County-Mississippi-Cold-Cases.

14. *Enterprise-Journal*, August 25, 1969; *Clarion-Ledger*, August 27, 1969.

15. *Clarion-Ledger*, October 4, 1969.

16. *Enterprise-Journal*, October 2, 1969.

17. *New York Times*, April 2, 1978.

18. An impressive new study of another southern Mississippi town is William Sturkey, *Hattiesburg: An American City in Black and White* (Cambridge, MA: Harvard University Press, 2019).

19. Hodding Carter, *So the Heffners Left McComb* (Garden City, NY: Doubleday, 1965), 58.

20. There is no full treatment of the civil rights movement in McComb. On the city in the late 1950s and the 1960s, see Charles M. Payne, *I've Got the Light of Freedom: The Organizing Tradition and the Mississippi Freedom Struggle* (Berkeley and Los Angeles: University of California Press, 1995), 111–31. See also John Dittmer, *Local People: The Struggle for Civil Rights in Mississippi* (Urbana and Chicago: University of Illinois Press, 1994), 99–115; 266–71; 303–14.

21. Payne, *I've Got the Light of Freedom*, 112, 113.

22. *Freedom's Journal* (McComb, MS; August 24, 1964) 4:3. Mississippi Department of Archives and History, 323.1/F853f/1964. Four issues of this student newspaper were published in 1964 under the auspices of the Council of Federated Organizations. For an edited collection of *Freedom's Journal* and other freedom school newspapers, see William Sturkey and Jon N. Hale, eds., *To Write in the Light of Freedom: The Newspapers of the 1964 Mississippi Freedom Schools* (Jackson: University Press of Mississippi, 2015).

23. Quoted in Dittmer, *Local People*, 266.

24. Neither person who made these observations is willing to be named in this book.

25. Stephen A. Berrey, *The Jim Crow Routine: Everyday Performances of Race, Civil Rights, and Segregation in Mississippi* (Chapel Hill: University of North Carolina Press, 2015), 194.

26. For a new study of the state's legal system, see Joseph A. Ranney, *A Legal History of Mississippi: Race, Class, and the Struggle for Opportunity* (Jackson: University Press of Mississippi, 2019).

Chapter One

Note to the chapter epigraphs: Between 1945 and 1972, Oliver Emmerich, editor of the McComb *Enterprise-Journal*, reminded readers well over 1,200 times in that newspaper that it was a privilege to live in McComb; Bryant quoted in Trent Brown, "Introduction," Hodding Carter II, *So the Heffners Left McComb* (Jackson: University Press of Mississippi, 2016), xviii. Carter's book was originally published in 1965. Bryant's remark is also quoted on the Mississippi Freedom Trail marker outside his home in McComb; https://www.mississippimarkers.com/pike-county.html. On the commemoration of Mississippi's civil rights legacy through those markers, see Richard Rubin, "The Freedom Trail in Mississippi Is a Chronicle of Outrage and Courage," *New York Times*, September 10, 2018.

1. https://www2.census.gov/library/publications/decennial/1970/pcp1/02605992ch01.pdf. See also *Enterprise-Journal*, February 2, 1971. Pike County's population dropped 9.4 percent from 1960 to 1970, a trend that Mississippi had seen for decades. McComb's population in 1960 had been 12,020, while in 1970 it was 11,969, a decrease of only .4 percent. According to the 2010 U.S. Census, McComb's population was 12,790, about 66 percent of whom were African American and 31 percent of whom were white. On McComb's population in the 1960s, see Amy Schmidt, "McComb Civil Rights Movement," in Ted Ownby and Charles Reagan Wilson, ed., *The Mississippi Encyclopedia* (Jackson: University Press of Mississippi, 2017), 787.

2. Howard Zinn, *SNCC: The New Abolitionists* (Boston: Beacon Press, 1964), 65. Bob Zellner with Constance Curry, *The Wrong Side of Murder Creek: A White Southerner in the Freedom Movement* (Montgomery, AL: NewSouth Books, 2008), 150.

3. *New York Times*, September 27, 1964.

4. John F. Stover, "Colonel Henry S. McComb, Mississippi Railroad Adventurer," *Journal of Mississippi History* 17 (July 1955): 177–90. On the timber industry that drove much of the development of Pike County and surrounding areas, see Nollie Hickman, *Mississippi Harvest: Lumbering in the Longleaf Pine Belt, 1840–1915* (University: University of Mississippi, 1962).

5. On the early history of the area, see Martin J. Hardeman, *The Structure of Time: Pike County, Mississippi, 1815–1912* (New York: Peter Lang, 1999). As is common with most Mississippi towns, there is no comprehensive scholarly history of McComb. Two recent histories of Mississippi contain no indexed references to either McComb or Pike County. See Dennis J. Mitchell, *A New History of Mississippi* (Jackson: University Press of Mississippi, 2014); Westley F. Busbee, Jr., *Mississippi: A History*, 2nd ed. (Malden, MA: Wiley Blackwell, 2015). On the history of the railroad and

farming in Pike County, see James L. McCorkle, Jr., "The Illinois Central R.R. and the Mississippi Commercial Vegetable Industry," *Journal of Mississippi History* 29 (May 1977): 155–72. On the broader context of the state in the late nineteenth century, see Bradley G. Bond, *Political Culture in the Nineteenth-Century South: Mississippi, 1839–1900* (Baton Rouge: Louisiana State University Press, 1995).

6. *New York Times*, October 2–6, 1911.

7. For the railroad museum's website, see http://www.mcrrmuseum.com/.

8. For a brief description of White's BAWI program, see Mitchell, *A New History of Mississippi*, 345–46.

9. "Pike County," *Mississippi Encyclopedia*, 997–98; *Enterprise-Journal*, December 1, 1958.

10. [Sylvia F. Cook?], *January 10, 1975: A Day to Remember, A Day to Forget* (McComb, MS: *Enterprise-Journal*, 1975), 4.

11. *Austin American-Statesman*, July 10, 1994.

12. Hodding Carter, *So the Heffners Left McComb* (Garden City, NY: Doubleday, 1965), 57.

13. Tom Hayden affidavit, COFO Records, Series 1, Box 1, Folder 18, Pike County, Z 1867.000 S, Mississippi Department of Archives and History.

14. This description of McComb is informed by John Dittmer, *Local People: The Struggle for Civil Rights in Mississippi* (Urbana and Chicago: University of Illinois Press, 1994), 99–100; and Carter, *So the Heffners Left McComb*, 52–58.

15. For the changes in Pike County population, see https://www.census.gov/population/cen counts/ms190090.txt.

16. Interview with Rita Watts, July 25, 2018.

17. *A Day to Remember, A Day to Forget*, 4.

18. *Enterprise-Journal*, January 3, 1969.

19. *Enterprise-Journal*, March 17, 1964. The McComb Garden Club still sponsors the annual Azalea Festival: *Enterprise-Journal*, March 2, 2018.

20. *A Day to Remember, A Day to Forget*, 3.

21. For a recent work that emphasizes the work of the national government in making those times ones that people remember so fondly, see David Goldfield, *The Gifted Generation: When Government Was Good* (New York: Bloomsbury, 2017).

22. See, for example, *Enterprise-Journal*, November 25, 1955.

23. Mac Gordon, *Hometown: A Remembrance* (Magnolia, MS: Magnolia Gazette Publishing Company, 2011), 15. The book carries an extended subtitle: "How a small town newspaper and ordinary citizens joined together in the 1960s to end racial violence in McComb, Mississippi." On children's education in the etiquette of Jim Crow, see LeeAnn G. Reynolds, *Maintaining Segregation: Children and Racial Instruction in the South, 1920–1955* (Baton Rouge: Louisiana State University Press, 2017).

24. Anne Moody grew up in Centreville, about forty miles from McComb. See her classic autobiography, *Coming of Age in Mississippi* (New York: Dial Press, 1968).

25. Carter, *So the Heffners Left McComb*, 53.

26. *Enterprise-Journal*, March 8, 1963.

27. *Enterprise-Journal*, February 4, 1964.

28. *Freedom's Journal* (McComb, MS; August 3, 1964) 2:3. Mississippi Department of Archives and History, 323.1/F853f/1964.

29. Kathryn Stockett, *The Help: A Novel* (New York: G. P. Putnam's Sons, 2009). For a nuanced fictional imagining of the relationship between a white Mississippi woman and her African American maid, see Ellen Douglas, *Can't Quit You, Baby* (New York: Scribner's, 1988).

30. Gordon, *Hometown*, 14.

31. Mississippi Blues Trail marker, Summit Street, McComb; http://www.msbluestrail.org /blues-trail-markers/summit-street.

32. Black travelers of the era often consulted the *Green Book*, a guide to services available to them on the road. Editions of the 1950s and 1960s listed the Desoto Hotel and also the White Castle Hotel, located in Baertown. In the 1930s and 1940s, the Townsend, another hotel, had also operated on Summit Street. For the *Green Book*, see https://digitalcollections.nypl.org/collections /the-green-book#/?tab=about.

33. *Enterprise-Journal*, November 7, 2006.

34. "SNCC Biography: Bob Moses," in Michael Edmonds, ed., *Risking Everything: A Freedom Summer Reader* (Madison: Wisconsin Historical Society Press, 2014), 29.

35. Dittmer, *Local People*, 100.

36. Dittmer, *Local People*, 100–101.

37. Interview with C. C. Bryant, February 7, 1985; transcript available at: https://www.crmvet .org/nars/js_bryant.pdf.

38. Wesley C. Hogan, *Many Minds, One Heart: SNCC's Dream for a New America* (Chapel Hill: University of North Carolina Press, 2007), 56–57.

39. Charles M. Payne, *I've Got the Light of Freedom: The Organizing Tradition and the Mississippi Freedom Struggle* (Berkeley and Los Angeles: University of California Press, 1995), 118.

40. Judith E. Barlow, "C. C. Bryant: A Race Man Is What They Called Him," M.A. thesis, University of Mississippi, 2012.

41. Payne, *I've Got the Light of Freedom*, 117.

42. Nathaniel H. Lewis Oral History, University of Southern Mississippi Center for Oral History & Cultural Heritage; transcript available at https://digitalcollections.usm.edu/uncategorized /digitalFile_a14af499-c9e6-45dc-9a24-97ca58efc095/.

43. Wesley Hogan refers to "going to the registrar . . . in McComb, Mississippi, in the fall of 1961," a minor error, given the significance of McComb in memories of the civil rights movement. But the registrar was in fact in Magnolia, the county seat. Wesley Hogan, "Freedom Now: Nonviolence in the Southern Freedom Movement, 1960–1964," in Emilye Crosby, ed., *Civil Rights History from the Ground Up: Local Struggles, a National Movement* (Athens: University of Georgia Press, 2011), 185.

44. https://www.crmvet.org/nars/js_bryant.pdf.

45. Payne, *I've Got the Light of Freedom*, 116.

46. *Freedom's Journal*, (McComb, MS; July 24, 1964) 1:4. Mississippi Department of Archives and History, 323.1/F853f/1964.

47. *Enterprise-Journal*, August 28, 1961.

48. *Enterprise-Journal*, August 31, 1961. The arresting officers were Eddie Smith and Richard

Rowley. Rowley would become police chief later in the decade. Rowley was also the arresting officer in the Woolworth's sit-in.

49. *Enterprise-Journal*, August 31, 1961; Dittmer, *Local People*, 107.

50. Dittmer, *Local People*, 106.

51. Hogan, *Many Minds, One Heart*, 61.

52. Payne, *I've Got the Light of Freedom*, 126–27.

53. Zellner recalled thinking, "So this is the way I die—like a football being kicked in a scrimmage." Zellner, *The Wrong Side of Murder Creek*, 163.

54. Payne, *I've Got the Light of Freedom*, 124–25; Hogan, *Many Minds, One Heart*, 61–65; Dittmer, *Local People*, 110–15.

55. Zinn, *SNCC*, 77.

56. J. Oliver Emmerich, *Two Faces of Janus: The Saga of Deep South Change* (Jackson: University Press of Mississippi, 1973), 104–5; 128. Charges against Milton J. Stayton, the oil worker who attacked Emmerich on December 3, 1961, were eventually dismissed because "the arrest of the defendant was improperly carried out." Stayton was represented by Breed Mounger, a formidable defense attorney from nearby Walthall County. See *Enterprise-Journal*, September 16, 1963; *New York Times*, December 4, 1961. On Emmerich, see David R. Davies, "J. Oliver Emmerich and the McComb *Enterprise-Journal*," in Davies, ed., *The Press and Race: Mississippi Journalists Confront the Movement* (Jackson: University Press of Mississippi, 2001), 111–34. See also David R. Davies, "J. Oliver Emmerich and the McComb *Enterprise-Journal*: Slow Change in McComb, 1964," *Journal of Mississippi History* 57:1 (March, 1995): 1–23. On the Mississippi press in the period, see Susan Weill, *In a Madhouse's Din: Civil Rights Coverage by Mississippi's Daily Press, 1948–1968* (Westport, CT: Praeger, 2002).

57. *Enterprise-Journal*, November 30, 1961. The fullest account of the Freedom Rides is Raymond Arsenault, *Freedom Riders: 1961 and the Search for Racial Justice* (New York: Oxford University Press, 2006).

58. Four young McComb white men were arrested for those attacks: Haskell Boyd, twenty; Earl Ratcliff, twenty-six; Claude McKenzie, twenty-one; and Johnny Thames, twenty. They were charged with disturbing the peace. *Enterprise-Journal*, December 1, 1961.

59. Sitton quoted in Kathleen Woodruff Wickam, "Dean of the Civil Rights Reporters: A Conversation with Claude Sitton," *Journalism History* 40:2 (July 2014): 122.

60. The fullest scholarly treatment of the civil rights movement in Pike County remains Payne, *I've Got the Light of Freedom*, 111–31; and Dittmer, *Local People*, 99–115; 266–671; 303–14. On 1964, see also Bruce Watson, *Freedom Summer: The Savage Season That Made Mississippi Burn and Made America a Democracy* (New York: Viking, 2010), 86–87; 135–36; 263–64; Joseph Crespino, *In Search of Another Country: Mississippi and the Conservative Counterrevolution* (Princeton, NJ: Princeton University Press, 2007), 112–13; 119–30; 155–56.

61. Joseph Crespino, "Civilities and Civil Rights in Mississippi," in Ted Ownby, ed., *Manners and Southern History* (Jackson: University Press of Mississippi, 2007), 114–36; quote at 115.

62. *Enterprise-Journal*, February 5, 1963.

63. "The Present Day Ku Klux Klan Movement," 90th Congress, 2nd Session, House Doc-

ument #377; text available at https://archive.org/stream/ThePresent-dayKuKluxKlanMovemen-tReportNinetiethCongressFirst/HUAC1_djvu.txt.

64. David Cunningham, "Shades of Anti-Civil Rights Violence: Reconsidering the Ku Klux Klan in Mississippi," in Ted Ownby, ed., *The Civil Rights Movement in Mississippi* (Jackson: University Press of Mississippi, 2013), 181. Establishing a precise count of violent acts in McComb or the Klan involvement in those acts remains a challenge. As the House Un-American Activities Committee Klan report notes: "From April to October 1964, more than 25 bombings and/or acts of arsons took place in the vicinity of McComb, Miss. While the methods of carrying out these violent acts showed a remarkable degree of similarity, the committee was unable to establish each act as the responsibility of a klan or its members. Committee investigation, together with sworn testimony, however, definitely established klan involvement in the majority of the crimes." See "The Present Day Ku Klux Klan Movement," 90th Congress, 2nd Session, House Document #377; text available at https://archive.org/stream/ThePresent-dayKuKluxKlanMovementReportNineti-ethCongressFirst/HUAC1_djvu.txt.

65. Cleveland Sellers with Robert Terrell, *The River of No Return: The Autobiography of a Black Militant and the Life and Death of SNCC* (New York: Morrow, 1973), 48.

66. Sitton quoted in Kathleen Woodruff Wickam, "Dean of the Civil Rights Reporters: A Conversation with Claude Sitton," *Journalism History* 40:2 (July 2014): 121–25.

67. *Enterprise-Journal*, May 29, 1964.

68. *Enterprise-Journal*, April 6, 1964.

69. For a photograph of the bombed Society Hill Missionary Baptist Church and the quote from the sheriff, see Michael Edmonds and Stephen Haller, "Images from Freedom Summer, 1964," *Southern Quarterly* 52:1 (Fall 2014): 53.

70. *Enterprise-Journal*, May 6, 1992.

71. Nicholas Von Hoffman, *Mississippi Notebook* (New York: David White, 1964), 32.

72. For interviews with major figures in the McComb civil rights movement, see the McComb Legacies website; http://mccomblegacies.org/. The website is a cooperative effort of local people and McComb public school students; see William Sturkey and Jon N. Hale, *To Write in the Light of Freedom: The Newspapers of the 1964 Mississippi Freedom Schools* (Jackson: University Press of Mississippi, 2015), 42. For the recollections of Brenda Travis, one of the leaders of the student movement, see Brenda Travis with John Obee, *Mississippi's Exiled Daughter: How My Civil Rights Baptism under Fire Shaped My Life* (Montgomery, AL: New South Books, 2018). See also Cynthia Loren Lamkin, "Perceptions of Segregation, Desegregation, and Integration from Burgland High School Students in McComb, Mississippi," Ph.D. dissertation, University of Southern Mississippi, 2016.

73. For Bryant's affidavit, see *Mississippi Black Paper* (Jackson: University Press of Mississippi, 2018), 109. Orig. ed. 1965. A dozen more people provided affidavits of that summer's violence. See COFO Records, Series 1, Box 1, Folder 18—Pike County, Z 1867.000 S, Mississippi Department of Archives and History. Black armed resistance to white violence has generated significant scholarly debate. See Akinyele Omowale Umoja, *We Will Shoot Back: Armed Resistance in the Mississippi Freedom Movement* (Chapel Hill: University of North Carolina Press, 2013). For a nuanced study

of the uses and limits of such resistance, see Emilye Crosby, "'It Wasn't the Wild West': Keeping Local Studies in Self-Defense Historiography," in Crosby, ed., *Civil Rights History from the Ground Up: Local Struggles, a National Movement* (Athens: University of Georgia Press, 2011), 194–255.

74. For a copy of that action, see https://www.crmvet.org/docs/640000_sncc_mcc_pikecivilaction.pdf.

75. For a list of "civil rights incidents" in the McComb area from April through November, 1964, compiled by COFO, see https://www.crmvet.org/info/mccomb1964.pdf.

76. Tom Hayden affidavit, COFO Records, Series 1, Box 1, Folder 18, Pike County, Z 1867.000 S, Mississippi Department of Archives and History.

77. Carter, *So the Heffners Left McComb.*

78. *Enterprise-Journal,* October 1, 1964. For a list of the arrested men, the charges against them, and the disposition of those charges, see https://www.crmvet.org/info/mccombbomber64.pdf. The nine men sentenced by Judge Watkins were Paul D. Wilson, Billy Earl Wilson, Jimmy P. Wilson, Gerald Lawrence, Hilton Dunaway, Ernest F. Zeeck, John Paul Westbrook, Murphy J. Duncan, and Emory Allen Lee. The latter three pled no contest to the charges. A tenth man who was arrested, Charles Avery Womack, had not been indicted by the grand jury. The eleventh man arrested, Sterling L. Gillis, was also to be sentenced by Judge Watkins, but that sentencing was to come "when he is able to get out of the state mental hospital at Whitfield and face the court." *Enterprise-Journal,* October 23, 1964. One of the few published sources to offer a detailed discussion of these men is Gordon, *Hometown,* 189–92.

79. Dittmer, *Local People,* 311. *Enterprise-Journal,* October 23, 1964; *Clarion-Ledger,* October 24, 1964.

80. *Enterprise-Journal,* October 28, 1964.

81. http://www.jacksonfreepress.com/news/2014/jun/18/violent-summer-when-klansmen-and-tyranny-stalked-m/

82. Transcript of *Today Show* interview, AU 68, TR3, Mississippi Department of Archives and History.

83. *Enterprise-Journal,* May 31, 1974. McDew quoted in Zinn, *SNCC,* 77.

84. The best study of black political participation in Mississippi in these years is Chris Danielson, *After Freedom Summer: How Race Realigned Mississippi Politics, 1965–1986* (Gainesville: University of Florida Press, 2011). Danielson's book emphasizes the continuing significance of race in state-level Mississippi politics of the period. He notes that by the mid-1980s, white-majority Pike County had two black supervisors, up from a total of zero during the period of the Andrews case; Danielson, *After Freedom Summer,* 166.

85. Jason Sokol, *There Goes My Everything: White Southerners in the Age of Civil Rights, 1945–1975* (New York: Knopf, 2006), 111.

86. Dittmer, *Local People,* 267.

87. Bill Minor quoted in Davies, "J. Oliver Emmerich and the McComb *Enterprise-Journal,*" 132; Gordon, *Hometown,* 207.

88. *Austin American-Statesman,* July 10, 1994.

89. http://www.mdah.ms.gov/arrec/digital_archives/sovcom/result.php?image=images/png /cd07/048940.png&otherstuff=6|53|0|30|1|1|1|48235|.

Chapter Two

1. *Enterprise-Journal*, August 25, 1969; *Clarion-Ledger*, August 24, 1969. Details of the physical remains are inconsistent in these two early accounts, with the *Clarion-Ledger* reporting an estimated height of 5'8," a twenty-five inch waist, and a twenty-eight-inch bust. Estimates of some of these measurements apparently were taken from the clothing found on the scene, given the deteriorated condition of the remains. The estimated height was taken from the body itself. One other inconsistent detail is that the *Enterprise-Journal* reported that a spent bullet was found on the scene, while the *Clarion-Ledger* wrote that the only bullet recovered was the one found in the body's nasal cavity. Some of these inconsistencies stem from the fact that the *Clarion-Ledger's* initial story ran on the day after the discovery of the body, while the *Enterprise-Journal*, which did not publish on weekends, ran its first story two days later.

2. *Enterprise-Journal*, August 25, 1969.

3. *Enterprise-Journal*, November 10, 2009.

4. *Enterprise-Journal*, August 25, 1969.

5. A recent study of Mississippi's criminal justice system argues that in the Jim Crow era, the "coroner system . . . was controlled by the white power structure. It was a critical tool for preserving the racial status quo." The authors maintain that Mississippi coroners of the period were simply "incompetent." See Radley Balko and Tucker Carrington, *The Cadaver King and the Country Dentist: A True Story of Injustice in the American South* (New York: Public Affairs, 2018), 59–60.

6. https://www.sos.ms.gov/Elections-Voting/Documents/CandidateQualifications.pdf.

7. *Enterprise-Journal*, August 27, 1969.

8. *Enterprise-Journal*, September 2, 1969.

9. *Enterprise-Journal*, September 19, 1969; the *Shreveport (LA) Times*, September 20, 1969; the *Times* reported that "two .30 caliber cartridge hulls" were discovered near the body, either a reporting or a typographical error or a reference to shell casings other than the ones from the .38-caliber weapon that killed Andrews. *Clarion-Ledger*, September 20, 1969.

10. *Enterprise-Journal*, March 25, 1957.

11. *Enterprise-Journal*, September 19, 1969; September 25, 1969. Lawrence "Uncle Bud" Varnado was the proprietor of Uncle Bud's Cabin, a well-known watering hole for residents of Pike and Lincoln Counties. Uncle Bud's Cabin was located on Highway 51, just south of Osyka and over the state line into Louisiana.

12. Interview with Justice James Kitchens, August 1, 2017.

13. *Enterprise-Journal*, January 28, 1963; January 25, 1968.

14. Without exception, the cousins of Tina Andrews with whom I spoke insisted that they not be identified in this book.

15. *Enterprise-Journal*, November 11, 1965. Interview with a cousin of Tina Andrews, August 6, 2018. The source wishes to remain anonymous.

16. Interviews with two members of the extended Andrews family, summer, 2018. Neither person wishes to be named in this book.

17. *Enterprise-Journal*, July 14, 1969.

18. *Enterprise-Journal*, August 13, 1969.

19. *Enterprise-Journal,* August 28, 1961; August 29, 1961.

20. Interview with Jackie Brown Andrews, July 16, 2017.

21. *Clarion-Ledger,* October 3, 1969; *Enterprise-Journal,* October 2, 1969, and October 15, 1969.

22. For a survey of broader southern developments in a national context, see James C. Cobb, *The South and America since World War II* (New York and Oxford: Oxford University Press, 2011).

23. Elana Levine, *Wallowing in Sex: The New Sexual Culture of 1970s American Television* (Durham, NC: Duke University Press, 2007). On the sexual revolution of the 1960s and 1970s, see John Heidenry, *What Wild Ecstasy: The Rise and Fall of the Sexual Revolution* (New York: Simon & Schuster, 1997); David Allyn, *Make Love, Not War: The Sexual Revolution, an Unfettered History* (Boston: Little, Brown, 2000).

24. Whitney Strub, *Perversion for Profit: The Politics of Pornography and the Rise of the New Right* (New York: Columbia University Press, 2011), 149.

25. http://www.jrsa.org/projects/Historical.pdf

26. http://www.disastercenter.com/crime/mscrimn.htm

27. *Enterprise-Journal,* October 6, 1969.

28. See William P. Hustwit, *Integration Now: Alexander v. Holmes and the End of Jim Crow Education* (Chapel Hill: University of North Carolina Press, 2019); Natalie G. Adams and James H. Adams, *Just Trying to Have School: The Struggle for Desegregation in Mississippi* (Jackson: University Press of Mississippi, 2018).

29. Prince, *Balancing the Scales,* 90, 102.

30. For surveys of the United States in the 1970s, see Peter N. Carroll, *It Seemed Like Nothing Happened: The Tragedy and Promise of America in the 1970s* (New York: Holt, Rinehart & Winston, 1982); Bruce Schulman, *The Seventies: The Great Shift in American Culture, Society, and Politics* (New York: Free Press, 2001); Edward D. Berkowitz, *Something Happened: A Political and Cultural Overview of the Seventies* (New York: Columbia University Press, 2006). For events of the 1970s in a broader perspective, see Thomas Borstelmann, *The 1970s: A New Global Perspective from Civil Rights to Economic Inequality* (Princeton, NJ: Princeton University Press, 2012).

31. *Enterprise-Journal,* January 2, 1969.

32. *Clarion-Ledger,* October 4, 1969; *Enterprise-Journal,* November 14, 1969.

33. *Enterprise-Journal,* October 27, 1969.

34. *Enterprise-Journal,* August 21, 1970.

35. *Enterprise-Journal,* August 21, 1970.

36. *Enterprise-Journal,* January 15, 1969.

Chapter Three

1. *Enterprise-Journal,* January 3, 1967; January 11, 1967; April 18, 1955.

2. *Enterprise-Journal, The Old McComb, Mississippi Story,* 976.2232 044, no. 1, Mississippi Department of Archives and History. The work is a collection of editorials, photographs, and stories published in the newspaper that year. Its frank purpose was to demonstrate the newspaper's effort "to bulwark the community with responsible journalism" during that period.

3. On the Child Development Group and the Head Start programs, see Crystal R. Sanders, *A Chance for Change: Head Start and Mississippi's Black Freedom Struggle* (Chapel Hill: University of North Carolina Press, 2016).

4. http://www.mdah.ms.gov/arrec/digital_archives/sovcom/result.php?image=images/png /cd02/008793.png&otherstuff=1|116|0|13|1|1|1|8579|

5. 1971 trial transcript, 424; *Enterprise-Journal*, March 25, 2005. Ruby Patricia Thomas, the daughter of Mr. and Mrs. Dale Ginn, married Clifton O. Lamkin, Jr. By the mid-1970s, they were the parents of three daughters. Pat Lamkin, now Patricia Bueto, is a retired nurse; as of 2019, she lives in McComb. *Enterprise-Journal*, December 26, 1972; June 29, 1976; September 8, 1996.

6. *State-Times Advocate* (Baton Rouge), March 18, 1971.

7. *Enterprise-Journal*, March 17, 1971, and March 18, 1971; *Clarion-Ledger*, March 18, 1971; *The Town Talk* (Alexandria, LA), March 18, 1971; *Alabama Journal* (Montgomery, AL), March 18, 1971; *Monroe (LA) News-Star*, March 18, 1971; *Greenwood (MS) Commonwealth*, March 18, 1971; *Daily World* (Opelousas, LA), March 18, 1971; *State Times Advocate* (Baton Rouge), March 18, 1971, and March 19, 1971; *Times-Picayune* (New Orleans), March 18, 1971.

8. Indictment of Ted Fleming and Richard McIntosh, Pike County Circuit Court File, #11,468.

9. "Tina Marie Andrews Case: Part Three, The Investigation and the Trial," Pike County Cold Cases, Facebook Page, August 13, 2011; *Clarion-Ledger*, March 19, 1971; *State-Times Advocate* (Baton Rouge), March 18, 1971.

10. *Enterprise-Journal*, March 17, 1971; *State-Times Advocate* (Baton Rouge) March 18, 1971; *Times-Picayune* (New Orleans), March 18, 1971; *Town Talk* (Alexandria, LA), March 18, 1971; *Greenwood Commonwealth* (Greenwood, MS), March 18, 1971; *Hattiesburg American*, March 18, 1971; *Delta Democrat-Times*, March 18, 1971.

11. http://www.mdah.ms.gov/arrec/digital_archives/sovcom/result.php?image=images/png /cd01/006886.png&otherstuff=2|36|2|38|4|1|1|6712|; *New York Times*, September 27, 1964.

12. Dittmer, *Local People*, 266.

13. https://archive.org/stream/WKKKKOM/5587107%20—%20Plans%20°f%20Klan%20 Groups%20to%20Infiltrate%20Law%20Enforcement%20Agencies_djvu.txt.

14. *Enterprise-Journal*, October 30, 1964.

15. *Enterprise-Journal*, March 17, 1971.

16. *Enterprise-Journal*, March 18, 1971; *Clarion-Ledger*, March 18, 1971; *Monroe (LA) News-Star*, March 18, 1971; *Delta Democrat-Times*, March 21, 1971.

17. *Clarion-Ledger*, March 19, 1971; *Enterprise-Journal*, July 5, 1968.

18. *Enterprise-Journal*, July 2, 2017.

19. *Enterprise-Journal*, August 16, 2006.

20. *Enterprise-Journal*, February 25, 1970.

21. *Clarion-Ledger*, March 23, 1971; *Enterprise-Journal*, March 22, 1971, and March 23, 1971.

22. *Enterprise-Journal*, March 17, 1971; March 18, 1971.

23. *Enterprise-Journal*, August 23, 1963; November 24, 1965; May 11, 1966; October 26, 1966.

24. Biographical information on Fleming and McIntosh is drawn from issues of the *Enterprise-Journal*, as well as from contemporary city directories.

25. *Enterprise-Journal*, April 7, 1959.

26. *Enterprise-Journal*, August 26, 1965.

27. *Enterprise-Journal*, March 31, 1958.

28. *Enterprise-Journal*, May 6, 1966. Several community organizations recognized a mother of the year. See that same issue of the newspaper for two other honorees.

29. *Enterprise-Journal*, November 14, 1993.

30. *Clarion-Ledger*, March 23, 1971.

31. All existing motions in this case are available at the Pike County Circuit Court, File #11,468. Relevant entries are also available in the General Docket #7, Criminal, Circuit Court, Pike County, Mississippi. *Enterprise-Journal*, March 22, 1971; March 23, 1971; March 24, 1971; March 25, 1971.

32. *Enterprise-Journal*, July 11, 1975.

33. Livingston Hall, Yale Kamisar, Wayne R. La Fave, and Jerold H. Israel, *Modern Criminal Procedure* 3rd ed. (St. Paul, MN: West Publishing Company, 1969), 1189.

34. *Enterprise-Journal*, March 29, 1971; March 30, 1971.

35. Pike County Circuit Court, File #11,468.

36. *Enterprise-Journal*, March 30, 1982.

37. *Enterprise-Journal*, March 30, 1982.

38. *Enterprise-Journal*, April 1, 1982.

39. Pike County Circuit Court, File #11,468.

40. Pike County Circuit Court, File #11,468.

41. *Enterprise-Journal*, March 25, 1971; March 29, 1971; March 30, 1971; *Advocate* (Baton Rouge), March 27, 1971.

42. *Enterprise-Journal*, March 25, 1971.

43. *Enterprise-Journal*, March 25, 1971.

44. *Enterprise-Journal*, February 19, 1969.

45. *Enterprise-Journal*, March 25, 1971.

46. *Enterprise-Journal*, April 2, 1971.

47. Pike County Circuit Court, File #11,468.

48. *Enterprise-Journal*, April 5, 1971; *Hattiesburg American*, April 6, 1971; *Daily World* (Opelousas, LA), April 6, 1971; *Clarion-Ledger*, April 6, 1971; *Greenwood Commonwealth*, April 6, 1971.

49. Interview with Justice James Kitchens, August 1, 2017.

50. Interview with Justice James Kitchens, August 1, 2017.

51. *Enterprise-Journal*, April 5, 1971; *Advocate* (Baton Rouge), April 6, 1971.

Chapter Four

1. *Enterprise-Journal*, March 25, 2005; *Enterprise-Journal*, November 8, 2015. For the Mississippi Legislature's resolution honoring Pigott, see http://billstatus.ls.state.ms.us/documents/2016/pdf/SC/SC0532SG.pdf.

2. https://courts.ms.gov/news/2015/11%2006%2015Joe%20Pigott.php.

3. *Enterprise-Journal*, March 25, 2005.

4. *Enterprise-Journal*, September 7, 1949.

5. https://www.legacy.com/obituaries/clarionledger/obituary.aspx?page=lifestory&pid=17635 0723. Interview with Brad Pigott, October 27, 2017.

6. In various accounts of the story published over the years, Barnes' age is sometimes listed as twenty-one and at other times as twenty-five or twenty-six.

7. *Enterprise-Journal*, April 17, 1951; April 18, 1951. The Barnes murder case was extraordinarily complex and well merits an extended study. Mac Gordon, whose father, Charles Gordon, diligently reported the story, writes that a Jackson filmmaker is currently working on the Barnes story. See *Clarion-Ledger*, January 12, 2019.

8. On one of the cases stemming from the shooting of Barnes, which eventually wound up before the Mississippi Supreme Court, see https://law.justia.com/cases/mississippi/supreme -court/1951/38282–0.html.

9. *Enterprise-Journal*, March 25, 2005.

10. *Enterprise-Journal*, October 25, 1951; *Enterprise-Journal*, March 25, 2005.

11. *Enterprise-Journal*, March 25, 2005.

12. *Enterprise-Journal*, May 4, 1971; June 24, 1971.

13. *Enterprise-Journal*, June 1, 1971.

14. Kevin M. Kruse and Julian E. Zelizer, *Fault Lines: A History of the United States since 1974* (New York: W.W. Norton, 2019), 44.

15. *Enterprise-Journal*, February 13, 1970.

16. *Enterprise-Journal*, February 16, 1970.

17. *Enterprise-Journal*, November 3, 1970.

18. J. Oliver Emmerich, *Two Faces of Janus: The Saga of Deep South Change* (Jackson: University Press of Mississippi, 1973), vii, viii.

19. *Enterprise-Journal*, May 4, 1971.

20. *Enterprise-Journal*, June 7, 1971.

21. *Enterprise-Journal*, June 9, 1971.

22. Brad Pigott to Trent Brown, e-mail, May 11, 2018.

23. *Enterprise-Journal*, March 19, 1955.

24. *Enterprise-Journal*, August 19, 1971.

25. *Enterprise-Journal*, April 21, 1971.

26. *Enterprise-Journal*, May 24, 1971; September 23, 1998.

27. *Enterprise-Journal*, October 27, 1970.

28. Pike County Mississippi Cold Case Facebook Page; https://www.facebook.com/Pike -County-Mississippi-Cold-Cases.

29. *Enterprise-Journal*, October 29, 1970.

30. *Enterprise-Journal*, January 14, 1971.

31. *Enterprise-Journal*, January 26, 1971.

32. *Enterprise-Journal*, February 10, 1971.

33. http://www.mdah.ms.gov/arrec/digital_archives/sovcom/imagelisting.php?foldercheck box%5B%5D=652%7C6%7C77%7C%7C0&searchimages=Submit+Query.

34. *Hattiesburg American*, June 2, 1971; *Enterprise-Journal*, June 22, 1971.

35. *Enterprise-Journal,* June 22, 1971.

36. *Enterprise-Journal,* June 28, 1971.

37. *Enterprise-Journal,* June 28, 1971; July 1, 1971; July 2, 1971.

38. Peter Guralnick, *Lost Highways: Journeys and Arrivals of American Musicians* (New York: Harper & Row, 1979), 240. On Richard Nixon's admiration and use of country music, see "Country, Cash Win White House," *Billboard* (May 2, 1970), 61. *Enterprise-Journal,* July 12, 1971.

39. *Enterprise-Journal,* July 12, 1971.

40. http://digital.wustl.edu/e/eop/eopweb/car0015.0445.017hoddingcarteriii.html.

41. *Enterprise-Journal,* January 29, 1960; February 3, 1960; August 1, 1960; October 10, 1960; June 6, 1961; May 9, 1962; April 5, 1963; May 3, 1963; May 29, 1963; July 10, 1963.

42. *Enterprise-Journal,* March 18, 2001.

43. *Enterprise-Journal,* June 27, 1969.

44. See Stephanie R. Rolph, *Resisting Equality: The Citizens' Council, 1954–1989* (Baton Rouge: Louisiana State University Press, 2018); Neil R. McMillen, *The Citizens' Council: Organized Resistance to the Second Reconstruction, 1954–1964,* rev. ed. (Urbana: University of Illinois Press, 1994). In the 1960s, McComb mayor Gordon Burt was a president of the Pike County Citizens' Council; he had been a charter member of the organization. See *Mississippi Black Paper* (Jackson: University Press of Mississippi, 2018), 66 (orig. ed. 1965); *Enterprise-Journal,* January 12, 1961, and October 22, 1962. A McComb attorney, Bert Jones, was a Citizens' Council member. He practiced law in partnership with J. Gordon Roach, who as circuit judge would hear the Tina Andrews murder trial in 1971. See *Enterprise-Journal,* April 4, 1962. Roach was not only a member of the Citizens' Council; he was a member of the board of directors of the county chapter. See *Enterprise-Journal,* May 14, 1962; that article provides a full list of the county Citizens' Council board members of that era. One of them, Phillip D. Brady, would be a member of the McComb city board into the 1970s. See also *Enterprise-Journal,* June 21, 1963. Burt was reelected as Citizens' Council president after he became mayor. Another local attorney with longtime Citizens' Council ties was L. S. "Mac" McClaren, who served terms as state representative and state senator representing Pike County. See *Enterprise-Journal,* May 10, 1962.

45. *Enterprise-Journal,* July 27, 1971.

46. *Enterprise-Journal,* February 26, 1974; March 14, 1975.

47. *Enterprise-Journal,* September 30, 1971.

48. *Enterprise-Journal,* October 4, 1971.

49. *Clarion-Ledger,* October 14, 1971; *Delta Democrat-Times,* October 14, 1971.

50. Richard McIntosh, Motion for a Subpoena Duces Tecum, October 26, 1971, Pike County Circuit Court File, Case #11,468; J. Gordon Roach, Order, October 26, 1971, PCCCF, Case # 11,468. Of the Andrews case, Prince says: "I remember the case but my activity was in producing the school records. Beyond that I am blank." Julian Prince to Trent Brown, email, October 1, 2018.

51. *Enterprise-Journal,* April 7, 1971.

52. *Enterprise-Journal,* October 12, 1971.

53. *Enterprise-Journal,* November 1, 1971.

54. Interview with Carroll Case, May 8, 2018. Case's remark seeks to characterize the attitude

of some local people toward Andrews, Lambert, and their families, and in no way represents his own opinion of them.

Chapter Five

1. https://www.hmdb.org/marker.asp?marker=49943. On the early history of Pike County, see Luke Ward Conerly, *Pike County, Mississippi, 1798–1876* (Nashville: Brandon Printing Company, 1909). On the move of the county seat from Holmesville to Magnolia, see Martin J. Hardeman, *The Structure of Time: Pike County, Mississippi, 1815–1912* (New York: Peter Lang, 1999), 41.

2. *Enterprise-Journal*, June 24, 1965.

3. In Mississippi, felony trials such as that of McIntosh were heard in the Circuit Court, while the Chancery Court heard matters of equity, guardianship, wills, and domestic matters such as divorce and custody; https://courts.ms.gov/aboutcourts/aboutthecourts.php.

4. https://www.census.gov/prod/www/decennial.html.

5. *Enterprise-Journal*, October 28, 1971.

6. *Enterprise-Journal*, October 29, 1971.

7. *Enterprise-Journal*, October 28, 1971; *Clarion-Ledger*, October 29, 1971; *Hattiesburg American*, October 29, 1971; *Daily Herald* (Biloxi, MS), October 29, 1971; *Times Picayune* (New Orleans), October 30, 1971.

8. *Enterprise-Journal*, October 29, 1971; *Clarion-Ledger*, October 29, 1971. Other state newspapers, including the *Hattiesburg American* and Greenville's *Delta Democrat-Times*, also provided brief coverage of the case through 1971. None of that coverage provides much detail beyond that offered in the *Enterprise-Journal*. The *Delta Democrat-Times*, along with other newspapers, pointed out that the case would be heard by a "biracial jury." *Delta Democrat-Times*, October 29, 1971.

9. *Enterprise-Journal*, October 29, 1971.

10. *Enterprise-Journal*, October 29, 1971.

11. *Enterprise-Journal*, October 29, 1971; *Clarion-Ledger*, October 30, 1971; *Hattiesburg American*, October 30, 1971.

12. Pike County Board of Supervisors, Meeting Minutes, April 19, 1971, pp. 367–80, Pike County Courthouse.

13. Like many women of the era, Patricia "Patsy" Taylor Harvey was referred to publicly almost always by her husband's name. She died in 2013. Dr. Marvin V. Harvey died in 2002. See https://www.findagrave.com/memorial/106889764/patricia-harvey.

14. On Harvey, see *Enterprise-Journal*, September 14, 1966; on Austin, see *Enterprise-Journal*, February 6, 2011; on Brumfield, see *Enterprise-Journal*, April 29, 1996; on Speed, see *Enterprise-Journal*, February 4, 1964, and May 25, 2007; on Wilson, see *Enterprise-Journal*, August 30, 1962, and August 10, 2003. Ole Miss football fans may remember "The Ballad of Archie Who," a 1969 song honoring Rebel great Archie Manning. Wilson was co-author of that song; see *Enterprise-Journal*, December 3, 1969. On Alexander, see *Enterprise-Journal*, October 29, 1971; on Harold Williams, see *Enterprise-Journal*, March 8, 2009.

15. Biographical information on all jurors is drawn largely from the local newspaper, either from contemporary stories in which they were featured or from obituaries published in later years. On Andrews, see *Enterprise-Journal*, August 12, 1988, and August 29, 1988. On McGowan, see *Enterprise-Journal*, October 13, 2004. On Williams, see *Enterprise-Journal*, January 16, 1962. On Gardner, see *Enterprise-Journal*, August 12, 2009. Of the twelve jurors, Luther Carr is the only one I have been unable to identify. He was, however, a white man.

16. In the year 2019, a black Mississippian who had faced six trials for a 1996 quadruple murder argued that his 2010 conviction at the hands of a jury of eleven whites and one black represented a racially biased stacking of the jury against him. See https://abcnews.go.com/Politics/blacks-kicked-off-juries-mississippi-death-row-inmate/story?id=61771926. See also https://www.theatlantic.com/ideas/archive/2019/03/flowers-v-mississippi-jurors-removed-because-race/585094/. As in other states, in Mississippi courts a defense attorney or a state's attorney could move to exclude a potential juror "for cause" (being a friend or a relative of the defendant, for instance) or via an allowed number of peremptory challenges, in which case the attorney does not need specifically to state the reason for striking a potential juror.

17. Clifton McGowan, telephone interview with Trent Brown, April 8, 2019.

18. Clifton McGowan, telephone interview with Trent Brown, April 8, 2019.

19. Interview with Justice James Kitchens, August 1, 2017.

20. Clifton McGowan, telephone interview with Trent Brown, April 8, 2019.

21. *Enterprise-Journal*, March 25, 2005.

22. Interview with Justice James Kitchens, August 1, 2017.

23. *Enterprise-Journal*, August 25, 1969.

24. Wallace appeared as an expert witness in a variety of trials around the country in the 1960s and 1970s. See, for example, the *Morning News* (Wilmington, DE), October 25, 1969; *Casper (WY) Star-Tribune*, November 5, 1969; *The Bee* (Danville, VA), May 9, 1970; *Silver City (NM) Daily Press*, March 8, 1972.

25. Accounts of the witnesses' testimony and quotations from those witnesses is drawn largely from the transcript of the trial. The *Enterprise-Journal* also contained detailed accounts of the testimony.

26. In newspaper coverage of the two trials, official documents in the court case file, and even in published obituaries of family members, Mullen's name appears in an unaccountable variety of spellings. For "Winifred Mullen," see *Enterprise-Journal*, September 19, 1969; March 23, 1971; *Clarion-Ledger*, September 20, 1969. For "Winifred Mullin," see *Enterprise-Journal*, November 1, 1971; November 22, 1971. For "Mrs. M.L. Mullen," see *Enterprise-Journal*, October 2, 1969; *Clarion-Ledger*, October 3, 1969. For "Winifred Andrew Mullen," see *Clarion-Ledger*, September 20, 1969. For "Mrs. Winifred Andrews Mullens," see *Hattiesburg American*, April 5, 1972. For "Winnie Fred Mullen," see her mother's obituary in *Enterprise-Journal*, July 11, 2002. For "Winnifred Mullen," see her brother's obituary in *Times-Picayune* (New Orleans), November 3, 2014. For "Winefred Andrews Mullin," see a motion by McIntosh's attorney William Watkins in Pike County Circuit Court Case #11,468.

27. *Enterprise-Journal*, October 29, 1971.

28. Stewart (1901–97) was a forensic anthropologist of international reputation. His work

helped to advance both the legal and academic acceptance of his field. After his death, he was featured with a retrospective and a symposium on his career in the *Journal of Forensic Sciences* 45, no. 2 (March 2000). The annual award for outstanding contributions to the field of physical forensic anthropology given by the American Academy of Forensic Sciences is named in his honor. See https://news.aafs.org/section-news/the-t-dale-stewart-award-nominations-are-due-january-1/. For an obituary, see *New York Times*, October 30, 1997.

29. 1971 trial transcript, 202, 206.

30. 1971 trial transcript, 203.

31. Marie Ussing Nylen continued for years her affiliation with the Dental Institute of the National Institute of Health. Not as active an expert witness as Stewart, she nevertheless offered testimony in similar cases around the country in the 1960s and 1970s. See, for example, *Pensacola (FL) News Journal,* February 28, 1979.

32. Interview with Justice James Kitchens, August 1, 2017.

33. 1971 trial transcript, 218, 224, 238, 243.

34. 1971 trial transcript, 246–48.

35. 1971 trial transcript, 254–58.

36. 1971 trial transcript, 261.

37. Interview with Wayne Dowdy, May 22, 2018.

38. 1971 trial transcript, 260–63.

39. 1971 trial transcript, 264.

40. 1971 trial transcript, 266.

41. 1971 trial transcript, 267–68.

42. 1971 trial transcript, 273.

43. 1971 trial transcript, 274.

44. *Enterprise-Journal,* June 3, 1944; September 25, 1959; March 17, 1969.

45. 1971 trial transcript, 271.

46. 1971 trial transcript, 276–77.

47. *Enterprise-Journal,* August 2, 1971.

48. 1971 trial transcript, 279–80.

Chapter Six

1. The *Enterprise-Journal* reported that Lambert gave her birthdate as April 11, 1957. But according to the trial transcript, she told B. D. Statham that she was born on April 11, 1956. She also told him that she was "twelve or thirteen, I guess," in August 1969. 1971 trial transcript, 302.

2. https://www.findagrave.com/memorial/98237631/pat-harrison-lambert.

3. For George Ann Lambert's obituary, see *Enterprise-Journal,* August 3, 2003.

4. 1971 trial transcript, 310–13. There is evident confusion here, as she could not have dropped out of school in January 1969, as B. D. Statham suggested, because of what had happened to her and Tina Andrews in August 1969. Unless otherwise noted, direct quotations in this chapter are drawn from the 1971 trial transcript.

5. On contemporary anxieties over southern girls' sexuality, see Susan K. Cahn, *Sexual Reckonings: Southern Girls in a Troubling Age* (Cambridge, MA: Harvard University Press, 2007).

6. 1971 trial transcript, 280.

7. *McComb and Magnolia, Mississippi City Directory, Including Fernwood and Summit* (Richmond, VA: R. L. Polk, 1969).

8. Interview with Carroll Case, July 24, 2018.

9. 1971 trial transcript, 281–83.

10. 1971 trial transcript, 282. *Advocate* (Baton Rouge), October 30, 1971.

11. The person preparing the transcript of the trial, not a native of McComb, gives the name of the restaurant as "Mr. Swifts." 1971 trial transcript, 283.

12. 1971 trial transcript, 284.

13. Interview with Carroll Case, May 8, 2018. The person making this observation was Carroll Case's future wife.

14. 1971 trial transcript, 284–85.

15. Neither of these people was willing to speak with me for attribution. Both spoke with me in 2018, showing that at least to some people in the area, speaking on the record about the case still entails potential risk of retribution.

16. 1971 trial transcript, 285–87.

17. 1971 trial transcript, 287–88.

18. 1971 trial transcript, 287.

19. 1971 trial transcript, 288.

20. 1971 trial transcript, 365–68.

21. 1971 trial transcript, 289.

22. 1971 trial transcript, 291.

23. 1971 trial transcript, 291–97.

24. 1971 trial transcript, 297.

25. General Docket #7, Criminal, Circuit Court, Pike County, Mississippi.

26. 1971 trial transcript, 445.

27. *Clarion-Ledger,* October 31, 1971.

28. 1971 trial transcript, 302–6.

29. 1971 trial transcript, 305.

30. 1971 trial transcript, 317.

31. 1971 trial transcript, 317–19.

32. 1971 trial transcript, 319–20.

33. 1971 trial transcript, 326.

34. 1971 trial transcript, 326.

35. *Enterprise-Journal,* November 1, 1971.

36. Telephone interview with Clifton McGowan, April 15, 2019. McGowan added that throughout the trial, he could never shake the impression that Lambert seemed to be somehow in danger.

37. 1971 trial transcript, 341–43.

38. 1971 trial transcript, 344; 346; 349–51.

39. 1971 trial transcript, 353–56.

40. 1971 trial transcript, 361–62.

41. 1971 trial transcript, 364.

42. 1971 trial transcript, 402, 405. *State-Times Advocate* (Baton Rouge), November 1, 1971; *Daily Herald* (Biloxi, MS), November 2, 1971.

43. 1971 trial transcript, 409.

44. 1971 trial transcript, 405.

45. 1971 trial transcript, 399–400.

46. 1971 trial transcript, 419–20.

47. 1971 trial transcript, 422.

48. 1971 trial transcript, 426; 429–30.

49. 1971 trial transcript, 443.

50. 1971 trial transcript, 457.

51. Tom P. Brady, *Black Monday* (Winona, MS: Association of Citizens' Councils, 1955), 12.

Chapter Seven

1. *Enterprise-Journal,* November 1, 1971; *Clarion-Ledger,* November 1, 1971; *Delta Democrat-Times,* November 2, 1971; 1971 trial transcript, 471–72.

2. 1971 trial transcript, 472–73.

3. 1971 trial transcript, 490–95; *Enterprise-Journal,* November 1, 1971.

4. 1971 trial transcript, 496–506; *Enterprise-Journal,* November 1, 1971.

5. 1971 trial transcript, 508.

6. 1971 trial transcript, 510. Telephone interview with Clifton McGowan, April 8, 2019; April 15, 2019.

7. 1971 trial transcript, 516–18.

8. 1971 trial transcript, 518–19.

9. 1971 trial transcript, 546–78.

10. *Enterprise-Journal,* November 1, 1971.

11. 1971 trial transcript, 529–32; *Enterprise-Journal,* November 1, 1971; *Hattiesburg American,* November 2. 1971; *Daily World* (Opelousas, LA), November 2, 1971.

12. *Enterprise-Journal,* November 1, 1971.

13. 1971 trial transcript, 533–36.

14. 1971 trial transcript, 534–36.

15. 1971 trial transcript, 537; 545.

16. *Enterprise-Journal,* November 1, 1971.

17. 1971 trial transcript, 580–86.

18. 1971 trial transcript, 588.

19. 1971 trial transcript, 590.

20. 1971 trial transcript, 592.

21. 1971 trial transcript, 591–92.

22. 1971 trial transcript, 593.

23. 1971 trial transcript, 593–94.

24. *State-Times* (Baton Rouge), March 22, 1969; March 27, 1969. The *State-Times* was a morning newspaper; the *Advocate* was published in the afternoon.

25. *Advocate* (Baton Rouge), September 30, 1969; January 27, 1970; *State-Times*, January 27, 1970; *State of Louisiana vs. Michael W. Howell, Rollin L. Copelan, and Richard McIntosh*, #70,265, 19th Judicial District, East Baton Rouge Parish, Docket Entry for January 26, 1970.

26. "Even if the Baton Rouge charge had resulted in a single conviction of 'carnal knowledge of a juvenile,' it is unlikely that a judge would have properly allowed admission of that single conviction. Only when there is an earlier 'pattern' of prior bad acts substantially similar to the act being charged (here, killing a female juvenile) would the prior acts be admissible." Even then, a defense attorney might have argued that introducing such a conviction might have been prejudicial to a jury. In short, the Baton Rouge arrest gave Joe Pigott nothing that he could develop in court. Brad Pigott to Trent Brown, e-mail, March 22, 2019.

27. *State-Times*, March 19, 1971; *Advocate*, March 19, 1971.

28. *Advocate* (Baton Rouge), March 19, 1971.

29. 1971 trial transcript, 596–97.

30. 1971 trial transcript, 597.

31. 1971 trial transcript, 597–98.

32. 1971 trial transcript, 600–602.

33. 1971 trial transcript, 603–4.

34. 1971 trial transcript, 605–13.

35. 1971 trial transcript, 614–19.

36. 1971 trial transcript, 620–22.

37. 1971 trial transcript, 622–27.

38. 1971 trial transcript, 627–32.

39. 1971 trial transcript, 634.

40. 1971 trial transcript, 635–36. *Hattiesburg American*, November 2, 1971; *Daily World* (Opelousas, LA), November 2, 1971; *Clarion-Ledger*, November 2, 1971; *Advocate* (Baton Rouge), November 2, 1971; *Times Picayune* (New Orleans), November 2, 1971; *Daily Herald* (Biloxi, MS), November 2, 1971.

41. *Clarion-Ledger*, October 31, 1971.

42. *Enterprise-Journal*, November 2, 1971.

43. Telephone interview with Clifton McGowan, April 8, 2019; April 15, 2019.

44. Telephone interview with Clifton McGowan, April 8, 2019; April 15, 2019.

45. Telephone interview with Clifton McGowan, April 8, 2019; April 15, 2019.

46. *Enterprise-Journal*, September 7, 1942; September 19, 1944; August 15, 1946; January 10, 1947.

47. *Enterprise-Journal*, September 12, 1947; June 30, 1949; July 13, 1950; May 6, 1954; October 2, 1953; March 7, 1955; September 30, 1955; June 26, 1957.

48. *Enterprise-Journal*, January 16, 1969; October 30, 1970; November 20, 1970; October 22, 1971.

49. *Enterprise-Journal*, May 20, 1966. Sheriffs kept a percentage of the taxes that they collected, a system that was of course admired by the sheriffs themselves, but also one that had attracted criticism.

50. *Enterprise-Journal*, February 6, 2011.

51. *Enterprise-Journal*, November 3, 1971.

52. James C. Cobb, *The South and America since World War II* (New York and Oxford: Oxford University Press, 2011), 117.

53. *Enterprise-Journal*, October 22, 1971. A coda of sorts is available for the James shooting. In 2016, Mrs. James, by then Shirley Wilson Tolliver, was a candidate for election commissioner in Pike County's district five. A manslaughter conviction did not prevent anyone in Mississippi from running for public office, although some other felony convictions, such as bribery or forgery, did. Mrs. Tolliver was not successful in that race, but Pike County voters were more forgiving in similar cases, as in 2017 the mayor of Magnolia had been elected despite a previous manslaughter conviction. *Enterprise-Journal*, October 23, 2016; January 27, 2017.

Chapter Eight

1. *Enterprise-Journal*, December 31, 1971.

2. *Advocate* (Baton Rouge), April 8, 1972. Because the 1972 trial of McIntosh resulted in his acquittal, it is unlikely that a transcript of that trial was ever made. The Pike County Circuit Court file on the case contains no transcript, but it contained no transcript of the 1971 trial, either. That file does contain a Court Reporter's Fee Bill for the preparation of the 1971 trial transcript, but no bill for a 1972 transcript. See Pike County Circuit Court, File #11,468. Justice James Kitchens, who prosecuted the 1972 trial, believes that no transcript of the second trial was ever prepared. Interview with Justice James Kitchens, August 1, 2017.

3. *Enterprise-Journal*, November 22, 1971.

4. *Enterprise-Journal*, March 16, 1972.

5. *Enterprise-Journal*, May 25, 1971.

6. *Enterprise-Journal*, July 12, 1971.

7. Interview with Justice James Kitchens, August 1, 2017.

8. https://courts.ms.gov/appellatecourts/sc/scjustices.php; https://ballotpedia.org/Jim_Kitchens; https://www.clarionledger.com/story/news/politics/2016/01/04/kitchens-supreme-court/78258392/.

9. *Enterprise-Journal*, August 4, 1971.

10. *Enterprise-Journal*, March 16, 1972.

11. *Enterprise-Journal*, March 20, 1972.

12. Richard Nixon, "What Has Happened to America?" *Reader's Digest* (October 1967: 49–54); available at http://college.cengage.com/history/ayers_primary_sources/nixon_1967.htm. On Nixon's use of the "law and order" argument in his campaigns and in his presidency, see Stephen E. Ambrose, *Nixon: The Triumph of a Politician, 1962–1972* (New York: Simon & Schuster, 1989), 125–26; 144–45; 260–65; 369–70; 373–77.

13. John A. Farrell, *Richard Nixon: The Life* (New York: Doubleday, 2017), 330. See also Kevin Phillips, *The Emerging Republican Majority* (New Rochelle, NY: Arlington House, 1969).

14. Interview with Carroll Case, May 25, 2018.

15. *Delta Democrat-Times*, March 30, 1972; *Enterprise-Journal*, March 29, 1972; *Clarion-Ledger*, March 31, 1972.

16. *Enterprise-Journal*, April 4, 1972.

17. *Enterprise-Journal*, April 3, 1972; *Clarion-Ledger*, October 23, 1970; December 29, 2013.

18. *Enterprise-Journal*, April 3, 1972.

19. *Enterprise-Journal*, February 2, 1972.

20. *Enterprise-Journal*, April 3, 1972.

21. *Enterprise-Journal*, April 3, 1972.

22. *Enterprise-Journal*, April 3, 1972.

23. *Enterprise-Journal*, April 3, 1972.

24. *Enterprise-Journal*, July 26, 2017.

25. Interview with Justice James Kitchens, August 1, 2017.

26. *Enterprise-Journal*, April 3, 1972.

27. For copies of the subpoenas for the 1972 trial, see Pike County Circuit Court, File #11,468.

28. *Enterprise-Journal*, April 4, 1972.

29. Biographical information on the jurors is drawn from contemporary issues of the *Enterprise-Journal* and from obituaries later published in that newspaper.

30. On Alford, see *Enterprise-Journal (E-J)*, June 7, 1987; March 31, 1989; June 11, 2009. On Reeves, see *E-J*, December 6, 1961; January 3, 1967; November 10, 1991. On Hayman, see *E-J*, October 5, 1944; September 3, 1989; May 26, 2014. On Moore, see *E-J*, February 16, 953; August 11, 1959; August 3, 1997. On Morgan, see *E-J*, March 7, 1966; November 10, 1970; December 14, 1972; May 14, 2007. On Hughes, see *E-J*, May 12, 2003; https://www.findagrave.com/memorial/90691335/ernest-w-hughes. It is possible that this juror was actually Hughes's son, also named Ernest W. Hughes. On the son, see *E-J*, June 12, 2016. Mrs. T. R. Quinn appears to be Mrs. Tommy Ray Quin, the wife of a substantial beef farmer. See *E-J*, September 21, 1953. In that story, the Quins are pictured with their children, including a daughter, Betty Ann. In 1966, Betty Ann Quinn married and was identified in the *Enterprise-Journal* as the daughter of Mr. and Mrs. T. R. Quinn. See *E-J*, April 11, 1966. My characterization of Mrs. Quinn as "middle-aged" is an estimate based upon her having a daughter of marriage age in 1966. The variant spellings of "Quin" and "Quinn" are as given in the local newspaper.

31. On Nunnery, see *Enterprise-Journal*, October 19, 1982. On Matthews, see *E-J*, December 18, 1970; November 12, 1995. On Carter, see *E-J*, January 6, 1965; August 8, 1985.

32. Copies of all subpoenas are included in Pike County Circuit Court, File #11,468.

33. *Clarion-Ledger*, April 5, 1972; *Hattiesburg American*, April 5, 1972; *Greenwood Commonwealth*, April 6, 1972; *Daily Herald* (Biloxi), April 5, 1972; *Enterprise-Journal (E-J)*, April 4, 1972. *E-J* characterized the testimony as "similar to that in the first trial," while the *Clarion-Ledger* reported that some witnesses "gave much the same testimony as in an earlier trial."

34. *Enterprise-Journal*, April 5, 1972.

35. *Enterprise-Journal*, April 6, 1972; *Hattiesburg American*, April 6, 1972; *Clarion-Ledger*, April 6, 1972.

36. Telephone interview with juror from 1972 trial, July 22, 2018. The juror insisted that his name not be used in this book.

37. *Enterprise-Journal*, April 5, 1972. For the defense's subpoena of those reports, see Pike County Circuit Court, File #11,468.

38. *Enterprise-Journal*, April 5, 1972.

39. *Enterprise-Journal*, April 5, 1972.

40. Interview with Carroll Case, August 26, 2018; interview with Jackie Brown Andrews, May 25, 2017. *Enterprise-Journal*, December 14, 1979.

41. Interview with Emily Sue Williams, July 24, 2018.

42. *Enterprise-Journal*, April 5, 1972.

43. *Enterprise-Journal*, April 5, 1972; *Greenwood Commonwealth*, April 6, 1972; *Clarion-Ledger*, April 6, 1972; *Enterprise-Journal*, April 6, 1972; *Hattiesburg American*, April 6, 1972.

44. *Enterprise-Journal*, June 7, 1963.

45. *Enterprise-Journal*, April 6, 1972.

46. *Enterprise-Journal*, April 6, 1972. Pike County Circuit Court, File #11,468.

47. *Enterprise-Journal*, April 7, 1972.

48. *Daily World* (Opelousas, LA), April 7, 1972; *Clarion-Ledger*, April 7, 1972; *Hattiesburg American*, April 7, 1972; *Enterprise-Journal*, April 7, 1972.

49. *Clarion-Ledger*, April 7, 1972; *Hattiesburg American*, April 7, 1972; *Enterprise-Journal*, April 7, 1972.

50. Instruction No. 3 for State, State of Mississippi vs. Richard McIntosh, Pike County Circuit Court File #11,468.

51. For defense instructions to the jury, see Pike County Circuit Court File #11,468.

52. *Enterprise-Journal*, April 7, 1972; *Daily World* (Opelousas, LA), April 7, 1972; *Clarion-Ledger*, April 7, 1972; *Hattiesburg American*, April 7, 1972; *Daily Herald* (Biloxi), April 7, 1972.

53. *Enterprise-Journal*, April 7, 1972; *Advocate* (Baton Rouge), April 8, 1972; *Enterprise-Journal*, April 10, 1972.

54. Interview with Carroll Case, July 24, 2018.

55. Interview with Jackie Brown Andrews, June 1, 2017.

56. Interview with Emily Sue Williams, May 25, 2018.

57. *Enterprise-Journal*, May 31, 1974.

58. http://blog.gulflive.com/mississippi-press-news/2018/06/tate_reeves_honors_former _jack.html. In 1992, Maples was indicted on forty-four felony charges, but those charges were subsequently dismissed after a second grand jury considered them; *Enterprise-Journal*, June 26, 1992.

59. General Docket #7, Criminal, Circuit Court, Pike County, Mississippi.

60. *Enterprise-Journal*, April 12, 1972.

61. *Enterprise-Journal*, January 3, 1972.

Chapter Nine

1. *Enterprise-Journal*, March 25, 2005. Quotations from Pigott in the following paragraphs are drawn from this same article.

2. *Enterprise-Journal*, March 27, 2005.

3. *Enterprise-Journal*, May 6, 1992.

4. Telephone interview with 1972 trial juror, June 23, 2018. The juror insisted that his name not be used in this book.

5. *Enterprise-Journal*, April 26, 1972; *Times Picayune* (New Orleans), April 28, 1972.

6. Interview with Wayne Dowdy, May 22, 2018.

7. City of McComb, Board Meeting Minutes, April 25, 1972.

8. *Enterprise-Journal*, April 26, 1972.

9. *Enterprise-Journal*, April 26, 1972.

10. *Enterprise-Journal*, June 30, 1975.

11. *Enterprise-Journal*, July 26, 1974.

12. *Enterprise-Journal*, April 26, 1972; May 3, 1972.

13. *Enterprise-Journal*, May 4, 1972.

14. [Sylvia F. Cook?], *January 10, 1975: A Day to Remember, A Day to Forget* (McComb, MS: Enterprise-Journal, 1975,), 7.

15. *Enterprise-Journal*, February 6, 2011; April 30, 1976; *Clarion-Ledger,* May 6, 1975.

16. [Cook?], *A Day to Remember, A Day to Forget,* 74.

17. *Enterprise-Journal*, March 3, 1978.

18. *Enterprise-Journal*, March 3, 1978.

19. *Enterprise-Journal*, March 3, 1978.

20. *Enterprise-Journal*, February 19, 1975.

21. *Enterprise-Journal*, August 6, 1975.

22. *Enterprise-Journal*, July 15, 1979.

23. *Enterprise-Journal*, August 8, 1979.

24. *Enterprise-Journal*, August 12, 1984.

25. *Enterprise-Journal*, July 25, 1960. Pike County Chancery Court, Bill of Complaint, July 8, 1960, Pike County Courthouse.

26. https://www.findagrave.com/memorial/60949086/agnes-ryan-fleming.

27. *Enterprise-Journal*, October 19, 1989.

28. *Enterprise-Journal*, March 8, 1987; *Enterprise-Journal*, June 27, 2000.

29. *Enterprise-Journal*, May 21, 2010.

30. Interview with Emily Sue Williams, May 25, 2018.

31. *Enterprise-Journal*, December 17, 1987.

32. *Enterprise-Journal*, May 31, 1968.

33. Interview with Emily Sue Williams, July 24, 2018.

34. *Enterprise-Journal*, January 29, 1979.

35. *Enterprise-Journal*, October 14, 1990; *Enterprise-Journal*, October 4, 1992.

36. *Enterprise-Journal*, June 13, 2008.

37. *Enterprise-Journal,* May 10, 2015.

38. *Enterprise-Journal,* August 15, 1999.

39. Pike County Chancery Court, Suit #24,865.

40. *Enterprise-Journal,* April 13, 1983.

41. https://www.dignitymemorial.com/obituaries/metairie-la/fred-andrews-6183378.

42. *Enterprise-Journal,* September 13, 1984.

43. Interview with Carroll Case, July 24, 2018.

44. *Enterprise-Journal,* July 11, 2002.

45. *Enterprise-Journal,* July 11, 1975.

46. *Enterprise-Journal,* April 25, 1968; September 27, 1968; May 29, 1974.

47. *Enterprise-Journal,* January 21, 1982; August 27, 1975; April 16, 1976; April 28, 1978; September 13, 1981.

48. *Enterprise-Journal,* August 9, 1988; September 28, 1989; October 27, 1989; October 23, 1990; September 28, 1992; July 21, 1994.

49. *Enterprise-Journal,* September 28, 1992; November 7, 1991; March 13, 1991; June 6, 1991.

50. *Enterprise-Journal,* May 30, 1995; March 3, 1997; March 27, 2019.

51. *Clarion-Ledger,* February 14, 2008; *Enterprise-Journal,* February 14, 2008; https://www.legacy.com/obituaries/clarionledger/obituary.aspx?n=william-f-watkins&pid=103375368.

52. Interview with Carroll Case, July 25, 2018.

53. One of Butler's teammates on the 1951 Liberty High School Rebels football squad was Billy Jack Caston, the man who would in 1961 beat civil rights activist Robert Moses in Amite County. *Clarion-Ledger,* October 8, 1951. Butler's play at quarterback would earn him a place on a 1954 state all-star team. *Enterprise-Journal,* May 26, 1954; September 2, 1955.

54. *Clarion-Ledger,* October 29, 1966; August 16, 1967. *Enterprise-Journal,* November 28, 1966.

55. *Enterprise-Journal,* August 19, 1964; November 18, 1964; December 2, 1964; July 13, 1965; November 7, 1968; August 12, 1970.

56. *Clarion-Ledger,* January 12, 1980; December 15, 1982. *Enterprise-Journal,* January 13, 1980; February 6, 1980. *Clarion-Ledger,* January 5, 1984; January 9, 1988; January 29, 1988. *Enterprise-Journal,* January 5, 1984; January 15, 1984.

57. *Enterprise-Journal,* December 15, 1988; April 11, 1995. *Clarion-Ledger,* July 6, 1995.

58. *Enterprise-Journal,* July 4, 1999; January 11, 2004. *Clarion-Ledger,* January 10, 2004.

59. *Enterprise-Journal,* November 26, 2009. *Clarion-Ledger,* November 27, 2009.

60. *Enterprise-Journal,* October 17, 1980.

61. *Clarion-Ledger,* May 27, 2007. *Enterprise-Journal,* March 25, 2005.

62. *Enterprise-Journal,* November 26, 2009.

63. *Enterprise-Journal,* June 13, 2011.

64. *Enterprise-Journal,* January 3, 1990.

65. *Enterprise-Journal,* March 6, 1996.

66. *Enterprise-Journal,* September 19, 1991.

67. Carroll Case, e-mail to Trent Brown, July 7, 2018.

68. *Enterprise-Journal,* January 8, 1975.

69. *Enterprise-Journal,* September 8, 1978.

70. *Enterprise-Journal,* June 26, 1989.

71. *Enterprise-Journal,* August 23, 1978.

72. https://www.findagrave.com/memorial/161096878/jimmie-nell-wolfe; https://www.find agrave.com/memorial/98237462/robert-alex-lambert.

73. *Enterprise-Journal,* February 25, 1996.

74. *Enterprise-Journal,* March 5, 1997.

75. https://www.facebook.com/billie.bordelon. James and Billie Jo Bordelon had two children, William Curtis Bordelon and Susan Denise Bordelon Brock; *Enterprise-Journal,* February 26, 1996.

76. https://k106country.wordpress.com/2017/03/20/mccomb-music-heritage-festival/; http://mccombarts.com/event/mccomb-music-heritage-festival/.

77. http://msbluestrail.org/blues-trail-markers/summit-street.

78. Information on guided tours and a printable driving tour of the city available at: http://mccomblegacies.org/history/.

79. http://www.wlbt.com/story/38469249/mccomb-city-elections-bring-historical-power -shift/. By 2018, the United States Census Bureau estimated, the demographic breakdown of the McComb population was 70 percent African American and 29 percent white; see https://www .census.gov/quickfacts/fact/table/mccombcitymississippi,pikecountymississippi/PST045218.

80. *Enterprise-Journal,* March 14, 1975.

81. https://www.facebook.com/search/top/?q=pike%20county%20mississippi%20cold%20 cases&epa=SEARCH_BOX.

Chapter Ten

1. Among those people were journalists, attorneys, and immediate members of Andrews's family. I have respected the privacy of some of them by not naming them here. Others I do mention in the body of this chapter. When I do refer specifically to people who did not wish to speak with me, I do so only to show my efforts to reconstruct the story of Tina Andrews, not to criticize their wish for privacy.

2. Interview with Emily Sue Williams, July 24, 2018.

3. For the photograph, see https://www.facebook.com/Pike-County-Mississippi-Cold-Cases -201706329882839/.

4. This source is one of those people who would not speak with me for attribution in this book.

5. James W. Kitchens to Trent Brown, June 22, 2017.

6. Interview with Justice James Kitchens, August 1, 2017. Quotations from Kitchens in the following paragraphs are drawn from this interview.

7. *New York Times,* June 8, 2000. Ernest Avants was convicted in 2003 of the 1966 slaying of Ben Chester White. It was the first federal murder conviction in a civil rights–era revived case. *Clarion-Ledger,* April 21, 2004.

8. Interview with Dee Bates, May 21, 2018. All quotations from Bates here are taken from our two in-person conversations, one in 2017 and the other in 2018.

9. http://bioguide.congress.gov/scripts/biodisplay.pl?index=D000466.

10. *Enterprise-Journal,* February 10, 1969.

11. *Enterprise-Journal,* March 25, 2005.

12. Interview with Wayne Dowdy, May 22, 2018. *Enterprise-Journal,* November 26, 1969.

13. *Enterprise-Journal,* 30 August 2018; https://www.vicksburgpost.com/2018/08/29/mccomb-fires-4-top-employees-hires-replacements-bnx/. The City Board hired Damian Gatlin, a Lincoln County Sheriff's Department investigator, as chief. Gatlin, the *Enterprise-Journal* pointed out, had grown up in "in White Acres in McComb." So of course had Richard McIntosh.

14. Interview with Wayne Dowdy, May 22, 2018.

15. Interview with Justice James Kitchens, August 1, 2017.

16. Interview with Wayne Dowdy, May 22, 2018.

17. Interview with Wayne Dowdy, May 22, 2018.

18. Interview with Wayne Dowdy, May 22, 2018.

19. Interview with Wayne Dowdy, May 22, 2018.

20. Interview with Wayne Dowdy, May 22, 2018.

21. John Gordon Roach, Jr., e-mail to Trent Brown, July 17, 2018.

22. James W. Younger to Trent Brown, June 28, 2018.

23. Federal Bureau of Investigation to Trent Brown, June 27, 2018.

24. Interview with Carroll Case, May 21, 2018.

25. Carroll Case, *The Slaughter: An American Atrocity* (n.p.: FBC, Inc., 1998).

26. *Enterprise-Journal,* August 23, 1998.

27. Interview with Carroll Case, May 21, 2018.

28. Interview with Carroll Case, May 21, 2018.

29. Interview with Carroll Case, May 21, 2018.

30. Interview with Carroll Case, May 21, 2018.

31. *Enterprise-Journal,* July 2, 2018.

32. Interview with Bennie Hayman, July 25, 2018.

33. Interview with Bennie Hayman, July 25, 2018.

34. Interview with Bennie Hayman, July 25, 2018.

35. Interview with Bennie Hayman, July 25, 2018. *Enterprise-Journal,* September 3, 1989.

36. Interview with Bennie Hayman, July 25, 2018.

37. Interview with Bennie Hayman, July 25, 2018.

38. Interview with Bennie Hayman, July 25, 2018.

39. The source asks that her name not be included in this book.

Conclusion

1. *State-Times Advocate* (Baton Rouge), March 19, 1971; *Advocate* (Baton Rouge), March 19, 1971.

2. Howard Smead, *Blood Justice: The Lynching of Mack Charles Parker* (New York: Oxford University Press, 1984).

3. See Joseph Crespino, "The Strange Career of Atticus Finch," *Southern Cultures* 6: 2, 9–29, and *Atticus Finch, The Biography: Harper Lee, Her Father, and the Making of an American Icon* (New York: Basic Books, 2018).

4. Interview with Justice Jim Kitchens, August 1, 2017.

5. 1971 trial transcript, 588.

6. 1971 trial transcript, 341–43. For copies of subpoenas to Henderson, see the case file, Pike County Circuit Court Case #11,468. In 1969, Henderson was sixteen years old. Perhaps the state decided that she would not make an effective witness. In 1962, Henderson was a special education student in the McComb public schools. She died in 2012. *Enterprise-Journal*, May 31, 1962; September 10, 2012.

7. *Enterprise-Journal*, August 25, 1969.

8. *Enterprise-Journal*, January 3, 1972.

9. George Orwell, *The Road to Wigan Pier* (New York: Harcourt, Brace, 1958), 52. Orig. ed. 1937.

10. Among the many books written on the murder of Emmett Till, two recent studies are Devery S. Anderson, *Emmett Till: The Murder that Shocked the World and Propelled the Civil Rights Movement* (Jackson: University Press of Mississippi, 2015); and Timothy B. Tyson, *The Blood of Emmett Till* (New York: Simon & Schuster, 2017). On the reopening of the Till case, see *New York Times*, July 12, 2018. To see how a historian can uncover a deep history of murder and racial control in a small Mississippi place, see Jason Morgan Ward, *Hanging Bridge: Racial Violence and America's Civil Rights Century* (New York: Oxford University Press, 2016). See also Karen L. Cox, *Goat Castle: A True Story of Murder, Race, and the Gothic South* (Chapel Hill: University of North Carolina Press, 2017).

11. *Enterprise-Journal*, March 10, 1982.

12. Paul Hendrickson, *Sons of Mississippi: A Story of Race and Its Legacy* (New York: Knopf, 2003), 16.

Index

Page numbers in italics refer to photographs.

Addison, Thelma, murder charges against, 198

African Americans. *See* blacks

Alexander, F. David (juror in 1971 McIntosh trial), 100, 101

Alford, Wendell H. (juror in 1972 McIntosh trial), 182

Allen, Eddie, murder charge against, 171

Amite County (Mississippi), 243; voter registration in, 24–25, 26, 35–36

Andrews, Corrine, bombing of home, 33

Andrews, Donna (sister of Tina), 3, 43, 189, 213, 250; author's attempt to contact, 249; Stietenroth contacts, 186, 187; witness in McIntosh trials, 67, 68, 69, 110–14, 150, 183, 256

Andrews, Doris Havard (mother of Tina), 3, 43, 211–12, 213

Andrews, Freddie (brother of Tina), 43, 113, 157, 212

Andrews, Fred Paul (father of Tina), 43, 44–45, 211–12, 212–13, 250

Andrews, Herbert (juror in 1971 McIntosh trial), 101, 102

Andrews, Karey (uncle of Tina), 44–45, 213, 240

Andrews, Tina Marie, *137*; burial, 47; death certificate, 250–51; gravesite, *141*, 174–75, 251; home, *142*, 201; memory of, 224–25; reputation, 1–2, 15, 98, 120, 162–63, 195, 226–27; school records, 1, 92, 106–7, 110–11, 149–50, 256, 282n50; seen with Stietenroth, 188–89; social class status, 12, 93, 96–97, 115, 265

Andrews, Tina Marie, murder of, 6–8, 39–52; discovery of body, 8–9, 39, 51, 236; events leading up to, 4–6, 118–20, 128–29; evidence in, 229–30, 255–56; identification of remains, 3, 41–43, 65, 92, 97, 99–100, 106–9, 114–15, 148–51, 163, 184–85, 194, 277n1; investigation into, 10, 50–52, 84–85; Kitchens on, 227–31; men arrested and indicted for, 9, 10–11, 12; motive for, 252–53; multiple types of information, 256–58; no convictions for, 200, 234; no eyewitness to, 98, 259–60; records of, 228–29, 239, 242, 243; reopening case, 233; rumors surrounding, 120, 166–68, 196, 225–27, 238, 253; weapon used, 43, 51, 228–29, 277n9. *See also* Fleming, Teddy J. "Ted" (murder suspect); McIntosh, Richard (murder suspect); McIntosh, Richard (murder suspect): 1971 trial of; McIntosh, Richard (murder suspect): 1972 trial of; oil field crime scene

Andrews, Winifred (sister of Tina). *See* Mullen, Winifred Andrews (sister of Tina)

Andrews family, 43, 174, 249–50; post-trial life, 211–13; reputation of, 15, 113, 120, 195, 261–63; silence of, 59–60, 120, 175, 196, 222–23; social class status, 12, 44, 96, 107, 111–13, 114

Austin, Emily (wife of Thomas), 168–69

Austin, Thomas B. (juror in 1971 McIntosh trial), 101, 166, 167–71, 206

Avants, Ernest, conviction of, 294n7

Baker, James (Rev.), bombing of home, 34

Barnes, Hattie Lee, murder charge against, 75–76, 281n6, 281n7

Bates, Dee (Pike County District Attorney), 232–34

Bates, Freddie, bombing of home, 33

Bellipani, Bobby (brother-in-law of Ted Fleming), 8, 190, 236

Berrey, Stephen, 13

Berry, Marion (SNCC worker), 25, 26

blacks: in McComb, 17, 20–22, 84, 220–21, 294n79; serving on juries, 71–72, 96, 100–103, 167–68, 182–84, 245, 284n16. See also civil rights movement; desegregation; integration; Jim Crow laws: blacks' resistance to; violence: racial; voter registration

bombings: Klan involvement in, 89, 179; 1964 campaign of, 9, 11, 32–34, 36, 53, 56, 76–77, 232, 275n64. See also civil rights movement: whites' resistance to; violence

Bordelon, Billie Jo Lambert. See Lambert, Billie Jo (friend of Tina)

Bordelon, James (husband of Billie Jo), 243–44

Brady, Thomas (judge), 76, 134

Bratley, Forrest G. (pathologist), testimony of, 150–51

Brown, Ossie B. (Baton Rouge defense attorney), 159

Browning, Katie (juror in McIntosh's 1972 trial), 183

Brumfield, Charles E. (juror in 1971 McIntosh trial), 101

Brumfield, Robert (Chamber of Commerce president), 11, 36

Bryant, C. C. (NAACP activist), 14, 23, 24, 25, 26, 27, 33

Bryant, Ora Lee (cafe owner), 32

Burgland High School (McComb) walk-out, 27

Burt, Gordon (mayor), 21, 30, 80, 282n44

Butler, Donald (highway patrol investigator), 215–16, 236–37, 293n53; and Andrews murder investigation, 42, 51, 185–89; and McColgan Hotel burglary, 179, 180, 181; testimony in McIntosh trials, 99, 105, 184

Carter, Hodding, II (journalist), 16–17, 33

Carter, Hodding, III (journalist), 90

Carter, J. J. (juror in 1972 McIntosh trial), 183

Case, Carroll (McComb banker and writer), interview, 239–42

Caston, Billy Jack, attack on Robert Moses, 26, 293n53

Citizens' Council, 89–90, 91, 282n44

civil rights movement: in Pike County, 35, 95; whites' resistance to, 9–13, 16, 22–37, 53, 56, 78, 89–91, 179, 254. See also desegregation; integration; Ku Klux Klan (KKK); sit-in demonstrations; voter registration

class, social, 15, 147, 210; as issue in McIntosh trials, 12, 96, 115, 150, 167, 174, 201, 253–54, 255, 261–63. See also Andrews, Tina Marie: social class status; Lambert, Billie Jo (friend of Tina): social class status; whites: social class divisions among; working class

Cobb, James, 171

Copelan, Rollin, 154, 158–59

Council of Federated Organizations (COFO), 32, 87, 270n22

Craft, Lamar, murder of, 75–76

Crespino, Joseph, 30

crime rate, 35, 48, 177–78

Croft Metals Inc. (McComb), union organizing at, 87–88

Cunningham, David, 30

Deep South, 10, 18, 36; social and cultural changes in, 47–50, 80–81, 206. See also Mississippi desegregation, 49, 216; bus, 28–29; school, 36, 75, 89–90, 92. *See also* integration

direct action protests, 25–26, 27. *See also* civil rights movement; sit-in demonstrations

Dittmer, John, 22

Douglas, C. H. (mayor), 28–29

Dowdy, Wayne (defense attorney for Ted Fleming), 64, 65, 66, 67–70, 73, 176, 222, 234–38

Dunagin, Charles (reporter), 50, 51, 86–87, 181

Emmerich, Oliver (newspaper editor), 18, 28, 31, 80–81, 92–93, 195, 198, 274n56

Evers, Charles (candidate for Mississippi governor), 171

Felder, Gerald, 189

Fentress, Sam (photographer), attack on, 29

Fleming, Agnes Bellipanni (wife of Ted), 191, 208, 209, 236

Fleming, Alton (brother of Ted), 60, 191

Fleming, Teddy J. "Ted" (murder suspect), 136, 160, 254; alibi for, 191; death of, 223, 232; indictment of, 55–56, 57–58, 60, 77, 116, 170, 197; Lambert identifies, 118, 119–20; never stands trial, 64, 66; *nolle prosequi* dismissal of charges, 193, 203–4, 232, 236, 255; post-indictment life, 204–5, 207–9; Richard McIntosh denies knowing in 1969, 155, 255–56; state's case against, 92, 243; suspension from police force, 56, 57, 73

Fortenberry, Glen (Pike County Circuit Clerk), 73

Fortenberry, Ray (boyfriend of Donna Andrews), 189

Freedom Riders, 28–29, 53, 87, 274n58

Freedom Summer (1964), 30, 31–38

F. W. Woolworth store (McComb), sit-in demonstration in, 25, 26, 47, 53, 273–74n48

Gardner, J. C. (juror in 1971 McIntosh trial), 101

gender: as issue in McIntosh trials, 96, 108–9, 134, 253–54, 255, 261; values regarding, 10, 105, 199. *See also* women

Gillis, Norman, Jr. (attorney), 64, 113

Gillis Drug Store (McComb), 2, 113, 207; burglary of, 179–81

Gordon, Charles (reporter), 75, 245

Gordon, Mac (reporter), 37

Green Book (travel guide for blacks), 273n32

Guy, George (police chief), 25, 56, 80, 85

Haffey, Thomas J. (city clerk), testimony of, 148

Hammons, Ronald Aubrey, manslaughter charge against, 171–72

Hardy, John (SNCC worker), 24

Harvey, Esco, questioning of, 161

Harvey, M. V. (doctor), 100, 179

Harvey, Mrs. M. V. (jury foreman for 1971 McIntosh trial), 100–101, 179, 283n13

Hayes, Curtis (civil rights demonstrator), 25, 26, 47

Hayman, B. C. "Bennie" (juror in 1972 McIntosh trial), 182–83, 244–47

Heffner family, harassment of, 33

Henderson, Beverly, possible identity of third girl, 127–28, 184, 257–58, 296n6

Hendrickson, Paul, 265–66

Hines, Noel Francis (aka Paul St. John), Mc-Colgan Hotel burglary, 179–81, 197

Hoaglund, Cy (F.B.I. agent), 40

Hogan, Wesley, 23

Holifield, Eve (professional prostitute), 180–81

Hoover, J. Edgar (F.B.I. director), 34

Howell, Michael, 154; aggravated rape arrest, 158–59

Hughes, Ernest W. (juror in 1972 McIntosh trial), 182, 183

Illinois Central Railroad, 15, 22

integration, 23, 220, 221. *See also* blacks: serving on juries; civil rights movement;

integration (*continued*)
desegregation; schools: integration of; sit-in demonstrations

James, Shirley Mae, murder charge against, 171, 172, 289n53
Jenkins, Howard (juror in 1972 McIntosh trial), 182, 183
Jim Crow laws, 78, 134, 220; blacks' resistance to, 11, 17, 20, 22–38, 48–49, 89–90, 198–99, 254, 265; legal system under, 71–72, 231, 277n5. *See also* segregation
Johnson, Paul B., Jr. (governor), 35
jurors, selection of, 69–72; in McIntosh trials, 95, 97, 100–104, 167, 173, 224, 284n15. *See also* blacks: serving on juries

Kennedy, Joseph P. (Pike County coroner), testimony of, 148–49
Kitchens, James W. (Jim, Pike County District Attorney and Mississippi Supreme Court justice), 83, 135, 175–76, 197; and indictment of McIntosh and Fleming, 58; interview with, 227–31; on jury selection system, 70–71, 72, 103–4; and McColgan Hotel burglary, 179–80, 181; and 1972 McIntosh trial, 108, 173, 177, 183, 189, 190, 202–3; and Ted Fleming case, 193
Kratzschmar, George (father of Billie Jo Lambert's baby), 184, 240–41
Kruse, Kevin, 78
Ku Klux Klan (KKK), 11, 24, 27, 37–38, 90, 199, 275n64; and Andrews murder case, 228–29; growth of, 29–31; law enforcement personnel as members of, 56, 72–73; and McComb centennial celebration, 178–79; rallies, 35, 88–89. *See also* civil rights movement: whites' resistance to

Lambert, Billie Jo (friend of Tina), 174, 218–20, 285n1; account of night of Andrews's

murder, 4–8, 116, 118–20, 128–29, 224, 227–28, 261; author's attempt to contact, 243–44; confides in Pat Lamkin, 54, 129, 132, 219; fear of retribution, 241, 286n15, 286n36; home, 142, 201; meetings with Pigott, 54, 67, 77, 116; 1971 McIntosh trial testimony, 116–34, 147, 156–57, 165, 187–88; 1972 McIntosh trial testimony, 185, 190–91, 192, 194–95; reputation, 15, 98, 120, 124, 131, 227–28, 261–63; Richard McIntosh visits, 123, 156–57; school records, 92, 149–50, 285n4; social class status, 4, 96, 116–17; unwed mother, 97, 117, 125–26, 184; witness for state, 55, 65–69, 96–97, 202–3, 236, 252, 253, 259
Lambert, George Ann Welch (Billie Jo's mother), 116–17, 219
Lambert, Pat Harrison (Billie Jo's father), 116, 219
Lambert, Robert Alex (Billie Jo's son), murder of, 219
Lambert family, 96, 261–63
Lamkin, Pat Thomas (friend of Billie Jo), 279n5; Billie Jo confides in, 54, 129, 132, 219; calls Joe Pigott, 54, 69, 129, 261; witness in McIntosh trials, 67–68, 69, 184
Lampton, Dunn (Pike County District Attorney), 230, 233
law and order, 171, 199; maintaining, 27, 53, 84, 93, 177–78; police role in, 58, 78, 79; whites' passion for, 10–13, 37–38, 50, 81–82, 88, 90, 91
law enforcement agencies, 29–30, 35, 72, 147, 231. *See also* police force (McComb); sheriff's department (Pike County)
Lawson, Robert "Tot" (Pike County sheriff), 83, 86, 180, 213, 216–18; and Andrews murder investigation, 8–9, 40, 42, 50–51, 55, 68, 105, 189; conversations with Austin, 167–68, 170–71. *See also* sheriff's department (Pike County)

Lee, Herbert, murder of, 26
Lewis, Ike (activist), 26, 27
Loden, Timothy (Rev.), 47

Magnolia (Mississippi), 94–95, 222, 248–49
Maples, Darwin (judge), 291n58; presides over 1972 McIntosh trial, 182, 196–97
Matthews, Ernest (juror in 1972 McIntosh trial), 182, 183
Mayer, W. T. (doctor), cross burned in yard, 33
McClanahan, Clyde, arrest of, 50
McColgan Hotel (McComb), burglary of, 179–81, 197
McComb (Mississippi), 14–38; centennial celebration, 178–79, 195, 198; downtown, 2, 45, 46, 143, 145, 207, 220–22, 247–48; east section, 4, 116–17, 128, 210; geographic location, 17–18; national image, 11–12, 30, 32; population, 1, 14, 271n1, 294n79; race relations, 16–17, 20–22, 37, 43, 84, 117–18, 232; schools, 1, 19–20, 27, 81, 269n2; segregation in, 4, 9–13, 14, 15, 20–21, 49; social and cultural changes, 47–50, 80–81, 85–88, 91, 93, 206, 267; tornado of 1975, 206; violence in, 9–13; White Acres housing development, 62, 210; white male power base, 12, 225, 261. See also bombings; Pete's Place (bar and grill, McComb); Pike County (Mississippi); Tiger's Den (teenage club, McComb)
McComb Cotton Mills, 15–16
McCrea (Louisiana) music festival, 86–87
McDew, Chuck (SNCC worker), 26, 27, 36
McGowan, Clifton (juror in 1971 McIntosh trial), 100, 101, 102, 103, 167, 168
McIntosh, Elma Evans (mother of Richard), 62, 210
McIntosh, Richard (murder suspect), 61–64, 138, 254–55; alibi, 190; author's attempt to contact, 244; charged as accessory to

aggravated rape in Baton Rouge, 158–60, 288n26; costs of defense, 192–93; denies knowing Fleming in 1969, 155, 255–56; indictment of, 55–56, 57–60, 77, 116, 170, 197, 249; Lambert identifies, 119–20, 121; post-trials life, 204–5, 209–11; state's case against, 111–12, 126–27, 131, 133, 242–43, 255; suspension from police force, 56, 57, 73, 192; trials of, 58, 59, 60, 61, 65–66, 200; visits Lambert's house, 156–57
—1971 trial, 94–172; character witnesses, 163, 256; defense, 92, 147–63; deliberations of jury, 103–5, 165; Lambert's testimony, 116–34, 147, 156–57, 165, 187–88; mistrial declared, 147, 165–66, 168, 172, 173, 193; own testimony, 154–63; selection of jury, 70, 95, 97, 100–103, 167, 284n15; state's case against, 124, 147–48, 149, 162–65, 165–68; transcript, 205, 229, 269n1, 289n2
—1972 trial, 173–200; character witnesses, 191, 256; defense, 185–90, 193–94; Lambert's testimony, 185, 190–91, 192, 194–95; newspaper coverage, 195; no transcript, 229, 289n2; selection of jury, 173, 182–84, 224, 245; state's case against, 184, 191–92, 231; verdict of not guilty, 192, 193, 194–95, 196, 203, 245–46, 255, 264
McIntosh, Richard (father of Richard), 61–62
Minor, Bill (reporter), 37
Mississippi: court system in, 255, 283n3; national image of, 81–82; race relations in, 1, 14, 264–67, 276n84. See also Magnolia (Mississippi); McComb (Mississippi); Pike County (Mississippi)
Mississippi State Sovereignty Commission, 53, 56, 86
Moody, Anne, 272n24
Moore, Thomas Earl (juror in 1972 McIntosh trial), 182, 183
Morgan, Harold E. (juror in 1972 McIntosh trial), 182, 183

Moses, Robert (SNCC leader), 24, 26, 27, 49, 293n53

Mounger, Breed, Sr. (defense attorney for Ted Fleming), 64–65, 69–70, 274n56

Mullen, Winifred Andrews (sister of Tina), 3, 43, 213, 250, 284n26; testimony in 1971 McIntosh trial, 67, 106–7

National Association for the Advancement of Colored People (NAACP), 22–23, 24

Nettles, Dorothy Marie (McIntosh's former girlfriend), testimony in McIntosh trials, 151–54, 158, 165, 190

Nixon, Richard (U.S. President), 177–78

Nunnery, Jessie Mae (juror in 1972 McIntosh trial), 182, 183

Nylen, Marie U. (expert witness), 285n31; testimony in McIntosh trials, 107, 108–9, 185

oil field crime scene: Butler's map of, 99, 186; discovery of body in, 8, 39–42, 139; Lambert's return to, 122, 132; McIntosh's feelings about, 155, 161–62, 163–64; place for romantic encounters, 6, 51, 121, 253; present-day appearance of, 144, 201–2, 223

Otken Elementary School (McComb), 1, 269n2. See also schools: McComb

Owens, Webb (NAACP worker), 23, 24

Parker, Jack (friend of Richard McIntosh), testimony of, 163–65

Parker, Mack Charles, murder of, 254

Parklane Academy (McComb), 81. See also schools: McComb

Patterson, Zach (mayor), 22

Payne, Charles, 11, 24, 26

Pete's Place (bar and grill, McComb), 114, 201

Pettey, Claude (dentist), testimony in 1971 McIntosh trial, 105, 109–10

Phillips, Kevin, 177, 178

Pigott, Brad (son of Joe), 75, 232

Pigott, Joe Ned (Pike County District Attorney and judge), 32, 74–78, 91, 104, 135, 168, 169; and Andrews murder investigation, 8, 40, 41, 42, 43–44, 51, 52, 202–3; appointed defense attorney for Hines, 180; attempts to rein in violence, 72–73; becomes judge, 82, 214, 233; death of, 231; finishes service as district attorney, 173, 175; and indictment of McIntosh and Fleming, 57–58; Lamkin's call to, 54, 69, 129, 261; meetings with Lambert, 54, 67, 77, 116; and 1971 McIntosh trial, 95, 97–98, 101–2, 109, 117–18, 122–27, 133, 149–51, 153–54, 158–65, 167, 288n26

Pike County (Mississippi), 16, 184, 240, 248; civil rights movement, 35, 95; Cold Cases Facebook page, 225–26; County Courthouse, 94, 95, 140; grand jury, 55, 57, 91; justice system, 71–72; oral tradition in, 224–25; population, 1, 14, 15, 17, 93, 271n1; social and cultural changes in, 47–50, 178, 207; social class distinctions in, 12, 15, 147, 219; violence in, 9–13, 171–72. See also Magnolia (Mississippi); McComb (Mississippi)

Pike County Circuit Court, 9, 47, 73, 82, 91, 92, 203, 219; and 1971 McIntosh trial, 121, 151; and 1972 McIntosh trial, 177–179, 181, 197

police force (McComb), 27, 53–56, 145, 181, 229; and Andrews murder investigation, 68, 170, 249, 260–61; blacks' view of, 101–2, 248; contingent at 1971 McIntosh trial, 103, 114, 190; dealing with Freedom Riders, 28–29; as members of the Ku Klux Klan, 56, 72; response to Freedom Summer, 31–32, 33; suspects are members of, 54–55, 57–58, 77–79, 96–97, 101–2, 118, 122, 128, 130, 156, 190, 203

Prince, Julian (school superintendent), 49, 92, 149, 150, 282n50

Quinn, Alyene (cafe owner and activist), 24, 34

Quinn, Mrs. T. R. (juror in 1972 McIntosh trial), 182, 183

race, 10, 105; as issue in McIntosh trials, 167, 201, 254, 264–67. *See also* blacks; McComb (Mississippi): race relations; violence: racial; whites

Reconstruction period, 17, 200

Reed, Ronnie (Tiger's Den employee), testimony of, 162–63

Reeves, Ralph L. (jury foreman in 1972 McIntosh trial), 182, 192, 224

Reeves, Robert (Pike County prosecutor), 76, 176; finishes service as county prosecutor, 173, 175; and 1971 McIntosh trial, 82–83, 95, 110, 126, 150, 166, 167

respectability, 10, 199; as issue in McIntosh trials, 96, 98, 114, 116, 150, 261–63; as issue in Tina Andrews's murder, 15, 113, 115

Roach, J. Gordon (judge), 58–59, 171, 198, 282n44; dismisses charges against Ted Fleming, 193; health problems, 181–82; and jury deliberation, 69–70; and McColgan Hotel burglary trial, 180–81; and 1972 McIntosh trial, 48–49, 79, 83, 178; presides over 1971 McIntosh trial, 91, 95, 99, 102, 104–5, 109, 114, 124–25, 133, 147–51, 163, 165, 196; pretrial rulings, 63, 66, 73

Roach, John Gordon, Jr. (Pike County prosecuting attorney), 83, 235, 238; and 1972 McIntosh trial, 173, 175; other cases prosecuted by, 171, 180, 197

Robinson, Reggie (SNCC worker), 24

Rowley, Richard (police chief), 42, 80, 85, 173, 218; dealing with civil rights activists, 47, 273–74n48; and McColgan Hotel prostitution ring, 180–81; sends police contingent to first McIntosh trial, 103, 114. *See also* police force (McComb)

schools, 31, 53; integration of, 49, 81, 90, 92, 207, 226, 269n3; McComb, 1, 19–20, 27, 81, 269n2

segregation: black challenges to, 23–37, 93, 265; dismantling, 78; maintenance of, 17, 23, 30; in McComb, 4, 9–13, 14, 15, 20–21, 81. *See also* desegregation; Jim Crow laws

Sellers, Cleveland (activist), 31

Sharpling, John (police lieutenant): investigation of Andrews murder, 42, 68, 84–85, 160; lawsuit against, 32

Shelton, Robert (Klan leader), 30–31, 88, 89

sheriff's department (Pike County), 27, 32, 33–34, 35. *See also* Lawson, Robert "Tot" (Pike County sheriff)

Sherrod, Charles (SNCC worker), 26

sit-in demonstrations, 25, 26, 47, 53, 273–74n48. *See also* civil rights movement

Sitton, Claude (reporter), 29, 31

Slaughter, Joseph, murders Robert Alex Lambert, 219–20

Smith, Eddie (police officer), 32, 273–74n48

SNCC. *See* Student Nonviolent Coordinating Committee (SNCC), voter registration project

Sokol, Jason, 36

Speed, Clarence A. (juror in 1971 McIntosh trial), 100, 101

Spillman, Wayne (friend of Richard McIntosh), 155

Statement of Principles (McComb business and civic leaders), 37, 76–77

Statham, B. D. (defense attorney for Richard McIntosh), 63–64, 94, 136, 213; discrediting Billie Jo Lambert, 65–66, 227, 228; Dowdy's recollections of, 237–38; Hayman's recollections of, 246–47; and jury selection system, 71, 72; motions filed by, 67, 69–70; and 1971 McIntosh trial, 95, 97–102, 106–14, 120, 122, 124–34, 147–58, 162–65; and 1972 McIntosh trial, 175, 182–92; other cases handled by, 171, 197

Stayton, Milton J.: attack on Oliver Emmerich, 274n56

Steele, Vernon E.: interviewed by Butler and Lawson, 189

Stewart, Edsel (doctor): testimony in 1971 McIntosh trial, 105

Stewart, T. Dale (expert witness), 284–85n28; testimony in McIntosh trials, 107–8, 184–85

Stietenroth, Norman (McComb resident), 186–89

Strub, Whitney, 48

Student Nonviolent Coordinating Committee (SNCC), voter registration project, 24–27

Talbert, Bobbie (activist), 26

third girl (unidentified person accompanying Tina and Billie Jo), 4, 5, 118–19, 127, 128, 184, 257–59, 296n6

Thornhill, Emmitt (segregationist), 16, 35, 37–38, 88

Thornhill, J. Emmitt, Jr., 56

Tiger's Den (teenage club, McComb), 3–4, 5, 47, 113, 146, 162–63, 201, 270n7

Timmons, Reesie (F.B.I. agent), 39–40, 49

To Kill a Mockingbird (Lee), comparing Andrews's case to, 254–55

Travis, Brenda (activist), 26, 27

unions, 15, 16, 22, 87–88

United Klans of America (UKA). See Ku Klux Klan (KKK)

Varnado, Lawrence "Uncle Bud," 43, 277n11

violence: in Pike County, 9–13, 171–72; racial, 9–13, 14, 78, 87, 134, 254, 275n4; working class-related, 11, 16, 38, 219. See also bombings; civil rights movement: whites' resistance to; Jim Crow laws: blacks' resistance to; Ku Klux Klan (KKK)

voter registration, 22, 24–27, 31, 35–36, 171, 273n43

Wade, Pete (businessman), 114

Wallace, Frederick (F.B.I. agent), 284n24; testimony in McIntosh trials, 105–6, 185

Wallace, George (1968 presidential candidate), 177–78

Waller, William (candidate for Mississippi governor), 171

Washington, Wade, murder charges against, 197–98

Watkins, Hollis (civil rights demonstrator), 25, 26, 47

Watkins, W. H., Jr. (judge), 34–35, 38, 58, 276n78

Watkins, William Franklin (defense attorney for Richard McIntosh), 64, 213–15; discrediting Billie Jo Lambert, 65–66; motions filed by, 63, 69–70; and 1971 McIntosh trial, 95, 147, 154; and 1972 McIntosh trial, 175, 182, 186, 192, 241; other cases handled by, 171, 197

Wells, Roosevelt, murder charges against, 197, 198

White, Ben Chester, murder of, 294n7

White, Hugh (governor), 16

whites, 17, 21; social class divisions among, 9–13, 15, 36, 49, 88, 90, 116; tensions among, 10, 38, 199–200; working-class, 15–16, 199, 261–62. See also civil rights movement: whites' resistance to; law and order: whites' passion for

Williams, Bobby (former McComb police officer), testimony in 1972 McIntosh trial, 190–91

Williams, Claude, Jr. (juror in 1971 McIntosh trial), 100, 101, 102

Williams, Harold L. (juror in 1971 McIntosh trial), 100, 101

Williams, Mike (assistant chief of police), 85

Williams, Sue (McComb resident), recollections of Andrews and Stietenroth, 188–89

Wilson, Lamont M. (juror in 1971 McIntosh trial), 100, 101, 167, 283n14

Wilson, Paul Dewey (arrested for bombings), 34

Wolfe, Jimmie Nell Lambert (sister of Billie
Jo), 133, 219
women: black, 21, 120; missing from Mc-
Comb in August 1969, 8; serving on juries,
71–72, 100, 182, 192, 195, 245, 247; white,
134. *See also* gender
working class, 12, 183; violence related to, 11,
16, 38, 219; white, 15–16, 199, 261–62. *See*

also class, social; McComb (Mississippi):
east section

Zackery, Michael, murder charges against,
197
Zelizer, Julian, 78
Zellner, Bob (SNCC worker), 27
Zinn, Howard, 14